T0336524

Financial Modeling and Valuation

Founded in 1807, John Wiley & Sons is the oldest independent publishing company in the United States. With offices in North America, Europe, Australia, and Asia, Wiley is globally committed to developing and marketing print and electronic products and services for our customers' professional and personal knowledge and understanding.

The Wiley Finance series contains books written specifically for finance and investment professionals as well as sophisticated individual investors and their financial advisors. Book topics range from portfolio management to e-commerce, risk management, financial engineering, valuation, and financial instrument analysis, as well as much more.

For a list of available titles, visit our website at www.WileyFinance.com.

Financial Modeling and Valuation

A Practical Guide to Investment Banking and Private Equity

Second Edition

PAUL PIGNATARO

WILEY

Copyright © 2022 by Paul Pignataro. All rights reserved.

Published by John Wiley & Sons, Inc., Hoboken, New Jersey.
Published simultaneously in Canada.

No part of this publication may be reproduced, stored in a retrieval system, or transmitted in any form or by any means, electronic, mechanical, photocopying, recording, scanning, or otherwise, except as permitted under Section 107 or 108 of the 1976 United States Copyright Act, without either the prior written permission of the Publisher, or authorization through payment of the appropriate per-copy fee to the Copyright Clearance Center, Inc., 222 Rosewood Drive, Danvers, MA 01923, (978) 750-8400, fax (978) 750-4470, or on the web at www.copyright.com. Requests to the Publisher for permission should be addressed to the Permissions Department, John Wiley & Sons, Inc., 111 River Street, Hoboken, NJ 07030, (201) 748-6011, fax (201) 748-6008, or online at http://www.wiley.com/go/permission.

Limit of Liability/Disclaimer of Warranty: While the publisher and authors have used their best efforts in preparing this work, they make no representations or warranties with respect to the accuracy or completeness of the contents of this work and specifically disclaim all warranties, including without limitation any implied warranties of merchantability or fitness for a particular purpose. No warranty may be created or extended by sales representatives, written sales materials or promotional statements for this work. The fact that an organization, website, or product is referred to in this work as a citation and/or potential source of further information does not mean that the publisher and authors endorse the information or services the organization, website, or product may provide or recommendations it may make. This work is sold with the understanding that the publisher is not engaged in rendering professional services. The advice and strategies contained herein may not be suitable for your situation. You should consult with a specialist where appropriate. Further, readers should be aware that websites listed in this work may have changed or disappeared between when this work was written and when it is read. Neither the publisher nor authors shall be liable for any loss of profit or any other commercial damages, including but not limited to special, incidental, consequential, or other damages.

For general information on our other products and services or for technical support, please contact our Customer Care Department within the United States at (800) 762-2974, outside the United States at (317) 572-3993 or fax (317) 572-4002.

Wiley also publishes its books in a variety of electronic formats. Some content that appears in print may not be available in electronic formats. For more information about Wiley products, visit our website at www.wiley.com.

Library of Congress Cataloging-in-Publication Data:

Names: Pignataro, Paul, author.
Title: Financial modeling and valuation : a practical guide to investment
  banking and private equity / Paul Pignataro.
Description: Second edition. | Hoboken, New Jersey : John Wiley & Sons,
  [2022] | Series: Wiley finance series | Includes index.
Identifiers: LCCN 2021056643 (print) | LCCN 2021056644 (ebook) | ISBN
  9781119808893 (cloth) | ISBN 9781119808909 (adobe pdf) | ISBN
  9781119808879 (epub)
Subjects: LCSH: Investment banking.
Classification: LCC HG4534 .P54 2022 (print) | LCC HG4534 (ebook) | DDC
  332.66—dc23/eng/20211201
LC record available at https://lccn.loc.gov/2021056643
LC ebook record available at https://lccn.loc.gov/2021056644

Cover design: Wiley
Cover image: © duncan1890/Getty Images

SKY10033120_021022

To my wife, Carmen, for her love and support, enabling me to find the time to write this book and to juggle a multitude of ventures, I am ever grateful.

Contents

CHAPTER 3
The Balance Sheet

Preface

The markets are vast and complex—not only the United States but also the global markets. Stocks, bonds, mutual funds, derivatives, options—yes, choices are endless, literally. Everyone wants to make money. Yet, throughout the past years we have faced tremendous market swings, leaving investors (and their money) floundering in a sea of lost hopes and few investors with a plethora of wealth. Many of these market anomalies and swings are dependent on, and in a sense dictated by, the investor – you. The investor plays a part in setting the current stock price. The reaction of the investor can aid in determining the success of an initial public offering (IPO). Yes, the collective psychology of the market as a whole plays a major role, but if the everyday investor were better equipped with the proper tools to understand the underlying fundamentals of a rational investment, smarter investment decisions could be made, more rational investments would be made, and the markets would be a more efficient environment.

This book sets out to give any investor the fundamental tools to help determine if a stock investment is a rational one, and if a stock price is under-valued, overvalued, or appropriately valued. These fundamental tools are used by investment banks, private equity firms, and Wall Street analysts.

We will evaluate Amazon, determining its current financial standing, projecting its future performance, and estimating a target stock price. We will further assess if this is a viable investment, but more importantly, give you the tools and concepts to make your own rational investment decisions. We will have you step into the role of an analyst on Wall Street to give you a first-hand perspective and understanding of how the modeling and valuation process works with the tools you need to create your own analyses.

This is a guide designed for investment banking and private equity professionals to be used as a refresher or handbook, or for individuals looking to enter into the investment banking or private equity field. Whether you are valuing a potential investment or business, the tools demonstrated in this book are extremely valuable in the process.

THE AMAZON CASE STUDY

We will analyze Amazon throughout this book. Amazon is an American multinational technology company headquartered in Seattle, Washington. It is currently the second-largest retailer in the world.[1] Through its online and physical stores, Amazon provides hundreds of millions of products sold either directly or via third-party sellers, and manufactures and sells various electronic devices including Kindle, Fire tablet, Fire TV, Echo, Ring, and other devices. Amazon is also involved in a host of technology and internet-focused ventures and initiatives, including Amazon Web Services, intelligent virtual assistance, cloud computing, and live-streaming via Amazon Prime. Amazon also develops and produces media content, and the list of Amazon's offerings continues to expand. If we want to invest in Amazon, how do we determine the viability of such an investment? In order to ensure profitability from a stock investment, we need to understand what the future stock price of Amazon could be. Obviously, stock price fluctuations are largely based on public opinion. However, there is a technical analysis used by Wall Street analysts to help determine and predict the stock price of a business.

This technical analysis is based on three methods:

1. Comparable company analysis
2. Discounted cash flow analysis
3. Precedent transaction analysis

Each of these methods view Amazon from three very different technical perspectives. Individually, these methods could present major flaws. However, it is the common belief that looking at all of these methods together will help us understand the technical drivers supporting Amazon's current stock price. Using Amazon as the example, we will construct all three of the listed analyses and all the supporting analyses exactly as a Wall Street analyst would. We will then have the ability to interpret from the analysis if Amazon is undervalued, overvalued, or appropriately valued. If the company is determined to be undervalued, that may suggest the stock price is lower than expected. We can potentially invest in the business and hope the stock price in time will increase. If the company is determined to be overvalued, that may suggest the stock price is higher than expected. In this case it may not make sense to invest in the business, as the

---

[1]David Marcotte, "2021 Top 50 Global Retailers," National Retail Federation (March 24, 2021), https://nrf.com/blog/2021-top-50-global-retailers.

stock price in time could potentially decrease. We are assuming in these cases there has been no unusual or unpredictable activity or announcements in Amazon's business or in the stock market. Such activity or announcements would affect the stock price above and beyond what the technical analysis predicts.

It is important to note that the modeling methodology presented in this book is just one view. The analysis of Amazon and its results do not directly reflect my belief, but rather, a possible conclusion for instructional purposes only based on limiting the most extreme of variables. There are other possibilities and paths I have chosen not to include in this book but could have also been sufficient. Many ideas presented here are debatable, and I welcome the debate. The point is to understand the methods, and further, the concepts behind the methods to properly equip you with the tools to drive your own analyses.

HOW THIS BOOK IS STRUCTURED

This book is divided into two parts:

1. Financial Statements and Projections
2. Valuation

In Part One, we will build a complete financial model of Amazon. We will analyze the company's historical performance and step through techniques to make accurate projections of the business's future performance. The goal of this section is not only to understand how to build a model of Amazon, but also to extract the modeling techniques used by analysts and to apply those techniques to any investment.

Once we have a good understanding of Amazon's past and future performance, Part Two will help us interpret the company's financials into a valuation analysis using the methods mentioned previously. You may skip directly to Part Two if your needs do not require building a complete financial model.

It is important to note it is not 100 percent necessary to have a full-scale model in order to conduct a valuation analysis, but it is recommended. Valuation techniques are based on a summary of the company's performance. In this case, to be complete, we will use the model of the company built in Part One to extract the necessary summary information and to conduct the valuation analysis. However, you could technically use summary information as well.

The book is designed to have you build your own model on Amazon step-by-step. The model template can be found on the companion website associated with this book and is titled "NYSF—Amazon—Template.xls." To access the website, go to www.wiley.com/go/pignataro (password: investment).

One

Financial Statements and Projections

Financial modeling is the fundamental building block of analysis in investment banking. We will take a look at Amazon and analyze its financial standing, building a complete financial model as it would be done by Wall Street analysts.

The goals of this section are:

1. Understanding financial statements
   a. Concepts
   b. Historical analysis
   c. Making projections
   d. Model flow between the statements
2. Developing the ability to build a complete financial model of Amazon

It is recommended that a financial model be built on six major components:

1. Income statement
2. Cash flow statement
3. Balance sheet
4. Depreciation schedule
5. Working capital
6. Debt schedule

The first three are the major statements: income statement, cash flow statement, and balance sheet. The latter three help support the flow and continuity of the first three. It is also not uncommon to have even more supporting schedules, depending on the required analysis. Notice the first six tabs in the model template ("NYSF—Amazon—Template.xls"). Each reflects the six major model components. Please use the template and follow along as we build the model together.

CHAPTER 1

The Income Statement

The income statement measures a company's profit (or loss) over a specific period of time. A business is generally required to report and record the sales it generates for tax purposes. And, of course, taxes on sales made can be reduced by the expenses incurred while generating those sales. Although there are specific rules that govern when and how those expense reductions can be utilized, there is still a general concept:

$$\text{Profit} = \text{Revenue} - \text{Expenses}$$

A company is taxed on profit. So:

$$\text{Net Income} = \text{Profit} - \text{Tax}$$

However, income statements have grown to be quite complex. The multifaceted categories of expenses can vary from company to company. As analysts, we need to identify major categories within the income statement in order to facilitate proper analysis. For this reason, one should always categorize income statement line items into nine major categories:

1. Revenue (sales)
2. Cost of goods sold
3. Operating expenses
4. Other income
5. Depreciation and amortization
6. Interest
7. Taxes
8. Non-recurring and extraordinary items
9. Distributions

No matter how convoluted an income statement is, a good analyst would categorize each reported income statement line item into one of these nine categories. This will allow an analyst to easily understand the major categories that drive profitability in an income statement and can further allow him or her to compare the profitability between several different companies—an analysis very important in determining relative valuation. This book assumes you have some basic understanding of accounting, so we will just briefly recap the line items.

REVENUE

Revenue is the sales or gross income a company has made during a specific operating period. It is important to note that when and how revenue is recognized can vary from company to company and may be different from the actual cash received. Revenue is recognized when "realized and earned," which is typically when the products sold have been transferred or once the service has been rendered.

COST OF GOODS SOLD

Cost of goods sold (COGS) is the direct costs attributable to the production of the goods sold by a company. These are the costs most directly associated to the revenue. This is typically the cost of the materials used in creating the products sold, although some other direct costs could be included as well.

Gross Profit

Gross profit is not one of the nine categories listed, as it is a totaling item. Gross profit is the revenue less COGS and is helpful in determining the net value of the revenue after COGS is removed. One common metric analyzed is gross profit margin, which is the gross profit divided by the revenue. We will calculate these totals and metrics for Amazon later in the chapter.

A business that sells cars, for example, may have manufacturing costs. Let's say we sell a car for $20,000, and we manufacture the cars in-house. We must purchase $5,000 in raw materials to manufacture the car. If we sell one car, $20,000 is our revenue and $5,000 is the COGS. That leaves us with $15,000 in gross profit, or a 75% gross profit margin. Now let's say in the first quarter of operations we sell 25 cars. That's 25 × $20,000, or

$500,000 in revenue. Our COGS is 25 × $5,000, or $125,000, which leaves us with $375,000 in gross profit.

Car Co.	1Q 2021
Revenue	500,000.0
COGS	125,000.0
Gross Profit	375,000.0
% Gross Profit Margin	75%

OPERATING EXPENSES

Operating expenses are expenses incurred by a company as a result of performing its normal business operations. These are the relatively indirect expenses related to generating the company's revenue and supporting its operations. Operating expenses can be broken into several other major subcategories, the most common of which are:

1. **Selling, General, and Administrative (SG&A).** These are all selling expenses and all general and administrative expenses of a company. Examples are employee salaries and rents.
2. **Advertising and Marketing.** These are expenses relating to any advertising or marketing initiatives the company employs. Examples are print advertising and Google Adwords.
3. **Research and Development (R&D).** These are expenses relating to furthering the development of the company's product or services.

Let's say in our car business, we have employees to whom we have paid $75,000 in total in the first quarter. We also have rents to pay of $2,500, and we ran an advertising initiative that cost us $7,500. Finally, let's assume we have employed some R&D efforts to continue to improve the design of our car that cost roughly $5,000 per quarter. Using the previous example, our simple income statement looks like this:

Car Co.	1Q 2021
Revenue	500,000.0
COGS	125,000.0
Gross Profit	375,000.0
% Gross Profit Margin	75%

(Continued)

Operating Expenses	
SG&A	77,500.0
Advertising	7,500.0
R&D	5,000.0
Total Operating Expenses	**90,000.0**

OTHER INCOME

Companies can generate income that is not core to their business. As this income is taxable, it is recorded on the income statement. However, since it is not core to business operations, it is not considered revenue. Let's take the example of the car company. A car company's core business is producing and selling cars. However, many car companies also generate income in another way: financing. If a car company offers its customers the ability to finance the payments on a car, those payments come with interest. The car company receives that interest. That interest is taxable and is considered additional income. However, as that income is not core to the business, it is not considered revenue; it is considered other income.

Another common example of other income is *income from noncontrolling interests,* also known as *income from unconsolidated affiliates.* This is income received when one company has a noncontrolling interest investment in another company. So when a company (Company A) invests in another company (Company B) and receives a minority stake in Company B, Company B distributes a portion of its net income to Company A. Company A records those distributions received as other income.

EBITDA

Earnings before interest, taxes, depreciation, and amortization (EBITDA) is a very important measure among Wall Street analysts. We will later see its many uses as a fundamental metric in valuation and analysis. It can be calculated as Revenue – COGS – Operating Expenses + Other Income.

It is debatable whether other income should be included in EBITDA. There are two sides to the argument:

1. *It should be included in EBITDA.* If a company produces other income, it should be represented as part of EBITDA, and other income should be listed above our EBITDA total. The argument here is that

other income, although not core to revenue, is still in fact operating and should be represented as part of the company's operations. There are many ways of looking at this. Taking the car example, we can maybe assume that the financing activities, although not core to revenue, are essential enough to the overall profitability to be considered as part of EBITDA.

2. *It should not be included in EBITDA.* If a company produces other income, it should not be represented as part of EBITDA, and other income should be listed below our EBITDA total. The argument here is that although it is a part of the company's profitability, it is not core enough to the operations to be incorporated as part of the company's core profitability.

Determining whether to include other income as EBITDA is not so simple and clear cut. It is important to consider if the other income is consistent and reoccurring. If it is not, the case can more likely be made that it should not be included in EBITDA. It is also important to consider the purpose of your particular analysis. For example, if you are looking to acquire the entire business, and that business will still be producing that other income even after the acquisition, then maybe it should be represented as part of EBITDA. Or maybe that other income will no longer exist after the acquisition, in which case it should not be included in EBITDA. As another example, if you are trying to compare EBITDA with the EBITDA of other companies, then it is important to consider if the other companies also produce that same other income. If not, then maybe it is better to keep other income out of the EBITDA analysis, to make sure there is a consistent comparison among all of the company EBITDAs.

Different banks and firms may have different views on whether other income should or should not be included in EBITDA. Even different industry groups within the same firm have been found to have different views on this topic. As a good analyst, it is important to come up with one consistent defensible view, and stick to it.

Let's assume in our car example the other income will be part of EBITDA.

Car Co.	1Q 2021
Revenue	500,000.0
COGS	125,000.0
Gross Profit	**375,000.0**
% Gross Profit Margin	*75%*

(*Continued*)

Operating Expenses	
SG&A	77,500.0
Advertising	7,500.0
R&D	5,000.0
Total Operating Expenses	**90,000.0**
Other Income	1,000.0
EBITDA	**286,000.0**
EBITDA Margin	*57%*

Notice we have also calculated EBITDA margin, which is defined as EBITDA / Revenue.

DEPRECIATION AND AMORTIZATION

Depreciation is the accounting for the aging and depletion of fixed assets over a period of time. Amortization is the accounting for the cost basis reduction of intangible assets (intellectual property such as patents, copyrights, and trademarks, for example) over their useful life. It is important to note that not all intangible assets are subject to amortization. We will discuss depreciation and amortization (D&A) in Chapter 4.

EBIT

Similar to EBITDA, earnings before interest and taxes (EBIT) is also utilized in valuation. EBIT is EBITDA – Depreciation and Amortization. So let's assume the example car company has $8,000 in D&A each quarter. So:

Car Co.	1Q 2021
EBITDA	286,000.0
EBITDA Margin	*57%*
D&A	8,000.0
EBIT	278,000.0
EBIT Margin	*56%*

Notice we have also calculated EBIT margin, which is defined as EBIT divided by revenue.

INTEREST

Interest is composed of interest expense and interest income. Interest expense is the cost incurred on debt that the company has borrowed. Interest income is commonly the income received from cash held in savings accounts, certificates of deposits, and other investments.

Let's assume the car company had $1MM in loans and incurs 10% of interest per year on those loans. So the car company has $100,000 in interest expense per year, or $25,000 per quarter. We can also assume that the company has $50,000 of cash and generated 1% of interest income on that cash per year ($500), or $125 per quarter.

Often, the interest expense is netted against the interest income as net interest expense.

EBT

Earnings before taxes (EBT) can be defined as EBIT – Net interest.

Car Co.	1Q 2021
EBIT	278,000.0
EBIT Margin	56%
Interest Expense	25,000.0
Interest Income	125.0
Net Interest Expense	24,875.0
EBT	253,125.0
EBT Margin	51%

Notice we have also calculated EBT margin, which is defined as EBT divided by revenue.

TAXES

Taxes are the financial charges imposed by the government on the company's operations. Taxes are imposed on earnings before taxes, as defined previously. In the car example, we can assume the tax rate is 35%.

Net Income

Net income is defined as EBT – Taxes. The complete income statement follows.

Car Co.	1Q 2021
Revenue	500,000.0
COGS	125,000.0
Gross Profit	**375,000.0**
% Gross Profit Margin	*75%*
Operating Expenses	
SG&A	77,500.0
Advertising	7,500.0
R&D	5,000.0
Total Operating Expenses	**90,000.0**
Other Income	1,000.0
EBITDA	**286,000.0**
EBITDA Margin	*57%*
D&A	8,000.0
EBIT	**278,000.0**
EBIT Margin	*56%*
Interest Expense	25,000.0
Interest Income	125.0
Net Interest Expense	**24,875.0**
EBT	**253,125.0**
EBT Margin	*51%*
Tax	88,593.75
Tax Rate (%)	*35%*
Net Income	164,531.25

NON-RECURRING AND EXTRAORDINARY ITEMS

Non-recurring and extraordinary items or events are expenses or incomes that are either one-time or not pertaining to everyday core operations. Gains or losses on sales of assets, or from business closures, are examples of non-recurring events. Such non-recurring or extraordinary events can be scattered about in a generally accepted accounting principles (GAAP) income statement, and so it is the job of a good analyst to identify these items and move them to the bottom of the income statement in order to have EBITDA, EBIT, and net income line items that represent everyday, continuous operations. We call this "clean" EBITDA, EBIT, and net income. However, we do not want to eliminate those non-recurring or extraordinary items completely, so we move them to this section. From here on out, we will refer to both "non-recurring" and "extraordinary" items simply as "non-recurring items" to simplify.

DISTRIBUTIONS

Distributions are broadly defined as payments to equity holders. These payments can be in the form of dividends or noncontrolling interest payments, to name the major two.

Noncontrolling interests is the portion of the company or the company's subsidiary that is owned by another outside person or entity. If another entity (Entity A) owns a noncontrolling interest in the company (Entity B), Entity B must distribute a portion of Entity B's earnings to Entity A. (We will discuss noncontrolling interests in more detail later in the book.)

Net Income (as Reported)

Because we have recommended moving some non-recurring line items into a separate section, the net income listed prior is effectively an adjusted net-income, which is most useful for analysis, valuation, and comparison. However, it is important still to represent a complete net income with all adjustments included to match the original given net income. So, it is recommended to have a second net income line as a "sanity check," defined as:

Net income − Non-recurring events − Distributions

SHARES

A company's shares outstanding reported on the income statement can be reported as basic or diluted. The basic share count is a count of the number of shares outstanding in the market. The diluted share count is the number of shares outstanding in the market plus any shares that would be considered outstanding today if all option and warrant holders that are in-the-money decided to exercise on their securities. The diluted share count is best thought of as a "What if?" scenario. If all the option and warrant holders who could exercise would, how many shares would be outstanding now?

Earnings per Share (EPS)

Earnings per share (EPS) is defined as the net income divided by the number of shares outstanding. A company typically reports a basic EPS and a diluted EPS, divided by basic shares or diluted shares, respectively. It is important to note that each company may have a different definition on what exactly to include in net income when calculating EPS. In other words, is net income before or after noncontrolling interests used? Or before or after dividends? For investors, it is common to use net income before dividends have been paid but after noncontrolling interest investors have been paid. However, we recommend backing into the company's historical EPS to identify the exact formula they are using. We will illustrate this process with Amazon next.

$$\text{Basic EPS} = \text{Net income} / \text{Basic shares}$$
$$\text{Diluted EPS} = \text{Net income} / \text{Diluted shares}$$

AMAZON'S INCOME STATEMENT

There are several ways to obtain a public company's financial information. We would first recommend going to the company's website and locating the "Investor Relations" section. Amazon's website has a lot of menu options and links, and the layout can change, but as of writing this book, the Investor Relations link can be found toward the bottom of their website under the "Get to Know Us" section. See Figure 1.1. One can also google "Amazon Investor Relations" to get to its site.

The "SEC Filings" section takes you to Amazon's government filings. I tend to prefer a company's SEC filing over the Annual Report as the SEC filing may not contain all exhibits that could provide extra and important detail (Figure 1.2).

To obtain the latest annual SEC filing (Figure 1.3), or the "10-K," select the dropdown box "Annual Filings" under "Group" and "2021" under "Filing Year." You can then select the pdf icon to download the document.

You can also go to the US Securities and Exchange Commission (SEC) website (www.sec.gov), where all public company filings are published, and search for Amazon's specific filings.

Note that by the time this book is published, Amazon may have changed its website. If so, you can download a copy of the 2020 Amazon 10-K on the

FIGURE 1.1 Amazon's Home Page

FIGURE 1.2 Amazon's Investor Relations

companion website associated with this book, or you can simply rely on the exhibits and examples throughout this book.

If you have downloaded the correct document, scroll down to locate the income statement. Make sure you have identified the company's complete *income statement* and not its *financial summary*. These are easy to confuse.

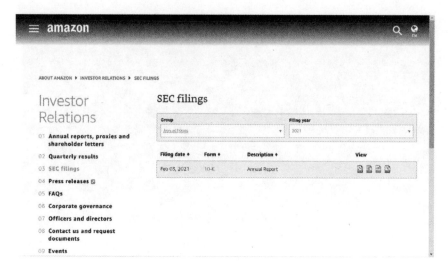

FIGURE 1.3 Amazon's SEC Filings

The financial summary does contain income statement information, but it is not as detailed as the actual income statement. The financial summary also typically contains a longer period (5–10 years) of historical data, whereas the more-detailed income statement typically contains only two or three years' worth. Figure 1.4 is Amazon's financial summary section, taken from page 18 of the company's 10-K. You can easily see that it does not contain all the necessary line items such as costs and expenses to properly create a model. You will also notice that it is labeled as "Selected Consolidated Financial Data."

If you continue to scroll through the filing, you will find the complete income statement on page 39. You will also notice that it is properly labeled as "Consolidated Statements of Operations." We will use the income statement found in Figure 1.5 to analyze Amazon's historical financial position. It is standard to have three years of financials in a company model, so we will create a model from years 2018–2020.

Revenue

When looking at the income statement in Figure 1.5, you want to first identify all the major line items as referenced earlier in this chapter, beginning with sales. We can see that Amazon has two lines of Revenues: "Net Product Sales" and "Net Service Sales." We will list both separately.

Item 6. *Selected Consolidated Financial Data*

The following selected consolidated financial data should be read in conjunction with the consolidated financial statements and the notes thereto in Item 8 of Part II, "Financial Statements and Supplementary Data," and the information contained in Item 7 of Part II, "Management's Discussion and Analysis of Financial Condition and Results of Operations." Historical results are not necessarily indicative of future results.

			Year Ended December 31,		
	2016	2017 (1)	2018	2019	2020
			(in millions, except per share data)		
Statements of Operations:					
Net sales	$ 135,987	$ 177,866	$ 232,887	$ 280,522	$ 386,064
Operating income	$ 4,186	$ 4,106	$ 12,421	$ 14,541	$ 22,899
Net income (loss)	$ 2,371	$ 3,033	$ 10,073	$ 11,588	$ 21,331
Basic earnings per share (2)	$ 5.01	$ 6.32	$ 20.68	$ 23.46	$ 42.64
Diluted earnings per share (2)	$ 4.90	$ 6.15	$ 20.14	$ 23.01	$ 41.83
Weighted-average shares used in computation of earnings per share:					
Basic	474	480	487	494	500
Diluted	484	493	500	504	510
Statements of Cash Flows:					
Net cash provided by (used in) operating activities (3)	$ 17,203	$ 18,365	$ 30,723	$ 38,514	$ 66,064

			December 31,		
	2016	2017	2018	2019 (4)	2020
			(in millions)		
Balance Sheets:					
Total assets	$ 83,402	$ 131,310	$ 162,648	$ 225,248	$ 321,195
Total long-term obligations	$ 20,301	$ 45,718	$ 50,708	$ 75,376	$ 101,406

(1) We acquired Whole Foods Market on August 28, 2017. The results of Whole Foods Market have been included in our results of operation from the date of acquisition.

(2) For further discussion of earnings per share, see Item 8 of Part II, "Financial Statements and Supplementary Data — Note 1 — Description of Business, Accounting Policies, and Supplemental Disclosures"

(3) As a result of the adoption of new accounting guidance, we retrospectively adjusted our consolidated statements of cash flows to add restricted cash to cash and cash equivalents, which restated cash provided by operating activities by $(69) million in 2016 and 2017.

(4) As a result of the adoption of new accounting guidance on January 1, 2019, we recognized lease assets and liabilities for operating leases with terms of more than twelve months. Prior period amounts were not adjusted and continue to be reported in accordance with our historic accounting policies.

FIGURE 1.4   Amazon's Five-Year Financial Summary

AMAZON.COM, INC.
CONSOLIDATED STATEMENTS OF OPERATIONS
(in millions, except per share data)

		Year Ended December 31,	
	2018	**2019**	**2020**
Net product sales	$ 141,915	$ 160,408	$ 215,915
Net service sales	90,972	120,114	170,149
Total net sales	232,887	280,522	386,064
Operating expenses:			
Cost of sales	139,156	165,536	233,307
Fulfillment	34,027	40,232	58,517
Technology and content	28,837	35,931	42,740
Marketing	13,814	18,878	22,008
General and administrative	4,336	5,203	6,668
Other operating expense (income), net	296	201	(75)
Total operating expenses	220,466	265,981	363,165
Operating income	12,421	14,541	22,899
Interest income	440	832	555
Interest expense	(1,417)	(1,600)	(1,647)
Other income (expense), net	(183)	203	2,371
Total non-operating income (expense)	(1,160)	(565)	1,279
Income before income taxes	11,261	13,976	24,178
Provision for income taxes	(1,197)	(2,374)	(2,863)
Equity-method investment activity, net of tax	9	(14)	16
Net income	$ 10,073	$ 11,588	$ 21,331
Basic earnings per share	$ 20.68	$ 23.46	$ 42.64
Diluted earnings per share	$ 20.14	$ 23.01	$ 41.83
Weighted-average shares used in computation of earnings per share:			
Basic	487	494	500
Diluted	500	504	510

See accompanying notes to consolidated financial statements.

FIGURE 1.5 Amazon's Income Statement

Now is a good time to open the model template titled "NYSF—Amazon—Template.xls." Notice the first six tabs each represent a financial schedule we will build to properly analyze the business. A well-built model contains at least these six major statements:

1. Income statement
2. Cash flow statement
3. Balance sheet
4. Depreciation schedule
5. Working capital schedule
6. Debt schedule

For this chapter, we will focus on the Income Statement tab. In this tab, we can enter the three years of each revenue stream, as shown in Figure 1.5. We will simply *hardcode* or type the numbers directly into the model as represented in the 10-K.

Before doing so, it is important to mention the first two important rules of modeling etiquette:

1. All hardcoded numbers and assumption drivers should be entered in blue font.
2. All formulas should be entered in black font.

When we mention hardcoded numbers, we mean numbers that are typed directly into a cell (that is, not links or formulas). All other formulas in the model are dependent on hardcodes, so should remain black. So, for example, the historical numbers we will now enter are hardcoded. These should be colored blue. However, the formulas that are simply summing hardcoded numbers should be in black font, as those are formulas. This is a standard on the Street and makes a model easier to analyze. It is important to be able to quickly zero in on the numbers and assumptions that drive the model projections (the blue numbers).

So, in Row 7, marked "Net Product Sales," we can type in 141,915; 160,408; and 215,915 for 2018, 2019, and 2020, or cells D7, E7, and F7, respectively. Remember to color the font of these blue, as they are hard codes. Later, we will look to the company's historical trends as a clue to estimating projections. So, let's calculate the historical growth of the company's net sales. The formula for growth in a current year is:

$$\text{Current Year Growth} = \text{Current Year/Previous Year} - 1$$

So we can calculate the 2019 net sales growth by entering the following into Cell E8:

Calculating 2019 Net Sales Growth (Cell E8)

Excel Keystrokes	Description
type "="	Enters into "formula" mode
select Cell E7	2019 Net Product Sales
type "/"	Divides
select Cell D7	2018 Net Product Sales
type "-1"	Subtracts 1
type "Enter"	End
Formula Result	=E7/D7−1

This should give you a 13.0% net sales growth in 2019. This process can be repeated for the net sales in 2020, or you can simply cut and paste the 2020 formula and copy it to the right. There are several ways to copy formulas to the right:

1. Click and drag the 2019 formula over to 2020. With the mouse, you can select the bottom right corner of Cell E8, and while holding down the left mouse button, you can drag the formula over to Cell F8.
2. Select the 2019 Growth in Cell E8. Select "Copy" from the menu bar (or hit "Ctrl" + "C"). Then select the 2020 Growth (Cell F8), and select "Paste" from the menu bar (or hit "Ctrl" + "V").
3. Preferred method:
   a. Highlight both the 2019 Growth in Cell E8 and the empty 2020 Growth in Cell F8. This can be done two ways:
      i. With the mouse: By selecting Cell E8, making sure to select the center of the cell, not the bottom right corner, and while holding down the left mouse button continue to move the mouse to the right, or;
      ii. With the keyboard: By selecting Cell E8, then holding down the "Shift" key while tapping the right arrow until the desired cells are selected.
   b. Hit "Ctrl" + "R, " which stands for "copy right."

Modeling Tip

We strongly recommend you use keyboard hotkeys (such as "Ctrl" + "R") as often as possible. The more comfortable you become with using the keyboard as opposed to the mouse, the more efficient a modeler you will become. (Please see Appendix 3 for a list of Excel hotkeys.)

TABLE 1.1 Amazon Historical Net Sales

Consolidated Income Statements (in US$ millions except per share amounts)

	Actuals		
Period Ending December 31	2018A	2019A	2020A
Revenue			
Net product sales	141,915.0	160,408.0	215,915.0
Y/Y growth (%)		13.0%	34.6%

Note that there is also a hotkey called "Ctrl" + "D," which stands for "copy down." Unfortunately, there is no "copy left" or "copy up." (See Table 1.1.)

We can now continue by entering the "Net Service Sales" numbers, and calculating the respective growth as we had done with the net sales.

We can then total the two sales line items into the total net sales line in Row 11. (See Table 1.2.)

Calculating 2018 Total Net Sales (Cell D11)

Excel Key Strokes	Description
type "="	Enters into "formula" mode
select Cell D7	2018 Net Product Sales
type "+"	Adds
select Cell D9	2018 Net Service Sales
type "Enter"	End
Formula result	=D7+D9

TABLE 1.2 Amazon Historical Total Net Sales

Consolidated Income Statements (in US$ millions except per share amounts)

	Actuals		
Period Ending December 31	2018A	2019A	2020A
Revenue			
Net product sales	141,915.0	160,408.0	215,915.0
Y/Y growth (%)		13.0%	34.6%
Net service sales	90,972.0	120,114.0	170,149.0
Y/Y growth (%)		32.0%	41.7%
Total Net Sales	232,887.0	280,522.0	386,064.0
Y/Y net sales growth (%)		20.5%	37.6%

This will give us $232,887.0 in total net sales for Amazon in 2018. We can now calculate total net sales' growth using the same growth formulas, as already demonstrated. We can also copy these formulas to the right through 2020 using one of the previous copy methods. (See Table 1.2.)

Getting to EBITDA

Below the revenue section we see "Operating Expenses," the first of which is "Cost of Sales." When referencing the categories earlier in this chapter, we see "Cost of Sales" clearly as category 2, "Cost of Goods Sold," and the rest as category 3, "Operating Expenses." I always recommend listing each cost line item as the company has done in an operating expense section, much like what we had done with revenue.

Digging up Depreciation

When identifying all expenses on an income statement, it is important to also locate the depreciation expense. Companies that have depreciating assets would generally record that depreciation as an expense to reduce taxes. So, if a company has depreciation, it should be represented on the income statement. However, not every company lists depreciation as a separate line item. A good analyst needs to do some more hunting to locate depreciation. Amazon certainly depreciates its assets. If you are unsure if the company you are analyzing depreciates assets, you should research the company's assets. An easy way to begin is by performing a word search for "depreciation" on the company's 10-K, or you can go to the cash flow statement to see if a depreciation line item exists. Depreciation is located in several places in the company's 10-K. In Figure 1.6, we use the example from page 38. This is the company's cash flow statement. You can clearly see there is a line item right after the "Adjustments to reconcile net income to net cash from operating activities" section titled "*Depreciation* and amortization of property and equipment and capitalized content costs, operating lease assets, and other." The existence of this line item clearly indicated depreciation is present, but just not separated out in the income statement. It is often the case that depreciation will show up directly on the cash flow statement yet not on the income statement. We will discuss why that may be the case in the next chapter when we learn about how the cash flow statement works.

In Figure 1.6, we can see depreciation and amortization for the consolidated business is $15,341, $21,789, and $25,251 for 2018, 2019, and 2020, respectively.

Once we have identified depreciation, we must determine where that depreciation is in the income statement. We have proven depreciation exists,

AMAZON.COM, INC.

CONSOLIDATED STATEMENTS OF CASH FLOWS

(in millions)

	Year Ended December 31,		
	2018	2019	2020
CASH, CASH EQUIVALENTS, AND RESTRICTED CASH, BEGINNING OF PERIOD	$ 21,856	$ 32,173	$ 36,410
OPERATING ACTIVITIES:			
Net income	10,073	11,588	21,331
Adjustments to reconcile net income to net cash from operating activities:			
Depreciation and amortization of property and equipment and capitalized content costs, operating lease assets, and other	15,341	21,789	25,251
Stock-based compensation	5,418	6,864	9,208
Other operating expense (income), net	274	164	(71)
Other expense (income), net	219	(249)	(2,582)
Deferred income taxes	441	796	(554)
Changes in operating assets and liabilities:			
Inventories	(1,314)	(3,278)	(2,849)
Accounts receivable, net and other	(4,615)	(7,681)	(8,169)
Accounts payable	3,263	8,193	17,480
Accrued expenses and other	472	(1,383)	5,754
Unearned revenue	1,151	1,711	1,265
Net cash provided by (used in) operating activities	30,723	38,514	66,064
INVESTING ACTIVITIES:			
Purchases of property and equipment	(13,427)	(16,861)	(40,140)
Proceeds from property and equipment sales and incentives	2,104	4,172	5,096
Acquisitions, net of cash acquired, and other	(2,186)	(2,461)	(2,325)
Sales and maturities of marketable securities	8,240	22,681	50,237
Purchases of marketable securities	(7,100)	(31,812)	(72,479)
Net cash provided by (used in) investing activities	(12,369)	(24,281)	(59,611)
FINANCING ACTIVITIES:			
Proceeds from short-term debt, and other	886	1,402	6,796
Repayments of short-term debt, and other	(813)	(1,518)	(6,177)
Proceeds from long-term debt	182	871	10,525
Repayments of long-term debt	(155)	(1,166)	(1,553)
Principal repayments of finance leases	(7,449)	(9,628)	(10,642)
Principal repayments of financing obligations	(337)	(27)	(53)
Net cash provided by (used in) financing activities	(7,686)	(10,066)	(1,104)
Foreign currency effect on cash, cash equivalents, and restricted cash	(351)	70	618
Net increase (decrease) in cash, cash equivalents, and restricted cash	10,317	4,237	5,967
CASH, CASH EQUIVALENTS, AND RESTRICTED CASH, END OF PERIOD	$ 32,173	$ 36,410	$ 42,377

See accompanying notes to consolidated financial statements.

FIGURE 1.6 Amazon's Cash Flow Statement

and we assume it must be somewhere in the income statement, although not directly shown. Be careful not to simply add the depreciation expense to the income statement. The depreciation amounts we have found previously are most likely buried in one of the expense items we have already identified. But how do we know which expense line item contains depreciation? Unfortunately, in many cases, it is not easy to tell.

A quick word search on depreciation in the 10-K reveals this quote under the "Technology and Content" expense section (page 45):

TECHNOLOGY AND CONTENT

Technology and content costs include payroll and related expenses for employees involved in the research and development of new and existing products and services, development, design, and maintenance of our stores, curation and display of products and services made available in our online stores, and infrastructure costs. Infrastructure costs include servers, networking equipment, and data center related depreciation and amortization, rent, utilities, and other expenses necessary to support AWS and other Amazon businesses. Collectively, these costs reflect the investments we make in order to offer a wide variety of products and services to our customers.

This is the only expense item that makes mention of depreciation. However, this is not the best and most complete indicator that all of the depreciation expense has been combined in the "Technology and Content" expense item.

Quite often, depreciation is a part of the cost of goods sold or sales, general, and administrative expenses, or spread out between the two. It is also often that one cannot identify exactly where depreciation is buried. It should be comforting to know, however, that whether we end up extracting the depreciation expense from cost of goods sold; sales, general, and administrative expenses; or both, it will not affect our EBITDA, which is most crucial for our valuation.

So, since the only mention of depreciation is in the "Technology and Content" section, we will assume depreciation should be removed from this line item. When we get to this line item, we will reduce the amount of those expenses by the value of depreciation.

We now have enough information to lay out a historical income statement for three years down to EBITDA.

Cost of Goods Sold

Amazon reports COGS as "Cost of Sales," and records 139,156, 165,536, and 233,307, for 2018, 2019, and 2020, respectively. Let us type those numbers into Cells D14, E14, and F14 now.

Notice there is a metric, "COGS as a % of Net Sales," in row 15. We will discuss later how calculating an expense as a percentage of revenue may or may not be a good indicator of future performance. To best prepare us for that discussion, let's calculate this metric now. The 2018 COGS as a percentage of net sales will be:

Calculating 2018 COGS as a % of Net Sales (Cell D15)

Excel Keystrokes	Description
type "="	Enters into "formula" mode
select Cell D14	2018 COGS
type "/"	Divides
select Cell D11	2018 Total Net Sales
type "Enter"	End
Formula Result	=D14/D11

This gives us 59.8% in 2018. We can now copy this formula to the right.

Gross Profit

Gross profit is revenue less cost of goods sold.

Calculating 2018 Gross Profit (Cell D16)

Excel Keystrokes	Description
type "="	Enters into "formula" mode
select Cell D11	2018 Total Net Sales
type "-"	Subtracts
select Cell D14	2018 COGS
Type "Enter"	End
Formula Result	=D11-D14

We can calculate the gross profit margin as explained earlier in this chapter.

Calculating 2018 Gross Profit Margin (Cell D17)

Excel Keystrokes	Description
type "="	Enters into "formula" mode
select Cell D16	2018 Gross Profit
type "/"	Divides
select Cell D11	2018 Total Net Sales
type "Enter"	End
Formula Result	=D16/D11

We can copy both formulas to the right and move on to operating expenses (see Table 1.3).

TABLE 1.3   Amazon Historical Gross Profit

Consolidated Income Statements (in US$ millions except per share amounts)

Period Ending December 31	Actuals		
	2018A	2019A	2020A
Revenue			
Net product sales	141,915.0	160,408.0	215,915.0
Y/Y growth (%)		13.0%	34.6%
Net service sales	90,972.0	120,114.0	170,149.0
Y/Y growth (%)		32.0%	41.7%
Total Net Sales	232,887.0	280,522.0	386,064.0
Y/Y net sales growth (%)		20.5%	37.6%
Cost of Goods Sold			
Cost of Goods Sold	139,156.0	165,536.0	233,307.0
COGS as a % of net sales	59.8%	59.0%	60.4%
Gross Profit	93,731.0	114,986.0	152,757.0
Gross profit margin (%)	40%	41%	40%

Fulfillment

In row 19, we can hardcode the three historical years for fulfillment expenses. We should have $34,027, $40,232, and $58,517 in years 2018, 2019, and 2020, respectively. We can then calculate fulfillment as a % of net sales as explained earlier in this chapter.

Calculating 2018 Fulfillment as a % of Net Sales (Cell D20)

Excel Keystrokes	Description
type "="	Enters into "formula" mode
select Cell D19	2018 Fulfillment
type "/"	Divides
select Cell D11	2018 Total Net Sales
type "Enter"	End
Formula Result	=D19/D11

We can copy both formulas to the right and move on to the next expense line item.
See Table 1.4 as a guide.

Technology and Content

Given the previous discussion on depreciation, we have assumed the depreciation expense is contained within Technology and Content. So in row 21, we should hardcode the technology and content expenses *less* the depreciation expense. We had earlier identified depreciation expense to be $15,341, $21,789, and $25,251 for 2018, 2019, and 2020, respectively. In 2018, for example, we should have $28,837 − 15,341. Then 2019 would be $35,931 − 21,789, and for 2020, $42,740 − 25,251. We can calculate these expenses as a percentage of net sales, as we did with the Fulfillment.

Calculating 2018 Technology and Content as a % of Net Sales (Cell D22)

Excel Keystrokes	Description
type "="	Enters into "formula" mode
select Cell D21	2018 Technology and Content
type "/"	Divides
select Cell D11	2018 Total Net Sales
type "Enter"	End
Formula Result	=D21/D11

TABLE 1.4   Amazon Historical EBITDA

Consolidated Income Statements (in US$ millions except per share amounts)

Period Ending December 31	Actuals		
	2018A	2019A	2020A
Revenue			
Net product sales	141,915.0	160,408.0	215,915.0
Y/Y growth (%)		*13.0%*	*34.6%*
Net service sales	90,972.0	120,114.0	170,149.0
Y/Y growth (%)		*32.0%*	*41.7%*
Total Net Sales	**232,887.0**	**280,522.0**	**386,064.0**
Y/Y net sales growth (%)		*20.5%*	*37.6%*
Cost of Goods Sold			
Cost of Goods Sold	139,156.0	165,536.0	233,307.0
COGS as a % of net sales	*59.8%*	*59.0%*	*60.4%*
Gross Profit	**93,731.0**	**114,986.0**	**152,757.0**
Gross profit margin (%)	*40%*	*41%*	*40%*
Operating Expenses			
Fulfillment	34,027.0	40,232.0	58,517.0
Fulfillment as a % of net sales	*14.6%*	*14.3%*	*15.2%*
Technology and Content	13,496.0	14,142.0	17,489.0
Technology and content as a % of net sales	*5.8%*	*5.0%*	*4.5%*
Marketing	13,814.0	18,878.0	22,008.0
Marketing as a % of net sales	*5.9%*	*6.7%*	*5.7%*
General and administrative	4,336.0	5,203.0	6,668.0
General and administrative as a % of net sales	*1.9%*	*1.9%*	*1.7%*
Other operating expense (income), net	296.0	201.0	(75.0)
Other operating expense as a % of net sales	*0.1%*	*0.1%*	*0.0%*
Total operating expenses	**65,969.0**	**78,656.0**	**104,607.0**
EBITDA	**27,762.0**	**36,330.0**	**48,150.0**
EBITDA margin (%)	*11.9%*	*13.0%*	*12.5%*

We can copy both formulas to the right and move on to the next expense line item. See Table 1.4 as a guide.

Marketing, General and Administrative, Other Operating Expense (Income), Net

The next three expense line items can be hardcoded as we have done with the Fulfillment expenses. For each line item, we can then calculate the respective margins. (See Table 1.4 as a guide.)

Once complete, all expense line items can be totaled.

Total Operating Expenses

We can now total each of these operating expense line items, taking care not to include the margin metrics.

Calculating 2018 Total Operating Expenses (Cell D29)

Excel Keystrokes	Description
type "="	Enters into "formula" mode
select Cell D19	Selects the first expense, "Fulfillment"
type "+"	Adds
select Cell D21	Selects the next expense, "Technology and Content"
type "+"	Adds
select Cell D23	Selects the next expense, "Marketing"
type "+"	Adds
select Cell D25	Selects the next expense, "General and Administrative"
type "+"	Adds
select Cell D27	Selects the next expense, "Other Operating Expense"
type "Enter"	End
Formula Result	=D19+D21+D23+D25+D27

Copy this formula to the right.

EBITDA

We can now calculate EBITDA as gross profit less the operating expenses.

Calculating 2018 EBITDA (Cell D30)

Excel Keystrokes	Description
type "="	Enters into "formula" mode
select Cell D16	2018 Gross Profit
type "-"	Subtracts
select Cell D29	2018 Total Operating Expenses
type "Enter"	End
Formula Result	=D16-D29

We can calculate the EBITDA margin.

Calculating 2018 EBITDA Margin (Cell D31)

Excel Keystrokes	Description
type "="	Enters into "formula" mode
select Cell D30	2018 EBITDA
type "/"	Divides
select Cell D11	2018 Total Net Sales
type "Enter"	End
Formula Result	=D30/D11

We can copy both formulas to the right. (See Table 1.4.)

Beyond EBITDA

Once we have EBITDA, we can continue identifying the rest of Amazon's income statement line items.

Depreciation and Amortization

We have already identified the depreciation. We can hardcode $15,341, $21,789, and $25,251 for 2018, 2019, and 2020, respectively into Row 32. See Table 1.5.

TABLE 1.5   Amazon Historical EBIT

Consolidated Income Statements (in US$ millions except per share amounts)

| | Actuals | | |
Period Ending December 31	2018A	2019A	2020A
EBITDA	27,762.0	36,330.0	48,150.0
EBITDA margin (%)	*11.9%*	*13.0%*	*12.5%*
Depreciation and amortization	15,341.0	21,789.0	25,251.0
EBIT	12,421.0	14,541.0	22,899.0
EBIT margin (%)	*5.3%*	*5.2%*	*5.9%*

EBIT

EBIT is EBITDA less depreciation. We can also calculate the EBIT margin, as we have done previously.

Calculating 2018 EBIT (Cell D33)

Excel Keystrokes	Description
type "="	Enters into "formula" mode
select Cell D30	2018 EBITDA
type "-"	Subtracts
select Cell D32	2018 Depreciation
type "Enter"	End
Formula Result	=D30-D32

We can calculate the EBIT margin.

Calculating 2018 EBIT Margin (Cell D34)

Excel Keystrokes	Description
type "="	Enters into "formula" mode
select Cell D33	2018 EBIT
type "/"	Divides
select Cell D11	2018 Total Net Sales
type "Enter"	End
Formula Result	=D33/D11

See Table 1.5.

Other Income

We can now hardcode other income. It is important here to consider the impact that other income has on the income statement. Notice how every expense line item is shown as a positive number even though the expense is *reducing* net income. Sometime, other line items like other income or non-recurring events are also listed as positive but may be *increasing* net income. This can lead to much confusion and erroneous reporting. My strong recommendation is, no matter how these line items are represented on the original set of financials, to simply show every expense or reduction in net income as positive (of course, except for revenue), and every income or increase in net income as negative. This will first ensure one who is analyzing the financials can at a glance identify which line items are actually increasing versus reducing income and second keep a consistent formulae flow in that EBITDA, EBIT, and net income are always subtracting from each individual line item. Had we not adjusted to this consistent logic we would have to add some line items and subtract others – and this can lead to common mistakes. We will, at the end of the income statement, make sure we can match the Net Income we calculate to Amazon's net income to ensure all is flowing properly.

Here it clearly states by the line-item name "Other Income" (expense), that an expense is shown in parenthesis. I would like to stick to the logic of the other above expenses showing an expense as a positive number. So, in 2018, "183" should be hardcoded; and the opposite for 2019, "(203)" where the positive number is actually income. (See Table 1.6.)

TABLE 1.6 Amazon Historical EBT

Consolidated Income Statements (in US$ millions except per share amounts)

Period Ending December 31	Actuals		
	2018A	2019A	2020A
EBIT	12,421.0	14,541.0	22,899.0
EBIT margin (%)	*5.3%*	*5.2%*	*5.9%*
Other Income	183.0	(203.0)	(2,371.0)
Interest			
Interest expense	1,417.0	1,600.0	1,647.0
Interest income	(440.0)	(832.0)	(555.0)
Net Interest Expense	977.0	768.0	1,092.0
Earnings before Tax (EBT)	11,261.0	13,976.0	24,178.0
EBT margin (%)	*4.8%*	*5.0%*	*6.3%*

Interest

Amazon, like most companies, reports interest expense separate from interest income. As already mentioned with other income, some companies report interest expense as a positive number and others as a negative number. I strongly recommend staying consistent with the logic of all expenses shown as positive. (See Table 1.6.)

Now we can sum both the interest expense and interest income together to calculate net interest expense in line 39.

Calculating 2018 Net Interest Expense (Cell D39)

Excel Keystrokes	Description
type "="	Enters into "formula" mode
select Cell D37	2018 Interest Expense
type "+"	Adds
select Cell D38	2018 Interest Income
type "Enter"	End
Formula Result	=D37+D38

Note typing "Alt" + "=" is a quick way to sum up line items in sequence. Refer to Table 1.6 as a guide.

EBT

Remember the formulas:

$$EBIT - Other\ Income - Interest = EBT$$

$$EBT\ margin = EBT\ /\ Total\ Revenue$$

Calculate EBT and refer to Table 1.6 as a guide.

This number should match the "Income before income taxes" from Amazon's income statement. This is a good "sanity check" to be sure all hardcoded numbers have been properly input and everything is flowing correctly. (See Table 1.7.)

Taxes

Take note of the total number of taxes on Amazon's income statement, listed as "Provision for Income Taxes." After hardcoding, we can calculate the tax

TABLE 1.7 Amazon Historical Net Income from Continuing Operations

Consolidated Income Statements (in US$ millions except per share amounts)

Period Ending December 31	Actuals		
	2018A	2019A	2020A
Earnings before Tax (EBT)	11,261.0	13,976.0	24,178.0
EBT margin (%)	*4.8%*	*5.0%*	*6.3%*
Income tax expense	1,197.0	2,374.0	2,863.0
All-in effective tax rate (%)	*10.6%*	*17.0%*	*11.8%*
Net Income from Continuing Operations	10,064.0	11,602.0	21,315.0

rate, necessary for our projections and further analysis, as taxes divided by EBT. Refer to Table 1.7.

Calculating 2018 Tax Rate (Cell D43)

Excel Keystrokes	Description
type "="	Enters into "formula" mode
select Cell D42	2018 Income Tax Expense
type "/"	Divides
select Cell D40	2018 EBT
type "Enter"	End
Formula Result	=D42/D40

We can now copy this formula to the right.

Net Income from Continuing Operations

Remember, EBT – Taxes = Net Income. (See Table 1.7.)

Non-Recurring and Extraordinary Items

Amazon has not clearly defined any non-recurring or extraordinary items. I kept this section in the model with some standard examples of line items you might see in an income statement. Leave them "0" for this model. You can then total each line item into the "Total Non-Recurring Events" line item.

Net Income (after Non-Recurring Events)

We now calculate the net income after non-recurring events as net income from continuing operations less non-recurring events. (See Table 1.8.)

Distributions

The next line item in Amazon's income statement after tax is Equity-method investment activity (net of tax). This is effectively noncontrolling interest. Be careful of the flow, as $9MM in 2018 is actually increasing the net income. So to stay within our standard practice of having an *expense* as positive and *income* as negative, we want to reverse the signs hardcoding "(9)" in 2018 and so on for the next years.

Although Amazon does not pay dividends, I left the line item here in row 53 to illustrate where it should be located, as it is a relatively common line item to have. This can stay hardcoded at "0." (See Table 1.8.)

Net Income (as Reported)

We can now calculate the net income (as reported) as net income (after non-recurring events) less equity method investment activity and dividends.

TABLE 1.8   Amazon Historical Net Income

Consolidated Income Statements (in US$ millions except per share amounts)

		Actuals	
Period Ending December 31	2018A	2019A	2020A
Non-Recurring Events			
Discontinued operations	0.0	0.0	0.0
Extraordinary items	0.0	0.0	0.0
Effect of accounting changes	0.0	0.0	0.0
Other items	0.0	0.0	0.0
Total Non-Recurring Events	0.0	0.0	0.0
Net Income (after Non-Recurring Events)	10,064.0	11,602.0	21,315.0
Equity-method investment activity, net of tax	(9.0)	14.0	(16.0)
Dividends paid on common stock	0.0	0.0	0.0
Net Income (as Reported)	10,073.0	11,588.0	21,331.0

This net income should match with the net income on Amazon's income statement in the 10-K. This again is a great way to make sure that you not only have every line item properly hardcoded into the model but have all income and expenses properly flowing in the correct direction. (See Table 1.8.)

Shares and EPS

We can now hardcode in the basic and diluted shares as Amazon has reported into Rows 59 and 60 before calculating EPS. We can then calculate the basic EPS by dividing the net income (as reported) by the number of basic shares outstanding, and the diluted EPS by dividing the net income (as reported) by the number of diluted shares outstanding. The purpose of calculating EPS here is to ensure we have metrics that match what the company reported for accuracy in our analysis. It is, however, common to calculate EPS using our adjusted net income depending on the purpose of the analysis.

Calculating 2018 Basic EPS (Cell D56)

Excel Keystrokes	Description
type "="	Enters into "formula" mode
select Cell D54	2018 Net Income (as reported)
type "/"	Divides
select Cell D59	2018 Basic Shares
type "Enter"	End
Formula Result	=D54/D59

We repeat the same process for the diluted EPS, using diluted shares in place of basic shares.

Calculating 2018 Diluted EPS (Cell D57)

Excel Keystrokes	Description
type "="	Enters into "formula" mode
select Cell D54	2018 Net Income (as reported)
type "/"	Divides
select Cell D60	2018 Diluted Shares
type "Enter"	End
Formula Result	=D54/D60

TABLE 1.9 Amazon Historical EPS

Consolidated Income Statements (in US$ millions except per share amounts)

	Actuals		
Period Ending December 31	2018A	2019A	2020A
Earnings per Share (EPS)			
Basic	20.68	23.46	42.66
Diluted	20.15	22.99	41.83
Average Common Shares Outstanding			
Basic	487	494	500
Diluted	500	504	510 ·

We now have a complete historical income statement for Amazon. We are now ready to make projections. (See Table 1.9.)

Notice that although the net income matches the Amazon financials, the EPS is slightly off in some cases. This is likely because the share count given is rounded to millions. Had we been given actual share counts, we could match EPS to the decimal. This is not a significant issue, as EPS is not used throughout the model; this is just output for valuation. The small difference will not affect our analysis.

INCOME STATEMENT – MAKING PROJECTIONS

Making projections is no easy task. One needs to spend much time understanding and researching the core business model, how it generates revenue, its cost structure, and beyond to best get a handle on the next years of its performance. Ideally, a Wall Street research analyst will have had years of experience following and keeping close watch on the business, and would have a good handle on its future trends in order to make good projections. That being said, there are methods to make fair generalizations, though broad, but strong enough to use as tools to assess overall company valuation. Remember: A good model is a functional and flexible one, and is one that is designed to easily be adjusted, to grow, and to evolve as we gain more knowledge and insight into the inner workings of business, therefore slowly honing a perfect valuation.

Revenue

Revenue, for example, can be quite difficult to predict. Amazon posted $386,064 million in 2020 total net sales, a 37.6% increase from 2019. How will we know what revenue will be in 2021? The truth is, it is almost impossible to be 100% sure. We will need to make an assumption with the understanding that that assumption will come with a degree of uncertainty, and may therefore change.

So how can you best make rational predictions for 2021? It is important to research and understand the company's business model, gathering as much information as you can to make your own best judgment. Revenue, for example, is almost always driven by a product of pricing and volume. So, when thinking about projecting revenue, your research should focus on understanding the company's pricing and volume. What initiatives is the company taking to increase its volume in 2021? Is it increasing its advertising? Is it acquiring other businesses or customers? What outside forces could affect the company's pricing model? Is it increasing its prices? Is it facing tremendous market competition and must lower its prices?

In addition to the research, we recommend the following sources:

1. *Investor presentations.* Try to look for a recent investor presentation on the investor relations section of the company website. These presentations are typically designed to explain recent and future performance to existing or future investors of the company's stock. These presentations can contain high-level projections.
2. *Earnings calls.* One can easily find when the next earnings call is on the investor relations section of the website. At the earnings call, you can listen to the management speak about the company's most recent financial performance. Management also sometimes gives guidance on the company's future performance.
3. *Wall Street research.* If you can get your hands on an equity research report written by a Wall Street analyst who has followed the company for several years, that report would contain estimated future performance.
4. *Data sources.* Yahoo! Finance, Thomson, First Call, and Bloomberg are examples of data sources that contain Wall Street consensus estimates. Yahoo! Finance is a free resource, so, if you do not have access to a paid service, this can serve as a good reference.

These are just several examples of where one can get guidance. We recommend not depending on any one single source of information, but gathering as many sources as you can and cross-checking with your research to make the strongest educated estimates possible.

For purposes of this analysis, and knowing that the research can take a considerable amount of time, we can take a first-guess assumption and leave the detailed research for once the model is complete. We can, for example, assume that revenue will continue to grow at its historical 37.6% rate into 2021.

We can also go to a data source such as Yahoo! Finance. One can, for example, go to finance.yahoo.com and type "AMZN" (the ticker for Amazon) in the "Quote Lookup" bar. There is a lot of great information here that can be used as a first cut assumption. It is not the best source, but it is a free source, so it is a good starting point.

You can now select "Analysis" in the menu bar. This data is a consensus by several Wall Street analysts who follow Amazon. (See Figure 1.7.) The second table from the top, titled "Revenue Est," gives us the consensus revenue. On the far right, we can see the average revenue estimates for 2021 and 2022 are $490.35Bn and $581.65Bn, respectively. It is also important to note the high and low estimates underneath the average.

As a "first cut," we should expect our projected revenue to be within the high and low range, and near the average. (It does not have to match exactly.) So, our earlier assumption of taking 2020's 37.6% growth for 2021 ($386,064 × 1.376) will give us $531,224 – significantly above the average and well above even the high estimate of $508.88. So, for Amazon's case,

yahoo! finance | Search for news, symbols or companies

Summary | Company Outlook | Chart | Conversations | Statistics | Historical Data | Profile | Financials | **Analysis** | Options

Currency in USD

Earnings Estimate	Current Qtr. (Jun 2021)	Next Qtr. (Sep 2021)	Current Year (2021)	Next Year (2022)
No. of Analysts	36	36	46	46
Avg. Estimate	12.21	12.92	55.74	72.09
Low Estimate	9.77	6.84	42.68	45.11
High Estimate	15.18	17.7	71.13	96.53
Year Ago EPS	10.3	12.37	41.83	55.74

Revenue Estimate	Current Qtr. (Jun 2021)	Next Qtr. (Sep 2021)	Current Year (2021)	Next Year (2022)
No. of Analysts	36	36	45	45
Avg. Estimate	115.17B	118.7B	490.35B	581.65B
Low Estimate	112.15B	110.97B	473.77B	547.19B
High Estimate	120.76B	123.56B	508.88B	612.25B
Year Ago Sales	88.91B	96.14B	386.06B	490.35B
Sales Growth (year/est)	29.50%	23.50%	27.00%	18.60%

FIGURE 1.7   Yahoo! Finance AMZN Estimates

taking the last year's revenue growth may be too aggressive. Notice at the bottom of the table a consensus revenue growth estimate is provided for the two years of 27.0% and 18.6% for 2021 and 2022, respectively. These percentages are quite a drop from the prior year's 37.6%. It's not unusual to see growth percentages, especially if they are so large, to scale down over time; we can use this to our benefit when projecting after the next two years. Let's use these consensus projections for now. This, of course, needs to be adjusted based on all our further research on the company. So, we will note that our assumptions are pending further research.

Note that the information found online changes frequently. If you find this information online yourself, it is likely to have changed. If you are building the model as you are reading this book, which we recommend, you should use the data in the exhibits found in this book to match your numbers to our solution.

In this model, we are going to project the total revenue, not the individual revenue line items "Net product sales" and "Net service sales." It is up to you to decide how detailed you would like your analysis to be. In many cases, revenue can be broken out by product, volume, and even geography. It is also not uncommon to have a completely separate revenue schedule and analysis that will feed into the income statement. Let's keep our revenue projections at this high level for now until we decide further detail is needed.

We can now start inputting our revenue projections into Excel.

So, we can type 27.0% into Cell G12. 27.0% as a hardcode and an assumption driver; remember to color the font blue. This percentage will drive the actual 2021 total net sales projection. We want the 2021 total net sales to be driven off our assumption or:

$$2021 \text{ Total Net Sales} = 2020 \text{ Total Net Sales} \times$$
$$(1 + 2021 \text{ Net Sales Growth Assumption}\%)$$

Calculating 2021 Total Net Sales (Cell G11)

Excel Keystrokes	Description
type "="	Enters into "formula" mode
select Cell F11	2020 Total Net Sales
type "*"	Multiplies
type "(1+"	Begins the $(1 + x\%)$ portion of the formula
select Cell G12	2021 Growth Assumption
type ")"	Closes the $(1 + x\%)$ portion of the formula
type "Enter"	End
Formula Result	=F11*(1+G12)

This will give us 2021 total revenue of $490,301.3. Notice this is very close to the average revenue projection in 2021 from Figure 1.7.

We can copy the revenue growth formula (Cell G11) to the right all the way through to 2025. We don't want to copy G12, however, because we will be adjusting these assumptions each year.

Using the analyst estimates, we can hardcode the 18.6% for the 2022 estimate into cell H12, giving us a 2022 net sales value of $581,497.3, again right in line with the analyst estimates.

What can we now do for the next years? One idea is to find a trend for the year-over-year reduction in net sales growth. Let's calculate what that would be for 2021 and 2022 and assess. We first want to create a new line in the template underneath the "Y/Y Net Sales Growth (%)" line.

A quick way to add a row is by moving the cursor to row 13 where we want the new row to be located. The "Add row" option may be in a different location depending on which version of Excel you have. For the Microsoft 365 version, it is located in "Home," "Insert," then "Insert Sheet Row." You can also try using the hotkeys: while holding down "Shift," tap the "Spacebar" and let go of all keys. This will highlight the entire row. Now you can use the hotkey combination "Ctrl" + "Shift" + "+," which adds a row. Once the row has been added, we can title it "Y/Y Growth (%) Decline" in cell C13. "Ctrl" + "I" is a quick way to italicize the title. We can then calculate the percentage decline in 2021 and 2022 for analysis.

Calculating 2021 Total Net Sales % Decline (Cell G13)

Excel Keystrokes	Description
type "="	Enters into "formula" mode
select Cell G12	2021 Total Net Sales Growth (%)
type "/"	Divides
select Cell F12	2020 Total Net Sales Growth (%)
type "-1"	Finalizes the percent change calculation
type "Enter"	End
Formula Result	= G12 / F12 - 1

We can copy this formula *one cell* to the right into H13; we don't want to copy into 2023 because we will be making our own assumptions after 2022.

This should give a 28.2% *decline* in 2021 and a 31.1% *decline* in 2022. So, there is a fairly consistent projected decline of ~30% that we can model going forward. We can use this projected decline to estimate future revenue growth.

Let's simply take the 31.1% projected decline forward by linking Cell I13 from Cell H13; Cell I13 will read "=H13." Even though the assumption in Cell I13 is not a hardcode, we still want to color it blue to indicate it is an assumption driver.

Note: Another option would be to just type "31.1%" into cell I13. I chose to link directly in, which I prefer, so that it is completely explicit where the assumption is coming from. Just be aware that if you type "31.1%" into the model as opposed to linking in from cell H13, your numbers will be slightly different due to rounding of the decimal. I would recommend linking the cell in as I have done so you can tie to the rest of the numbers in the book.

We can also now copy cell I13 to the right all the way through 2025 since we will continue this same assumption going forward. Some may feel it is easier to have rounded the decline down to an even 30%. That would have also been okay; it's a small difference so this will not impact the billion-dollar value estimate at the end of this analysis.

Now that we have hardcoded growth percent decline estimated, we can calculate our projected revenue growth for 2023.

Calculating 2023 Y/Y Net Sales Growth (Cell I12)

Excel Keystrokes	Description
type "="	Enters into "formula" mode
select Cell H12	2022 Y/Y Net Sales Growth (%)
type "*"	Multiplies
type "(1+"	Begins the $(1 + x\%)$ portion of the formula
select Cell I13	2023 Assumption
type ")"	Closes the $(1 + x\%)$ portion of the formula
type "Enter"	End
Formula Result	=H12*(1+I13)

This would give us a 12.8% sales growth and $656,006.5MM sales in 2023.

We can copy Cell I12 and I13 to the right all the way through 2025. (See Table 1.10.)

Cost of Goods Sold

Next let's look at the costs. Again, fully understanding and researching each cost is important in best estimating its future performance. However, such

TABLE 1.10 Amazon Projected Revenue

Consolidated Income Statements (in US$ millions except per share amounts)

| | Actuals | | | | Estimates | | | |
Period Ending December 31	2018A	2019A	2020A	2021E	2022E	2023E	2024E	2025E
Revenue								
Net product sales	141,915.0	160,408.0	215,915.0					
Y/Y growth (%)		*13.0%*	*34.6%*					
Net service sales	90,972.0	120,114.0	170,149.0					
Y/Y growth (%)		*32.0%*	*41.7%*					
Total Net Sales	232,887.0	280,522.0	386,064.0	490,301.3	581,497.3	656,006.5	713,912.0	757,323.5
Y/Y net sales growth (%)		*20.5%*	*37.6%*	*27.0%*	*18.6%*	*12.8%*	*8.8%*	*6.1%*
Y/Y growth (%) decline				*(28.2%)*	*(31.1%)*	*(31.1%)*	*(31.1%)*	*(31.1%)*

detail may be as difficult to project as the revenue. There are a couple of ways to estimate future costs. First, it is important to consider whether the costs are fixed or variable. A fixed cost is relatively static and may grow a certain percentage year over year. Rent, for example, can be considered a fixed cost as it may only increase 5–10% each year, independent of the growth in revenue. In contrast, a variable cost will increase in direct proportion to the growth of the business, most commonly determined by the revenue growth. In other words, if the revenue is increasing by 10%, the costs will also increase by 10%. If the revenue decreases by 4%, the costs will also decrease by 4%.

Quite often, cost of goods sold is considered a variable cost. If your revenue is declining, you are most likely selling less product, so your costs should also be decreasing. Conversely, if your revenue is increasing, you are most likely selling more product, so cost of goods sold should be increasing in direct proportion to the revenue. There are, however, exceptions. For example, a revenue increase could be due to an increase in pricing, not because more product has been sold. In this case maybe costs should not be increasing at all (no change in volume). Or, a further twist, maybe the company is raising its prices because the manufacturer who is providing raw materials has raised its prices, so effectively both revenue and costs should be increasing proportionally. This is where a deeper understanding of the company's business model and cost structure comes in handy.

Historical trends can help us determine how best to make initial projections, with the knowledge that we can later tweak as we build a more fundamental understanding of the business. If we analyze the historical cost of goods sold as a percentage of revenue over the past three years, we notice the costs have been around 60% of total revenue each year. This consistent trend is a strong indicator that the cost of goods sold could be variable, growing at the same rate as revenue. If the percentages had not been consistent over the past three years, further research would need to be done to better understand the reasons for the variability. The company could have significantly changed its business model or taken other initiatives to significantly increase or decrease its costs in relation to its revenue. In that case, one could listen to the last earnings call or earnings release to get management's views on whether costs of goods sold is expected to increase or decrease.

So, for next year, we want to make an assumption based on the prior year's trends, adjusted based on our research. There are several common methods:

1. Take an average percentage of the last three years.
2. Take a maximum percentage of the last three years (conservative approach).
3. Take a minimum percentage of the last three years (aggressive approach).
4. Take the last year's percentage.
5. Have the percentages steadily increase or decrease year over year.

Note that these are five of the most common methods, but you may look for and identify other trends that may work better based on the individual company's past performance such as percentages decreasing for the next year then staying constant for the next four years.

We always recommend a conservative approach as long as the most conservative approach is within logical reason, so we immediately eliminate option #3. We acknowledge that taking the average over the past three years (option #1) can be a good approach, but we notice that the maximum percentage of the last three years also happens to be the same as the last year's percentage, which satisfies two conditions (options #2 and #4), which is preferred. We do acknowledge that the percentages are slightly increasing year over year, but caution that a further increase without solid evidence could be too much of an increase. So let's take 60.4% as the projection for 2021–2025. Note that all of the methods in the list can be considered accurate; our recommended approach is simply a suggestion. Remember, the point is to build out a complete model with broad assumptions, then go back and tweak such assumptions as you research and get a stronger understanding of the business.

We can link cell F16 into cell G16 by typing "=F16" into cell G16. Or you can simply select Cell G16, type the equals sign, then select cell F16 and hit enter. We will make this blue because, although it is not a hardcode, it is an assumption.

Now we can calculate the projections. The formula for projecting cost of goods sold in 2021 will be:

2021 COGS = 2021 COGS as a % of net sales × 2021 Total net sales

Calculating 2021 COGS (Cell G15)

Excel Keystrokes	Description
type "="	Enters into "formula" mode
select Cell G16	2021 COGS as a % of Net Sales
type "*"	Multiplies
select Cell G11	2021 Total Net Sales
type "Enter"	End
Formula Result	=G16*G11

This will give us 2021 COGS of $296,299.9. We can copy Cell G15 and G16 to the right all the way through 2025. We can also now calculate future gross profit and the gross profit margin. We have already calculated these formulas in 2010 through 2012, so we can just copy Cells F17 and F18 through 2025 as well. (See Table 1.11.)

TABLE 1.11 Amazon Projected Gross Profit

Consolidated Income Statements (in US$ millions except per share amounts)

Period Ending December 31	Actuals			Estimates				
	2018A	2019A	2020A	2021E	2022E	2023E	2024E	2025E
Cost of Goods Sold								
Cost of Goods Sold	139,156.0	165,536.0	233,307.0	296,299.9	351,411.7	396,439.2	431,432.8	457,667.3
COGS *as a % of net sales*	59.8%	59.0%	60.4%	60.4%	60.4%	60.4%	60.4%	60.4%
Gross Profit	93,731.0	114,986.0	152,757.0	194,001.4	230,085.6	259,567.3	282,479.2	299,656.2
Gross profit margin (%)	40%	41%	40%	40%	40%	40%	40%	40%

Operating Expenses

This same procedure can be repeated for each cost item on the income statement: conducting adequate research, analyzing the historical trends, and considering whether each cost is fixed or variable in order to best determine which of the five methods should be used to project the costs forward.

Let's analyze the company's fulfillment expense. If we look at the historical expense as a percentage of revenue over the past three years, we notice the costs were 14.6%, 14.3%, and 15.2% for 2018, 2019, and 2020, respectively. The costs have been slightly bouncing around; it is not certain if the 2019 drop to 14.3 was a one-time dip or if the 15.2 was a defined increase that will continue. This is where further research may reveal a management discussion on these expenses clarifying. Unfortunately, I could not find any clear determination on 2021 outlook. An average of the three years would give us 14.7, which may be a good assumption. However, taking the maximum of the past three years is most conservative, which we like. It is also the same as the least-year approach. I always prefer when more than one method points to the same assumption. So, let's go with the maximum or last-year approach for now, which both point to 15.2, keeping in mind that taking the average or using another approach would not necessarily be wrong; we can always go back and tweak our model as we get to know more about the company.

We can take the 2020 15.2% as our future assumption for 2021–2025. Link cell F21 into cell G21, by typing "=F21" in cell G21. Then we can use the formula below to make our projections.

$$2021 \text{ Fulfillment} = 2021 \text{ Fulfillment as a \% of Net Sales} \times 2021 \text{ Total Net Sales}$$

Calculating 2021 Fulfillment (Cell G20)

Excel Keystrokes	Description
type "="	Enters into "formula" mode
select Cell G21	2021 Fulfillment as a % of Net Sales
type "*"	Multiplies
select Cell G11	2021 Total Net Sales
type "Enter"	End
Formula Result	=G11*G21

This gives us $74,316.6 in 2021. We can copy Cells G20 and G21 to the right.

We can repeat this procedure for each operating expense, namely, "Technology and Content," "Marketing," "General and Administrative," and "Other operating expense (income), net." For each expense, take the 2020 percentage of net sales as the future assumption and use that assumption to calculate the projected expense. Let's go through it one more time for "Technology and Content." For the rest, you can look to Table 1.12 as a guide.

We can take the 2020 4.5% as our future assumption for 2021–2025. Link cell F23 into cell G23, by typing "=F23" in cell G23. Then we can use the formula below to make our projections.

$$2021 \text{ Technology and Content} = 2021 \text{ Technology and Content}$$
$$\text{as a \% of Net Sales} \times 2021 \text{ Total Net Sales}$$

Calculating 2021 Technology and Content (Cell G22)

Excel Keystrokes	Description
type "="	Enters into "formula" mode
select Cell G23	2021 Technology and Content as a % of Net Sales
type "*"	Multiplies
select Cell G11	2021 Total Net Sales
type "Enter"	End
Formula Result	=G11*G23

This gives us $22,211.0 in 2021. We can copy Cells G22 and G23 to the right.

Repeat this for all Operating Expenses using Table 1.12 as a guide.

We can then copy the Total Operating Expenses, EBITDA, and EBITDA margin % formulas to the right through 2025, cells F30, F31, and F32. We now have an Amazon model complete up through EBITDA. (See Table 1.13.)

Depreciation and Amortization

When building a complete financial model it is recommended to leave projected depreciation empty for now. We will build a depreciation schedule that will contain projected depreciation expense to be linked in here. We can, however, copy the EBIT and EBIT margin % formulas, rows 34 and 35, from 2020 to the right through 2025. (See Table 1.13.)

TABLE 1.12 Amazon Projected Operating Expenses

Consolidated Income Statements (in US$ millions except per share amounts)

| | | Actuals | | | | | Estimates | | |
Period Ending December 31	2018A	2019A	2020A	2021E	2022E	2023E	2024E	2025E
Operating Expenses								
Fulfillment	34,027.0	40,232.0	58,517.0	74,316.6	88,139.5	99,433.1	108,210.0	114,790.0
Fulfillment as a % of net sales	14.6%	14.3%	15.2%	15.2%	15.2%	15.2%	15.2%	15.2%
Technology and Content	13,496.0	14,142.0	17,489.0	22,211.0	26,342.3	29,717.6	32,340.8	34,307.3
Technology and Content as a % of net sales	5.8%	5.0%	4.5%	4.5%	4.5%	4.5%	4.5%	4.5%
Marketing	13,814.0	18,878.0	22,008.0	27,950.2	33,148.9	37,396.4	40,697.3	43,172.1
Marketing as a % of net sales	5.9%	6.7%	5.7%	5.7%	5.7%	5.7%	5.7%	5.7%
General and administrative	4,336.0	5,203.0	6,668.0	8,468.4	10,043.5	11,330.4	12,330.5	13,080.3
General and administrative as a % of net sales	1.9%	1.9%	1.7%	1.7%	1.7%	1.7%	1.7%	1.7%
Other operating expense (income), net	296.0	201.0	(75.0)	(95.3)	(113.0)	(127.4)	(138.7)	(147.1)
Other operating expense as a % of net sales	0.1%	0.1%	0.0%	0.0%	0.0%	0.0%	0.0%	0.0%
Total Operating Expenses	65,969.0	78,656.0	104,607.0	132,850.9	157,561.2	177,750.0	193,439.9	205,202.6

TABLE 1.13 Amazon Projected EBITDA and EBIT

Consolidated Income Statements (in US$ millions except per share amounts)

Period Ending December 31	Actuals			Estimates				
	2018A	2019A	2020A	2021E	2022E	2023E	2024E	2025E
EBITDA	27,762.0	36,330.0	48,150.0	61,150.5	72,524.5	81,817.3	89,039.3	94,453.6
EBITDA margin (%)	11.9%	13.0%	12.5%	12.5%	12.5%	12.5%	12.5%	12.5%
Depreciation and amortization	15,341.0	21,789.0	25,251.0					
EBIT	12,421.0	14,541.0	22,899.0	61,150.5	72,524.5	81,817.3	89,039.3	94,453.6
EBIT margin (%)	5.3%	5.2%	5.9%	12.5%	12.5%	12.5%	12.5%	12.5%

Other Income

Next we have "Other income." In order to properly project this line item, we would need a better understanding of what exactly "Other income" is. "Other" is quite vague and could be a composite of many varying line items. Further research reveals this note from page 29 of the 10-K:

"The primary components of other income (expense), net are related to equity warrant valuations, equity securities valuations and adjustments, and foreign currency."

Although this is not the most explicit explanation, we can get the sense that this income is related to securities, foreign currency, items that may be dependent on market dynamics. Quite often you will come across these line items that will not be clearly identified and may prove to be difficult to project. In such instances we recommend several possible methods to project such line items.

Seven Methods of Projections   Again, there will be times where we will come across many line items that are difficult to define and, moreover, difficult to project. In the example of "Other Income," knowing that the line item may be dependent on market fluctuations, it can be very difficult if not impossible to accurately project. However, in my experience, no matter how the projections of a particular line item could ultimately be derived, there are seven common ways to project a line item:

1. Conservative (the maximum of the past three years)
2. Aggressive (the minimum of the past three years)
3. Average (the average of the past three years)
4. Last year (recent performance)
5. Repeat the cycle
6. Year-over-year growth
7. Project out as a percentage of an income statement or balance sheet line item

These are similar to the five methods mentioned earlier. However, those methods were relating to projecting variable operating expenses driven by revenue generation, so we had a better idea of their nature. These more-complete seven methods apply to projecting all, including more obscure line items such as Other Income that may depend on market fluctuations.

1. *Conservative.* A greater expense would be more conservative. So, taking the maximum amount from the last three years may not be the most accurate, but it is a conservative approach. You can use the "maximum" formula in Excel. For example, "=max(x, y, z)" will give you the largest amount of x, y, and z.

2. *Aggressive.* This is probably not the most recommended method, but it is a possible method, so we will note it. Assuming lower expenses is more aggressive, we would take the minimum amount from the last three years. You can use the "minimum" formula in Excel; "=min(x, y, z)" will give you the minimum amount of *x, y,* and *z*.

3. *Average.* This is a popular method, but be warned that quite often, the average of the past three years does not always give the best indication of next year's performance, especially if one of the past three years was unusual. We mention this specifically, as we see many analysts using the average method as the safety method. We recommend better to carefully go through all various methods before considering the average method. You can use the "average" formula in Excel; "=average(x, y, z)" will give you the average amount of *x, y,* and *z*.

4. *Last year.* This is based on the underlying assumption that the company's performance last year is most indicative of its future performance. If one does not know the business or the specific line item well, it may not be easy to determine if this is the correct method to use. However, a combination of this method and the conservative method is a quite useful indicator. In other words, if last year's performance also happens to be the most conservative of the last three years, then we have two supporting methodologies that point to the same number. The more support we have, the better.

5. *Repeat the cycle.* Quite often, the last three years' numbers will be quite volatile, swinging from positive to negative or from a very small value to a large value. Although it is often difficult to identify exactly why, some companies can plan more significant cash flow events every second or third year. For example, companies can make larger capital expenditure investments every third year, and smaller investments in the other years. In this case, you may want to continue this trend. The easiest way to do this is to have the projected 2021 year to equal the first historical year (2018). This way, when copied right, 2022 will equal the 2019 value, 2023 will equal the 2020 value, and so on.

6. *Year-over-year growth.* Here we can assume some year-over-year growth rate to project the line item going forward. The growth rate can be dependent on what exactly that "other" line item is. If it is rent, for example, we can assume the rent will increase by a standard 5% each year. You can also take a look at the historical trends much like what we had done with revenue and apply those trends to the projections.

7. *Project out as a percentage of an income statement or balance sheet line item.* "Other" line items can sometimes grow dependent on another income statement or balance sheet line item. For example, if "other" is made up of employee salaries, you may want to project this line item based on a percentage of SG&A. One way to determine if this can be an appropriate method is by looking at the historical percentage of SG&A. If the percentages have been fairly consistent over the past three years, then this could be a good indication.

It is also important to add comments in Excel describing the exact method you are using. A good analyst should always add explicit detail and explanations to assumptions to the model for clarity.

It is not easy to determine exactly which method to use. But it is important to note that quite often these "other" items are insignificant to the overall valuation. To prove this, choose one of the previous methods, and highlight that line item to be revisited once the model and valuation is complete. Then, try to change your assumptions using one of the methods and see if it significantly changes your valuation. If it does, it is worth further research.

So to give you a good idea as to the thought process, let's walk through how to analyze the "Other Income" line item.

■ **Conservative:** The conservative method, the maximum of three years, would give us 183 from 2018. We like conservative models, so this may be the way to go, but we should first consider all options.

■ **Aggressive:** An aggressive approach is not recommended. So let's cross this one out.

■ **Average:** The average method could work, but 2020 is extremely large compared to the prior two years. In fact, there may have been an extraordinary or one-time event in 2020. So the average in this case will not be the best indicator of next year's performance, as 2020 will skew the results.

■ **Last year:** Last year's value of (2,371) seems to be unusually large, and is income, not an expense, which would be *very* conservative. Let's rule this one out.

■ **Repeat the cycle:** Repeat the cycle is a method to consider, as the 2018 value of 182 is positive yet the 2019 value is negative. It is often the case when line items are dependent on securities that one sees positive and negative swings. Whether it's related to buying securities in one year and selling off in the next, or readjusting valuation up in one year and down in the next, the idea of positive and negative swings for this line item may work, with the exception of 2020's unusually large income.

- **Year-over-year growth:** Given the volatility of these numbers, there are clearly no smooth growth trends.
- **Project out as a percentage of an income statement or balance sheet line item:** Given this line item is dependent on market valuation and currency, as opposed to operating line items that are based on revenue growth, we don't believe this would be an accurate method. Therefore, we should also cross this one off.

So, we are left with conservative or repeat the cycle. Since this line item is based off of market dynamics, valuation, currency, I would expect this to continue to swing from positive to negative in the future. Although I typically prefer 100% conservative models, these swings are inevitable. To prove this further, I pulled up some prior reports from Amazon's investor relations site to be sure there were continued historical swings, and there were. The only exception is the large $2.5Bn 2020 income, which I will assume to be extraordinary. So, I will choose the "repeat the cycle" method but make an exception to repeat only 2018 and 2019 going forward.

This is not an easy decision, as there is not too much support for analysis; if it gives more comfort, we can highlight this assumption, and once the model is complete, try to run the projections both ways to see if that changes our analysis. This will make the process 100% thorough.

So, I would take G36 and link it from D36, effectively taking the 2018 *expense* for 2021. I would then take H36 and link it from E36, taking the 2019 *income* for 2022. Now if we were to copy this to the right, the 2020 assumption would come into play; we want to skip this assumption as an outlier. So, I recommend taking the 2021 assumption for 2023, linking I36 from G36. This can be copied to the right to continue the cycle. This may sound confusing, so please refer to Figure 1.8, where I have laid out the proper formulas for reference.

	2021E	2022E	2023E	2024E	2025E
Formula	=D36	=E36	=G36	=H36	=I36
Value	183	(203)	183	(203)	183

FIGURE 1.8   Amazon Projected Other Income

Modeling Tip

We strongly recommend saving deeper research until the model is completely linked through. I have often seen analysts one or two days after receiving a model assignment still researching the company to best home in on revenue and cost assumptions. It is, as a result, not excusable to mention to your superior that you are still conducting research, when asked to see the model and there is no model to review. It is preferable to first have a completely linked model with even the most general assumptions, and then later go back to tweak and hone assumptions.

Interest Income

When building a complete financial model, it is recommended to leave projected interest expense and interest income empty. We will build a debt schedule that will help us better project interest expense and interest income to be linked in here. We can, however, copy the net interest expense, EBT and EBT margin % formulas, rows 40, 41, and 42, from 2020 to the right through 2025. See Table 1.14.

Taxes

We typically look at the historical taxes as a percentage of EBT to make our projections. However, you may note the historical tax projections are quite low and volatile. First, a low 10.6% in 2018, jumping to a slightly more reasonable 17% in 2019, back down to 11.8% in 2020. Note the typical statutory tax rate in the U.S. is 35%; understand that companies may benefit from several areas of deductions to reduce that rate. This needs some further research. Performing a word search on "Tax Rate" in the 2020 10-K reveals some notes on deductions but no explanation on the actual rate reduction. I would imagine, given the 2020 pandemic, the company taxes may not be standard. Performing the same word search on the 2019 10-K reveals the following note from page 63:

"This amount was primarily comprised of the remeasurement of federal net deferred tax liabilities resulting from the permanent reduction in the US statutory corporate tax rate to 21% from 35%."

So here Amazon disclosed a 21% tax rate. This seems a bit more reasonable than the 2020 11.8%. For a second strong data point, the company

TABLE 1.14 Amazon Projected EBT

Consolidated Income Statements (in US$ millions except per share amounts)

Period Ending December 31	Actuals				Estimates				
	2018A	2019A	2020A	2021E	2022E	2023E	2024E	2025E
Other Income	183.0	(203.0)	(2,371.0)	183.0	(203.0)	183.0	(203.0)	183.0
Interest								
Interest expense	1,417.0	1,600.0	1,647.0					
Interest income	(440.0)	(832.0)	(555.0)					
Net Interest Expense	977.0	768.0	1,092.0	0.0	0.0	0.0	0.0	0.0
Earnings before Tax (EBT)	11,261.0	13,976.0	24,178.0	60,967.5	72,727.5	81,634.3	89,242.3	94,270.6
EBT margin (%)	*4.8%*	*5.0%*	*6.3%*	*12.4%*	*12.5%*	*12.4%*	*12.5%*	*12.4%*

released their first quarterly report while I was writing this book. Pulling up their Q1 income statement, I calculated an implied tax rate of 20.99%, which, of course, rounds up to 21% – exactly what was stated in 2019.

So let's use 21.0%, hardcoding into Cell G44. We can then calculate the projected income tax expense.

Calculating 2021 Income Tax Expense (Cell G43)

Excel Keystrokes	Description
type "="	Enters into "formula" mode
select Cell G44	2021 Tax Rate %
type "*"	Multiplies
select Cell G41	2021 EBT
type "Enter"	End
Formula Result	=G44*G41

This gives us an income tax expense of $12,803.2. We can copy cells G43 and G44 to the right. (See Table 1.15)

Cell F45 ("Net Income from Continuing Operations") can now be copied through 2025.

You may have noticed that the 2021 taxes appear very high compared to 2020. Remember, we still do not have depreciation and interest expense in our projections. Once those are linked in, the tax expense will be reduced.

Non-Recurring Events

We have no identified non-recurring events for Amazon, so we can just copy the 0 assumptions, totals, and the "Net Income (after non-recurring events)" Cells F47 through F52 to the right.

Distributions

Equity Method Investment Activity   The next line "Equity Method Investment Activity, net of Tax" is difficult to project. As it is related to equity, or possibly valuation, like with "Other Income" we will have to turn to the seven methods. And with the same logic as with "Other Income," because both were based on equity fluctuations, we see once again positive and negative swings. So, without further deduction, we can easily see the "repeat the cycle" method can work here.

So, we can have G53 as "=D53" and we can copy this to the right.

TABLE 1.15 Amazon Projected Net Income

Consolidated Income Statements (in US$ millions except per share amounts)

Period Ending December 31	Actuals			Estimates				
	2018A	2019A	2020A	2021E	2022E	2023E	2024E	2025E
Earnings before Tax (EBT)	11,261.0	13,976.0	24,178.0	60,967.5	72,727.5	81,634.3	89,242.3	94,270.6
EBT margin (%)	4.8%	5.0%	6.3%	12.4%	12.5%	12.4%	12.5%	12.4%
Income Tax Expense	1,197.0	2,374.0	2,863.0	12,803.2	15,272.8	17,143.2	18,740.9	19,796.8
All-in effective tax rate (%)	10.6%	17.0%	11.8%	21.0%	21.0%	21.0%	21.0%	21.0%
Net Income from Continuing Operations	10,064.0	11,602.0	21,315.0	48,164.3	57,454.7	64,491.1	70,501.4	74,473.8
Non-Recurring Events								
Discontinued operations	0.0	0.0	0.0	0.0	0.0	0.0	0.0	0.0
Extraordinary items	0.0	0.0	0.0	0.0	0.0	0.0	0.0	0.0
Effect of accounting changes	0.0	0.0	0.0	0.0	0.0	0.0	0.0	0.0
Other items	0.0	0.0	0.0	0.0	0.0	0.0	0.0	0.0
Total Non-Recurring Events	0.0	0.0	0.0	0.0	0.0	0.0	0.0	0.0
Net Income (after Non-Recurring Events)	10,064.0	11,602.0	21,315.0	48,164.3	57,454.7	64,491.1	70,501.4	74,473.8
Income attributable to equity method investments	(9.0)	14.0	(16.0)	(9.0)	14.0	(16.0)	(9.0)	14.0
Dividends paid on common stock	0.0	0.0	0.0	0.0	0.0	0.0	0.0	0.0
Net Income (as Reported)	10,073.0	11,588.0	21,331.0	48,173.3	57,440.7	64,507.1	70,510.4	74,459.8

Dividends Since Amazon does not pay dividends, we can simply carry the "0" to the right.

We can now copy F55, the Net Income (as reported) to the right. (See Table 1.15.)

Shares

Basic Shares Outstanding Before calculating earnings per share on rows 57 and 58, we need projected share counts. The best way to project the share count is to first get the most current count of basic shares outstanding. This comes from the first page of the most recent filing (in this case, the Amazon 10-Q report). You can find such additional reports for Amazon by selecting "SEC Filings" in the investor relations section of its website. (See Figure 1.9.)

Adjusting the "Group" dropdown box to "Quarterly Filings" reveals the 10-Q dated April 30, 2021. The bottom of the first page of this report lists the share count of 504,323,736. (See Figure 1.10.) We will use this as the 2021 basic share count in Cell G60. Note that we need to divide this number by 1,000,000 in order to be at equivalent units as the prior years, or hardcode "504.323736."

Diluted Shares Outstanding and the Treasury Method Diluted shares outstanding is a count of all the shares outstanding in the market plus any stock options or warrants that are exercisable today. What if every stock option

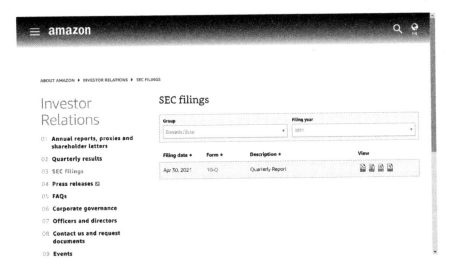

FIGURE 1.9 Amazon SEC Filings

Washington, D.C. 20549

FORM 10-Q

(Mark One)

☒   QUARTERLY REPORT PURSUANT TO SECTION 13 OR 15(d) OF THE SECURITIES EXCHANGE ACT OF 1934

For the quarterly period ended March 31, 2021

or

☐   TRANSITION REPORT PURSUANT TO SECTION 13 OR 15(d) OF THE SECURITIES EXCHANGE ACT OF 1934

For the transition period from   to   .
Commission File No. 000-22513

AMAZON.COM, INC.

(Exact name of registrant as specified in its charter)

Delaware	91-1646860
(State or other jurisdiction of incorporation or organization)	(I.R.S. Employer Identification No.)

410 Terry Avenue North, Seattle, Washington 98109-5210
(206) 266-1000
(Address and telephone number, including area code, of registrant's principal executive offices)

Securities registered pursuant to Section 12(b) of the Act:

Title of Each Class	Trading Symbol(s)	Name of Each Exchange on Which Registered
Common Stock, par value $.01 per share	AMZN	Nasdaq Global Select Market

Indicate by check mark whether the registrant (1) has filed all reports required to be filed by Section 13 or 15(d) of the Securities Exchange Act of 1934 during the preceding 12 months (or for such shorter period that the registrant was required to file such reports), and (2) has been subject to such filing requirements for the past 90 days.   Yes ☒   No ☐

Indicate by check mark whether the registrant has submitted electronically every Interactive Data File required to be submitted pursuant to Rule 405 of Regulation S-T during the preceding 12 months (or for such shorter period that the registrant was required to submit such files).   Yes ☒   No ☐

Indicate by check mark whether the registrant is a large accelerated filer, an accelerated filer, a non-accelerated filer, a smaller reporting company, or an emerging growth company. See the definitions of "large accelerated filer," "accelerated filer," "smaller reporting company," and "emerging growth company" in Rule 12b-2 of the Exchange Act.

Large accelerated filer	☒	Accelerated filer	☐
Non-accelerated filer	☐	Smaller reporting company	☐
		Emerging growth company	☐

If an emerging growth company, indicate by check mark if the registrant has elected not to use the extended transition period for complying with any new or revised financial accounting standards provided pursuant to Section 13(a) of the Exchange Act. ☐

Indicate by check mark whether the registrant is a shell company (as defined in Rule 12b-2 of the Exchange Act).   Yes ☐   No ☒

504,323,736 shares of common stock, par value $0.01 per share, outstanding as of April 21, 2021

FIGURE 1.10   Amazon 10-Q

holder who holds in-the-money option contracts decides to exercise on those options today? How many shares would be in the market? The diluted share count attempts to estimate that number of shares. There are several resources we can use to obtain the total number of Walmart diluted shares outstanding, but the best way to obtain that diluted share count is to calculate the number ourselves. The best starting point is to pull the most recently reported annual report. Although the Amazon quarterly report is more recent, the quarterly report typically does not contain the option and warrant detail. But it is always worth taking a look first. Now, to get a count of diluted shares, we need to find all notes regarding options and warrants that may be held. Unfortunately performing a quick word search on "options" does not reveal much valuable information. We could also try "warrants" or simply "stock" to uncover some option tables, but nothing is revealed. Ideally, we would get an option table that would indicate all the in-the-money options available. Note in my previous book on Walmart that

(Shares in thousands)	Restricted Stock and Performance Share Awards		Restricted Stock Rights		Stock Options[1]	
	Shares	Weighted-Average Grant-Date Fair Value Per Share	Shares	Weighted-Average Grant-Date Fair Value Per Share	Shares	Weighted-Average Exercise Price Per Share
Outstanding at February 1, 2011	13,617	$52.33	16,838	$47.71	33,386	$49.35
Granted	5,022	55.03	5,826	47.13	2,042	42.90
Vested/exercised	(3,177)	51.26	(3,733)	47.26	(13,793)	50.22
Forfeited or expired	(2,142)	52.55	(1,310)	47.92	(1,483)	48.01
Outstanding at January 31, 2012	13,320	$53.56	17,621	$47.76	20,152	$48.21
Exercisable at January 31, 2012					13,596	$50.49

(1) Includes stock option awards granted under the Stock Incentive Plan of 2010, the Colleague Share Ownership Plan 1999 and the ASDA Sharesave Plan 2000.

FIGURE 1.11   Walmart Option Table

there is a good example of an options table and an analysis on converting stock options for projections. I've added Walmart's option table here as an example of what to look for.

Figure 1.11 represents all outstanding options and their respective exercise price. If the options are "in-the-money" (meaning the options are exercisable) or the current stock price is above the exercise price, then technically these options could be exercised and should be included into our diluted share count. Now, the Walmart stock price was $61.36 on January 31, 2012, which was well above any of the strike prices indicated. Notice, however, that only 13,596 of the shares were exercisable. Why not all? It is most likely because many of the stock options listed previously have certain restrictions, such as timing, preventing one from exercising the stock.

If you recall from the beginning of the Making Projections section in this chapter, I mention several valuable resources for making projections. One, which we are using most often, is the filings; the other was market data (we used Yahoo! Finance as an easy example). We have yet to look into investor presentations. If you go to the "Quarterly Results" section of the Amazon's investor relations site, you will find several documents, including "Presentation." The investor presentation is another valuable resource as it sometimes contains projected information from company management. Because we are looking for stock option information, we would like to use the latest presentation filed, which at the time of writing this book was as of Q1 2021. (See Figure 1.12.)

Q1 2021 Financial Results
Conference Call Slides

FIGURE 1.12   Amazon Q1 2021 Presentation

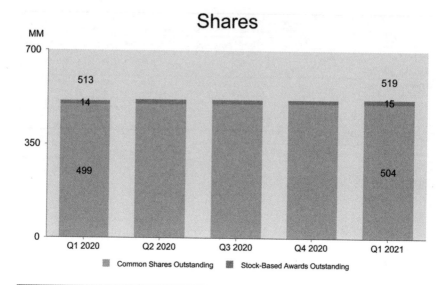

Efficiently Managing Dilution

FIGURE 1.13   Amazon Shares

Scrolling down to page 6 reveals a very valuable share chart. See Figure 1.13. Each bar displays the number of shares outstanding in orange and above in blue, the diluted options. The rightmost bar, for Q1 2021, indicates 15MM options outstanding. Although it would be ideal to have more concrete data – a table with a full breakout like Walmart had in Figure 1.11 – this is also direct from the company and the best information we can get at this time. Again, a good analyst would highlight this assumption and continue to research as new and more specific data emerge. So let's use this information for our diluted share count. In Cell G61 we can simply type "=G60+15." It is very important when making an assumption like this that the source is noted.

We can have 2022 simply link from 2021 by having H60 equal to G60 and H61 equal to G61. Copy to the right. (See Table 1.16.)

Earnings per Share

We can calculate the projected earnings per share using the same formulas as the historical. It is easiest to just copy the formulas over to the right, from Cells F57 and F58. (See Table 1.16.)

We now have as much of the income statement as we can complete at this point. (See Table 1.17.)

We will continue on to the cash flow and revisit tweaking the income statement assumptions once the model is complete.

TABLE 1.16 Amazon Projected Earnings per Share

Consolidated Income Statements (in US$ millions except per share amounts)

| Period Ending December 31 | Actuals | | | | | Estimates | | |
	2018A	2019A	2020A	2021E	2022E	2023E	2024E	2025E
Earnings per Share (EPS)								
Basic	20.68	23.46	42.66	95.52	113.90	127.91	139.81	147.64
Diluted	20.15	22.99	41.83	92.76	110.61	124.21	135.77	143.38
Average Common Shares Outstanding								
Basic	487	494	500	504	504	504	504	504
Diluted	500	504	510	519	519	519	519	519

TABLE 1.17   Amazon Projected Income Statement

Consolidated Income Statements (in US$ millions except per share amounts)

Period Ending December 31	Actuals			Estimates				
	2018A	2019A	2020A	2021E	2022E	2023E	2024E	2025E
Revenue								
Net product sales	141,915.0	160,408.0	215,915.0					
Y/Y growth (%)		13.0%	34.6%					
Net service sales	90,972.0	120,114.0	170,149.0					
Y/Y growth (%)		32.0%	41.7%					
Total Net Sales	232,887.0	280,522.0	386,064.0	490,301.3	581,497.3	656,006.5	713,912.0	757,323.5
Y/Y net sales growth (%)		20.5%	37.6%	27.0%	18.6%	12.8%	8.8%	6.1%
Y/Y growth (%) decline				(28.2%)	(31.1%)	(31.1%)	(31.1%)	(31.1%)
Cost of Goods Sold								
Cost of goods sold	139,156.0	165,536.0	233,307.0	296,299.9	351,411.7	396,439.2	431,432.8	457,667.3
COGS as a % of net sales	59.8%	59.0%	60.4%	60.4%	60.4%	60.4%	60.4%	60.4%
Gross Profit	93,731.0	114,986.0	152,757.0	194,001.4	230,085.6	259,567.3	282,479.2	299,656.2
Gross profit margin (%)	40%	41%	40%	40%	40%	40%	40%	40%
Operating Expenses								
Fulfillment	34,027.0	40,232.0	58,517.0	74,316.6	88,139.5	99,433.1	1,08,210.0	1,14,790.0
Fulfillment as a % of net sales	14.6%	14.3%	15.2%	15.2%	15.2%	15.2%	15.2%	15.2%

Technology and content	13,496.0	14,142.0	17,489.0	22,211.0	26,342.3	29,717.6	32,340.8	34,307.3
Technology and content as a % of net sales	*5.8%*	*5.0%*	*4.5%*	*4.5%*	*4.5%*	*4.5%*	*4.5%*	*4.5%*
Marketing	13,814.0	18,878.0	22,008.0	27,950.2	33,148.9	37,396.4	40,697.3	43,172.1
Marketing as a % of net sales	*5.9%*	*6.7%*	*5.7%*	*5.7%*	*5.7%*	*5.7%*	*5.7%*	*5.7%*
General and administrative	4,336.0	5,203.0	6,668.0	8,468.4	10,043.5	11,330.4	12,330.5	13,080.3
General and administrative as a % of net sales	*1.9%*	*1.9%*	*1.7%*	*1.7%*	*1.7%*	*1.7%*	*1.7%*	*1.7%*
Other operating expense (income), net	296.0	201.0	(75.0)	(95.3)	(113.0)	(127.4)	(138.7)	(147.1)
Other operating expense as a % of net sales	*0.1%*	*0.1%*	*0.0%*	*0.0%*	*0.0%*	*0.0%*	*0.0%*	*0.0%*
Total Operating Expenses	65,969.0	78,656.0	104,607.0	132,850.9	157,561.2	177,750.0	193,439.9	205,202.6
EBITDA	27,762.0	36,330.0	48,150.0	61,150.5	72,524.5	81,817.3	89,039.3	94,453.6
EBITDA margin (%)	*11.9%*	*13.0%*	*12.5%*	*12.5%*	*12.5%*	*12.5%*	*12.5%*	*12.5%*
Depreciation and amortization	15,341.0	21,789.0	25,251.0					
EBIT	12,421.0	14,541.0	22,899.0	61,150.5	72,524.5	81,817.3	89,039.3	94,453.6
EBIT margin (%)	*5.3%*	*5.2%*	*5.9%*	*12.5%*	*12.5%*	*12.5%*	*12.5%*	*12.5%*
Other income	183.0	(203.0)	(2,371.0)	183.0	(203.0)	183.0	(203.0)	183.0

(Continued)

TABLE 1.17 (*Continued*)

Consolidated Income Statements (in US$ millions except per share amounts)

Period Ending December 31	Actuals			Estimates				
	2018A	2019A	2020A	2021E	2022E	2023E	2024E	2025E
Interest								
Interest expense	1,417.0	1,600.0	1,647.0					
Interest income	(440.0)	(832.0)	(555.0)					
Net Interest Expense	977.0	768.0	1,092.0	0.0	0.0	0.0	0.0	0.0
Earnings before Tax (EBT)	11,261.0	13,976.0	24,178.0	60,967.5	72,727.5	81,634.3	89,242.3	94,270.6
EBT margin (%)	4.8%	5.0%	6.3%	12.4%	12.5%	12.4%	12.5%	12.4%
Income tax expense	1,197.0	2,374.0	2,863.0	12,803.2	15,272.8	17,143.2	18,740.9	19,796.8
All-in effective tax rate (%)	10.6%	17.0%	11.8%	21.0%	21.0%	21.0%	21.0%	21.0%
Net Income from Continuing Operations	10,064.0	11,602.0	21,315.0	48,164.3	57,454.7	64,491.1	70,501.4	74,473.8
Non-recurring events								
Discontinued operations	0.0	0.0	0.0	0.0	0.0	0.0	0.0	0.0
Extraordinary items	0.0	0.0	0.0	0.0	0.0	0.0	0.0	0.0
Effect of accounting changes	0.0	0.0	0.0	0.0	0.0	0.0	0.0	0.0

Other items	0.0	0.0	0.0	0.0	0.0	0.0	0.0	0.0
Total Non-recurring Events	**0.0**	**0.0**	**0.0**	**0.0**	**0.0**	**0.0**	**0.0**	**0.0**
Net Income (after Non-recurring Events)	**10,064.0**	**11,602.0**	**21,315.0**	**48,164.3**	**57,454.7**	**64,491.1**	**70,501.4**	**74,473.8**
Income attributable to equity method investments	(9.0)	14.0	(16.0)	(9.0)	14.0	(16.0)	(9.0)	14.0
Dividends paid on common stock	0.0	0.0	0.0	0.0	0.0	0.0	0.0	0.0
Net Income (as Reported)	**10,073.0**	**11,588.0**	**21,331.0**	**48,173.3**	**57,440.7**	**64,507.1**	**70,510.4**	**74,459.8**
Earnings per Share (EPS)								
Basic	20.68	23.46	42.66	95.52	113.90	127.91	139.81	147.64
Diluted	20.15	22.99	41.83	92.76	110.61	124.21	135.77	143.38
Average common shares outstanding								
Basic	487	494	500	504	504	504	504	504
Diluted	500	504	510	519	519	519	519	519

The Cash Flow Statement

The cash flow statement is a measure of how much cash a company has produced or spent over a period of time. Although an income statement shows profitability, that profit may or may not result in actual cash gain. This is because many income statement items that are recorded do not necessarily result in an effect on cash. For example, when a sale is made, a customer can pay in cash or on credit. If a company has $10MM in sales, and all customers have paid in cash, then the company has actually generated $10MM in cash. But, if a company has $10MM in sales on credit, then although the revenue has been recorded on the income statement, cash has not been received. The cash flow statement aims to determine how much cash was actually generated, which is broken out into three segments:

- Cash from operating activities
- Cash from investing activities
- Cash from financing activities

The sum of all the cash generated (or spent) from operating activities, from investing activities, and from financing activities results in the total amount of cash spent or received in a given period.

CASH FROM OPERATING ACTIVITIES

Cash from operating activities is a representation of how much cash was generated from net income or profit. We explained earlier how revenue could be received in cash or on credit. As revenue is a source of income, if a portion of that revenue is on credit, we need to make an adjustment to net income based on how much of that revenue is actually cash. Similarly, expenses recorded on the income statement could be cash expenses (they have been paid) or non-cash expenses (they have not been paid). Let's take a billing invoice on an operating expense such as office supplies as an example. Once the invoice is received (a bill we have to pay), we would need to record this on the income statement, even if we had not actually paid that bill yet. Having this expense on our income statement would bring our profitability down. But, when looking at cash available, that bill should not be included as we did not pay it. So, for cash flow from operations, we would add that expense back to the net income, effectively reversing the expense effects.

Example:

Income Statement	
Revenue (collected in cash)	10,000,000.0
SG&A (invoice we did not pay)	2,000,000.0
Net Income	**8,000,000.0**
Cash Flow	
Net Income	**8,000,000.0**
Add back SG&A	2,000,000.0
Cash from Operations	**10,000,000.0**

This should make logical sense. We've collected $10MM in cash from our sales; we received an invoice of $2MM, but we did not pay that invoice. The invoice is expensed properly on the income statement, but we do not want to include that in our cash analysis, as it did not yet affect our cash. So, we add that expense back to the net income. The cash from operations rightfully shows we still have $10MM in cash.

Now, let's say of the $10MM in revenue, only $8MM was cash sales, and $2MM was sold on credit. The income statement looks exactly the same, but the cash flow statement is different. If we had only collected $8MM of that $10MM of revenue in cash, then we would need to subtract the $2MM of revenue we did not collect from the net income.

Income Statement	
Revenue (only $8MM collected in cash)	10,000,000.0
SG&A (invoice we did not pay)	2,000,000.0
Net Income	**8,000,000.0**
Cash Flow	
Net Income	**8,000,000.0**
Subtract revenue we did not collect in cash	(2,000,000.0)
Add back SG&A we did not pay	2,000,000.0
Cash from Operations	**8,000,000.0**

This analysis may seem trivial in the previous example, but it is important to understand the methodology as we apply this to more complex income statements. In general, cash from operating activities is generated by taking net income and removing all the non-cash items.

Or, in its most fundamental form, cash from operations as demonstrated is:

Net Income + Expenses We Did Not Pay – Revenue We Did Not Receive

But it gets slightly more complex. To understand this completely, let's take a look at all of the components of an income statement and determine which items can be considered cash or non-cash.

Revenue

As we explained previously, if revenue is received on credit, this would be removed from net income. Note that the portion of revenue received on credit is called *accounts receivable*.

Cost of Goods Sold

Cost of goods sold (COGS) is the inventory costs related to the item sold. If it costs $50 to make a chair, for example, and we sell that chair for $100, then for each chair sold, we will record a $50 expense related to the manufacturing cost of the product; this is cost of goods sold. However, we must also reduce our inventory balance by $50 for each chair sold. A reduction in inventory results in a positive cash inflow in the cash from operations section on the cash flow statement. We will illustrate examples of this in the next section.

Operating Expenses

As explained with the $2MM invoice, if an expense received has not been paid, this would be added back to net income. The portion of operating expenses that has not been paid is called *accrued expenses*.

Depreciation

Depreciation is an expense that is never actually paid. As described earlier, it is accounting for the aging of assets. So, like any expense that is not cash, we add it back to net income when calculating cash flow from operations.

Interest

Interest expense is almost always paid in cash. There can be certain complex debt instruments that are an exception, but if a company cannot pay its interest, then generally it is considered defaulting on its debt. So, for this reason, we almost always consider interest as cash. Therefore, we would not add it back to net income on the cash flow statement.

Taxes

Taxes can be deferred in some situations, which will be discussed later. The portion of taxes that we expensed, but did not yet pay, is referred to as *deferred taxes*.

The following table summarizes the most common income statement line items and the related accounts if they can be deferred.

Net Income Line Item	Possible Deferrable Items?	Effect in Cash from Operations
Revenue	Yes	Changes in Accounts Receivable
Cost of Goods Sold	Yes	Changes in Inventory Changes in Accounts Payable
Operating Expenses	Yes	Changes in Accrued Expenses Changes in Prepaid Expenses
Depreciation	Yes	Depreciation
Interest	No	None (some exceptions)
Taxes	Yes	Deferred Taxes

Keeping with the theme demonstrated above, where we adjust the related revenue and expense items we did not pay or receive in cash from net income to get a measure of cash generated or spent, we can generalize this table toward cash flow from operating activities:

Cash from Operating Activities = Net Income + [Changes in Accounts Receivable + Changes in Inventory + Changes in Accounts Payable + Changes in Accrued Expenses + Changes in Prepaid Expenses] + Depreciation + Deferred Taxes

Although we will discuss this later, there is a definition [Changes in Accounts Receivable + Changes in Inventory + Changes in Accounts Payable + Changes in Accrued Expenses + Changes in Prepaid Expenses] called *changes in working capital,* so:

Cash from Operating Activities = Net Income + Depreciation + Deferred Taxes + Changes in Working Capital

Note the actual "changes" in each individual line item could be positive or negative. This will be explained in Chapter 5.

To be complete, cash from operating activities should include adjustments based on any and all income statement line items that are non-cash. So, you may see "+Other Non-Cash Items" at the end of the formula to capture those adjustments.

$$\text{Cash from Operating Activities} = \text{Net Income} + \text{Depreciation} + \text{Deferred Taxes} + \text{Other Non-Cash Items} + \text{Changes in Working Capital}$$

The important lesson here is to gain the conceptual understanding of how cash from operating activities is derived from the income statement. As we get into more complex case studies and analyses, and for due diligence purposes, you will learn that it is important to understand cash flow as derived from individual income statement line items, rather than memorizing a standard formula. The information in this section is the fundamental beginning of such analyses.

CASH FROM INVESTING ACTIVITIES

Now that we have a measure of cash generated from our operations, there are two other areas from which cash can be generated or spent: investing activities and financing activities. Cash from investing activities is cash generated or spent from buying or selling assets, businesses, or other investments or securities. More specifically, the major categories are:

- Capital expenditures (investments in property, plant, and equipment)
- Buying or selling assets
- Buying, selling, spinning off, or splitting off businesses or portions of business entities
- Investing in or selling marketable and nonmarketable securities

CASH FROM FINANCING ACTIVITIES

Cash from financing activities is defined as cash generated or spent from equity or debt. More specifically:

- Raising or buying back equity or preferred securities
- Raising or paying back debt
- Distributions to equity holders (non-controlling interests and dividends)

The sum of the cash from operating activities, cash from investing activities, and cash from financing activities gives us a total measure of how much cash is generated or has been spent over a given period.

Financial Statement Flows Example

Let's take a second, slightly deeper example walking through a complete sale process. We are a new company interested in selling chairs, so we open up a local retail shop. We will sell each chair for $100. It will cost approximately $50 in raw material to create one chair. So the first thing we will do is purchase enough raw material to build 10 chairs ($500). The simple flows are:

Cash Flow		Balance Sheet	
Net Income	0.0	Cash	(500.0)
Changes in Inventory (Purchase of Chairs)	(500.0)	Inventory	500.0
Total Changes in Cash	**(500.0)**		

No income has been generated. Cash is negative, as we have spent money to pay for the inventory. An inventory asset has been created on the balance sheet. We will discuss the balance sheet in its entirety later.

Now the cash balance in the balance sheet is −$500. We clearly do not have cash to pay for these raw materials, but the vendor is allowing us to defer the money owed to him until we are able to come up with the cash. So, we incur a liability to the vendor called *accounts payable*. The new flows will be:

Cash Flow		Balance Sheet	
Net Income	0.0	Cash	0.0
Changes in Inventory (Purchase of Chairs)	(500.0)	Inventory	500.0
Changes in Accounts Payable	500.0	Accounts Payable	500.0
Total Changes in Cash	**0.0**		

At the end of the transaction, the cash balance is zero, we have an asset of $500 in inventory, and we have a liability of $500 in payables due to the vendor.

Now, let's say one chair is sold for $100. Two things happen on the income statement:

1. Revenue is recorded for $100.
2. COGS is incurred of $50.

Let's walk through how each of these transactions flows through the income statement, cash flow statement, and balance sheet. It is recommended to focus on one transaction at a time, making sure each completely flows through all three statements before moving on to the next transaction.

If revenue is recorded at $100, then taxes are affected at, let's say, 40%, so $40, and the net income effect is $60:

Income Statement	
Revenue	100.0
Taxes (@ 40%)	(40.0)
Net Income	60.0

Next we move to the cash flow statement. Net income begins the cash flow statement, which is the $60 change. Nothing else on the cash flow statement is affected at this point so the total cash change is $60. On the balance sheet, the change in cash will affect our cash balance, which is an asset. And the net income change we will later learn affects our retained earnings.

Cash Flow	
Net Income	60.0
Total Changes in Cash	**60.0**

Balance Sheet	
Cash	60.0
Inventory	500.0
Accounts Payable	500.0
Retained Earnings (Net Income)	60.0

Now let's look at the COGS, which incurs a cost of $50. Let's look at the financial statement adjustments based on the COGS to get a complete representation of the sale. So, on the income statement, we will incur an expense of $50. As expenses are tax-deductible, taxes will reduce by $20, resulting in a net income reduction of $30:

Income Statement	
COGS	(50.0)
Taxes (@ 40%)	20.0
Net Income	(30.0)

Next, we move to the cash flow statement, which starts with net income. COGS is related to inventory. We need to reduce the inventory asset on the balance sheet to reflect the $50 of raw materials that have been sold, which results in a positive cash adjustment. So we will add a "Changes in Inventory" line of $50:

Cash Flow	
Net Income	**(30.0)**
Changes in Inventory	50.0
Total Changes in Cash	**20.0**

Balance Sheet Adjustments	
Cash	20.0
Inventory	(50.0)
Retained Earnings (Net Income)	(30.0)

For the balance sheet, the cash change from before will increase the cash asset balance. Inventory will reduce by $50 to reflect the raw materials sold. And the retained earnings will reduce by the net income change of −$30.

We can now combine the balance sheet adjustment to the total balance sheet.

Balance Sheet Adjustments	
Cash	20.0
Inventory	(50.0)
Retained Earnings (Net Income)	(30.0)

Balance Sheet	
Cash	80.0
Inventory	450.0
Accounts Payable	500.0
Retained Earnings (Net Income)	30.0

We will learn later what it means when we say the balance sheet balances. Here, it does balance, as the sum of the assets (80 + 450 = 530) less the liabilities (500) equals the shareholders' equity (30).

If you have little accounting experience, some of these adjustments may seem a bit confusing. Don't worry about this just yet. As you proceed through the next few chapters – specifically Chapter 3, which will give you a clearer understanding of the balance sheet – I recommend revisiting this example, as you should then have a much better understanding. I also recommend reviewing the additional exercises associated with each chapter, which can be found online.

Notice the previous sale was a cash sale. Let's now say that we have sold another chair, but this time the sale was on credit.

Income Statement	
Revenue	100.0
Taxes (@ 40%)	(40.0)
Net Income	**60.0**

Notice the income statement looks the same whether the sale was made in cash or on credit. The cash flow statement will be a little different. If the customer pays on credit, then we need to make an adjustment to the cash flow statement, as we did not yet receive that cash. Effectively, we need to subtract the portion of revenue we did not yet receive in cash, and we will create an accounts receivable asset account in the cash flow statement and balance sheet to represent the money owed to us.

Cash Flow	
Net Income	60.0
Changes in Accounts Receivable	(100.0)
Total Changes in Cash	**(40.0)**

Balance Sheet Adjustments	
Cash	(40.0)
Accounts Receivable	100.0
Retained Earnings (Net Income)	60.0

Notice the total cash change is −$40, which reflects the taxes owed on the sale. Because we have recorded the sale, even though we did not receive the cash on that sale yet, we still incur and pay taxes on that sale.

So we need to add these adjustments to the original balance sheet, giving us:

Balance Sheet Adjustments	
Cash	(40.0)
Accounts Receivable	100.0
Retained Earnings (Net Income)	60.0

Balance Sheet	
Cash	40.0
Inventory	450.0
Accounts Receivable	100.0
Accounts Payable	500.0
Retained Earnings (Net Income)	90.0

The cash balance, which was previously $80, has been reduced to $40, an accounts receivable account has been created, and the retained earnings increase from $30 to $90.

We can now make the adjustments to the COGS and inventory.

Income Statement	
COGS	(50.0)
Taxes (@ 40%)	20.0
Net Income	(30.0)

Cash Flow	
Net Income	(30.0)
Changes in Inventory	50.0
Total Changes in Cash	20.0

Balance Sheet Adjustments	
Cash	20.0
Inventory	(50.0)
Retained Earnings (Net Income)	(30.0)

And we can update the balance sheet:

Balance Sheet Adjustments	
Cash	20.0
Inventory	(50.0)
Retained Earnings (Net Income)	(30.0)

Balance Sheet	
Cash	60.0
Inventory	400.0
Accounts Receivable	100.0
Accounts Payable	500.0
Retained Earnings (Net Income)	60.0

Notice the COGS movements are also the same whether the purchase was made on cash or credit. The balance sheet balances, as the sum of the assets (60 + 400 + 100 = 560) less the liabilities (500) equals the shareholders' equity (60).

Now let's say we have sold the remaining eight chairs, four of which have been sold on credit. The income statement is:

Income Statement	
Revenue	800.0
Taxes (@ 40 %)	(320.0)
Net Income	480.0

Since four of the chairs were sold on credit, we need to remove the $400 from net income on the cash flow statement and adjust for the balance sheet.

Cash Flow	
Net Income	480.0
Changes in Accounts Receivable	(400.0)
Total Changes in Cash	**80.0**

Balance Sheet Adjustments	
Cash	80.0
Accounts Receivable	400.0
Retained Earnings (Net Income)	480.0

Adding these balance sheet adjustments to the total balance sheet gives us:

Balance Sheet Adjustments	
Cash	80.0
Accounts Receivable	400.0
Retained Earnings (Net Income)	480.0

Balance Sheet	
Cash	140.0
Inventory	400.0
Accounts Receivable	500.0
Accounts Payable	500.0
Retained Earnings (Net Income)	540.0

We can now make the adjustments for the COGS and inventory associated to the sale, which is $400. Remember: Regardless of whether the sale is made in cash or on credit, we still need to adjust for the COGS and removal of inventory.

Income Statement	
COGS	(400.0)
Taxes (@ 40%)	160.0
Net Income	**(240.0)**

Now we need to remove the $400 from inventory, which results in a positive cash adjustment on the cash flow statement. For the balance sheet, we need to adjust the inventory and cash accordingly.

Cash Flow	
Net Income	**(240.0)**
Changes in Inventory	400.0
Total Changes in Cash	**160.0**

Balance Sheet Adjustments	
Cash	160.0
Inventory	(400.0)
Retained Earnings (Net Income)	(240.0)

Adding these balance sheet adjustments to the total balance sheet gives us:

Balance Sheet Adjustments	
Cash	160.0
Inventory	(400.0)
Retained Earnings (Net Income)	(240.0)

Balance Sheet	
Cash	300.0
Inventory	0.0
Accounts Receivable	500.0
Accounts Payable	500.0
Retained Earnings (Net Income)	300.0

So now we have sold our entire inventory. Notice that we have $500 in payables due, but only $300 in cash. If we had collected on the accounts receivable from our customers, we would not have this problem. So, let's assume we finally collected on all the accounts receivable and we can pay down the payables. We collect $500 in accounts receivable:

Cash Flow		Balance Sheet Adjustments	
Net Income	**0.0**	Cash	500.0
Accounts Receivable	500.0	Accounts Receivable	(500.0)
Total Changes in Cash	**500.0**	Retained Earnings (Net Income)	0.0

The receivable asset goes away and cash is collected. Adding these balance sheet adjustments to the total balance sheet gives us:

Balance Sheet Adjustments		Balance Sheet	
Cash	500.0	Cash	800.0
Accounts Receivable	(500.0)	Inventory	0.0
Retained Earnings (Net Income)	0.0	Accounts Receivable	0.0
		Accounts Payable	500.0
		Retained Earnings (Net Income)	300.0

Notice that we did not make any changes to the income statement, as we did not create any income generating event here. We simply converted an asset into cash. We now have $800 in cash, enough to pay down our liabilities. We pay $500 in liabilities:

Cash Flow		Balance Sheet Adjustments	
Net Income	**0.0**	Cash	(500.0)
Accounts Payable	(500.0)	Accounts Payable	(500.0)
Total Changes in Cash	**(500.0)**	Retained Earnings (Net Income)	0.0

Adding these balance sheet adjustments to the main balance sheet gives us:

Balance Sheet Adjustments		Balance Sheet	
Cash	(500.0)	Cash	300.0
Accounts Payable	(500.0)	Inventory	0.0
Retained Earnings (Net Income)	0.0	Accounts Receivable	0.0
		Accounts Payable	0.0
		Retained Earnings (Net Income)	300.0

We have collected all our assets and paid down all our liabilities. Notice that at $100 per chair and a cost of $50 per chair, selling 10 chairs nets us ($1,000 – $500), or $500 pretax profit. At a 40% tax rate, the net profit on that sale is $300 ($500 – $200), exactly the amount of cash and net income we have in the balance sheet.

Don't get discouraged if you did not understand this example completely. As you read on and gain a more fundamental understanding of the underlying concepts involved, the example will become clearer. I recommend revisiting this example a few times as you continue reading.

AMAZON'S CASH FLOW STATEMENT

As we did with the income statement, let's lay out the historical numbers for Amazon's cash flow before making projections. On the income statement, we have regrouped a lot of the line items, and extracted some other line items, to get to comparable metrics Wall Street analysts use for analysis such as EBITDA. For the cash flow statement, it is recommended to lay out each item line by line in the order found on the company filings. There may be a couple of line items we will make adjustments to later for more complex reasons, but at this point, keeping with this general rule is best. Amazon's cash flow statement can be found on page 38 of the Amazon 10-K. (See Figure 2.1.)

Cash from Operating Activities

As mentioned earlier:

Cash from Operating Activities = Net Income + Depreciation + Deferred Taxes + Other Non-Cash Items + Changes in Working Capital

From Figure 2.1, we can certainly identify the top line as net income. Next is "Depreciation and Amortization." After, we have several non-cash adjustments starting with a line called "Stock-based compensation," and followed by two "other" non-cash line items, namely "Other operating expense (income), net" and "Other expense (income), net." These three line items can fall into the "Other Non-Cash Items" category in the general "Cash from Operating Activities" layout. After that, Amazon lists "Deferred income taxes."

Finally, there are five line items under the heading "Changes in Operating Assets and Liabilities." These are the working capital items that we will discuss later. Again, for the historical section, we can just list these line items exactly as Amazon has done. We have identified all of these line items properly; they make up the net income, depreciation, deferred taxes, other non-cash items, and working capital from our cash flow from operations formula.

Proceed to the "Cash Flow Statement" tab in the "NYSF – Amazon – Template.xls" model.

Since we already have net income and depreciation from the income statement, we can link in these line items from the income statement tab into the cash flow statement tab. The easiest way to link in from another tab is

AMAZON.COM, INC.
CONSOLIDATED STATEMENTS OF CASH FLOWS
(in millions)

	Year Ended December 31,		
	2018	2019	2020
CASH, CASH EQUIVALENTS, AND RESTRICTED CASH, BEGINNING OF PERIOD	$ 21,856	$ 32,173	$ 36,410
OPERATING ACTIVITIES:			
Net income	10,073	11,588	21,331
Adjustments to reconcile net income to net cash from operating activities:			
Depreciation and amortization of property and equipment and capitalized content costs, operating lease assets, and other	15,341	21,789	25,251
Stock-based compensation	5,418	6,864	9,208
Other operating expense (income), net	274	164	(71)
Other expense (income), net	219	(249)	(2,582)
Deferred income taxes	441	796	(554)
Changes in operating assets and liabilities:			
Inventories	(1,314)	(3,278)	(2,849)
Accounts receivable, net and other	(4,615)	(7,681)	(8,169)
Accounts payable	3,263	8,193	17,480
Accrued expenses and other	472	(1,383)	5,754
Unearned revenue	1,151	1,711	1,265
Net cash provided by (used in) operating activities	30,723	38,514	66,064
INVESTING ACTIVITIES:			
Purchases of property and equipment	(13,427)	(16,861)	(40,140)
Proceeds from property and equipment sales and incentives	2,104	4,172	5,096
Acquisitions, net of cash acquired, and other	(2,186)	(2,461)	(2,325)
Sales and maturities of marketable securities	8,240	22,681	50,237
Purchases of marketable securities	(7,100)	(31,812)	(72,479)
Net cash provided by (used in) investing activities	(12,369)	(24,281)	(59,611)
FINANCING ACTIVITIES:			
Proceeds from short-term debt, and other	836	1,402	6,796
Repayments of short-term debt, and other	(813)	(1,518)	(6,177)
Proceeds from long-term debt	182	871	10,525
Repayments of long-term debt	(155)	(1,166)	(1,553)
Principal repayments of finance leases	(7,449)	(9,628)	(10,642)
Principal repayments of financing obligations	(337)	(27)	(53)
Net cash provided by (used in) financing activities	(7,686)	(10,066)	(1,104)
Foreign currency effect on cash, cash equivalents, and restricted cash	(351)	70	618
Net increase (decrease) in cash, cash equivalents, and restricted cash	10,317	4,237	5,967
CASH, CASH EQUIVALENTS, AND RESTRICTED CASH, END OF PERIOD	$ 32,173	$ 36,410	$ 42,377

See accompanying notes to consolidated financial statements.

FIGURE 2.1 Amazon Cash Flow

to type equals in a cell and then key over to the tab with the data, or you can use "Ctrl"+"Page Up" or "Page Down" to toggle between tabs. For net income, in cell D7 type "=," then you can use the cursor to select the Income Statement tab, and select Cell D55. Hit Enter. This should take you back to Cell D7 on the Cash Flow Statement tab, which should read "='Income Statement'!D55." See Table 2.1.

We can do the same thing linking in depreciation and amortization from the income statement, starting in D8. The final cell should read "='Income Statement'!D33." We can copy cells D7 and D8 to the right. It's okay to copy them all the way through to 2025. Even though we are just focusing on historicals now, we will end up using the income statement projections as well.

Note: It's very important to avoid hardcoding the same number in two places; this is why I strongly recommend linking from the income statement into the cash flow statement as opposed to hardcoding net income and depreciation into the cash flow statement. This not only avoids error, but if

TABLE 2.1   Amazon Historical Cash Flow from Operating Activities

Consolidated Statements of Cash Flows (in US$ millions except per share amounts)

Period Ending December 31	Actuals		
	2018A	2019A	2020A
Cash Flows from Operating Activities			
Net income	10,073.0	11,588.0	21,331.0
Depreciation and amortization	15,341.0	21,789.0	25,251.0
Stock-based compensation	5,418.0	6,864.0	9,208.0
Other operating expense (income), net	274.0	164.0	(71.0)
Other expense (income), net	219.0	(249.0)	(2,582.0)
Deferred income taxes	441.0	796.0	(554.0)
Changes in Operating Working Capital			
Changes in inventory	(1,314.0)	(3,278.0)	(2,849.0)
Changes in accounts receivable	(4,615.0)	(7,681.0)	(8,169.0)
Changes in accounts payable	3,263.0	8,193.0	17,480.0
Changes in accrued expenses	472.0	(1,383.0)	5,754.0
Changes in unearned revenue	1,151.0	1,711.0	1,265.0
Net Changes in Working Capital	(1,043.0)	(2,438.0)	13,481.0
Total Cash from Operating Activities	30,723.0	38,514.0	66,064.0

the numbers happen to change on the income statement, if properly linked, they will automatically flow into the cash flow statement.

We can now hardcode out the rest of the historical cash flow from operating activities. (See Table 2.1 as a guide.)

We can also total the net changes in operating working capital, summing the four working capital line items (D14 through D18). The "Total Cash Flows from Operating Activities" line is a sum of all of the line items in the cash flows from operating activities section (D7 through D18). The totals should match the totals presented in the Amazon 10-K.

Calculating 2018 Net Changes in Operating Working Capital (Cell D19)

Excel Keystrokes	Description
type "="	Enters into "formula" mode
type "sum("	Begins "sum" formula
select Cell D14	Selects the first cell in series
type ":"	Indicates we want to include all cells from the first cell to the last cell in series
select Cell D18	Selects the last cell in series
type ")"	Ends "sum" formula
type "Enter"	End
Formula Result	=sum(D14:D18)

Note, you can also simply use the hotkey "alt"+"=" as a quick way to create the sum formula. Please repeat the above process to calculate the sum of Cells D7 through D18. Copy both of these formulas to the right. (See Table 2.1.)

Cash from Investing Activities

Here, the most important line item to identify is capital expenditures (CAPEX). Capital expenditures are important for valuation in the discounted cash flow analysis, as we will learn in Part Two of the book, on Valuation. The CAPEX is represented in the Amazon financials by the "Purchase of property and equipment" line. The rest of the lines can be laid out one by one. "Proceeds from property and equipment sales and incentives" is the sale and/or disposal of assets. "Business acquisitions, net of cash acquired" are investments and acquisitions of business or other entities that Amazon made. Both "Sales and maturities of marketable securities" and "Purchases of marketable securities" are related to the buying, selling, and maturing of liquid financial instruments that can quickly be converted into cash. Later we will discuss how best to project each of these line items.

We can list each line item line by line as Amazon has in the 10-K. (See Table 2.2.) We can then total line items in Cells D22 through D26 in the "Total Cash from Investing Activities" line, Cell D27.

Cash from Financing Activities

Again we want to lay out each item line by line – with one exception. Quite often, companies list the payments of debt instruments and the issuance of debt instruments as two separate line items. It will be much simpler if we combine the issuances and payments of like debt instruments. This will make the model flow more smoothly as we link information from the debt schedule into this section. The "Proceeds from short-term debt, and other" and "Repayments of short-term debt, and other" can be combined into simply "Short-term borrowings." The next two lines, "Proceeds from long-term debt" and "Repayments of long-term debt," can both be combined into "Long-term borrowings." The next lines, "Principal repayments of finance leases" and "Principal repayments of financing obligations," should be listed as is.

We can total the line items in Cells D29 through D32 in the "Total Cash from Financing Activities" line. (See Table 2.3.)

Notice in the Amazon cash flow statement that there is a line titled "Foreign Currency Effect on Cash, Cash Equivalents, and Restricted Cash," which is an adjustment made on foreign currency due to the company's international subsidiaries. This often comes up in multinational companies

TABLE 2.2   Amazon Historical Cash Flow from Investing Activities

Consolidated Statements of Cash Flows (in US$ millions except per share amounts)

		Actuals	
Period Ending December 31	2018A	2019A	2020A
Cash Flows from Investing Activities			
CAPEX [Purchase of property and equipment]	(13,427.0)	(16,861.0)	(40,140.0)
Proceeds from property and equipment sales and incentives	2,104.0	4,172.0	5,096.0
Business acquisitions, net of cash acquired	(2,186.0)	(2,461.0)	(2,325.0)
Sales and maturities of marketable securities	8,240.0	22,681.0	50,237.0
Purchases of marketable securities	(7,100.0)	(31,812.0)	(72,479.0)
Total Cash from Investing Activities	**(12,369.0)**	**(24,281.0)**	**(59,611.0)**

TABLE 2.3 Amazon Historical Cash Flow from Financing Activities

Consolidated Statements of Cash Flows (in US$ millions except per share amounts)

		Actuals	
Period Ending December 31	2018A	2019A	2020A
Cash Flows from Financing Activities			
Short-term borrowings (repayments)	73.0	(116.0)	619.0
Long-term borrowings (repayments)	27.0	(295.0)	8,972.0
Principal repayments of finance leases	(7,449.0)	(9,628.0)	(10,642.0)
Principal repayments of financing obligations	(337.0)	(27.0)	(53.0)
Total Cash from Financing Activities	(7,686.0)	(10,066.0)	(1,104.0)

outside of the three major cash flow statement categories. So, we need to hardcode this line item after the financing activities section in the cash flow statement, as Amazon has done. Once included, we can calculate the "Total Change in Cash and Cash Equivalents," by adding the "Cash from Operating Activities," "Cash from Investing Activities," "Cash from Financing Activities," and this "Foreign Currency Effect on Cash, Cash Equivalents, and Restricted Cash" line item (or D20+D27+D33+D34). We can copy this total to the right.

We should now have all the cash flow statement line items laid out over the three historical years. (See Table 2.4.)

TABLE 2.4 Amazon Historical Cash Flow

Consolidated Statements of Cash Flows (in US$ millions except per share amounts)

		Actuals	
Period Ending December 31	2018A	2019A	2020A
Cash Flows from Operating Activities			
Net income	10,073.0	11,588.0	21,331.0
Depreciation and amortization	15,341.0	21,789.0	25,251.0
Stock-based compensation	5,418.0	6,864.0	9,208.0
Other operating expense (income), net	274.0	164.0	(71.0)
Other expense (income), net	219.0	(249.0)	(2,582.0)
Deferred income taxes	441.0	796.0	(554.0)

(*Continued*)

TABLE 2.4   (*Continued*)

	Actuals		
Period Ending December 31	2018A	2019A	2020A
Changes in Operating Working Capital			
Changes in inventory	(1,314.0)	(3,278.0)	(2,849.0)
Changes in accounts receivable	(4,615.0)	(7,681.0)	(8,169.0)
Changes in accounts payable	3,263.0	8,193.0	17,480.0
Changes in accrued expenses	472.0	(1,383.0)	5,754.0
Changes in unearned revenue	1,151.0	1,711.0	1,265.0
Net Changes in Working Capital	(1,043.0)	(2,438.0)	13,481.0
Total Cash from Operating Activities	30,723.0	38,514.0	66,064.0
Cash Flows from Investing Activities			
CAPEX [Purchase of property and equipment]	(13,427.0)	(16,861.0)	(40,140.0)
Proceeds from property and equipment sales and incentives	2,104.0	4,172.0	5,096.0
Business acquisitions, net of cash acquired	(2,186.0)	(2,461.0)	(2,325.0)
Sales and maturities in marketable securities	8,240.0	22,681.0	50,237.0
Purchases of marketable securities	(7,100.0)	(31,812.0)	(72,479.0)
Total Cash from Investing Activities	(12,369.0)	(24,281.0)	(59,611.0)
Cash Flows from Financing Activities			
Short-term borrowings (repayments)	73.0	(116.0)	619.0
Long-term borrowings (repayments)	27.0	(295.0)	8,972.0
Principal repayments of finance leases	(7,449.0)	(9,628.0)	(10,642.0)
Principal repayments of financing obligations	(337.0)	(27.0)	(53.0)
Total Cash from Financing Activities	(7,686.0)	(10,066.0)	(1,104.0)
Foreign Currency Effect on Cash, Cash Equivalents, and Restricted Cash	(351.0)	70.0	618.0
Total Change in Cash and Cash Equivalents	10,317.0	4,237.0	5,967.0

CASH FLOW STATEMENT – MAKING PROJECTIONS

When making projections, many cash flow statement line items come from the depreciation schedule, working capital schedule, or debt schedule, so it is often recommended to complete the depreciation and working capital schedules first. (The debt schedule should always be done last.) But for purposes of continuity and in keeping the topic of this section to cash flow, let's project the *other* cash flow line items, and then we can move on to the depreciation and working capital schedules and link those appropriate line items back into the cash flow statement when done.

Cash from Operating Activities

Cash from operating activities begins with net income, which we have on the income statement. We have already linked in the net income historically, and you should have already copied net income all the way to the right.

Depreciation and Amortization   "Depreciation and amortization" and "Deferred taxes" ultimately come from the "Depreciation" schedule. But they first flow from the depreciation schedule into the income statement, and then into the cash flow statement. We have already linked in from the income statement when creating the historicals; just be sure this has been copied all the way to the right through 2025.

Stock-Based Compensation   "Stock-Based Compensation" refers to payment to employees with some form of equity. This is an adjustment to the cash flow statement as a non-cash expense to net income. This line item comes up often in company cash flow statements if they pay their employees in stock. Because it is known that this is a salary adjustment, this line item is an adjustment to the operating expenses. So although we could use the Seven Methods of Projections (see Chapter 1) to break down how best to project this line item, we can deduce that this can likely be projected as a percentage of operating expenses (or #7 of the seven methods), "Project out as a percentage of an income statement or balance sheet line item." If you suspect this may be an ideal method to project a particular line item, but you are not entirely sure, a great way to test the method is to calculate the percentages historically first. If the historical percentages are similar year to year, then that's a great indicator. If, however, the historical percentages vary widely, then this may not be the best method. So, to prove this method, let's first add a line and calculate the historical percentages.

We can first add a line underneath "Stock-Based Compensation" row 10. So after moving the cursor to line 10 we can hit "Shift" plus "Spacebar" to highlight the row. Let go of those keys, then hit the combination "Ctrl" plus "Shift" plus "+." This should add a blank line in row 10. So in C10 we can label the row as "% of Total Operating Expenses."

Note that some may think it more appropriate to use a percentage of "General and Administrative Expenses" as that often contains employee salaries. If you try to use that for the percentages, you will get percentages above 100% because the "Stock-Based Compensation" values are greater. So it's best to use the total operating expenses.

We can calculate our percentage in D10.

Calculating 2018 Percentage of Total Operating Expenses (Cell D10)

Excel Keystrokes	Description
type "="	Enters into "formula" mode
select Cell D9	2018 Stock-Based Compensation
type "/"	Divides
Select 'Income Statement' Tab	Moves to the Income Statement Sheet
select Cell D30	2018 Total Operating Expenses
type "Enter"	End
Formula Result	=D9/'Income Statement'!D30

You may need to format Cell D10 to display percentages and one decimal. "Ctrl"+"1" is a quick way to open up the "Format Cells" box. Here you can select "Percentage" as an option. This gives us 8.2% in 2018. We can now copy this formula to the right through 2020 only, giving us 8.7% and 8.8%. (See Table 2.5.)

So it looks like the historical years' percentages are quite similar, very similar in the last two. I believe it's safe to use the last year's 8.8% to drive our future projections. We can have G10 equal to F10 as our assumption. We can then use this percentage to back-calculate into our 2021 projection.

Calculating 2021 Stock-Based Compensation (Cell G9)

Excel Keystrokes	Description
type "="	Enters into "formula" mode
select Cell G10	2021 % Operating Expenses
type "*"	Multiplies
Select 'Income Statement' Tab	Moves to the Income Statement Sheet
select Cell G30	2021 Total Operating Expenses
type "Enter"	End
Formula Result	=G10*'Income Statement'!G30

We can then copy cells G9 and G10 to the right through 2025. (See Table 2.5.)

TABLE 2.5 Amazon Projected Stock-Based Compensation

Consolidated Statements of Cash Flows (in US$ millions except per share amounts)

Period Ending December 31	Actuals			Estimates				
	2018A	2019A	2020A	2021E	2022E	2023E	2024E	2025E
Cash Flows from Operating Activities								
Net income	10,073.0	11,588.0	21,331.0	48,173.3	57,440.7	64,507.1	70,510.4	74,459.8
Depreciation and amortization	15,341.0	21,789.0	25,251.0	0.0	0.0	0.0	0.0	0.0
Stock-based compensation	5,418.0	6,864.0	9,208.0	11,694.2	13,869.3	15,646.4	17,027.5	18,062.9
% of Total Operating Expenses	8.2%	8.7%	8.8%	8.8%	8.8%	8.8%	8.8%	8.8%

Other Operating Expense   Next we have a couple "other" line items. Again, we will come across many such line items that are difficult to define and, moreover, difficult to project. The first is "Other operating expense (income)." First, notice the same exact line item on the income statement. The numbers are slightly different due to the fact that this line item is making non-cash adjustments to the expense item on the income statement. In this situation, I would right away look to project this line item, just as we had done the income statement line item. One may question why not just project this line item as a percentage of the income statement line item. We could possibly do that too, but that would give you effectively the same number as both projections are ultimately based on Total Net Sales as a denominator.

So, we can first add a line underneath "Other Operating Expense" row 11. We can move the cursor to line 12, then hit "shift" plus "spacebar" to highlight the row. Let go of those keys, then use the combination "Ctrl" plus "shift" plus "+." This should add a blank line in row 12. So in C12, we can label the row as "% of Total Net Sales."

We can calculate our percentage in D12.

Calculating 2018 % of Total Net Sales (Cell D12)

Excel Keystrokes	Description
type "="	Enters into "formula" mode
select Cell D11	2018 Other Operating Expense
type "/"	Divides
Select 'Income Statement' Tab	Moves to the Income Statement Sheet
select Cell D11	2018 Total Net Sales
type "Enter"	End
Formula Result	=D11/'Income Statement'!D11

You may need to format Cell D11 to display percentages and one decimal. This gives us 0.1% in 2018. We can now copy this formula to the right through 2020 only, giving us 0.1% and 0.0%. (See Table 2.6.)

So it looks like the historical years' percentages are again quite similar, very similar in the last two. I believe it's safe to use the last year's 0.0% to drive our future projections. We can have G12 equal to F12 as our assumption. We can then use this percentage to back-calculate into our 2021 projection.

TABLE 2.6 Amazon Projected Cash from Operating Activities

Consolidated Statements of Cash Flows (in US$ millions except per share amounts)

	Actuals			Estimates				
Period Ending December 31	2018A	2019A	2020A	2021E	2022E	2023E	2024E	2025E
Cash Flows from Operating Activities								
Net income	10,073.0	11,588.0	21,331.0	48,173.3	57,440.7	64,507.1	70,510.4	74,459.8
Depreciation and amortization	15,341.0	21,789.0	25,251.0	0.0	0.0	0.0	0.0	0.0
Stock-based compensation	5,418.0	6,864.0	9,208.0	11,694.2	13,869.3	15,646.4	17,027.5	18,062.9
% of total operating expenses	*8.2%*	*8.7%*	*8.8%*	*8.8%*	*8.8%*	*8.8%*	*8.8%*	*8.8%*
Other operating expense (income), net	274.0	164.0	(71.0)	(90.2)	(106.9)	(120.6)	(131.3)	(139.3)
% of total net sales	*0.1%*	*0.1%*	*0.0%*	*0.0%*	*0.0%*	*0.0%*	*0.0%*	*0.0%*
Other expense (income), net	219.0	(249.0)	(2,582.0)	219.0	(249.0)	219.0	(249.0)	219.0
Deferred income taxes	441.0	796.0	(554.0)					
Changes in Operating Working Capital								
Changes in inventory	(1,314.0)	(3,278.0)	(2,849.0)					
Changes in accounts receivable	(4,615.0)	(7,681.0)	(8,169.0)					
Changes in accounts payable	3,263.0	8,193.0	17,480.0					
Changes in accrued expenses	472.0	(1,383.0)	5,754.0					
Changes in unearned revenue	1,151.0	1,711.0	1,265.0					
Net Changes in Working Capital	(1,043.0)	(2,438.0)	13,481.0	0.0	0.0	0.0	0.0	0.0
Total Cash from Operating Activities	30,723.0	38,514.0	66,064.0	59,996.3	70,954.1	80,251.8	87,157.6	92,602.4

Calculating 2021 Other Operating Expense (Cell G11)

Excel Keystrokes	Description
type "="	Enters into "formula" mode
select Cell G12	2021 % Total Net Sales
type "*"	Multiplies
Select 'Income Statement' Tab	Moves to the Income Statement Sheet
select Cell G11	2021 Total Net Sales
type "Enter"	End
Formula Result	=G12*'Income Statement'!G11

We can then copy cells G11 and G12 to the right through 2025. (See Table 2.6.)

Other Expense (Income) Now we have "Other Expense (income), net." Notice this line item also exists on the income statement, but as "Other Income (expense)." It's referring to the same line item except the signs in the name are reversed due to the nature of the flows from the cash flow and income statement. (In the cash flow statement, a positive number depicts a cash inflow, but on the income statement, a positive number is an expense.)

Notice also that the trends are similar, although the actual numbers are different, i.e., a positive cash flow, then a negative, then a very large (we assumed extraordinary) flow. Again, as this line item exists on the income statement, I would use the same logic to make our projections. Referring back to Chapter 1, we used the seven methods to deduce "repeat the cycle," avoiding 2021 as this seemed like a one-time flow. Let's use the same logic here. So, we can have G13 equal to D13, and H13 equal to E13. However, once we get to I13, we want to revert back to G13. So, I13 will be equal to G13 and this cell (I13) can be copied to the right. To be completely explicit, please see Figure 2.2 for the formulas in each cell and refer to Table 2.6.

	2021E	2022E	2023E	2024E	2025E
Formula	=D13	=E13	=G13	=H13	=I13
Value	219	(249)	219	(249)	219

FIGURE 2.2 Amazon Projected Other Expense (Income)

Deferred Taxes Since a large portion of deferred taxes is often dependent on PP&E and Depreciation methods, we will leave this line empty for now and discuss in the Depreciation chapter.

Changes in Operating Working Capital The next line items, "Changes in inventory," "Changes in accounts receivable," "Changes in accounts payable," "Changes in accrued expenses," and "Changes in unearned revenue" all come from the working capital schedule. So we can skip these line items for now and link them in once we complete those schedules.

We can still copy the net changes in operating working capital Cell F21 to the right.

We have to be careful to readjust our "Total Cash from Operating Activities" formula, as we now have assumption drivers in rows 10 and 12. As of now, these new percentages are calculating into our total cash values; they should not be contributing to our total. We should change the formula in D22 to add up each individual line item, skipping over the assumption drivers.

Recalculating 2018 Total Cash from Operating Activities (Cell D22)

Excel Keystrokes	Description
type "="	Enters into "formula" mode
Select Cell D7	2018 Net Income
type = "+"	Adds
Select Cell D8	2018 Depreciation and amortization
type = "+"	Adds
Select Cell D9	2018 Stock-based compensation
type = "+"	Adds
Select Cell D11	2018 Other operating expense (income), net
type = "+"	Adds
Select Cell D13	2018 Other expense (income), net
type = "+"	Adds
Select Cell D14	2018 Deferred income taxes
type = "+"	Adds
Select Cell D21	2018 Net changes in working capital
Type "Enter"	End
Formula result	=D7+D8+D9+D11+D13+D14+D21

We can copy this formula to the right.

This is all we can complete for now in the cash flow from operating activities section. (See Table 2.6.)

Cash from Investing Activities

Capital expenditures (CAPEX) is typically one of the few line items that management often gives guidance on. You can typically find company guidance by performing a word search on "capital expenditures." For example, in the previous book on Walmart, we uncovered the following note in its 10-K:

> We expect capital expenditures for property and equipment in fiscal 2013, excluding any business acquisitions, to range between $13.0 billion and $14.0 billion.

This was very helpful at the time. Unfortunately, we did not get the same guidance in Amazon's report due to the pandemic. A word search on "capital expenditures" in Amazon's 10-K revealed the following note:

> The COVID-19 pandemic and resulting global disruptions have caused significant market volatility. These disruptions can contribute to defaults in our accounts receivable, affect asset valuations resulting in impairment charges, and affect the availability of lease and financing credit as well as other segments of the credit markets. We have utilized a range of financing methods to fund our operations and capital expenditures and expect to continue to maintain financing flexibility in the current market conditions. However, due to the rapidly evolving global situation, it is not possible to predict whether unanticipated consequences of the pandemic are reasonably likely to materially affect our liquidity and capital resources in the future.

This isn't very helpful for us. Without guidance, we can still utilize the seven methods to make a rational assumption. It is often the case that CAPEX is analyzed as a percentage of sales (the % of an operating item method). Knowing that this is often utilized for CAPEX, let's calculate the percentages and see if they seem reasonable. Note that although CAPEX is often considered as a percentage of sales, this can be considered too aggressive. Quite often percent of sales is used as a default, but this may not be the most accurate representation. Some companies can spend, for example,

10% of sales on CAPEX as a policy of reinvestment in their business, but if you're a manufacturer with a lot of spare capacity coming out of a downturn, it wouldn't make sense to have massive CAPEX increases as a result of 20% annual revenue growth.

So, let's look at the historical CAPEX as a percentage of sales, and see if there is a solid trend.

We should add a line underneath the CAPEX line. In order to add a row, first we need to highlight a row by selecting any cell in row 25, holding down "Shift" and "Space bar," and letting go. Then hold down "Ctrl"+"Shift" + "+."

We can label this new row "CAPEX % of Revenue." Now let's take a look at the historical trend.

2018 CAPEX % of Revenue (Cell D25)

Excel Keystrokes	Description
type "="	Enters into "formula" mode
type "-"	We want CAPEX to be positive so we can calculate a positive percentage
Select Cell D24	2018 CAPEX
type = "/"	Divides
Select 'Income Statement' Tab	Moves to the Income Statement Sheet
Select Cell D11	2018 Total Net Sales
Type "Enter"	End
Formula result	=-D24/'Income Statement'!D11

Note: You may need to adjust the formatting to view the contents of cell D25 as a percentage.

This gives us 5.8% in 2018. If we copy this formula to the right two times, we notice the CAPEX raised slightly to 6.0% in 2019, then jumps to 10.4% in 2020. We need to investigate whether the 10.4% jump was a one-time jump or if the company is ready to significantly increase their CAPEX spend going forward. Unfortunately, they don't talk too much about it in their 10-K. We can, however, look to the Q1 2021 report to see if the CAPEX as a % of Total Net Sales drops back to ~6%. From Figure 2.3, page 3 of the Q1 2021 Cash Flow Statement, we can see the CAPEX spend was $12,082MM.

AMAZON.COM, INC.
CONSOLIDATED STATEMENTS OF CASH FLOWS
(in millions)
(unaudited)

	Three Months Ended March 31,		Twelve Months Ended March 31,	
	2020	2021	2020	2021
CASH, CASH EQUIVALENTS, AND RESTRICTED CASH, BEGINNING OF PERIOD	$ 36,410	$ 42,377	$ 23,507	$ 27,505
OPERATING ACTIVITIES:				
Net income	2,535	8,107	10,563	26,903
Adjustments to reconcile net income to net cash from operating activities:				
Depreciation and amortization of property and equipment and capitalized content costs, operating lease assets, and other	5,362	7,508	22,297	27,397
Stock-based compensation	1,757	2,306	7,347	9,757
Other operating expense (income), net	67	30	244	(108)
Other expense (income), net	565	(1,456)	451	(4,603)
Deferred income taxes	322	1,703	704	827
Changes in operating assets and liabilities:				
Inventories	1,392	(304)	(2,605)	(4,545)
Accounts receivable, net and other	1,262	(2,255)	(6,018)	(11,686)
Accounts payable	(8,044)	(8,266)	6,532	17,258
Accrued expenses and other	(2,761)	(4,060)	(1,213)	4,455
Unearned revenue	607	900	1,430	1,558
Net cash provided by (used in) operating activities	3,064	4,213	39,732	67,213
INVESTING ACTIVITIES:				
Purchases of property and equipment	(6,795)	(12,082)	(20,365)	(45,427)
Proceeds from property and equipment sales and incentives	1,367	895	4,970	4,624
Acquisitions, net of cash acquired, and other	(91)	(630)	(1,384)	(2,864)
Sales and maturities of marketable securities	11,626	17,826	31,664	56,437
Purchases of marketable securities	(15,001)	(14,675)	(39,938)	(72,153)
Net cash provided by (used in) investing activities	(8,894)	(8,666)	(25,053)	(59,383)
FINANCING ACTIVITIES:				
Proceeds from short-term debt, and other	617	1,926	1,934	8,105
Repayments of short-term debt, and other	(631)	(2,001)	(1,860)	(7,547)
Proceeds from long-term debt	76	111	842	10,560
Repayments of long-term debt	(36)	(39)	(1,140)	(1,556)
Principal repayments of finance leases	(2,600)	(3,406)	(10,013)	(11,448)
Principal repayments of financing obligations	(17)	(67)	(43)	(103)
Net cash provided by (used in) financing activities	(2,591)	(3,476)	(10,280)	(1,989)
Foreign currency effect on cash, cash equivalents, and restricted cash	(484)	(293)	(401)	809
Net increase (decrease) in cash, cash equivalents, and restricted cash	(8,905)	(8,222)	3,998	6,650
CASH, CASH EQUIVALENTS, AND RESTRICTED CASH, END OF PERIOD	$ 27,505	$ 34,155	$ 27,505	$ 34,155

See accompanying notes to consolidated financial statements.

FIGURE 2.3 Amazon Quarterly Cash Flow

Now from Figure 2.4, page 4 of the quarterly report, we can see the Q1 2021 Total Net Sales was $108,518MM. Dividing the CAPEX into the Net Sales gives us 11.1%. So it looks like, at least in the first quarter, Amazon is continuing its strong spend. Further, performing a word search on "capital expenditures" in the quarterly report reveals this note:

Cash capital expenditures were $5.4 billion and $11.2 billion during Q1 2020 and Q1 2021, which primarily reflect investments in additional capacity to support our fulfillment operations and in support of continued business growth in technology infrastructure (the majority of which is to support AWS), which investments we expect to continue over time.

My interpretation of this is that their CAPEX spend is due to an increase in infrastructure, which makes sense due to the increase in Amazon's business during the pandemic, and that they may continue to see such an increase in the future. So for now, let's use 11.1% as that's the most up-to-date guidance we have.

We can hardcode "11.1%" in Cell G25 and project 2021 CAPEX.

Note when hardcoding 11.1%: Make sure you have formatted the cells into percentages. If your cells have not been formatted as a percent and you type in "11.1%," Excel will convert that percentage into the decimal 0.111, which may appear as 0.1 in your Excel if it is rounding to the one decimal place.

2021 CAPEX (Cell G24)

Excel Keystrokes	Description
type "="	Enters into "formula" mode
type "-"	CAPEX should be negative; a cash outflow
Select Cell G25	2021 CAPEX % of Revenue
type = "*"	Multiplies
Select 'Income Statement' Tab	Moves to the Income Statement Sheet
Select Cell G11	2021 Total Net Sales
Type "Enter"	End
Formula Result	=-G25*'Income Statement'!G11

This gives us −$54,423.4 in 2021. We can now copy cells G24 and G25 to the right through 2025. We may want to dig deeper and assess whether that 11.1% spend will really continue indefinitely; we may want to scale this down over time. Let's leave the assumptions where they are for now; we can always reassess at the end of the model. (See Table 2.7.)

AMAZON.COM, INC.
CONSOLIDATED STATEMENTS OF OPERATIONS
(in millions, except per share data)
(unaudited)

	Three Months Ended March 31,	
	2020	2021
Net product sales	$ 41,841	$ 57,491
Net service sales	33,611	51,027
Total net sales	75,452	108,518
Operating expenses:		
Cost of sales	44,257	62,403
Fulfillment	11,531	16,530
Technology and content	9,325	12,488
Marketing	4,828	6,207
General and administrative	1,452	1,987
Other operating expense (income), net	70	38
Total operating expenses	71,463	99,653
Operating income	3,989	8,865
Interest income	202	105
Interest expense	(402)	(399)
Other income (expense), net	(406)	1,697
Total non-operating income (expense)	(606)	1,403
Income before income taxes	3,383	10,268
Provision for income taxes	(744)	(2,156)
Equity-method investment activity, net of tax	(104)	(5)
Net income	$ 2,535	$ 8,107
Basic earnings per share	$ 5.09	$ 16.09
Diluted earnings per share	$ 5.01	$ 15.79
Weighted-average shares used in computation of earnings per share:		
Basic	498	504
Diluted	506	513

See accompanying notes to consolidated financial statements.

FIGURE 2.4 Amazon Quarterly Income Statement

TABLE 2.7 Amazon CAPEX

Consolidated Statements of Cash Flows (in US$ millions except per share amounts)

Period Ending December 31	Actuals			Estimates				
	2018A	2019A	2020A	2021E	2022E	2023E	2024E	2025E
Cash Flows from Investing Activities								
CAPEX [Purchase of property and equipment]	(13,427.0)	(16,861.0)	(40,140.0)	(54,423.4)	(64,546.2)	(72,816.7)	(79,244.2)	(84,062.9)
% of Revenue	*5.8%*	*6.0%*	*10.4%*	*11.1%*	*11.1%*	*11.1%*	*11.1%*	*11.1%*

Proceeds from Property and Equipment Sales and Incentives This is related to a company selling off or disposing portions of their property or equipment. It is unclear exactly what they are doing, and a word search doesn't reveal much information, but it is most likely selling old equipment they are planning on replacing. Note that this can also be related to the sale of equipment from portions of businesses they have closed or are planning on closing. This is clearly an unknown and is difficult to project without further company guidance. We continue to recommend being conservative here. However, given the "non-recurring" nature of disposals, we can argue taking a minimum of the past three years is not conservative enough. Being more conservative could mean there are no more disposals. If we want to be most conservative, we can assume this will be zero in the future. Note that it also may be helpful to take a look at a quarterly report if one has been produced beyond the annual report. It may have more updated information. We will go with the most conservative approach, hardcoding "0" in for each projected year.

Items Based on Cash Available Some line items on the cash flow statement are driven by how much cash a business has available. Investments such as purchasing securities, for example, are not necessary to drive the operations of the business. But if the company has a surplus of cash, making such investments could be wise. Another example is a share buyback. A company can choose to buy back its shares as a way to increase value in its stock. However, if a company does not have a surplus of cash, buying back shares may not be the best or most feasible business decision. These items are almost impossible to predict. One recommendation is to highlight these line items red, project them zero for now, and revisit them once the model is complete and once we have a better idea of what the company's cash position could be. It is also important to do further research and listen to the company's latest conference call to see if cash management or future cash initiatives are discussed.

Business Acquisitions, Net of Cash Acquired Business acquisitions, net of cash acquired is a good example of an "item based on cash available." This is very difficult to predict. Most companies have investing activities that will be quite volatile such as this one. What's most difficult about such investing activities is that companies may only make large investments if they have the cash to do so. Amazon, for example, made a large investment in 2017 to acquire Whole Foods. When will the next big acquisition happen? What's the company's strategy? A quick word search on "Acquisition" reveals Note 5 from page 54 in the company 10-K. (See Figure 2.5.)

So, taking the conservative approach or the minimum would give us $2,461, indicating that Amazon will be making such acquisitions in the future. We cannot assume Amazon would have the need or financial capacity to make such acquisitions year after year, especially after the pandemic. This is an example of where one always needs to step back and research such line items in addition to selecting one of the earlier projection methods.

Note 5 — ACQUISITIONS, GOODWILL, AND ACQUIRED INTANGIBLE ASSETS

2018 Acquisition Activity

On April 12, 2018, we acquired Ring Inc. for cash consideration of approximately $839 million, net of cash acquired, and on September 11, 2018, we acquired PillPack, Inc. for cash consideration of approximately $753 million, net of cash acquired, to expand our product and service offerings. During 2018, we also acquired certain other companies for an aggregate purchase price of $57 million.

2019 Acquisition Activity

During 2019, we acquired certain companies for an aggregate purchase price of $315 million, net of cash acquired.

2020 Acquisition Activity

During 2020, we acquired certain companies for an aggregate purchase price of $1.2 billion, net of cash acquired, of which $1.1 billion was capitalized to in-process research and development intangible assets ("IPR&D").

The primary reason for all acquisitions was to acquire technologies and know-how to enable Amazon to serve customers more effectively. Acquisition-related costs were expensed as incurred.

Pro forma results of operations have not been presented because the effects of 2020 acquisitions, individually and in the aggregate, were not material to our consolidated results of operations.

FIGURE 2.5 Amazon Acquisition Activity

Although having some cash outflow here can be prudent, let's leave this one zero for now. Note that it is important to have a good high-level understanding of what the analysis is being created for to help judge where time should be spent conducting deeper research. We will learn later that CAPEX is the line item within the cash flow from investing activities section that has the greatest impact on our valuation. This may vary from analysis to analysis, but in this case it provides some comfort that although this line item is very difficult to predict, it should not have a huge impact on our overall valuation analysis.

Marketable Securities You will often see in the "Cash from Investing Activities" line items related to the purchasing and selling of securities for investment purposes. Marketable securities can be relatively easily bought, sold, or traded on public exchanges. This and the next line item, "Purchases of Marketable Securities," are related to the selling or maturing, and purchasing of such securities, respectively. Performing a word search on "marketable securities" reveals the following brief explanation:

As of December 31, 2019 and 2020, our cash, cash equivalents, restricted cash, and marketable securities primarily consisted of cash, AAA-rated money market funds, U.S. and foreign government and agency securities, and other investment grade securities.

As the combined purchasing and selling of securities give a better impression of the net impact on the market security balance, we can see that in 2018, the sum of the "Sales and Maturities in Marketable Securities" and "Purchases of Marketable Securities" was $1,140MM. In 2019, it was ($9,131)MM, and in 2020, ($22,242)MM. So analyzing the net balances shows a positive flow in 2018, a negative flow in 2019, and a much larger negative flow in 2020. (See Figure 2.6.)

As we discussed with "Other Expenses," which we suggested was based on market dynamics, you will often see positive and negative swings. However, the net of these two line items seems to be trending from positive to negative; I would expect to see a positive at some point. So, I referred to

	2018	2019	2020	Q1 2021
Net, Sales (Purchases) of Marketable Securities	1,140	(9,131)	(22,242)	3,151

FIGURE 2.6   Amazon Net Marketable Securities

	2021E	2022E	2023E	2024E	2025E
Formula	=D28	=E28	=G28	=H28	=I28
Value	8,240	22,681	8,240	22,681	8,240

FIGURE 2.7   Amazon Projected Sales and Maturities in Marketable Securities

	2021E	2022E	2023E	2024E	2025E
Formula	=D29	=E29	=G29	=H28	=I29
Value	(7,100)	(31,812)	(7,100)	(31,812)	(7,100)

FIGURE 2.8   Amazon Projected Purchases of Marketable Securities

the Q1 report to see if the trend continues. As per Figure 2.6, the net in Q1 2021 shows a positive $3,151. So for projections we can't assume a linear trend from positive down to negative. It is more likely to see positive and negative swings, and as with other income, I will assume 2020 showed an extraordinary outflow due to the pandemic and will for now follow the "repeat the cycle" case using 2018 and 2019, skipping 2020. Note the average or conservative methods could work here, but I prefer to replicate swings. The differences between each of these methods do not produce large enough results to greatly impact the overall company valuation. We can always reevaluate after the entire model is complete. See Figures 2.7 and 2.8.

We need to again be careful of the CAPEX assumption drivers calculating into the "Total Cash Flow from Investing Activities." So we need to change D30 to now add each individual line item skipping over row 25.

Recalculating 2018 Total Cash Flow from Investing Activities (Cell D30)

Excel Keystrokes	Description
type "="	Enters into "formula" mode
Select Cell D24	2018 CAPEX
type = "+"	Adds
Select Cell D26	2018 Proceeds from property and equipment sales and incentives
type = "+"	Adds

Select Cell D27	2018 Business acquisitions, net of cash acquired
type = "+"	Adds
Select Cell D28	2018 Sales and maturities in marketable securities
type = "+"	Adds
Select Cell D29	2018 Purchases of marketable securities
Type "Enter"	End
Formula result	=D24+D26+D27+D28+D29

We can now copy the this to the right. (See Table 2.8.)

Cash Flow from Financing Activities

Remember to think of the financing activities in three major sections:

1. Raising or buying back equity
2. Raising or paying down debt
3. Distributions

All items relating to debts, we will leave empty for now. These projected line items will ultimately come from the debt schedule, which will be discussed later. So the short-term borrowings, the long-term borrowings, the principal repayments of finance leases, and the principal repayments of financing obligations will all be empty. Note, since the finance leases and financing obligations are still interest-bearing securities, we treat them as debt for the purposes of modeling them out in the debt schedule. Also note that the company does not report any distributions. See the first edition of this book on Walmart for a good analysis on projecting dividends.

We can now copy Cell D36 through 2025.

Effect of Exchange Rate on Cash This line item is minimal and volatile. Let's use the repeat the cycle method given the volatility, although the average or "conservative" methods could work here as well. The values are very small and will have a minimal effect on our cash flow. Let's link Cell G37 to D37 (in Cell G37, we will have "=D37") and copy Cell G37 over to the right through 2025. (See Table 2.9.)

Our cash flow projections are complete, and we can now copy the total cash and cash equivalents formula from F38 over to the right through 2025. (See Table 2.10.)

There is a line at the bottom of the cash flow statement titled "Cash flow before debt paydown." This is utilized for the debt schedule. We will leave it empty for now and discuss that line item in Chapter 7.

TABLE 2.8 Amazon Cash Flow from Investing Activities

Consolidated Statements of Cash Flows (in US$ millions except per share amounts)

Period Ending December 31	Actuals			Estimates				
	2018A	2019A	2020A	2021E	2022E	2023E	2024E	2025E
Cash Flows from Investing Activities								
CAPEX [Purchase of property and equipment]	(13,427.0)	(16,861.0)	(40,140.0)	(54,423.4)	(64,546.2)	(72,816.7)	(79,244.2)	(84,062.9)
% of Revenue	5.8%	6.0%	10.4%	11.1%	11.1%	11.1%	11.1%	11.1%
Proceeds from property and equipment sales and incentives	2,104.0	4,172.0	5,096.0	0.0	0.0	0.0	0.0	0.0
Business acquisitions, net of cash acquired	(2,186.0)	(2,461.0)	(2,325.0)	0.0	0.0	0.0	0.0	0.0
Sales and maturities in marketable securities	8,240.0	22,681.0	50,237.0	8,240.0	22,681.0	8,240.0	22,681.0	8,240.0
Purchases of marketable securities	(7,100.0)	(31,812.0)	(72,479.0)	(7,100.0)	(31,812.0)	(7,100.0)	(31,812.0)	(7,100.0)
Total Cash from Investing Activities	(12,369.0)	(24,281.0)	(59,611.0)	(53,283.4)	(73,677.2)	(71,676.7)	(88,375.2)	(82,922.9)

TABLE 2.9 Amazon Projected Cash Flow from Financing Activities

Consolidated Statements of Cash Flows (in US$ millions except per share amounts)

Period Ending December 31	Actuals			Estimates				
	2018A	2019A	2020A	2021E	2022E	2023E	2024E	2025E
Cash Flow from Financing Activities								
Short-term borrowings (repayments)	73.0	(116.0)	619.0					
Long-term borrowings (repayments)	27.0	(295.0)	8,972.0					
Principal repayments of finance leases	(7,449.0)	(9,628.0)	(10,642.0)					
Principal repayments of financing obligations	(337.0)	(27.0)	(53.0)					
Total Cash Flow from Financing Activities	(7,686.0)	(10,066.0)	(1,104.0)	0.0	0.0	0.0	0.0	0.0
Foreign Currency Effect on Cash, Cash Equivalents, and Restricted Cash	(351.0)	70.0	618.0	(351.0)	70.0	618.0	(351.0)	70.0

TABLE 2.10 Amazon Projected Cash Flow Statement

Consolidated Statements of Cash Flows (in US$ millions except per share amounts)

Period Ending December 31	Actuals			Estimates				
	2018A	2019A	2020A	2021E	2022E	2023E	2024E	2025E
Cash Flows from Operating Activities								
Net income	10,073.0	11,588.0	21,331.0	48,173.3	57,440.7	64,507.1	70,510.4	74,459.8
Depreciation and amortization	15,341.0	21,789.0	25,251.0	0.0	0.0	0.0	0.0	0.0
Stock-based compensation	5,418.0	6,864.0	9,208.0	11,694.2	13,869.3	15,646.4	17,027.5	18,062.9
% of total operating expenses	8.2%	8.7%	8.8%	8.8%	8.8%	8.8%	8.8%	8.8%
Other operating expense (income), net	274.0	164.0	(71.0)	(90.2)	(106.9)	(120.6)	(131.3)	(139.3)
% of total net sales	0.1%	0.1%	0.0%	0.0%	0.0%	0.0%	0.0%	0.0%
Other expense (income), net	219.0	(249.0)	(2,582.0)	219.0	(249.0)	219.0	(249.0)	219.0
Deferred income taxes	441.0	796.0	(554.0)					
Changes in Operating Working Capital								
Changes in inventory	(1,314.0)	(3,278.0)	(2,849.0)					
Changes in accounts receivable	(4,615.0)	(7,681.0)	(8,169.0)					

Changes in accounts payable	3,263.0	8,193.0	17,480.0					
Changes in accrued expenses	472.0	(1,383.0)	5,754.0					
Changes in unearned revenue	1,151.0	1,711.0	1,265.0					
Net changes in working capital	(1,043.0)	(2,438.0)	13,481.0	0.0	0.0	0.0	0.0	0.0
Total Cash from Operating Activities	**30,723.0**	**38,514.0**	**66,064.0**	**59,996.3**	**70,954.1**	**80,251.8**	**87,157.6**	**92,602.4**
Cash Flows from Investing Activities								
CAPEX [Purchase of property and equipment]	(13,427.0)	(16,861.0)	(40,140.0)	(54,423.4)	(64,546.2)	(72,816.7)	(79,244.2)	(84,062.9)
% of revenue	*5.8%*	*6.0%*	*10.4%*	*11.1%*	*11.1%*	*11.1%*	*11.1%*	*11.1%*
Proceeds from property and equipment sales and incentives	2,104.0	4,172.0	5,096.0	0.0	0.0	0.0	0.0	0.0
Business acquisitions, net of cash acquired	(2,186.0)	(2,461.0)	(2,325.0)	0.0	0.0	0.0	0.0	0.0
Sales and maturities in marketable securities	8,240.0	22,681.0	50,237.0	8,240.0	22,681.0	8,240.0	22,681.0	8,240.0

(Continued)

TABLE 2.10 (*Continued*)

Consolidated Statements of Cash Flows (in US$ millions except per share amounts)

Period Ending December 31	Actuals			Estimates				
	2018A	2019A	2020A	2021E	2022E	2023E	2024E	2025E
Purchases of marketable securities	(7,100.0)	(31,812.0)	(72,479.0)	(7,100.0)	(31,812.0)	(7,100.0)	(31,812.0)	(7,100.0)
Total Cash from Investing Activities	(12,369.0)	(24,281.0)	(59,611.0)	(53,283.4)	(73,677.2)	(71,676.7)	(88,375.2)	(82,922.9)
Cash Flows from Financing Activities								
Short-term borrowings (repayments)	73.0	(116.0)	619.0					
Long-term borrowings (repayments)	27.0	(295.0)	8,972.0					
Principal repayments of finance leases	(7,449.0)	(9,628.0)	(10,642.0)					
Principal repayments of financing obligations	(337.0)	(27.0)	(53.0)					
Total Cash from Financing Activities	(7,686.0)	(10,066.0)	(1,104.0)	0.0	0.0	0.0	0.0	0.0
Foreign Currency Effect on Cash, Cash Equivalents, and Restricted Cash	(351.0)	70.0	618.0	(351.0)	70.0	618.0	(351.0)	70.0
Total Change in Cash and Cash Equivalents	10,317.0	4,237.0	5,967.0	6,361.9	(2,653.2)	9,193.1	(1,568.6)	9,749.5

CHAPTER **3**

The Balance Sheet

The balance sheet is a measure of a company's financial position at a specific point in time. The balance sheet's performance is broken up into three major categories: assets, liabilities, and shareholders' equity, where the company's total value of assets must always equal the sum of its liabilities or shareholders' equity.

$$\text{Assets} = \text{Liabilities} + \text{Shareholders' Equity}$$

ASSETS

An asset is a resource held to produce some economic benefit. Examples of assets are cash, inventory, accounts receivable, and property. Assets are separated into two categories: current assets and noncurrent assets.

Current Assets

A current asset is an asset whose economic benefit is expected to come within one year. Examples of common current assets follow.

Cash and Cash Equivalents Cash is currency on hand. Cash equivalents are assets that are readily convertible into cash, such as money market holdings, short-term government bonds or Treasury bills, marketable securities, and commercial paper. Cash equivalents are often considered as cash because they can be easily liquidated when necessary.

Accounts Receivable Accounts receivable (AR) is a sale made on credit. The revenue for the sale has been recognized, but the customer did not pay for the sale in cash. An asset is recorded for the amount of the sale and remains until the customer has paid. If AR increases by $100, for example, then we must have booked a sale. So, revenue increases by $100.

Income Statement	
Revenue	100.0
Taxes (@ 40%)	(40.0)
Net Income	**60.0**

The resulting net income increase of $60 flows to the cash flow statement. We then need to remove the $100 in AR, as an increase in AR of $100 results in a cash outflow of $100. Combined with the net income increase of $60, we have a total cash change of –$40.

Cash Flow			Balance Sheet	
Net Income	60.0	→	Cash	(40.0)
Changes in Accounts Receivable	(100.0)	→	Accounts Receivable	100.0
Total Changes in Cash	**(40.0)**	→	Retained Earnings (Net Income)	60.0

In the balance sheet, cash is reduced by $40, AR increases by $100, and retained earnings increases by $60. Note the relationship between the changes in accounts receivable on the cash flow statement and accounts receivable on the balance sheet: cash down, asset up. The balance sheet balances; total assets (–$40 + $100 = $60) less liabilities (0) equals retained earnings ($60).

When the customer finally pays, cash is received and the AR on the balance sheet is removed.

Cash Flow			Balance Sheet	
Net Income	**0.0**	→	Cash	100.0
Changes in Accounts Receivable	100.0	→	Accounts Receivable	(100.0)
Total Changes in Cash	**100.0**	→	Retained Earnings (Net Income)	0.0

Inventory   Inventory is the raw materials and goods that are ready for sale. When raw materials are acquired, inventory is increased by the amount of material purchased. Once goods are sold and recorded as revenue, the value of the inventory is reduced and a cost of goods sold expense (COGS) is recorded. Let's say, for example, we are selling chairs.

If inventory increases by $50, then we have most likely purchased inventory, resulting in a cash outflow. Cash reduces by $50 and an inventory asset is created. Note the relationship between the changes in inventory on the cash flow statement and inventory on the balance sheet: cash down, asset up.

Cash Flow		Balance Sheet	
Net Income	0.0	Cash	(50.0)
Changes in Inventory	(50.0)	Inventory	50.0
Total Changes in Cash	**(50.0)**	Retained Earnings (Net Income)	0.0

If inventory decreases by $50, it is most likely related to a sale of that inventory, which is expensed as COGS. Note the additional expense affects taxes and the resulting Net Income is –$30.

An asset sold results in a cash increase; when added to the –$30 of net income, it gives us a total $20 change in cash.

Income Statement	
COGS	(50.0)
Taxes (@ 40%)	20.0
Net Income	**(30.0)**

Cash Flow		Balance Sheet	
Net Income	(30.0)	Cash	20.0
Changes in Inventory	50.0	Inventory	(50.0)
Total Changes in Cash	**20.0**	Retained Earnings (Net Income)	(30.0)

Inventory is removed. Net income affects retained earnings. The balance sheet balances; total assets ($20 – $50 = –$30) less liabilities (0) equals retained earnings (–$30).

Prepaid Expense   Prepaid expense is an asset created when a company pays for an expense in advance of when it is billed or incurred. Let's say we decide to prepay rent expense by $100. Cash goes into a prepaid expense account. Note the relationship between the changes in prepaid expense on the cash flow statement and prepaid expense on the balance sheet: cash down, asset up.

Cash Flow		Balance Sheet	
Net Income	0.0	Cash	(100.0)
Changes in Prepaid Expense	(100.0)	Prepaid Expense	100.0
Total Changes in Cash	**(100.0)**	Retained Earnings (Net Income)	0.0

When the expense is actually incurred, it is then expensed in the SG&A account; after tax we get –$60 in net income.

Income Statement	
SG&A	(100.0)
Taxes (@ 40%)	40.0
Net Income	**(60.0)**

The –$60 in net income flows into retained earnings on the balance sheet. The prepaid expense asset reduces, causing a change in prepaid expense inflow.

Cash Flow		Balance Sheet	
Net Income	(60.0)	Cash	40.0
Changes in Prepaid Expense	100.0	Prepaid Expense	(100.0)
Total Changes in Cash	**40.0**	Retained Earnings (Net Income)	(60.0)

The balance sheet balances as the total Assets (40 – 100 = –60) less liabilities (0) equals shareholders' equity (–60).

Non-Current Assets

Non-current assets are not expected to be converted into cash within one year. Some examples of non-current assets are:

Property, Plant, and Equipment (PP&E)   PP&E are assets purchased in order to further the company's operations. Also known as *fixed assets*, examples of property, plant, and equipment (PP&E) are buildings, factories, and machinery.

Intangible Assets   An intangible asset is an asset that cannot be physically touched. Intellectual property, such as patents, trademarks, and copyrights, goodwill, and brand recognition, are all examples intangible assets.

LIABILITIES

A liability is any debt or financial obligation of a company. There are current liabilities and non-current liabilities.

Current Liabilities

Current liabilities are company debts or obligations that are owed within one year. Some examples of current liabilities follow.

Accounts Payable   Accounts payable is an obligation owed to a company's suppliers. If a company, for example, purchases $500 in raw materials from its supplier on credit, the company incurs a $500 account payable. The company increases the accounts payable by $500 until they pay the supplier.

Cash Flow		Balance Sheet	
Net Income	**0.0**	Cash	500.0
Changes in Accounts Payable	500.0	Accounts Payable	500.0
Total Changes in Cash	**500.0**	Retained Earnings (Net Income)	0.0

Once the supplier is paid, the accounts payable reduces by $500, and cash on the balance sheet goes down by $500. Note the relationship between the changes in accounts payable on the cash flow statement and accounts payable on the balance sheet: cash up, liability up.

Accrued Liabilities Accrued liabilities are expenses that have been incurred but have not yet been paid. If a company receives a utility bill of $1,000, for example, which is expensed under SG&A, an accrued liabilities account is also recorded for $1,000 in the balance sheet.

Income Statement	
SG&A	(1,000.0)
Taxes (@ 40%)	400.0
Net Income	**(600.0)**

After taxes, the net income effect is –$600, which flows to cash flow. Note the relationship between the changes in accrued liabilities on the cash flow statement and accrued liabilities on the balance sheet: cash up, liability up.

Cash Flow		Balance Sheet	
Net Income	**(600.0)**	Cash	400.0
Changes in Accrued Liabilities	1,000.0	Accrued Liabilities	1,000.0
Total Changes in Cash	**400.0**	Retained Earnings (Net Income)	(600.0)

One the bill has been paid, the accrued liabilities reduces, and cash in the balance sheet goes down by $1,000.

Cash Flow		Balance Sheet	
Net Income	**0.0**	Cash	(1,000.0)
Changes in Accrued Liabilities	(1,000.0)	Accrued Liabilities	(1,000.0)
Total Changes in Cash	**(1,000.0)**	Retained Earnings (Net Income)	0.0

Short-Term Debts Short-term debts are debts that come due within one year.

Non-Current Liabilities

Non-current liabilities are company debts or obligations due beyond one year. Some examples of non-current liabilities follow.

Long-Term Debts Long-term debts are debts due beyond one year.

Deferred Taxes Deferred taxes result from timing differences between net income recorded for generally accepted accounting principles (GAAP) and net income recorded for tax purposes. Deferred taxes can act as a liability or an asset. (We will discuss this further in the "Deferred Taxes" section in Chapter 4.)

Now may be a good time to review the example introduced in Chapter 2, "Financial Statement Flows Example." It was important to introduce the example early in the book so you can get a general idea of the impact of a sale in all three statements. But now you should have a more complete understanding of the line item flows.

AMAZON'S BALANCE SHEET

We should now hardcode in the historical balance sheet numbers for Amazon. Amazon's balance sheet line items can be listed just as the company has done. There will be a few adjustments we will make here, but we should go through them line-by-line. We use Amazon's balance sheet found on page 41 of the 10-K. (See Figure 3.1.) Please refer to the "Balance Sheet"

AMAZON.COM, INC.
CONSOLIDATED BALANCE SHEETS
(in millions, except per share data)

	December 31,	
	2019	2020
ASSETS		
Current assets:		
Cash and cash equivalents	$ 36,092	$ 42,122
Marketable securities	18,929	42,274
Inventories	20,497	23,795
Accounts receivable, net and other	20,816	24,542
Total current assets	96,334	132,733
Property and equipment, net	72,705	113,114
Operating leases	25,141	37,553
Goodwill	14,754	15,017
Other assets	16,314	22,778
Total assets	$ 225,248	$ 321,195
LIABILITIES AND STOCKHOLDERS' EQUITY		
Current liabilities:		
Accounts payable	$ 47,183	$ 72,539
Accrued expenses and other	32,439	44,138
Unearned revenue	8,190	9,708
Total current liabilities	87,812	126,385
Long-term lease liabilities	39,791	52,573
Long-term debt	23,414	31,816
Other long-term liabilities	12,171	17,017
Commitments and contingencies (Note 7)		
Stockholders' equity:		
Preferred stock, $0.01 par value:		
Authorized shares — 500		
Issued and outstanding shares — none	—	—
Common stock, $0.01 par value:		
Authorized shares — 5,000		
Issued shares — 521 and 527		
Outstanding shares — 498 and 503	5	5
Treasury stock, at cost	(1,837)	(1,837)
Additional paid-in capital	33,658	42,865
Accumulated other comprehensive income (loss)	(986)	(180)
Retained earnings	31,220	52,551
Total stockholders' equity	62,060	93,404
Total liabilities and stockholders' equity	$ 225,248	$ 321,195

FIGURE 3.1 Amazon Balance Sheet

tab in the model. Notice the balance sheet only contains two historical years, as opposed the three found on the income statement and cash flow statements. This is common. We could go back to prior reports to dig up 2018, but I do not believe this will be necessary for our analysis. We will just focus on 2019 and 2020.

Current Assets

"Cash and cash equivalents" and "Marketable securities" we can hardcode in. The asset section of the balance sheet almost always starts with a balance of the company's cash and securities that can easily be converted into cash. So in the balance sheet for 2019 and 2020, for "Cash and cash equivalents," enter $36,092 and $42,122 into Cells D8 and E8, respectively. The same can be done with "Marketable securities," hardcoding $18,929 and $42,274 into Cells D9 and E9. See Table 3.1.

We can next hardcode "Inventories" and "Accounts receivables, net and other." We will discuss these line items in more detail when projecting in the working capital schedule. Finally, we can easily total the historical current assets in cell D12 as "=SUM(D8:D11)," or by using the hotkey combination "Alt" plus "=". We can copy this formula to the right. (See Table 3.1.)

Non-Current Assets

The first line in the non-current assets section is property and equipment. This line item is most important when projecting our depreciation in the depreciation schedule. For now, we can hardcode in the 2019 and 2020 values, $72,705 and $113,114, into Cell D13 and E13, respectively.

TABLE 3.1 Amazon Historical Current Assets

Consolidated Balance Sheets (in US$ millions except per share amounts)		
On December 31	2019A	2020A
Assets		
Current Assets:		
Cash and cash equivalents	36,092.0	42,122.0
Marketable securities	18,929.0	42,274.0
Inventories	20,497.0	23,795.0
Accounts receivable, net and other	20,816.0	24,542.0
Total Current Assets	**96,334.0**	**132,733.0**

Operating Leases   Amazon has a substantial amount of both finance and operating leases. A note found on page 48 of the 10-K briefly describes the nature of these leases:

> We categorize leases with contractual terms longer than twelve months as either operating or finance. Finance leases are generally those leases that allow us to substantially utilize or pay for the entire asset over its estimated life. Assets acquired under finance leases are recorded in "Property and equipment, net." All other leases are categorized as operating leases. Our leases generally have terms that range from one to ten years for equipment and one to twenty years for property.

A portion of the operating leases are accounted for here as an asset. Let's hardcode $25,141 and $37,553 into 2019 and 2020, respectively.

Goodwill   Goodwill is an intangible asset that typically arises as a result of an acquisition. See my book titled *Mergers and Acquisitions* for a more robust explanation on goodwill. Let's list this as a separate item. So we can hardcode $14,754 and $15,017 into 2019 and 2020, respectively.

Other Assets   Other assets we can also hardcode in. Although it is not 100% clear what this line item is made up of, further research does mention it may consist of several items, including intangible assets and equity investments. Page 49 of the 10-K says:

> Included in "Other assets" on our consolidated balance sheets are amounts primarily related to video and music content, net of accumulated amortization; acquired intangible assets, net of accumulated amortization; certain equity investments; equity warrant assets; long-term deferred tax assets; and lease prepayments made prior to lease commencement.

So, we can hardcode the $16,314 and $22,778 into 2019 and 2020, respectively.

We can then total the asset section of the balance sheet. In Cell D17 we should have "=SUM(D12:D16)." This can be copied to the right to get what is shown in Table 3.2.

Current Liabilities

We can now continue listing the historical values for liabilities.

TABLE 3.2 Amazon Historical Total Assets

Consolidated Balance Sheets (in US$ millions except per share amounts)		
On December 31	2019A	2020A
Assets		
Current Assets:		
Cash and Cash Equivalents	36,092.0	42,122.0
Marketable Securities	18,929.0	42,274.0
Inventories	20,497.0	23,795.0
Accounts Receivable, Net and Other	20,816.0	24,542.0
Total Current Assets	**96,334.0**	**132,733.0**
Property, plant and equipment, net	72,705.0	113,114.0
Operating leases	25,141.0	37,553.0
Goodwill	14,754.0	15,017.0
Other assets	16,314.0	22,778.0
Total Assets	**225,248.0**	**321,195.0**

We can hardcode the current liabilities, "Accounts Payable," "Accrued Expenses," and "Unearned Revenue" line by line, as we did with the current assets. We will learn more about projecting these current liabilities in the working capital section.

Short-Term Debt Notice we have in our model template a line item titled "Short-term debt." The company has not identified short-term debt separately in the current liabilities section. This is highly unusual as the company does have debt; it has at times identified certain debt as short term, but again has not isolated the current portion on their balance sheet. We left the item here for future reference and will revisit once we dig into the company's debts in more detail.

We can then total current liabilities in Cell D24 as "=SUM(D20:D23)." We can copy this formula to the right. (See Table 3.3.)

Non-Current Liabilities

The company has three non-current liability line items, "Long-term lease liabilities," "Long-term debt," and "Other long-term liabilities." The first two are related to the company's financial obligations, which we will dig into as we discuss the debt schedule. Let's hardcode these as is.

TABLE 3.3 Amazon Historical Liabilities

Consolidated Balance Sheets (in US$ millions except per share amounts)		
On December 31	2019A	2020A
Liabilities		
Current Liabilities:		
Accounts payable	47,183.0	72,539.0
Accrued expenses and other	32,439.0	44,138.0
Short-term debt	0.0	0.0
Unearned revenue	8,190.0	9,708.0
Total Current Liabilities	87,812.0	1,26,385.0
Long-term lease liabilities	39,791.0	52,573.0
Long-term debt	23,414.0	31,816.0
Other long-term liabilities	12,171.0	17,017.0
Total Liabilities	163,188.0	227,791.0

Other Long-Term Liabilities "Other long-term liabilities" is a combination of several liabilities. Again, we will find many line items noted as "Other," which could be vague or a composite of several individual line items. A note from page 50 of the 10-K says:

> Included in "Other long-term liabilities" on our consolidated balance sheets are liabilities primarily related to financing obligations, asset retirement obligations, deferred tax liabilities, unearned revenue, tax contingencies, and digital video and music content.

Let's simply hardcode these three line items as is. We can total the entire liability section in Cell D28 as "=SUM(D24:D27)." We can copy this sum to the right. (See Table 3.3.)

Shareholders' Equity

The shareholders' equity section of the balance sheet can be thought of in two major segments:

1. *Equity.* This can include common stock, preferred stock, or treasury stock.
2. *Earnings.* This can include:

a. Retained earnings. This is the portion of net income of the business that has not been distributed out to equity holders.
b. Other comprehensive income or loss. These are the unrealized gains or losses not included in standard net income. These unrealized gains or losses can be due to securities available for sale, derivatives, foreign currency adjustments due to foreign subsidiaries, or pension adjustments, to name a few.

Amazon lists a preferred stock line item, but it is zero, so we will simply hardcode zero into this row.

Next, we have "Common stock," "Treasury stock," and "Additional Paid-in capital."

Common Stock and Additional Paid-in Capital We recommend combining "Common stock" and "Additional paid-in capital" as one. Shares are assigned to them with a "par value, " representing some base value the shares are initially worth. This par value is quite nominal – for example, $0.10 per share, or $0.1 per share. Once the shares are issued in the market, the price issued less this par value is the "capital in excess of par value." For example, let's say we want to raise 500 shares in the market. If we issue the shares into the market at $20 per share, the total value of funds raised is $20 × 500, or $10,000. However, if our shares had a $0.10 par value, we record this issuance in the shareholders' equity on the balance sheet in two lines: the par value at $50 (500 × $0.10) and the difference between the par value and the funds raised ($9,950) under "Additional paid-in capital," sometimes abbreviated as "APIC."

For modeling purposes, it is just as easy to combine these line items as long as both the par value and the APIC are referring to the same type of security. So in our balance sheet we will have $5 + $33,658 for 2019 common stock, and $5 + $42,865 in 2020 (Row 31).

Treasury Stock, Accumulated Other Comprehensive Loss and Retained Earnings We now list "Treasury stock," "Accumulated other comprehensive income (loss)," and "Retained earnings" as Amazon has it. We will then get "Total Shareholders' Equity" in Row 35, summing Rows 30 through 34.

Finally we can total our liabilities and equity by summing Row 35 and Row 28. So in Cell D36 we will have: "=D35+D28." We can copy this to the right. Notice the "Balance" Row 38, which tests to be sure the total assets equals the sum of the total liabilities and equity. This should read "Y" at this point. (See Table 3.4.)

TABLE 3.4   Amazon Historical Balance Sheet

Consolidated Balance Sheets (in US$ millions except per share amounts) On December 31	2019A	2020A
Assets		
Current Assets:		
Cash and cash equivalents	36,092.0	42,122.0
Marketable securities	18,929.0	42,274.0
Inventories	20,497.0	23,795.0
Accounts receivable, net and other	20,816.0	24,542.0
Total current assets	96,334.0	132,733.0
Property, plant and equipment, net	72,705.0	1,13,114.0
Operating leases	25,141.0	37,553.0
Goodwill	14,754.0	15,017.0
Other assets	16,314.0	22,778.0
Total Assets	225,248.0	321,195.0
Liabilities		
Current Liabilities:		
Accounts payable	47,183.0	72,539.0
Accrued expenses and other	32,439.0	44,138.0
Short-term debt	0.0	0.0
Unearned revenue	8,190.0	9,708.0
Total current liabilities	87,812.0	126,385.0
Long-term lease liabilities	39,791.0	52,573.0
Long-term debt	23,414.0	31,816.0
Other long-term liabilities	12,171.0	17,017.0
Total Liabilities	163,188.0	227,791.0
Stockholders' equity		
Preferred stock	0.0	0.0
Common stock par value + additional paid-in-capital	33,663.0	42,870.0
Treasury stock	(1,837.0)	(1,837.0)
Accumulated other comprehensive income (loss)	(986.0)	(180.0)
Retained earnings	31,220.0	52,551.0
Total Stockholders' Equity	62,060.0	93,404.0
Total Liabilities & Stockholders' Equity	225,248.0	321,195.0
SUPPLEMENTAL DATA:		
Balance? (Y/N)	Y	Y

CHAPTER 4

Depreciation Schedule

Depreciation is accounting for the aging of assets.

Depreciation is an income tax deduction that allows a taxpayer to recover the cost or other basis of certain property. It is an annual allowance for the wear and tear, deterioration, or obsolescence of the property.

Most types of tangible property (except, land), such as buildings, machinery, vehicles, furniture, and equipment are depreciable. Likewise, certain intangible property, such as patents, copyrights, and computer software is depreciable.

—from IRS.gov

So, in other words, as a company owns and utilizes an asset, its value will most likely decrease. As we discussed in the balance sheet, if an asset value reduces, there must be another change to one of the other line items in the balance sheet to offset the asset reduction. Accounting rules state that the reduction in asset value can be expensed, with the idea being that the asset's aging or "wear and tear" was partly to do with utilization of the asset to produce or generate revenue. If the item is expensed, net income is reduced – which in turn will reduce the retained earnings in the shareholders' equity section of the balance sheet.

Let's take an example of an asset that has a depreciation expense of $5,000. Depreciation expense reduces net income after taxes, as per the following example. Net income drives the cash flow statement, but since depreciation is a non-cash expense, it is added back to cash.

Income Statement		Cash Flow	
Depreciation	(5,000.0)	Net Income	(3,000.0)
Taxes (@ 40%)	2,000.0	Depreciation	5,000.0
Net Income	(3,000.0)	Total Changes in Cash	2,000.0

In the balance sheet, net income drives retained earnings. Depreciation will lower the value of the asset being depreciated (the PP&E, which stands for "Property, Plant, and Equipment," is the balance sheet line item that typically contains the business's assets).

Cash Flow	
Net Income	**(3,000.0)**
Depreciation	5,000.0
Total Changes in Cash	**2,000.0**

Balance Sheet Adjustments	
Cash	2,000.0
PP&E	(5,000.0)
Retained Earnings (Net Income)	(3,000.0)

There are several methods allowed to depreciate assets. Each has its benefits under certain conditions. We will learn about the most popular methods and how they are utilized in this chapter. The major two categories are:

1. Straight-line depreciation
2. Accelerated depreciation

STRAIGHT-LINE DEPRECIATION

The straight-line method of depreciation evenly ages the asset by the number of years that asset is expected to last—its useful life. For example, if we purchased a car for $50,000, and that car has a useful life of 10 years, the depreciation would be $5,000 per year. So, next year the asset will have depreciated by $5,000 and its value would be reduced to $45,000. In the following year, the asset will be depreciated by another $5,000 and be worth $40,000. By Year 10, the asset will be worth zero and have been fully depreciated.

One can also assign a residual value (also known as scrap value) to an asset, which is some minimal value an asset can be worth after the end of its useful life. So, for example, if the car after Year 10 can be sold for $1,000 for spare parts, then $1,000 is the residual value. In this case, by Year 10, the value of the car should be $1,000, not zero. In order to account for residual value into the depreciation formula, we need to depreciate the value of the car less this residual value, or $50,000 – $1,000, which is $49,000. The depreciation will now be $4,900 per year, which means the next year the value of the car will be $44,100. By Year 10, the final value of the car will be $1,000. The definition for straight-line depreciation is:

Depreciation = (Fair Value of Asset – Residual Value) / Useful Life

ACCELERATED DEPRECIATION

Accelerating depreciation allows a greater depreciation expense earlier in the life of the asset, and a lower depreciation in the later years. The most common reason for accelerating depreciation is that a higher depreciation expense will produce a lower taxable net income, and therefore lower taxes. There are several methods for accelerating depreciation, the most common of which are:

- Declining balance
- Sum of the year's digits
- Modified Accelerated Cost Recovery System (MACRS)

Declining Balance

The declining balance method takes a percentage of the net property balance each year. The net property balance is reduced each year by the depreciation expensed in that particular year.

The percentage applied is calculated by dividing 1 by the life of the asset times an accelerating multiplier:

$$1 \text{ / Useful Life} \times \text{Accelerating Multiplier}$$

The multiplier is most commonly 2.0 or 1.5.

In the car example from earlier, the asset has a life of 10 years. If we assume 2.0 as the accelerating multiplier, then the declining balance percentage is:

$$1 / 10 \times 2 = 20\%$$

We will apply 20% to the net property balance each year to calculate the accelerated depreciation of the car. So, 20% of $50,000 is $10,000. The net balance is $40,000 ($50,000 − $10,000). In Year 2, we will apply 20% to the $40,000, which gives us $8,000. The new net balance is $32,000 ($40,000 − $8,000). In Year 3, we will apply 20% to the $32,000 to get $6,400. (See Table 4.1.)

TABLE 4.1   Declining Balance Example

Period Ending December 31	2021E	2022E	2023E	2024E	2025E
Net property, plant & equipment	50,000.0	40,000.0	32,000.0	25,600.0	20,480.0
Accelerated depreciation (%)	20%	20%	20%	20%	20%
Depreciation expense	10,000.0	8,000.0	6,400.0	5,120.0	4,096.0

Sum of the Year's Digits

To calculate the sum of the year's digits method, we first take the sum of the digits from 1 to the life of the asset. For example, an asset with a useful life of 10 will have a sum of 55 (1+2+3+4+5+6+7+8+9+10). For Year 1, the percentage will be 10/55, or 18.18%. For Year 2, the percentage will be 9/55, or 16.36%. Year 3 is 8/55, or 14.55%, and so on. This percentage is applied to the base value of the asset and is not reduced by the depreciation each year like in the declining balance method.

$$\text{Year 1 depreciation} = \$50,000 \times 18.18\% \text{ or } \$9,090$$
$$\text{Year 2 depreciation} = \$50,000 \times 16.36\% \text{ or } \$8,180$$
$$\text{Year 3 depreciation} = \$50,000 \times 14.54\% \text{ or } \$7,270$$
$$\text{Year 4 depreciation} = \$50,000 \times 12.73\% \text{ or } \$6,365$$
$$\text{Year 5 depreciation} = \$50,000 \times 10.91\% \text{ or } \$5,455$$

Notice in Table 4.2 that we are basing the future depreciation on the original balance each year. This differs from the declining balance method, where we recalculate the net property balance each year.

Modified Accelerated Cost Recovery System (MACRS)

MACRS is the US tax method of depreciation. The MACRS method is a predefined set of percentages based on the asset's useful life. These percentages are applied to the base value of the asset each year. (You can look up these percentages on irs.gov.)

There are several conventions used, each with a different set of calculated percentages, including half-year convention and mid-quarter convention. The differences in conventions are dependent on when exactly the asset is placed in service and starts depreciating. The half-year convention, shown in Table 4.3, assumes the asset is not placed in service and does not begin depreciating until midyear.

TABLE 4.2   Sum of the Year's Digits Example

Period Ending December 31	2021E	2022E	2023E	2024E	2025E
Net property, plant & equipment	50,000.0				
Accelerated depreciation (%)	18.18%	16.36%	14.54%	12.73%	10.91%
Depreciation expense	9,090.0	8,180.0	7,270.0	6,365.0	5,455.0

TABLE 4.3 MACRS Half-Year Convention

	Depreciation rate for recovery period					
Year	3-year	5-year	7-year	10-year	15-year	20-year
1	33.33%	20.00%	14.29%	10.00%	5.00%	3.750%
2	44.45	32.00	24.49	18.00	9.50	7.219
3	14.81	19.20	17.49	14.40	8.55	6.677
4	7.41	11.52	12.49	11.52	7.70	6.177
5		11.52	8.93	9.22	6.93	5.713
6		5.76	8.92	7.37	6.23	5.285
7			8.93	6.55	5.90	4.888
8			4.46	6.55	5.90	4.522
9				6.56	5.91	4.462
10				6.55	5.90	4.461
11				3.28	5.91	4.462
12					5.90	4.461
13					5.91	4.462
14					5.90	4.461
15					5.91	4.462
16					2.95	4.461
17						4.462
18						4.461
19						4.462
20						4.461
21						2.231

When looking at the three-year percentages in Table 4.3, notice that the first percentage is actually lower (33.33%) than the next year's percentage of 44.45%, which is not really accelerating. The midyear convention assumes the asset is not placed in service, and so does not start depreciating until midyear, so an adjustment has been made to that first percentage.

TABLE 4.4 MACRS Mid-Quarter Convention Placed in Service in First Quarter

Year	Depreciation rate for recovery period					
	3-year	5-year	7-year	10-year	15-year	20-year
1	58.33%	35.00%	25.00%	17.50%	8.75%	6.563%
2	27.78	26.00	21.43	16.50	9.13	7.000
3	12.35	15.60	15.31	13.20	8.21	6.482
4	1.54	11.01	10.93	10.56	7.39	5.996
5		11.01	8.75	8.45	6.65	5.546
6		1.38	8.74	6.76	5.99	5.130
7			8.75	6.55	5.90	4.746
8			1.09	6.55	5.91	4.459
9				6.56	5.90	4.459
10				6.55	5.91	4.459
11				0.82	5.90	4.459
12					5.91	4.460
13					5.90	4.459
14					5.91	4.460
15					5.90	4.459
16					0.74	4.460
17						4.459
18						4.460
19						4.459
20						4.460
21						0.565

The mid-quarter convention, as shown in Table 4.4, assumes the asset starts depreciating in the middle of the quarter. So here the starting percentage of 58.33% is higher than that of the half-year convention. Because the asset is placed in service in the first quarter rather than mid-year, the asset will begin depreciating earlier, and will therefore have a greater depreciation expense by the end of the first year.

There are also mid-quarter convention tables where the asset is placed in service in the second, third, and fourth quarters.

TABLE 4.5 Modified Accelerated Cost Recovery System

Period Ending December 31	2021E	2022E	2023E	2024E	2025E
Net property, plant & equipment	50,000.0				
Accelerated depreciation (%)	17.50%	16.50%	13.20%	10.56%	8.45%
Depreciation expense	8,750.0	8,250.0	6,600.0	5,280.0	4,225.0

Determining which table to use really depends on when the assets are placed in service, which is most likely unobtainable information. So, by default, we typically use the mid-quarter convention where the asset is placed in service in the first quarter, as it results in the greatest depreciation expense in the first year. It is always recommended to consult an asset appraiser and a tax professional to be sure you are using the correct methods of depreciation.

For an asset with a 10-year useful life, using Table 4.4, we would apply 17.50% to the value of the asset. For Year 2, the percentage will be 16.50%. See Table 4.5:

Year 1 depreciation = $50,000 × 17.50%, or $8,750

Year 2 depreciation = $50,000 × 16.50%, or $8,250

Year 3 depreciation = $50,000 × 13.20%, or $6,600

Year 4 depreciation = $50,000 × 10.56%, or $5,280

Year 5 depreciation = $50,000 × 8.45%, or $4,225

Note that quite often there are differences between the income statement reported for generally accepted accounting principles (GAAP) purposes and the income statement for tax purposes. One of the major differences can be the method of depreciation. Common depreciation methods under US GAAP include straight line, declining balance, and sum of the year's digits. Tax accounting uses the Modified Accelerated Cost Recovery System (MACRS). The differences in the net income caused by using a different depreciation method when filing GAAP reports versus tax statements can cause a *deferred tax liability*. We will discuss this in the next section.

DEFERRED TAXES

Deferred Tax Asset

A deferred tax asset is defined as an asset on a company's balance sheet that may be used to reduce income tax expense. A deferred tax asset is most commonly created after receiving a net operating loss (NOL), which occurs when a company's expenses exceed its sales. The IRS allows a company to offset the loss against taxable income in another year. The NOL can be carried back 2–5 years or carried forward up to 20 years. Note that the number of years a company can carry back or carry forward a loss depends on several business factors, which need to be considered by the IRS on a case-by-case basis. More information on the specific criteria can be found at www.irs.gov. It is always strongly recommended to verify with a certified accountant or tax professional.

NOL Carryback Example

Income Statement	2018	2019	2020
EBT	750.0	1,500.0	(1,000.0)
Taxes (@ 40%)	(300.0)	(600.0)	0.0
Net Income	450.0	900.0	(1,000.0)

The company in this example suffered a net loss in 2020. So, they file for a two-year carryback, which allows the company to offset the 2020 loss by receiving a refund on taxes paid in the prior two years. So that $1,000 loss becomes a balance from which taxes can be deducted in other years.

NOL Applied to 2018	
Beginning Balance	1,000.0
Taxable Income	750.0
Tax Refund (@ 40%)	300.0
NOL Balance	250.0

We first apply the $1,000 loss to the $750 of taxable income in 2018, which results in a $300 refund. This leaves us with $250 ($1,000 – $750) of NOLs left to apply to 2019.

NOL Applied to 2019	
Beginning Balance	250.0
Taxable Income	1,500.0
Tax Refund (@ 40%)	100.0
NOL Balance	0.0

In 2019, we have $1,500 of taxable income. However, with only $250 in NOLs left, we can only receive a refund on $250 of the $1,500. So that's a $100 refund ($250 × 40%). Combined with the $300 refund, we have a total of $400 refunded.

If the company had little or no taxable income in the prior years, a company can elect to carry forward the net operating losses for up to 20 years depending on various considerations. Let's take another example, where after the two-year carryback credits have been applied an NOL balance still exists.

Income Statement	2018	2019	2020
EBT	100.0	200.0	(1,000.0)
Taxes (@ 40%)	(40.0)	(80.0)	0.0
Net Income	60.0	120.0	(1,000.0)

The company in this example also suffered a net loss in 2020. The company files for a two-year carryback, which allows the company to offset the 2020 loss by receiving a refund on taxes paid in the prior two years.

NOL Applied to 2018	
Beginning Balance	1,000.0
Taxable Income	100.0
Tax Refund (@ 40%)	40.0
NOL Balance	900.0

So we first apply the $1,000 loss to the $100 taxable income in 2018, which results in a $40 refund. This leaves us with $900 ($1,000 – $100) of NOLs left to apply to 2019.

NOL Applied to 2019	
Beginning Balance	900.0
Taxable Income	200.0
Tax Refund (@ 40%)	80.0
NOL Balance	700.0

In 2019, we have $200 of taxable income. Applying the NOL will result in an $80 refund, or $120 in total refunds when combined with the 2018 tax refund. Notice we still have $700 in NOLs left. These can be used to offset future taxes. This $700 balance becomes a deferred tax asset until it is used or no longer usable.

Deferred Tax Liability

A deferred tax liability is caused by temporary accounting differences between the income statement filed for GAAP purposes and the income statement for tax purposes. One common cause of a deferred tax liability is by differing methods of depreciation in a GAAP income statement versus that in a tax income statement. A company can produce a GAAP set of financials using straight-line depreciation, for example, yet have a tax set of financials using the MACRS method of depreciation. This causes a deferred tax liability, reducing taxes in the short term.

Let's take a simple example of a company with $100,000 earnings before interest, taxes, depreciation, and amortization (EBITDA). For GAAP purposes, let's assume we will use the straight-line depreciation of $5,000 ($50,000/10). Let's also say we have decided to accelerate the depreciation for tax purposes using the MACRS method of depreciation. For an asset with a 10-year useful life, the accelerated depreciation is $8,750 (17.5% × $50,000). This will create the income statements shown in Table 4.6 for GAAP and for tax purposes.

The GAAP income statement in the left column shows a lower depreciation expense and shows $95,000 in earnings before taxes (EBT). The right column, however, the tax income statement, shows a higher depreciation expense, because it has been accelerated. This creates a lower EBT of $91,250, and results in $1,500 ($38,000 − $36,500) of lower taxes. Now, the GAAP reported taxes of $38,000, which is the larger amount, is the tax number we see in a company's annual report or 10-K. The lower taxes filed for tax purposes is the amount of tax filed to the IRS that we actually have to pay this year. So, the difference between the taxes reported and the taxes we paid ($1,500) becomes a non-cash item. Just like any expense that we did not yet pay in cash, this non-cash portion of taxes is added back to net income in the cash flow statement. This is a deferred tax liability.

Note that this is a great method to use in order to free up cash in the short term. The deferred tax amount of $1,500 calculated previously can

TABLE 4.6 Income Statements for GAAP and Tax Purposes

Income Statement	GAAP (Straight Line Depreciation)	Tax (MACRS Depreciation)
EBITDA	100,000.0	100,000.0
Depreciation	(5,000.0)	(8,750.0)
EBIT	95,000.0	91,250.0
Interest	0.0	0.0
EBT	95,000.0	91,250.0
Taxes (@ 40%)	(38,000.0)	(36,500.0)
Net Income	57,000.0	54,750.0

also be calculated by subtracting the accelerated depreciation expense from the straight line and multiplying by the tax rate.

$$\text{Deferred Tax Liability} = (\text{Accelerated Depreciation} - \text{Straight Line Depreciation}) \times \text{Tax\%}$$

or

$$(\$8,750 - \$5,000) \times 40\% = \$1,500$$

In modeling, we use this method, building a projected straight-line depreciation schedule, and an accelerated depreciation schedule. We then subtract the projected straight-line depreciation from the accelerated and multiply by the tax rate to get projected deferred tax. We will demonstrate this process with Amazon.

PROJECTING DEPRECIATION

We can now project straight-line depreciation, accelerated depreciation, and deferred taxes. The purposes of having a separate depreciation schedule are to allow us to project several methods of depreciation on groups of assets and to project deferred taxes without convoluting the income statement, cash flow statement, and balance sheet.

Straight-Line Depreciation

We need to consider depreciation on both the assets the company currently owns and its future property improvements that it is projecting to build (capital expenditures [CAPEX]). This will result in a "tiered" schedule, with depreciation stacking each time a new CAPEX improvement occurs.

We begin with the net value of its assets. We've already hardcoded Amazon's net assets into cell E13 of the balance sheet: $113,114.

A note on page 48 of the Amazon 10-K confirms the company uses the straight-line method of depreciation:

Depreciation and amortization is recorded on a straight-line basis over the estimated useful lives of the assets (generally the lesser of 40 years or the remaining life of the underlying building, three years prior to January 1, 2020, and four years subsequent to January 1, 2020, for our servers, five years for networking equipment, ten years for heavy equipment, and three to ten years for other fulfillment equipment).

We can now project depreciation for this net property value. Unfortunately there is difficulty here, as the reported property value is a combination of many different asset classes with different useful lives. The note above suggests useful lives spanning from 3 to 40 years. The best way to project future depreciation requires a list of *every* asset that the company owns, the useful life of *each* asset, *each* asset's original purchase value, and the year each asset was purchased. However, it is almost impossible to get this information.

One suggested method to project depreciation is to take a weighted average of the company's net asset value separated by asset class and the useful lives of each asset class, but there is a problem: We do not know when these assets were actually purchased.

The next best method is to analyze the historical depreciation trends. Amazon's depreciation has been $15,341, $21,789, and $25,251 in 2018, 2019, and 2020, respectively. Notice that implies a very significant 42.0% jump from 2018 to 2019 and a more reasonable but still quite high 15.9% jump from 2019 to 2020. The question is, what will the future trend be? It's reasonable to assume 42.0% is an outlier, but will the growth continue to be 15.9%? We can look to the Q1 report for a clue. See Figure 4.1.

We can use this in two ways: There is $27,397 in 12 months ending 2021 depreciation, which represents an 8.5% growth from 2020. Or, we can take just the three months and multiply by four. This is a touch more aggressive but another useful data point. That gives us $30,032 ($7,508 × 4), or an 18.9% growth from 2020. So definitely higher, but neither imply growth as high as 42.0%. We can at least prove that the 2019 growth was extreme and shoot for something between ~9% – 18% going forward. Note that this range is right around the 2020 growth of 15.9%.

We want to ensure we can continue this trend in the future. So, we will build the straight-line depreciation schedule with some broad useful life assumptions, then tweak those assumptions to approach projected depreciation levels that continue the same relative trend.

It is important to note that it is unusual to see a huge drop in depreciation unless the company has written down assets or sold assets, or unless a large portion of its assets have been fully depleted. Conversely, it is unusual to see a huge increase in depreciation unless the company has purchased a business or assets. With that noted, we should do some research to ensure there have not been any such significant events to the company's assets.

Let's begin modeling out the depreciation. It is recommended to actually pull the net property number from the balance sheet into the depreciation schedule. So we can start in cell G6 on the Depreciation schedule. We can then link in the 2020 net PP&E from the balance sheet by typing "=," toggling over to the balance sheet, selecting cell E13, and typing "Enter." Notice

CONSOLIDATED STATEMENTS OF CASH FLOWS
(in millions)
(unaudited)

	Three Months Ended March 31,		Twelve Months Ended March 31,	
	2020	2021	2020	2021
CASH, CASH EQUIVALENTS, AND RESTRICTED CASH, BEGINNING OF PERIOD	$ 36,410	$ 42,377	$ 23,507	$ 27,505
OPERATING ACTIVITIES:				
Net income	2,535	8,107	10,563	26,903
Adjustments to reconcile net income to net cash from operating activities:				
Depreciation and amortization of property and equipment and capitalized content costs, operating lease assets, and other	5,362	7,508	22,297	27,397
Stock-based compensation	1,757	2,306	7,347	9,757
Other operating expense (income), net	67	30	244	(108)
Other expense (income), net	565	(1,456)	451	(4,603)
Deferred income taxes	322	1,703	704	827
Changes in operating assets and liabilities:				
Inventories	1,392	(304)	(2,605)	(4,545)
Accounts receivable, net and other	1,262	(2,255)	(6,018)	(11,686)
Accounts payable	(8,044)	(8,266)	6,532	17,258
Accrued expenses and other	(2,761)	(4,060)	(1,213)	4,455
Unearned revenue	607	900	1,430	1,558
Net cash provided by (used in) operating activities	3,064	4,213	39,732	67,213
INVESTING ACTIVITIES:				
Purchases of property and equipment	(6,795)	(12,082)	(20,365)	(45,427)
Proceeds from property and equipment sales and incentives	1,367	895	4,970	4,624
Acquisitions, net of cash acquired, and other	(91)	(630)	(1,384)	(2,864)
Sales and maturities of marketable securities	11,626	17,826	31,664	56,437
Purchases of marketable securities	(15,001)	(14,675)	(39,938)	(72,153)
Net cash provided by (used in) investing activities	(8,894)	(8,666)	(25,053)	(59,383)
FINANCING ACTIVITIES:				
Proceeds from short-term debt, and other	617	1,926	1,934	8,105
Repayments of short-term debt, and other	(631)	(2,001)	(1,860)	(7,547)
Proceeds from long-term debt	76	111	842	10,560
Repayments of long-term debt	(36)	(39)	(1,140)	(1,556)
Principal repayments of finance leases	(2,600)	(3,406)	(10,013)	(11,448)
Principal repayments of financing obligations	(17)	(67)	(43)	(103)
Net cash provided by (used in) financing activities	(2,591)	(3,476)	(10,280)	(1,989)
Foreign currency effect on cash, cash equivalents, and restricted cash	(484)	(293)	(401)	809
Net increase (decrease) in cash, cash equivalents, and restricted cash	(8,905)	(8,222)	3,998	6,650
CASH, CASH EQUIVALENTS, AND RESTRICTED CASH, END OF PERIOD	$ 27,505	$ 34,155	$ 27,505	$ 34,155

FIGURE 4.1 Amazon Quarterly Cash Flow Statement

we have linked the 2020 balance sheet net PP&E value into the 2021 depreciation schedule. This is intentional. We assume the property balance at the end of 2020 is equal to the property balance at the beginning of 2021. It's that beginning 2021 property balance that will determine the depreciation expense that will be incurred during the year 2021.

We can now depreciate this. We discussed the wide range of useful lives for the assets that make up the PP&E for Amazon in the earlier note. Let's start with the midpoint, which is approximately 20 for now; we will later adjust this. There are two rows of useful life years (in the "Depreciation" tab, Rows 10 and 11, respectively) for the PP&E and CAPEX. We can enter our assumption of 20 into cell G10.

Rows 13 through 18 are where we will lay out the projected depreciation for both the PP&E and each CAPEX. The formula for straight-line depreciation is (Asset − Residual Value)/ Useful Life. For such a large group of assets, we will typically assume the residual value is zero. So, we can simply take the PP&E and divide it by our assumed useful life of 20.

PP&E Depreciation (Cell G13)

Excel Keystrokes	Description
type "="	Enters into "formula" mode
select G6	Net PP&E
type "/"	Divides
select G10	2021 PP&E Years
type "Enter"	End
Formula Result	=G6/G10

This will give us $5,655.7, which will be our depreciation each year over the life of the asset.

Notice that if we copy this formula to the right, as we had done with most formulas on the income statement and cash flow statement, we will receive an error message. This is because, as expected, the cell references also shift to the right as we copy our formula to the right. In other words, the formula "=G6/G10" becomes "=H6/H10" and so on. However, in this case we do not want the cell references to change. We want to be able to copy the formula to the right without changing the cell references. We can do this by adding a "$" before the column references in the original formula. The "$" anchors the cell references. There are three ways to edit cell G13:

1. Double-click the cell.
2. Hit "F2."
3. Edit the cell directly in the formula toolbar, which is located under the menu bar at the top of the spreadsheet.

△	A	B	C	D
1	Value	10	20	30
2		40	50	60
3	Formula	=B1	=C1	=D1
4		=B2	=C2	=D2
5	Result	10	20	30
6		40	50	60

△	A	B	C	D
1	Value	10	20	30
2		40	50	60
3	Formula	=$B1	=$B1	=$B1
4		=$B2	=$B2	=$B2
5	Result	10	10	10
6		40	40	40

FIGURE 4.2   Unanchored Formulas   **FIGURE 4.3**   Formulas with Anchored Columns

We can add "$" to each column reference, changing the formula from "=G6/G10" to "=$G6/$G10." We can now copy this formula to the right.

Notice we did not include, but could have included, the "$" before the row number as well, producing "=$G$6/$G$10." Doing so would have anchored the row references, but it would not make much difference here, as we are not going to copy this formula to other rows.

Anchoring Formula References   As a guide, a cell with a formula such as "=B1," when copied to the right, will change to "C1" in the second column and to "D1" in the third column, and so on (as shown in Figure 4.2).

However, if we include a dollar sign before the "B" ("=$B1"), copying this formula to the right will leave the "B" reference intact. (See Figure 4.3.) The formula will still read "=$B1" in the second and third columns, but we have only anchored the column reference, not the row reference. So, if we were to copy this formula down, the row reference will still change, reading "=$B2" in the second row.

We could have added a "$" to the row reference to keep this from happening. If we were to change the formula to "=$B$1," then we can copy this formula to the right or down and it will always read "=$B$1." (See Figure 4.4.)

Hitting "F4" while in edit mode of a cell is a quick way to add the "$" into these formulas.

After copying the depreciation formula to the right, the depreciation schedule should look like Table 4.7.

△	A	B	C	D
1	Value	10	20	30
2		40	50	60
3	Formula	=$B$1	=$B$1	=$B$1
4		=$B$1	=$B$1	=$B$1
5	Result	10	10	10
6		10	10	10

FIGURE 4.4   Formulas with Anchored Columns and Rows

TABLE 4.7 Amazon PP&E Depreciation

Depreciation (in US$ millions except per share amounts)

Period Ending December 31	2021E	2022E	2023E	2024E	2025E
			Estimates		
Property, Plant, & Equipment on Jan 1, 2021	113,114.0				
Capital Expenditures as of Jan 1 of Each Year					
Straight-line Depreciation					
Years					
Existing PP&E	20				
CAPEX					
Depreciation ($)					
Existing PP&E	5,655.7	5,655.7	5,655.7	5,655.7	5,655.7
2021 CAPEX					
2022 CAPEX					
2023 CAPEX					
2024 CAPEX					
2025 CAPEX					
Total Book Depreciation					

Now we can start inputting our CAPEX assumptions and CAPEX depreciation. *Remember:* We have already projected CAPEX in our cash flow statement, so we can use those projections and link them into the depreciation schedule. Notice the CAPEX projections in our cash flow statement are negative. When linking them in, we want to reverse the signs so they are represented as a positive number on the depreciation schedule. We want these formulas to be inserted into Row 7, so in cell G7 we can type "=-" (notice the "-" sign after the "=" sign), on the cash flow statement select the CAPEX in year 2021, cash flow statement cell G24, and hit "Enter." We should now have the 2021 projected CAPEX as a positive number in our depreciation schedule. We can copy this formula to the right. We do not want the "$" here, as we want those cell column references to shift to the right as we copy the formula to the right.

We can now depreciate each CAPEX, beginning with the 2021 $54,423.4. It is important to consider timing here. We are assuming the CAPEX will be built and completed in early 2021 and that there will be a full year of depreciation by the end of that year. We now need to make an assumption for the useful life of the CAPEX. As we discussed before, this range is extremely wide. Let's take the midpoint of approximately 20, as we had done with the PP&E, and we will adjust later.

Row 11 is reserved for our CAPEX useful life, so let's input 20 into cell G11. We can then create our 2021 CAPEX depreciation formula in Row 14.

2021 CAPEX Depreciation (Cell G14)

Excel Keystrokes	Description
type "="	Enters into "formula" mode
select G7	2021 CAPEX
hit "F4"	Adds "$" to cell
type "/"	Divides
select G11	2021 CAPEX Years
hit "F4"	Adds "$" to cell
type "Enter"	End
Formula Result	=$G$7/$G$11

This gives us $2,721.2 in depreciation from the 2021 CAPEX. This depreciation will, of course, occur every year for 20 years, so we need to copy this formula to the right. (See Table 4.8.)

We can now continue this process for the 2022 CAPEX. Note that as the 2022 CAPEX will not begin until 2022, the depreciation will not start until 2022. So, there will be no depreciation in 2021, or no formula in cell

TABLE 4.8 Amazon 2021 CAPEX Depreciation

Depreciation (in US$ millions except per share amounts)

Period Ending December 31	Estimates				
	2021E	2022E	2023E	2024E	2025E
Property, Plant, & Equipment on Jan 1, 2021	113,114.0				
Capital Expenditures as of Jan 1 of Each Year	54,423.4	64,546.2	72,816.7	79,244.2	84,062.9
Straight-line Depreciation Years					
Existing PP&E	20				
CAPEX	20				
Depreciation ($)					
Existing PP&E	5,655.7	5,655.7	5,655.7	5,655.7	5,655.7
2021 CAPEX	2,721.2	2,721.2	2,721.2	2,721.2	2,721.2
2022 CAPEX					
2023 CAPEX					
2024 CAPEX					
2025 CAPEX					
Total Book Depreciation					

G15. We will begin in cell H15. Let's continue to use 20 again, but it is important to keep this assumption separate from the useful life of the previous CAPEX in case we need to adjust the assumption later.

So, let's input 20 into cell H11. We can then create our 2022 CAPEX depreciation formula in Row 15.

2022 CAPEX Depreciation (Cell H15)

Excel Keystrokes	Description
type "="	Enters into "formula" mode
select H7	2022 CAPEX
hit "F4"	Adds "$" to cell
type "/"	Divides.
select H11	2022 CAPEX Years
hit "F4"	Adds "$" to cell
type "Enter"	End
Formula Result	=$H$7/$H$11

This depreciation will, of course, occur every year for 20 years, so we need to copy this formula to the right. (See Table 4.9.)

This pattern should continue for 2023 CAPEX, keeping 20 as the useful life assumption in cell I11.

2023 CAPEX Depreciation (Cell I16)

Excel Keystrokes	Description
type "="	Enters into "formula" mode
select I7	2023 CAPEX
hit "F4"	Adds "$" to cell
type "/"	Divides.
select I11	2023 CAPEX Years
hit "F4"	Adds "$" to cell
type "Enter"	End
Formula Result	=$I$7/$I$11

We copy this formula to the right. (See Table 4.10.)

And for 2024 CAPEX, we keep the useful life assumption at 20 in cell J11.

TABLE 4.9 Amazon 2022 CAPEX Depreciation

Depreciation (in US$ millions except per share amounts)

Period Ending December 31	2021E	2022E	2023E	2024E	2025E
			Estimates		
Property, Plant, & Equipment on Jan 1, 2021	113,114.0				
Capital Expenditures as of Jan 1 of Each Year	54,423.4	64,546.2	72,816.7	79,244.2	84,062.9
Straight-line Depreciation					
Years					
Existing PP&E	20				
CAPEX	20	20			
Depreciation ($)					
Existing PP&E	5,655.7	5,655.7	5,655.7	5,655.7	5,655.7
2021 CAPEX	2,721.2	2,721.2	2,721.2	2,721.2	2,721.2
2022 CAPEX		3,227.3	3,227.3	3,227.3	3,227.3
2023 CAPEX					
2024 CAPEX					
2025 CAPEX					
Total Book Depreciation					

TABLE 4.10 Amazon 2023 CAPEX Depreciation (in US$ millions except per share amounts)

Period Ending December 31	2021E	2022E	2023E	2024E	2025E
			Estimates		
Property, Plant, & Equipment on Jan 1, 2021	113,114.0				
Capital Expenditures as of Jan 1 of Each Year	54,423.4	64,546.2	72,816.7	79,244.2	84,062.9
Straight-line Depreciation					
Years					
Existing PP&E	20				
CAPEX	20	20	20		
Depreciation ($)					
Existing PP&E	5,655.7	5,655.7	5,655.7	5,655.7	5,655.7
2021 CAPEX	2,721.2	2,721.2	2,721.2	2,721.2	2,721.2
2022 CAPEX		3,227.3	3,227.3	3,227.3	3,227.3
2023 CAPEX			3,640.8	3,640.8	3,640.8
2024 CAPEX					
2025 CAPEX					
Total Book Depreciation					

2024 CAPEX Depreciation (Cell J17)

Excel Keystrokes	Description
type "=" "	Enters into "formula" mode
select J7	2024 CAPEX
hit "F4"	Adds "$" to cell
type "/"	Divides.
select J11	2024 CAPEX Years
hit "F4"	Adds "$" to cell
type "Enter"	End
Formula Result	=$J$7/$J$11

We copy this formula to the right. (See Table 4.11.)

For 2025 CAPEX we keep the useful life assumption at 20 in cell K11.

2025 CAPEX Depreciation (Cell K18)

Excel Keystrokes	Description
type "="	Enters into "formula" mode
select K7	2025 CAPEX
hit "F4"	Adds "$" to cell
type "/"	Divides
select K11	2025 CAPEX Years
hit "F4"	Adds "$" to cell
type "Enter"	End
Formula Result	=$K$7/$K$11

We can now total the depreciation expense in each year. Summing Rows 13 through 18, in cell G19 we will have "=SUM(G13:G18)." (See Table 4.12.) We can copy this formula to the right.

This gives us 2021 depreciation of $8,376.9. We can now analyze how this compares to the historical depreciation.

We discussed earlier that we expect growth to be somewhere between 9% and 18% based on historical trends and input from the latest quarterly report. The 2021 depreciation we projected is showing a steep decline from the previous year, so we need to make adjustments to our useful life assumptions. There are two major variables we can adjust: the useful life of the net PP&E or the useful life of the CAPEX. It is important to note that the depreciation of our net PP&E makes up the greater portion of the 2021

TABLE 4.11 Amazon 2024 CAPEX Depreciation

Depreciation (in US$ millions except per share amounts)

Period Ending December 31	2021E	2022E	2023E	2024E	2025E
			Estimates		
Property, Plant, & Equipment on Jan 1, 2021	113,114.0				
Capital Expenditures as of Jan 1 of Each Year	54,423.4	64,546.2	72,816.7	79,244.2	84,062.9
Straight-line Depreciation					
Years					
Existing PP&E	20				
CAPEX	20	20	20	20	
Depreciation ($)					
Existing PP&E	5,655.7	5,655.7	5,655.7	5,655.7	5,655.7
2021 CAPEX	2,721.2	2,721.2	2,721.2	2,721.2	2,721.2
2022 CAPEX		3,227.3	3,227.3	3,227.3	3,227.3
2023 CAPEX			3,640.8	3,640.8	3,640.8
2024 CAPEX				3,962.2	3,962.2
2025 CAPEX					
Total Book Depreciation					

TABLE 4.12 Amazon Total Book Depreciation

Depreciation (in US$ millions except per share amounts)

Period Ending December 31	2021E	2022E	Estimates 2023E	2024E	2025E
Property, Plant, & Equipment on Jan 1, 2021	113,114.0				
Capital Expenditures as of Jan 1 of Each Year	54,423.4	64,546.2	72,816.7	79,244.2	84,062.9
Straight-line Depreciation					
Years					
Existing PP&E	20				
CAPEX	20	20	20	20	20
Depreciation ($)					
Existing PP&E	5,655.7	5,655.7	5,655.7	5,655.7	5,655.7
2021 CAPEX	2,721.2	2,721.2	2,721.2	2,721.2	2,721.2
2022 CAPEX		3,227.3	3,227.3	3,227.3	3,227.3
2023 CAPEX			3,640.8	3,640.8	3,640.8
2024 CAPEX				3,962.2	3,962.2
2025 CAPEX					4,203.1
Total Book Depreciation	8,376.9	11,604.2	15,245.0	19,207.2	23,410.4

depreciation expense. So, we would recommend trying to adjust *downward* the useful life of the PP&E first. If we adjust cell G10 down to 15, we get $10,262.1 in total depreciation, which is still lower than the expected range calculated. If we bring it down further, to 10, we get $14,032.6, closer, but still showing a decline. If we drop the assumption to 5, we get $25,344. This is pretty much in line with the prior year. Let's try to bring it down one more year to 4. This gives us $30,999.7, a 22.8% growth over the prior year, now too high. So, let's go back to 5, representing flat growth, but knowing that we can still adjust the CAPEX to get to our overall target trend. We can hardcode "5" into cell G10.

Now we can look at our CAPEX useful life assumption. If we start to drop this down, this will bring up our total depreciation into the desired range. We can try to hardcode 15 into G11, which gives us $26,251, a 4.0% growth over the prior year. Let's drop it down to 10 to increase this growth further. This gives us $28,065.1, an 11.1% overall growth from 2020. This is now within the 9–18% range. Although this may be okay, I'd like to get that growth up a bit more into the midpoint of the range, so let try to drop it down one more to 9. This gives us $28,669.8, a 13.5% growth from 2020. If we drop down one more year to 8, we get a 16.5% growth, still in the range but at the high end. So let's stick with 9, closest to the midpoint of the range. This works. We can hardcode "9" into cell G11 and copy to the right. See Table 4.13.

This process has illustrated that adjusting the useful life for the net PP&E affects the overall balance of total depreciation. So, if our total depreciation is significantly low or high, we should first adjust the net PP&E useful life assumption. The CAPEX useful life affects the rate at which depreciation increases, so if the total depreciation is increasing too fast or too slow in the future, we should adjust the CAPEX useful life. It does take some practice to get comfortable with these drivers. We want to reiterate that this is not the most accurate way to project depreciation. The most accurate way is to have detailed data on all assets purchased: the cost, date purchased, and useful life of each. Given that this data is very difficult to obtain, we need to focus on the larger trends.

We can now link our straight-line total depreciation into our income statement. So, on the income statement, where we had left the projected depreciation empty ("Income Statement" tab, cell G33), we can type "=, " toggle back to the depreciation schedule, select cell G19, and hit "Enter." We can then copy income statement cell G23 to the right. Table 4.14 is the updated income statement with our depreciation linked in. Note once the depreciation is linked in, all values below will update (EBIT, EBT, Net Income) to reflect the additional expense.

TABLE 4.13 Adjusted Amazon Total Book Depreciation

Depreciation (in US$ millions except per share amounts)

Period Ending December 31	Estimates				
	2021E	2022E	2023E	2024E	2025E
Property, Plant, & Equipment on Jan 1, 2021	113,114.0				
Capital Expenditures as of Jan 1 of Each Year	54,423.4	64,546.2	72,816.7	79,244.2	84,062.9
Straight-line Depreciation					
Years					
Existing PP&E	5				
CAPEX	9	9	9	9	9
Depreciation ($)					
Existing PP&E	22,622.8	22,622.8	22,622.8	22,622.8	22,622.8
2021 CAPEX	6,047.0	6,047.0	6,047.0	6,047.0	6,047.0
2022 CAPEX		7,171.8	7,171.8	7,171.8	7,171.8
2023 CAPEX			8,090.7	8,090.7	8,090.7
2024 CAPEX				8,804.9	8,804.9
2025 CAPEX					9,340.3
Total Book Depreciation	28,669.8	35,841.6	43,932.4	52,737.3	62,077.6

TABLE 4.14 Amazon Income Statement with Depreciation Expense

Consolidated Income Statements (in US$ millions except per share amounts)

Period Ending December 31	Actuals			Estimates				
	2018A	2019A	2020A	2021E	2022E	2023E	2024E	2025E
Revenue								
Net Product Sales	141,915.0	160,408.0	215,915.0					
Y/Y growth (%)		*13.0%*	*34.6%*					
Net Service Sales	90,972.0	120,114.0	170,149.0					
Y/Y growth (%)		*32.0%*	*41.7%*					
Total Net Sales	**232,887.0**	**280,522.0**	**386,064.0**	**490,301.3**	**581,497.3**	**656,006.5**	**713,912.0**	**757,323.5**
Y/Y Net Sales Growth (%)		*20.5%*	*37.6%*	*27.0%*	*18.6%*	*12.8%*	*8.8%*	*6.1%*
Y/Y Growth (%) Decline				*(28.2%)*	*(31.1%)*	*(31.1%)*	*(31.1%)*	*(31.1%)*
Cost of goods sold								
Cost of goods sold	139,156.0	165,536.0	233,307.0	296,299.9	351,411.7	396,439.2	431,432.8	457,667.3
COGS as a % of net sales	*59.8%*	*59.0%*	*60.4%*	*60.4%*	*60.4%*	*60.4%*	*60.4%*	*60.4%*
Gross profit	**93,731.0**	**114,986.0**	**152,757.0**	**194,001.4**	**230,085.6**	**259,567.3**	**282,479.2**	**299,656.2**
Gross profit margin (%)	*40%*	*41%*	*40%*	*40%*	*40%*	*40%*	*40%*	*40%*

(Continued)

TABLE 4.14 (*Continued*)

Consolidated Income Statements (in US$ millions except per share amounts)

Period Ending December 31	Actuals			Estimates				
	2018A	2019A	2020A	2021E	2022E	2023E	2024E	2025E
Operating expenses								
Fulfillment	34,027.0	40,232.0	58,517.0	74,316.6	88,139.5	99,433.1	108,210.0	114,790.0
Fulfillment as a % of net sales	*14.6%*	*14.3%*	*15.2%*	*15.2%*	*15.2%*	*15.2%*	*15.2%*	*15.2%*
Technology and Content	13,496.0	14,142.0	17,489.0	22,211.0	26,342.3	29,717.6	32,340.8	34,307.3
Technology and Content as a % of net sales	*5.8%*	*5.0%*	*4.5%*	*4.5%*	*4.5%*	*4.5%*	*4.5%*	*4.5%*
Marketing	13,814.0	18,878.0	22,008.0	27,950.2	33,148.9	37,396.4	40,697.3	43,172.1
Marketing as a % of net sales	*5.9%*	*6.7%*	*5.7%*	*5.7%*	*5.7%*	*5.7%*	*5.7%*	*5.7%*
General and administrative	4,336.0	5,203.0	6,668.0	8,468.4	10,043.5	11,330.4	12,330.5	13,080.3
General and administrative as a % of net sales	*1.9%*	*1.9%*	*1.7%*	*1.7%*	*1.7%*	*1.7%*	*1.7%*	*1.7%*
Other operating expense (income), net	296.0	201.0	(75.0)	(95.3)	(113.0)	(127.4)	(138.7)	(147.1)

Other operating expense as a % of net sales	0.1%	0.1%	0.0%	0.0%	0.0%	0.0%	0.0%	0.0%
Total operating expenses	65,969.0	78,656.0	104,607.0	132,850.9	157,561.2	177,750.0	193,439.9	205,202.6
EBITDA	27,762.0	36,330.0	48,150.0	61,150.5	72,524.5	81,817.3	89,039.3	94,453.6
EBITDA margin (%)	11.9%	13.0%	12.5%	12.5%	12.5%	12.5%	12.5%	12.5%
Depreciation and amortization	15,341.0	21,789.0	25,251.0	28,669.8	35,841.6	43,932.4	52,737.3	62,077.6
EBIT	12,421.0	14,541.0	22,899.0	32,480.7	36,682.8	37,884.9	36,302.0	32,375.9
EBIT margin (%)	5.3%	5.2%	5.9%	6.6%	6.3%	5.8%	5.1%	4.3%
Other income	183.0	(203.0)	(2,371.0)	183.0	(203.0)	183.0	(203.0)	183.0
Interest								
Interest expense	1,417.0	1,600.0	1,647.0					
Interest income	(440.0)	(832.0)	(555.0)					
Net interest expense	977.0	768.0	1,092.0	0.0	0.0	0.0	0.0	0.0
Earnings before tax (EBT)	11,261.0	13,976.0	24,178.0	32,297.7	36,885.8	37,701.9	36,505.0	32,192.9
EBT margin (%)	4.8%	5.0%	6.3%	6.6%	6.3%	5.7%	5.1%	4.3%
Income tax expense	1,197.0	2,374.0	2,863.0	6,782.5	7,746.0	7,917.4	7,666.0	6,760.5
All-in effective tax rate (%)	10.6%	17.0%	11.8%	21.0%	21.0%	21.0%	21.0%	21.0%

(Continued)

147

TABLE 4.14 (*Continued*)

Consolidated Income Statements (in US$ millions except per share amounts)

Period Ending December 31	Actuals			Estimates				
	2018A	2019A	2020A	2021E	2022E	2023E	2024E	2025E
Net income from continuing operations	10,064.0	11,602.0	21,315.0	25,515.1	29,139.8	29,784.5	28,838.9	25,432.4
Non-recurring events								
Discontinued operations	0.0	0.0	0.0	0.0	0.0	0.0	0.0	0.0
Extraordinary items	0.0	0.0	0.0	0.0	0.0	0.0	0.0	0.0
Effect of accounting changes	0.0	0.0	0.0	0.0	0.0	0.0	0.0	0.0
Other items	0.0	0.0	0.0	0.0	0.0	0.0	0.0	0.0
Total non-recurring events	0.0	0.0	0.0	0.0	0.0	0.0	0.0	0.0
Net income (after non-recurring events)	10,064.0	11,602.0	21,315.0	25,515.1	29,139.8	29,784.5	28,838.9	25,432.4
Income attributable to equity method investments	(9.0)	14.0	(16.0)	(9.0)	14.0	(16.0)	(9.0)	14.0

Dividends paid on common stock	0.0	0.0	0.0	0.0	0.0	0.0	0.0	0.0
Net income (As reported)	10,073.0	11,588.0	21,331.0	25,524.1	29,125.8	29,800.5	28,847.9	25,418.4
Earnings per share (EPS)								
Basic	20.68	23.46	42.66	50.61	57.75	59.09	57.20	50.40
Diluted	20.15	22.99	41.83	49.15	56.08	57.38	55.55	48.95
Average common shares outstanding								
Basic	487	494	500	504	504	504	504	504
Diluted	500	504	510	519	519	519	519	519

TABLE 4.15 Amazon Cash Flow Statement Projections with Depreciation Expense

Consolidated Statements of Cash Flows (in US$ millions except per share amounts)

Period Ending December 31	Actuals			Estimates				
	2018A	2019A	2020A	2021E	2022E	2023E	2024E	2025E
Cash flows from operating activities								
Net income	10,073.0	11,588.0	21,331.0	25,524.1	29,125.8	29,800.5	28,847.9	25,418.4
Depreciation and amortization	15,341.0	21,789.0	25,251.0	28,669.8	35,841.6	43,932.4	52,737.3	62,077.6
Stock-based compensation	5,418.0	6,864.0	9,208.0	11,694.2	13,869.3	15,646.4	17,027.5	18,062.9
% of Total Operating Expenses	8.2%	8.7%	8.8%	8.8%	8.8%	8.8%	8.8%	8.8%
Other operating expense (income), net	274.0	164.0	(71.0)	(90.2)	(106.9)	(120.6)	(131.3)	(139.3)
% of Total Net Sales	0.1%	0.1%	0.0%	0.0%	0.0%	0.0%	0.0%	0.0%
Other expense (income), net	219.0	(249.0)	(2,582.0)	219.0	(249.0)	219.0	(249.0)	219.0
Deferred income taxes	441.0	796.0	(554.0)	(554.0)	(554.0)	(554.0)	(554.0)	(554.0)

Changes in operating working capital							
Changes in inventory	(1,314.0)	(3,278.0)	(2,849.0)				
Changes in accounts receivable	(4,615.0)	(7,681.0)	(8,169.0)				
Changes in accounts payable	3,263.0	8,193.0	17,480.0				
Changes in accrued expenses	472.0	(1,383.0)	5,754.0				
Changes in unearned revenue	1,151.0	1,711.0	1,265.0				
Net changes in working capital	(1,043.0)	(2,438.0)	13,481.0	0.0	0.0	0.0	0.0
Total cash from operating activities	30,723.0	38,514.0	66,064.0	65,463.0	77,926.8	88,923.6	97,678.4	105,084.7

Notice the depreciation expense also populates the cash flow statement, as we had previously linked the cash flow expense in from the income statement. (See Table 4.15.)

PROJECTING DEFERRED TAXES

Finally, we need to consider deferred taxes. As mentioned earlier, we often calculate deferred taxes as per GAAP versus tax accounting differences. However, as the company may be reporting only one set of financials, these differences may not exist. So it is uncertain in reality how the company will treat deferred taxes in the future. They can potentially go away altogether; we just don't know. Performing a word search on "deferred taxes" reveals a table found on page 63 of the 10-K (see Figure 4.5):

You can see from Figure 4.5 that Amazon's deferred taxes come from many items above and beyond simply depreciation and amortization; prior losses in the form of carryforwards and tax credits, for example. It is often common practice to model out accelerated depreciation in order to calculate deferred taxes. But because it is shown in Figure 4.5 that the deferred taxes come from other items as well, simply modeling out the depreciation won't give us the entire picture. If you would like to know how to model accelerated depreciation, please refer to the first edition book on Walmart.

So much like an "other" line item, this deferred tax item is derived from a variety of items that would be very difficult to model out one by one with the limited information presented in the 10-K. So, we should defer to the "Seven methods of projections" from Chapter 1. We feel it is best, as this is an unknown, to take the most conservative approach, which is also the same as the "last year" approach (we like it when two of the methods point to the same results). It is safe to say this deferred tax line does not have a large impact on the overall valuation, so we can keep this assumption for now and tweak later if needed. We can further, at the end of the analysis, try different approaches, and see if any of them changes the overall valuation to determine if it is even worthwhile belaboring the assumption. Let's have G13 be "=F13," and we can copy this to the right through 2025. (See Table 4.15.)

We can now proceed to the working capital schedule, which will help us complete the cash flow statement.

	December 31,	
	2019	2020
Deferred tax assets (1):		
Loss carryforwards U.S. - Federal/States	188	245
Loss carryforwards - Foreign	3,232	3,876
Accrued liabilities, reserves, and other expenses	1,373	2,457
Stock-based compensation	1,585	2,033
Depreciation and amortization	2,385	1,886
Operating lease liabilities	6,648	10,183
Other items	728	559
Tax credits	772	207
Total gross deferred tax assets	16,911	21,446
Less valuation allowances (2)	(5,754)	(5,803)
Deferred tax assets, net of valuation allowances	11,157	15,643
Deferred tax liabilities:		
Depreciation and amortization	(5,507)	(5,508)
Operating lease assets	(6,331)	(9,539)
Other items	(640)	(1,462)
Net deferred tax assets (liabilities), net of valuation allowances	$ (1,321)	$ (866)

FIGURE 4.5 Amazon Deferred Taxes

CHAPTER 5

Working Capital

Working capital is a measure of a company's current assets less its current liabilities.

Working Capital = Current Assets – Current Liabilities

- *Asset*: An asset is a resource held to produce some economic benefit. Examples of assets are cash, inventory, accounts receivable, and property.
- *Current asset*: A current asset is an asset whose economic benefit is expected to come within one year. Examples of current assets are cash, inventory, and accounts receivable.
- *Liability*: A liability is any debt or financial obligation of a company. Examples of liabilities are accounts payable, accrued expenses, long-term debt, and a deferred tax liability.
- *Current liability*: A current liability is a debt or financial obligation that is due within one year. Examples of current liabilities are accounts payable and accrued expenses.

So, the working capital, or the current assets less the current liabilities, helps us determine if cash coming in from our current assets will cover the liabilities that are coming due in the next 12 months. If working capital is positive, current assets are greater than the current liabilities, and we will potentially have more than enough funds to cover our liabilities coming due. If the working capital is negative, current assets are less than the current liabilities, and we do not have enough resources to pay our current liabilities, a working capital deficit. For this reason, working capital is regarded as a measure of a company's near-term liquidity.

OPERATING WORKING CAPITAL

For modeling purposes, we focus on a narrower definition of working capital called *operating working capital*. Operating working capital is also defined as current assets less current liabilities. However, we do not include cash and cash equivalents as part of current assets, and we do not include debts as part of current liabilities.

- *Cash equivalents*: Cash equivalents are assets that are readily convertible into cash, such as money market holdings, short-term government bonds or Treasury bills, marketable securities, and commercial paper. Cash equivalents are often considered as cash because they can be easily liquidated when necessary.

So, removing cash and cash equivalents, we are left with this for current assets:

- Accounts receivable
- Inventory
- Prepaid expenses

And removing debts, we are left with the following for current liabilities:

- Accounts payable
- Accrued expenses

Note that there are other possible current assets or current liabilities; these are a few of the most common items.

Each of these line items is most closely related to the company's operations. For example, accounts receivable is the portion of revenue we did not collect in cash, and accrued expenses is the portion of expenses we did not yet pay in cash. For this reason, operating working capital is a good measure of how much cash is coming in from the day-to-day operations. Another way to look at it is this: Operating working capital helps track how well a company is managing its cash generating from day-to-day operations. In contrast, working capital, because it includes cash, cash equivalents, and debts, may not give the clearest measure of just the day-to-day operations.

How do we know if the individual items are really performing well? If we see accounts receivable, for example, increasing year over year, this could mean we have an ever-growing collections problem. However, this could also mean that the accounts receivables are growing because the revenue is growing, which would be a good indicator of strong business growth. So it is not enough to look at these operating working capital line items independently in order to determine their performance; we need to compare these line items to some related income statement line item. We use a measure called "days" to track how well we are collecting our receivables or paying our payables. Days are measured by dividing the receivable or payable by its related income statement item and multiplying by 360.

For example, let's say in 2020 the accounts receivable balance is $25,000 and the revenue is $100,000.

Income Statement	
Revenue	100,000.0
COGS	10,000.0
Operating Expenses	85,000.0
EBITDA	**5,000.0**

Operating Working Capital	
Accounts Receivable	25,000.0
Inventory	7,500.0
Prepaid Expenses	1,000.0
Accounts Payable	12,500.0
Accrued Expenses	15,000.0
Net Working Capital	**6,000.0**

The accounts receivable divided by the revenue gives us 25%. So, 25% of our 2020 revenue has not yet been collected. We multiply this percentage by the number of days in one year to get an equivalent number representing how many days these receivables have been left outstanding: 25% × 360 = 90, so of the 2020 revenue, 90 days are outstanding. As a rule of thumb, many companies require customer receipts to be paid within 30 days. However, depending on the business 60, 90, or even more could be acceptable. Ninety could be considered high or it could be okay, depending on the business model and the product sold. Notice that we have used 360 days instead of 365. Either way is acceptable; however, we more commonly use 360 because this is divisible by 12, which would make the modeling simpler if we ever wanted to break the year column down into 12 months.

$$\text{Accounts Receivable Days} = \frac{\text{Accounts Receivable}}{\text{Revenue}} \times 360$$

It is important to note that we have made a simplifying assumption in this example for clarity. We took the last year's accounts receivable balance as the numerator in the calculation. In the actual analysis, it is important to take an average of the ending balances from the year being analyzed and the previous year. Because balance sheet items are balances at a specific point in time, averaging the current year and previous year's performance gives us a better indicator of measurement for the entire year. Income statement and cash flow items actually give us total performance over an entire period, so averaging doesn't apply. The complete formula for accounts receivable days in 2020 is:

$$2020 \text{ Accounts Receivable Days} =$$
$$\frac{\text{Average (2020 Accounts Receivables, 2019 Accounts Receivables)}}{2020 \text{ Revenue}} \times 360$$

Let's take another example using a liability (accrued expenses). Let's say the accrued expenses balance in 2020 is $15,000 and is made up of unpaid office rent. The 2020 income statement expense is $85,000. The accrued expenses of $15,000 divided by $85,000 gives us 17.6%. So, 17.6% of our 2020 expenses have not yet been paid. We multiply this percentage by the number of days in one year to get an equivalent number representing how many days these payables have been left outstanding: 17.6% × 360 = 63.4, so of the 2020 expense, 63.4 days are still outstanding, which could be considered too high in this case, especially considering rent should typically be paid every 30 days.

$$\text{Accrued Expenses Days} = \frac{\text{Accrued Expenses}}{\text{Operating Expenses}} \times 360$$

We again simplified the example for purposes of instruction. When performing the actual analysis, we take the average of the accrued expenses balance in the year being analyzed and the prior year.

$$2020 \text{ Accrued Expenses Days} =$$
$$\frac{\text{Average (2020 Accrued Expenses, 2019 Accrued Expenses)}}{2020 \text{ Operating Expenses}} \times 360$$

AMAZON'S OPERATING WORKING CAPITAL

Let's now take a look at Amazon's working capital line items. (See Figure 5.1.) We use Amazon's balance sheet, found on page 41 of the Amazon 10-K, to identify which are the proper current asset and current liability line items.

AMAZON.COM, INC.
CONSOLIDATED BALANCE SHEETS
(in millions, except per share data)

	December 31,	
	2019	2020
ASSETS		
Current assets:		
Cash and cash equivalents	$ 36,092	$ 42,122
Marketable securities	18,929	42,274
Inventories	20,497	23,795
Accounts receivable, net and other	20,816	24,542
Total current assets	96,334	132,733
Property and equipment, net	72,705	113,114
Operating leases	25,141	37,553
Goodwill	14,754	15,017
Other assets	16,314	22,778
Total assets	$ 225,248	$ 321,195
LIABILITIES AND STOCKHOLDERS' EQUITY		
Current liabilities:		
Accounts payable	$ 47,183	$ 72,539
Accrued expenses and other	32,439	44,138
Unearned revenue	8,190	9,708
Total current liabilities	87,812	126,385
Long-term lease liabilities	39,791	52,573
Long-term debt	23,414	31,816
Other long-term liabilities	12,171	17,017
Commitments and contingencies (Note 7)		
Stockholders' equity:		
Preferred stock, $0.01 par value:		
Authorized shares — 500		
Issued and outstanding shares — none	—	—
Common stock, $0.01 par value:		
Authorized shares — 5,000		
Issued shares — 521 and 527		
Outstanding shares — 498 and 503	5	5
Treasury stock, at cost	(1,837)	(1,837)
Additional paid-in capital	33,658	42,865
Accumulated other comprehensive income (loss)	(986)	(180)
Retained earnings	31,220	52,551
Total stockholders' equity	62,060	93,404
Total liabilities and stockholders' equity	$ 225,248	$ 321,195

FIGURE 5.1   Amazon Balance Sheet

Starting from the top of the balance sheet, we know cash is not included in operating working capital. Marketable securities is also not related to operating working capital, as it can be looked at as another form of "cash equivalents" – i.e., it can be readily converted into cash, as we described earlier.

The next two line items ("Inventories" and "Accounts receivable, net and other") are operating working capital line items.

On the liabilities side, there is "Accounts payable," "Accrued expenses and other," and "Unearned revenue," all of which are working capital line items.

So we have now identified the following line items from the balance sheet to be used in our operating working capital schedule:

- Inventories
- Accounts receivable, net and other
- Accounts payable
- Accrued expenses and other
- Unearned revenue

We can now proceed to the operating working capital schedule in the model and rework the schedule so that we have these six line items.

Inventories

Since we already have the historical receivables hardcoded in the balance sheet, we can link these rows into the operating working capital schedule. Let's proceed to the tab in the model titled "Operating Working Capital." At the top of the schedule (cell E7), we can link in the 2019 receivables in from the balance sheet by typing "=," toggling over to the Balance Sheet, selecting cell D10, and typing "Enter." We can copy this one cell to the right for 2020. (See Table 5.1.)

We now calculate the historical days, which will help us make better projection assumptions. Keeping in line with the earlier example, we can calculate inventory turnover days using the following formula:

$$2020 \text{ Inventory Turnover Days} =$$
$$\frac{\text{Average (2020 Inventories, 2019 Inventories)}}{2020 \text{ COGS}} \times 360$$

So, in operating working capital cell F8, we can follow these steps:

2020 Inventory Turnover Days (Cell F8)

Excel Keystrokes	Description
type "="	Enters into "formula" mode
type "average("	Creates the "Average" formula
select cell F7	2020 Inventories
type ", "	Separates the two values we want to average
select cell E7	2019 Inventories
type ")"	Completes the "Average" formula
type "/"	Divides
toggle over to the income statement and select cell F15	2020 COGS
type "*360"	Multiplies by 360
type "Enter"	End
Formula Result	=AVERAGE(F7, E7)/'Income Statement'!F15*360

This should give us 34.2 days.

TABLE 5.1 Amazon Historical Operating Working Capital Inventories

Operating Working Capital Schedule (OWC) (in US$ millions except per share amounts)

On December 31	Actuals				Estimates			
	2018A	2019A	2020A	2021E	2022E	2023E	2024E	2025E
Current Assets								
Inventories		20,497.0	23,795.0					
Inventory turnover days								
Accounts receivable, net and other								
Days receivable								
Total Current Assets								
Current Liabilities								
Accounts payable								
Days payable								
Accrued expenses and other								
Days payable								
Unearned revenue								
Unearned revenue days								
Total Current Liabilities								
Total Operating Working Capital								
Change in total operating working capital								
Match? (Y/N)								

Note: Do not copy this formula beyond 2020, as we will be providing our own assumption drivers for projections in 2021 This formula is solely for the purposes of calculating historical metrics.

Accounts Receivable, Net and Other

The same process can continue for the remaining operating working capital line items. We need to take care in understanding which income statement line item the operating working capital item is referring to. In some cases, this is obvious. For example, accounts receivable is almost always related to revenue and inventory is related to COGS.

So we can link in "Accounts Receivable" from row 11 on the balance sheet. In operating working capital cell E9, we can type "=," toggle over to the balance sheet, select cell D11, and hit "Enter." We can copy this one cell to the right for 2020. We can now calculate the receivable days:

2020 Accounts Receivable Days =

$$\frac{\text{Average (2020 Accounts Receivables, 2019 Accounts Receivables)}}{\text{2020 Total Net Sales}} \times 360$$

So, in operating working capital cell F10, we can follow these steps:

2020 Days Receivable (Cell F10)

Excel Keystrokes	Description
type "="	Enters into "formula" mode
type "average("	Creates the "Average" formula
select cell F9	2020 Accounts Receivable
type ", "	Separates the two values we want to average.
select cell E9	2019 Accounts Receivable
type ")"	Completes the "Average" formula
type "/"	Divides
toggle over to the income statement and select cell F11	2020 Total net sales
type "*360"	Multiplies by 360
type "Enter"	End
Formula Result	=AVERAGE(F9, E9)/'Income Statement'!F11*360

This should give us 21.1 days. We can now total the two "Current asset" line items into row 11, taking care not to include the "days" metric into the total. Cell E11 should read "=E7+E9."

We can copy cell E11 to the right to get what we have in Table 5.2.

Accounts Payable

We can now repeat this procedure for the current liability line items, "Accounts payable, " "Accrued expenses and other," and "Unearned revenue." We first link in "Accounts payable" from row 20 on the balance sheet. In operating working capital cell E13 we can type "=," toggle over to the balance sheet, select cell D20, and hit "Enter." We can copy this one cell to the right for 2020. Accounts payable is most commonly related to COGS, but it's worth a bit of research to be sure. Unfortunately, our research has not revealed any new information, so we will stay with the default assumption. We can calculate the historical days by this formula:

$$2020 \text{ Days Payable} =$$
$$\frac{\text{Average (2020 Accounts Payable, 2019 Accounts Payable)}}{2020 \text{ COGS}} \times 360$$

2020 Days Payable (Cell F14)

Excel Keystrokes	Description
type "="	Enters into "formula" mode
type "average("	Creates the "Average" formula
select cell F13	2020 Accounts Payable
type ", "	Separates the two values we want to average
select cell E13	2019 Accounts Payable
type ")"	Completes the "Average" formula
type "/"	Divides
toggle over to the income statement and select cell F15	2020 COGS
type "*360"	Multiplies by 360
type "Enter"	End
Formula Result	=AVERAGE(F13, E13)/'Income Statement'!F15*360

This gives us 92.4, and we can move on to accrued expenses.

TABLE 5.2 Amazon Historical Operating Working Capital Assets

Operating Working Capital Schedule (OWC) (in US$ millions except per share amounts)

On December 31	Actuals			Estimates				
	2018A	2019A	2020A	2021E	2022E	2023E	2024E	2025E
Current Assets								
Inventories		20,497.0	23,795.0					
Inventory turnover days			34.2					
Accounts receivable, net and other		20,816.0	24,542.0					
Days receivable			21.1					
Total Current Assets		41,313.0	48,337.0					
Current Liabilities								
Accounts payable								
Days payable								
Accrued expenses and other								
Days payable								
Unearned revenue								
Unearned revenue days								
Total Current Liabilities								
Total Operating Working Capital								
Change in total operating working capital								
Match? (Y/N)								

Accrued Expenses and Other

We first link in "Accrued expenses and other" from row 21 on the balance sheet. In working capital cell E15 we can type "=," toggle over to the balance sheet, select cell D21, and hit "Enter." We can copy this one cell to the right for 2020. Accrued expenses are commonly related to an operating expense, but we do not know exactly what operating expense this can relate to. Further research uncovers the following note from page 50 of the 2020 10-K:

> Included in "Accrued expenses and other" on our consolidated balance sheets are liabilities primarily related to leases and asset retirement obligations, payroll and related expenses, tax-related liabilities, unredeemed gift cards, customer liabilities, current debt, acquired digital media content, and other operating expenses.

This is a composite of several operating expense line items, so in this case, because there is not just one specific operating expense line item we can relate to, we will use the "Total Operating Expenses" from line 30 of the income statement.

We can calculate the historical days by this formula:

2020 Days Payable =

$$\frac{\text{Average (2020 Accrued Expenses, 2019 Accrued Expenses)}}{\text{2020 Total Operating Expenses}} \times 360$$

2020 Days Payable (Cell F16)

Excel Keystrokes	Description
type "="	Enters into "formula" mode
type "average("	Creates the "Average" formula
select cell F15	2020 Accrued Expenses
type ","	Separates the two values we want to average
select cell E15	2019 Accrued Expenses
type ")"	Completes the "Average" formula
type "/"	Divides
toggle over to the income statement and select cell F30	2020 Total Operating Expenses
type "*360"	Multiplies by 360
type "Enter"	End
Formula Result	=AVERAGE(F15, E15)/'Income Statement'!F30*360

This gives us 131.8 days.

Unearned Revenue

We are now left with "Unearned revenue," which we link in from row 23 in the balance sheet. In working capital cell E17 we can type "=," toggle over to the balance sheet, select cell D23, and hit "Enter." We can copy this one cell to the right for 2020. Unearned revenue is related to the net revenue or sales. So we can calculate the historical days by this formula:

2020 Unearned Revenue Days =

$$\frac{\text{Average (2020 Unearned Revenue, 2019 Unearned Revenue)}}{\text{2020 Total Net Sales}} \times 360$$

2020 Unearned Revenue Days (Cell F18)

Excel Keystrokes	Description
type "="	Enters into "formula" mode
type "average("	Creates the "Average" formula
select cell F17	2020 Unearned Revenue
type ", "	Separates the two values we want to average
select cell E17	2019 Unearned Revenue
type ")"	Completes the "Average" formula
type "/"	Divides
toggle over to the income statement and select cell F11	2020 Total Net Sales
type "*360"	Multiplies by 360
type "Enter"	End
Formula Result	=AVERAGE(F17, E17)/'Income Statement'!F11*360

This gives us 8.3 days. We can now total the three "Current liability" line items into row 19, taking care not to include the "days" metric into the total. Cell E19 should read "=E13+E15+E17."

The line directly underneath "Total Current Liabilities" ("Total Operating Working Capital") is calculated by subtracting the total current liabilities from total current assets. So, in cell E20 we can type "= E11-E19." We can copy both cell E19 and E20 to the right to get what we have in Table 5.3.

We can now start projecting the operating working capital schedule.

TABLE 5.3 Amazon Historical Operating Working Capital

Operating Working Capital Schedule (OWC) (in US$ millions except per share amounts)

| | | Actuals | | | | | Estimates | | |
On December 31	2018A	2019A	2020A	2021E	2022E	2023E	2024E	2025E
Current Assets								
Inventories		20,497.0	23,795.0					
Inventory turnover days			*34.2*					
Accounts receivable, net and other		20,816.0	24,542.0					
Days receivable			*21.1*					
Total Current Assets		41,313.0	48,337.0					
Current Liabilities								
Accounts payable		47,183.0	72,539.0					
Days payable			*92.4*					
Accrued expenses and other		32,439.0	44,138.0					
Days payable			*131.8*					
Unearned revenue		8,190.0	9,708.0					
Unearned revenue days			*8.3*					
Total Current Liabilities		87,812.0	126,385.0					
Total Operating Working Capital		(46,499.0)	(78,048.0)					
Change in total operating working capital								
Match? (Y/N)								

PROJECTING OPERATING WORKING CAPITAL

In order to project operating working capital, we will use the 2020 days calculated for each line item as an indicator of next year's operating working capital performance. It is also recommended to pull in 2018 and prior years' working capital numbers from previous Amazon reports for more color on historical days; we will stick to just the 2020 days for purposes of this analysis.

Receivables

I'd like to jump over inventory for a second and look at Receivables first because it's easier to conceptualize when beginning projections. The receivable days in 2020 were 21.1. Remember that 30 days is a typical range for receivables, so we are within line. Let's use this assumption going forward, so we can link cell G10 from F10 by having G10 "=F10." We can copy this to the right. In order to use the projected days to drive estimated accounts receivable, we need to reverse-engineer the standard receivable days formula used earlier:

2020 Accounts Receivable Days =

$$\frac{\text{Average (2020 Accounts Receivables, 2019 Accounts Receivables)}}{\text{2020 Total Net Sales}} \times 360$$

For 2021 the formula would read:

2021 Accounts Receivable Days =

$$\frac{\text{Average (2021 Accounts Receivables, 2020 Accounts Receivables)}}{\text{2021 Total Net Sales}} \times 360$$

Now we have receivable days (our projected assumption), and we want to solve for 2021 receivables. So we can divide both sides of the equation by 360, giving us:

$$\frac{\text{2021 Accounts Receivable Days}}{360} = \frac{\text{Average (2021 Accounts Receivables, 2020 Accounts Receivables)}}{\text{2021 Total Net Sales}}$$

We can multiply both sides of the equation by 2021 Total Net Sales, giving us:

$$\frac{2021 \text{ Accounts Receivable Days}}{360} \times 2021 \text{ Total Net Sales} =$$
$$\text{Average (2021 Accounts Receivables, 2020 Accounts Receivables)}$$

So, in order to get 2021 Receivables, the formula is:

$$\frac{2021 \text{ Accounts Receivable Days}}{360} \times 2021 \text{ Total Net Sales}$$

Note that we could have taken the formula a step further and readjusted for the "Average (2021 Receivables, 2020 Receivables)" component. However, for standard projections, the days we choose as our driver should technically be a representation of average and standard indicators. So adjusting for the average can be considered overengineering the analysis. However, there are some advanced analyses (e.g., backing into management's projections), where using the following formula is the only way to back into the exact metrics. So, for reference, we have done the analysis here.

First we convert the "average" formula into mathematical operations:

$$\frac{2021 \text{ Accounts Receivable Days}}{360} \times 2021 \text{ Total Net Sales} =$$
$$\frac{2021 \text{ Accounts Receivables} + 2020 \text{ Accounts Receivables}}{2}$$

We can multiply both sides of the equation by 2 to get:

$$\left\{ (2021 \text{ Accounts Receivable Days}) / 360 \times 2021 \text{ Total Net Sales} \right\} \times 2$$
$$= (2021 \text{ Accounts Receivables} + 2020 \text{ Accounts Receivables})$$

And we can subtract the 2020 Receivables from both sides of the equation:

$$2021 \text{ Accounts Receivables} = \left\{ \frac{2021 \text{ Accounts Receivable Days}}{360} \right.$$
$$\left. \times 2021 \text{ Total Net Sales} \right\} \times 2 - 2020 \text{ Accounts Receivables}$$

We will stick with the "2021 Receivable Days / 360 × 2021 Total Net Sales" formula to calculate the 2021 projections. Remember in the original basic formula (Receivables / Revenue × 360), the "Receivables / Revenue" part of the formula gives us a percentage. This percentage answers, "What percent of revenue booked is left outstanding?" Remember the first example in this chapter, where we had $25,000 of receivables after booking $100,000 in revenue, representing 25% of our revenue still outstanding. We then multiplied the percentage by 360 to convert into an estimated number of days outstanding. So in the example, 360 times 25% is 90 days. Now, in the reverse-engineered formula (2021 Receivable Days / 360 × 2021 Total Net Sales), the "2021 Receivable Days / 360" part of the formula backs into that percentage outstanding, or 90/360, giving us 25%. We simply multiply that percentage by the projected revenue to get future estimated receivables.

2021 Receivables (Cell G9)

Excel Keystrokes	Description
type "="	Begins the formula
select cell G10	2021 Days Receivable
type "/360"	Divides by 360
type "*"	Multiplies
toggle over to the income statement and select cell G11	2021 Total Net Sales
hit "Enter"	End
Formula Result	=G10/360*'Income Statement'!G11

This should give us $28,802.3. We can copy this formula to the right through 2025 to complete our receivables projections. (See Table 5.4.)

Inventories

We can repeat this process for each working capital line item. But remember, each item is related to different income statement line items, so let's go back to inventories:

$$2021 \text{ Inventories} = \frac{2021 \text{ Inventory Turnover Days}}{360} \times 2021 \text{ COGS}$$

In cell G8, we can use the 34.2 days, pulling in from F8 as our future assumption, to project the inventories. So cell G8 will read "=F8."

TABLE 5.4   Amazon Projected Operating Working Capital Receivables

Operating Working Capital Schedule (OWC) (in US$ millions except per share amounts)

On December 31	Actuals			Estimates				
	2018A	2019A	2020A	2021E	2022E	2023E	2024E	2025E
Current Assets								
Inventories		20,497.0	23,795.0					
Inventory turnover days			34.2					
Accounts receivable, net and other		20,816.0	24,542.0	28,802.3	34,159.6	38,536.5	41,938.1	44,488.3
Days receivable			21.1	21.1	21.1	21.1	21.1	21.1
Total Current Assets		41,313.0	48,337.0					
Current Liabilities								
Accounts payable		47,183.0	72,539.0					
Days payable			92.4					
Accrued expenses and other		32,439.0	44,138.0					
Days payable			131.8					
Unearned revenue		8,190.0	9,708.0					
Unearned revenue days			8.3					
Total Current Liabilities		87,812.0	1,26,385.0					
Total Operating Working Capital		(46,499.0)	(78,048.0)					
Change in total operating working capital								
Match? (Y/N)								

2021 Inventories (Cell G7)

Excel Keystrokes	Description
type "="	Begins the formula
select cell G8	2021 Inventory Turnover Days
type "/360"	Divides by 360
type "*"	Multiplies
toggle over to the income statement and select cell G15	2021 COGS
hit "Enter"	End
Formula Result	=G8/360*'Income Statement'!G15

This gives us $28,125.4. We can copy cells G7 and G8 to the right. We can also copy the total current assets cell F11, calculated earlier, over to the right to have our complete current asset projections. (See Table 5.5.)

Accounts Payable

We can now continue the process with the current liabilities, beginning with the accounts payable.

$$2021 \text{ Accounts Payable} = \frac{2021 \text{ Days Payable}}{360} \times 2021 \text{ COGS}$$

So, in cell G14, we can use the 92.4 days, pulling in from F14 as our future assumption. Note that 92.4 is high, but still close to the 30–90 day range. So cell G14 will read "=F14."

2021 Accounts Payable (Cell G13)

Excel Keystrokes	Description
type "="	Begins the formula
select cell G14	2021 Days Payable
type "/360"	Divides by 360
type "*"	Multiplies
toggle over to the income statement and select cell G15	2021 COGS
hit "Enter"	End
Formula Result	= G14/360*'Income Statement'!G15

This gives us $76,023.5. We can copy cells G13 and G14 to the right.

TABLE 5.5 Amazon Projected Operating Working Capital Current Assets

Operating Working Capital Schedule (OWC) (in US$ millions except per share amounts)

On December 31	Actuals			Estimates				
	2018A	2019A	2020A	2021E	2022E	2023E	2024E	2025E
Current Assets								
Inventories		20,497.0	23,795.0	28,125.4	33,356.7	37,630.9	40,952.5	43,442.8
Inventory turnover days			*34.2*	*34.2*	*34.2*	*34.2*	*34.2*	*34.2*
Accounts receivable, net and other		20,816.0	24,542.0	28,802.3	34,159.6	38,536.5	41,938.1	44,488.3
Days receivable			*21.1*	*21.1*	*21.1*	*21.1*	*21.1*	*21.1*
Total Current Assets		41,313.0	48,337.0	56,927.8	67,516.3	76,167.4	82,890.7	87,931.1
Current Liabilities								
Accounts payable		47,183.0	72,539.0					
Days payable			*92.4*					
Accrued expenses and other		32,439.0	44,138.0					
Days payable			*131.8*					
Unearned revenue		8,190.0	9,708.0					
Unearned revenue days			*8.3*					
Total Current Liabilities		87,812.0	1,26,385.0					
Total Operating Working Capital		(46,499.0)	(78,048.0)					
Change in total operating working capital								
Match? (Y/N)								

Accrued Expenses

Remember that we based Accrued Expenses off of Total Operating Expenses, so we use the following formula:

$$2021 \text{ Accrued Expenses} = \frac{2021 \text{ Days Payable}}{360} \times 2021 \text{ Total Operating Expenses}$$

So, we can pull F16 into G16 as our future assumption. Note 131.8 days is pretty high, well outside of the 30–90 day range. It is possible that some current liability line items have higher days – whether Amazon is holding longer bills to be paid, or they have a few line items that aren't getting paid that is pushing the entire days number up. Either way, let's stick with this assumption now for consistency. If we drop the number down to 90, for example, without strong reason, the balance will drop and we will later see it will cause a large cash inflow that may not be accurate. So cell G16 will read "=F16."

2021 Accrued Expenses (Cell G15)

Excel Keystrokes	Description
type "="	Begins the formula
select cell G16	2021 Days Payable
type "/360"	Divides by 360
type "*"	Multiplies
toggle over to the income statement and select cell G30	2021 Total Operating Expenses
hit "Enter"	End
Formula Result	= G16/360*'Income Statement'!G30

Here we get $48,626.4. We can copy cells G15 and G16 to the right. (See Table 5.6.)

Unearned Revenue

Unearned revenue is money received for a sale that had not yet been made. So by definition, we had based this item off of Revenue, and we notice it's a very low 8.3 days. This can make sense, as it is likely the case that only a very small amount of sales fall into this category. So we can stick with this assumption, having cell G18 equal to F18, and the formula will read:

2021 Unearned Revenue =

(2021 Unearned Revenue Days) / 360 × 2021 Total Net Sales

TABLE 5.6 Amazon Projected Operating Working Capital Schedule

Operating Working Capital Schedule (OWC) (in US$ millions except per share amounts)

On December 31	Actuals			Estimates				
	2018A	2019A	2020A	2021E	2022E	2023E	2024E	2025E
Current Assets								
Inventories		20,497.0	23,795.0	28,125.4	33,356.7	37,630.9	40,952.5	43,442.8
Inventory turnover days			34.2	34.2	34.2	34.2	34.2	34.2
Accounts receivable, net and other		20,816.0	24,542.0	28,802.3	34,159.6	38,536.5	41,938.1	44,488.3
Days receivable			21.1	21.1	21.1	21.1	21.1	21.1
Total Current Assets		41,313.0	48,337.0	56,927.8	67,516.3	76,167.4	82,890.7	87,931.1
Current Liabilities								
Accounts payable		47,183.0	72,539.0	76,023.5	90,163.8	1,01,716.8	1,10,695.3	1,17,426.5
Days payable			92.4	92.4	92.4	92.4	92.4	92.4
Accrued expenses and other		32,439.0	44,138.0	48,626.4	57,670.9	65,060.5	70,803.3	75,108.7
Days payable			131.8	131.8	131.8	131.8	131.8	131.8
Unearned revenue		8,190.0	9,708.0	11,365.2	13,479.2	15,206.3	16,548.5	17,554.8
Unearned revenue days			8.3	8.3	8.3	8.3	8.3	8.3
Total Current Liabilities		87,812.0	126,385.0	136,015.1	161,313.9	181,983.6	198,047.2	210,090.1
Total Operating Working Capital		(46,499.0)	(78,048.0)	(79,087.3)	(93,797.6)	(105,816.2)	(115,156.5)	(122,159.0)
Change in total operating working capital								
Match? (Y/N)								

2021 Unearned Revenue (Cell G17)

Excel Keystrokes	Description
type "="	Begins the formula
select cell G18	2021 Unearned Revenue Days
type "/360"	Divides by 360
type "*"	Multiplies
toggle over to the income statement and select cell G11	2021 Total Net Sales
hit "Enter"	End
Formula Result	=G18/360*'Income Statement'!G11

This gives us $11,365.2. We can copy cells G17 and G18 to the right. We can also copy the total current liabilities (cell F19) and total operating working capital (cell F20), calculated earlier, to the right through 2025 to get the operating working capital schedule. (See Table 5.6.)

OPERATING WORKING CAPITAL AND THE CASH FLOW STATEMENT

It is important to explain the relationship between operating working capital line items and cash flow line items. Remember: One of the reasons for creating an operating working capital schedule is to serve as a bridge between balance sheet items and cash flow items. Now that we have our operating working capital projections, we can link each of these line items into the operating working capital section of the cash flow statement (Cash Flow Statement rows 16–20).

Let's first discuss this relationship between operating working capital and cash flow. If inventory increases from one year to the next, this results in a cash outflow. For example, if we had $0 in inventory in 2019, and in 2020 our inventory balance increases to $1,000, we may have purchased inventory. If inventory is purchased, money is spent, so the cash flow relating to the inventory change is –$1,000. The same rules apply to all current assets within operating working capital. (Remember that cash is not included in operating working capital.) If accounts receivable increases from year to year, this results in a cash outflow.

But, what happens if a current asset account would decrease from year to year? If we have $1,500 in accounts receivable in 2019, for example, and that balance has reduced to $0 by 2020, we must have collected on our accounts receivable. In other words, if a customer who owed us money for a sale he or she made on credit pays us back, we have collected on those receivables. So, the receivables go down, and cash comes in. In this example, we have received cash of $1,500 from the reduction in accounts receivable. Similarly, if our inventory has reduced from, say, $2,000 in 2019 to $1,500 in 2020, we can assume we have sold that inventory and cash is received.

Current assets increase[1] (+) Cash flow decreases (–)

Current assets decrease[1] (–) Cash flow increases (+)

[1] *Note:* When referring to operating working capital current assets excludes cash. If cash as an asset would increase, then cash on the cash flow statement would certainly increase accordingly.

Current liabilities have the opposite effect on cash. Let's look at accrued liabilities, for example. If an accrued liability has increased from $1,000 in 2019 to $2,000 in 2020, this results in a positive cash flow. It's sort of hard to think through how an increase in a payable (an expense you have not yet paid) results in a positive cash flow line item, but remember that the cash flow from operations represents non-cash adjustments to the net income. So payables increasing from $1,000 to $2,000 mean we have more non-cash expenses that we should be adding back to net income. This "add back" is represented by a cash inflow. So an accounts payable account increasing from one year to the next results in a cash increase, or really cash being "added back" to the net income. Conversely, if the accrued liability account decreases, we have paid down that liability; cash decreases. If, for example, the accounts payable account was $7,500 in 2019 and is reduced to $0 in 2020, we have effectively paid off those expenses, resulting in a cash out-flow of –$7,500. An increase in current liabilities reflects an increase in cash and a decrease in current liabilities reflects a decrease in cash.

Current liabilities increase (+) Cash flow increases (+)

Current liabilities decrease (–) Cash flow decreases (–)

The cash flow statement operating working capital section refers to the cash flow impact based on the increase or decrease in each current asset and current liability from year to year. So we want to link the year-to-year changes of each working capital line item to the cash flow statement, taking care to properly adjust for the directional cash flows. Before we begin let's look at the total working capital. Row 21 of the operating working capital schedule ("Change in total operating working capital") represents the total change in operating working capital for each projected year. So in cell G21, we can subtract the 2020 total operating working capital from the 2021 total operating working capital, or type "=," select cell G20, type "–," and select cell F20. We can copy this formula to the right. This is showing that the operating working capital is decreasing from year to year.

Since operating working capital is defined as current assets (not including cash) less current liabilities (not including debts), it can be thought of as a net asset. So, total operating working capital acts like an asset in that if it is increasing from year to year, it represents a cash outflow, and if it is decreasing, it represents a positive cash flow. If Amazon's projected operating working capital is decreasing from year to year, we should see total changes in cash from working capital on the cash flow statement as positive.

The match formula in row 22 is another one of the several checks we have throughout the model. It may read "N" right now, as we have not yet properly linked the operating working capital line items to the cash flow statement. Once done properly, the match should read "Y." The match checks to make sure the total operating working capital changes (row 21) matches the operating working capital changes in the cash flow statement (cash flow statement row 21). In the cash flow statement, we will subtract each individual line item making up working capital and then total the changes. So, we are effectively calculating the same working capital in two different ways. This helps ensure we have our flows moving in the right direction. See the following graphic.

Operating Working Capital	2020	2021
Accounts Receivable	20,000.0	25,000.0
Inventory	5,000.0	7,500.0
Prepaid Expenses	1,250.0	1,000.0
Accounts Payable	10,000.0	12,500.0
Accrued Expenses	12,500.0	15,000.0
Net Working Capital	**3,750.0**	**6,000.0**
Changes in Net Working Capital		**2,250.0**

Cash Flow	2021
Accounts Receivable	(5,000.0)
Inventory	(2,500.0)
Prepaid Expenses	250.0
Accounts Payable	2,500.0
Accrued Expenses	2,500.0
Total Working Capital	**(2,250.0)**

Changes in Inventory

Let's link each operating working capital line item to the cash flow statement beginning with the inventories. On the cash flow statement, row 16 ("Changes in inventory") represents "Inventory," so we clearly want to link this in from the "Inventory" row in the operating working capital schedule. However, on the cash flow statement we want to show the year-to-year change, representing a proper inflow or outflow, depending on whether the item is an asset or a liability. We see that inventories in the operating working capital schedule have increased from 2020 to 2021. This should be represented as a cash outflow on the cash flow statement. So when we link the inventories from the operating working capital to the cash flow statement, we should link the "negative" changes from 2020 to 2021, or Cash Flow Changes in Inventory = – (2021 Inventories – 2020 Inventories).

2021 Changes in Inventory (Cash Flow Cell G16)

Excel Keystrokes	Description
type "="	Begins the formula
type "–("	Prepares to calculate the "Negative" change
select Operating Working Capital cell G7	2021 Inventories
type "–"	Subtracts
select Operating Working Capital cell F7	2020 Inventories
type ")"	Closes the parentheses
hit "Enter"	End
Formula Result	=-('Operating Working Capital'!G7- 'Operating Working Capital'!F7)

We can copy this formula to the right through 2025. (See Table 5.7.)

Accounts Receivable

Every current asset within the operating working capital works the same way, that is, we want to pull the "negative" change into the cash flow statement because of the relationship between current assets in the operating working capital and their effect on cash. Because accounts receivable is also increasing year over year, we should expect to see a cash outflow in the "Accounts Receivables" line item in the cash flow statement.

2021 Changes in Accounts Receivable (Cash Flow Cell G17)

Excel Keystrokes	Description
type "="	Begins the formula
type "–("	Prepares to calculate the "Negative" change
select Operating Working Capital cell G9	2021 Accounts Receivable
type "–"	Subtracts
select Operating Working Capital cell F9	2020 Accounts Receivable
type ")"	Closes the parentheses
hit "Enter"	End
Formula Result	=-('Operating Working Capital'!G9- 'Operating Working Capital'!F9)

We can copy this formula to the right through 2025. (See Table 5.7.)

TABLE 5.7 Amazon Projected Operating Working Capital Schedule

Operating Working Capital Schedule (OWC) (in US$ millions except per share amounts)

On December 31	Actuals			Estimates				
	2018A	2019A	2020A	2021E	2022E	2023E	2024E	2025E
Cash Flows from Operating Activities								
Net income	10,073.0	11,588.0	21,331.0	25,524.1	29,125.8	29,800.5	28,847.9	25,418.4
Depreciation and amortization	15,341.0	21,789.0	25,251.0	28,669.8	35,841.6	43,932.4	52,737.3	62,077.6
Stock-based compensation	5,418.0	6,864.0	9,208.0	11,694.2	13,869.3	15,646.4	17,027.5	18,062.9
% of total operating expenses	*8.2%*	*8.7%*	*8.8%*	*8.8%*	*8.8%*	*8.8%*	*8.8%*	*8.8%*
Other operating expense (income), net	274.0	164.0	(71.0)	(90.2)	(106.9)	(120.6)	(131.3)	(139.3)
% of total net sales	*0.1%*	*0.1%*	*0.0%*	*0.0%*	*0.0%*	*0.0%*	*0.0%*	*0.0%*
Other expense (income), net	219.0	(249.0)	(2,582.0)	219.0	(249.0)	219.0	(249.0)	219.0
Deferred income taxes	441.0	796.0	(554.0)	(554.0)	(554.0)	(554.0)	(554.0)	(554.0)
Changes in Operating Working Capital								
Changes in inventory	(1,314.0)	(3,278.0)	(2,849.0)	(4,330.4)	(5,231.3)	(4,274.1)	(3,321.7)	(2,490.2)
Changes in accounts receivable	(4,615.0)	(7,681.0)	(8,169.0)	(4,260.3)	(5,357.2)	(4,377.0)	(3,401.6)	(2,550.2)
Changes in accounts payable	3,263.0	8,193.0	17,480.0	3,484.5	14,140.4	11,553.0	8,978.5	6,731.2
Changes in accrued expenses	472.0	(1,383.0)	5,754.0	4,488.4	9,044.5	7,389.6	5,742.9	4,305.4
Changes in unearned revenue	1,151.0	1,711.0	1,265.0	1,657.2	2,113.9	1,727.1	1,342.3	1,006.3
Net Changes in Working Capital	(1,043.0)	(2,438.0)	13,481.0	1,039.3	14,710.2	12,018.6	9,340.4	7,002.4
Total Cash from Operating Activities	30,723.0	38,514.0	66,064.0	66,502.3	92,637.0	100,942.2	107,018.8	112,087.1

IDENTIFYING PROPER WORKING CAPITAL LINE ITEMS BETWEEN THE CASH FLOW AND BALANCE SHEET

It happens quite often that the line items we have identified as operating working capital as per the balance sheet do not exactly match the line items within the operating cash flow section in the cash flow statement. Our suggestion is to add rows as appropriate to properly include all working capital items in the cash flow statement for valuation purposes. Another approach is to consolidate like balance sheet items that may both be reflected in one cash flow working capital line item. Luckily the line items in Amazon's reports line up so no adjustments need to be made. See my book on Walmart for an example of how to make such adjustments when the line items do not match up.

Changes in Accounts Payable

For current liabilities, remember that an increase from year to year represents a cash inflow. So:

2021 Changes in Accounts Payable = 2021 Accounts Payable
– 2020 Accounts Payable

In other words this is a direct subtraction, not "-" as we had done with the current assets.

2021 Changes in Accounts Payable (Cash Flow Cell G18)

Excel Keystrokes	Description
type "="	Begins the formula
select Operating Working Capital cell G13	2021 Accounts Payable
type "–"	Subtracts
select Operating Working Capital cell F13	2020 Accounts Payable
hit "Enter"	End
Formula Result	='Operating Working Capital'!G13–'Operating Working Capital'!F13

This formula can be copied to the right through 2025. (See Table 5.7.)

Changes in Accrued Expenses

We can repeat the process for accrued expenses.

2021 Changes in Accrued Expenses (Cash Flow Cell G19)

Excel Keystrokes	Description
type "="	Begins the formula
select Operating Working Capital cell G15	2021 Accrued Expenses
type "–"	Subtracts
select Operating Working Capital cell F15	2020 Accrued Expenses
hit "Enter"	End
Formula Result	='Operating Working Capital'!G15- 'Operating Working Capital'!F15

This formula can be copied to the right through 2025. (See Table 5.7.)

Changes in Unearned Revenue

We can now link the unearned revenue.

2021 Changes in Unearned Revenue (Cash Flow Cell G20)

Excel Keystrokes	Description
type "="	Begins the formula
select Operating Working Capital cell G17	2021 Unearned Revenue
type "-"	Subtracts
select Operating Working Capital cell F17	2020 Unearned Revenue
hit "Enter"	End
Formula Result	='Operating Working Capital'!G17- 'Operating Working Capital'!F17

We can copy this formula to the right. (See Table 5.7.)

We notice that the "match" row 22 in the operating working capital schedule should now read "Y." Again, this is a check to ensure we are properly linking each year-to-year operating working capital line item change in the cash flow statement. It is easy to confuse the direction of flows when linking from the operating working capital into the cash flow statement. Having this check can help avoid that potential issue. We are now done with the working capital schedule and can continue to project the balance sheet.

CHAPTER 6

Balance Sheet Projections

Now that we have every line item listed on the balance sheet, and have completed both the depreciation and working capital schedule, we are ready to make our projections.

Cash Flow Statement Drives Balance Sheet vs. Balance Sheet Drives Cash Flow Statement

There are two common methods used when modeling financial projections:

1. *Balance sheet drives the cash flow statement.* The cash flow statement is derived from subtracting year-over-year balance sheet changes.
2. *Cash flow statement drives the balance sheet.* The balance sheet is projected based on how cash is being sourced or spent.

Although both methods are utilized often, we strongly recommend the second method, using the cash flow to drive the balance sheet. It is a more logical approach and has been proven to be less prone to errors. Further, the first method of back-solving into a cash flow statement can lead to an incomplete picture of each individual cash flow. Let's take PP&E, for example. The net PP&E value increases by capital expenditures (CAPEX) spend and decreases by depreciation. So if PP&E on the balance sheet is increasing by $1,000, how do we know how much of that change is attributable to depreciation versus CAPEX?

Cash Flow		Balance Sheet	2019	2020
Depreciation	?	Property, Plant, & Equipment	0.0	1,000.0
CAPEX	?			

One can possibly attribute that to CAPEX of $1,000.

Cash Flow	
Depreciation	0.0
CAPEX	(1,000.0)

Balance Sheet	2019	2020
Property, Plant, & Equipment	0.0	1,000.0

Or, CAPEX could be $1,500 and depreciation is $500, also resulting in the net $1,000 PP&E change.

Cash Flow	
Depreciation	500.0
CAPEX	(1,500.0)

Balance Sheet	2019	2020
Property, Plant, & Equipment	0.0	1,000.0

Further, we could have purchased $2,000 in assets and written down $500 in assets. Several possibilities could account for this change in PP&E. But the cash flow statement clearly shows depreciation and CAPEX, so we can look to the cash flow statement. For this reason, if we use the cash flow statement to create the projected balance sheet, we may have a more complete picture of the business.

Note: We understand in this example that additional research on CAPEX and depreciation can reveal how the PP&E is changing from year to year. However, this illustrates the possibility of other complex situations where important cash flows can be missed by back-calculating into the cash flow statement from the balance sheet.

We highly recommend following and adhering to the method we will discuss next. One of the major plights of a junior Wall Street analyst is keeping a balance sheet in balance. Remember: The formula Assets − Liabilities = Shareholders' Equity must always hold for a balance sheet to be in balance. The difficulty in balancing a balance sheet is the ability to individually make projections to each line item within the assets, liabilities, and shareholders' equity section, and to ensure the formula still holds.

When a balance sheet doesn't balance, error checking to find out what might be off can be a daunting task. This has been known to keep analysts up all night. However, with a clear and methodical approach to projecting a balance sheet, this task should no longer be so strenuous. Such all-nighters would be eliminated if one had a better conceptual understanding of the flows behind a balance sheet. With our methods, the maximum time it should take to error check an unbalanced balance sheet should be one hour, so we encourage you to read on.

The key to thinking about balance sheet projections is the cash flow statement. Cash flows affect assets, liabilities, and shareholders' equity items. If a company spends cash, it could have purchased an asset, or maybe it paid back a loan. Conversely, if a company receives cash, maybe it has sold an asset or has raised funds. We look to the cash flow statement to help determine how our assets, liabilities, and shareholders' equity are being affected. If cash is spent, that must mean an asset is increasing (except cash), or a liability or shareholders' equity is decreasing; if cash is received, that must mean an asset is decreasing (except cash), or a liability or shareholders' equity is increasing. So, to project balance sheet line items, we look to each balance sheet line item and ask ourselves two questions:

1. Which cash flow statement item or items are affecting this balance sheet item?
2. In what direction should this cash flow statement item be driving the balance sheet item? Should it be increasing or decreasing?

Assets

Let's take the "cash" line item on the balance sheet as an example. If 2020 cash was $1,000 and we want to project 2021 cash, we look to the two questions.

Cash Flow	2021
?	?

Balance Sheet	2020	2021
Cash	1,000.0	?

The cash flow item "Total change in cash and cash equivalents" affects the balance sheet cash. Also, a positive value of cash should naturally increase the total balance of cash on the balance sheet. So if the total change in cash and cash equivalents was $500, then the 2021 cash in the balance should be $1,500.

Cash Flow	2021
Total Change in Cash	500.0

Balance Sheet	2020	2021
Cash	1,000.0	1,500.0

So for 2021 cash on the balance sheet we would take the 2020 cash from the balance sheet and add the 2021 change in cash and cash equivalents from the cash flow statement, or:

2021 Balance Sheet Cash = 2020 Balance Sheet Cash + 2021 Total Change in Cash and Cash Equivalents

In the same way, we can project the 2021 cash for Amazon.

2021 Cash (Balance Sheet Cell F8)

Excel Keystrokes	Description
type "="	Begins the formula
select E8	2020 Cash
type "+"	Adds
select Cash Flow cell G38	2021 Total Change in Cash and Cash Equivalents
hit "Enter"	End
Formula Result	=E8+ 'Cash Flow Statement'!G38

This should give us $54,989.9. We can copy this formula to the right through 2025. (See Table 6.1.)

Inventories Let's skip over marketable securities and first look at inventories and accounts receivable only because we have already discussed these two line items in relation to the balance sheet when constructing the working capital schedule and it is important to finalize the complete relationship of these line items on all schedules.

Let's look at an inventories example and assume 2020 inventory is $1,500.

Cash Flow	2021		Balance Sheet	2020	2021
?	?	→	Inventories	1,500.0	?

To answer the first of the two questions, the cash flow item relating to inventories is Changes in Inventory in the working capital section of the cash flow statement. Let's say changes in inventory in 2021 is –$250. A negative change in working capital would imply that we had purchased some more inventory, so the inventories balance should increase from $1,500 to $1,750.

Cash Flow	2021		Balance Sheet	2020	2021
Changes in Inventory	(250.0)	→	Inventories	1,500.0	1,750.0

2021 Balance Sheet Inventories = 2020 Balance Sheet Inventories –
2021 Cash Flow Changes in Inventory

Notice here the formula structure is similar to the formula for cash, but we are using a "–" instead of a "+."

TABLE 6.1 Amazon Projected Balance Sheet Cash

Consolidated Balance Sheets (in US$ millions except per share amounts)

On December 31	2019A	2020A	2021E	2022E	2023E	2024E	2025E
					Estimates		
Assets							
Current assets:							
Cash and cash equivalents	36,092.0	42,122.0	54,989.9	74,019.7	103,903.2	122,195.8	151,430.0
Marketable securities							
Inventories							
Accounts receivable, net and other							
Total current assets							
Property, plant and equipment, net							
Operating leases							
Goodwill							
Other assets							
Total assets							

2021 Inventories (Balance Sheet Cell F10)

Excel Keystrokes	Description
type "="	Begins the formula
select E10	2020 Inventories
type "-"	Subtracts
select Cash Flow cell G16	2021 Changes in Inventory
hit "Enter"	End
Formula Result	=E10-'Cash Flow Statement'!G16

This gives us $28,125.4. We can copy this formula to the right through 2025.

Accounts Receivable In the same way, we can look at accounts receivable. Let's take an accounts receivable example and assume the 2020 accounts receivable balance sheet balance was $1,000.

Cash Flow	2021
?	?

Balance Sheet	2020	2021
Receivables	1,000.0	?

To answer the first question, it's the 2021 changes in accounts receivable line item in the operating working capital section of the cash flow statement that drives the balance sheet accounts receivable. Now remember the relationship between accounts receivable on the cash flow statement and the balance sheet, as discussed in the Working Capital chapter. If the cash change is positive, then we have collected on our accounts receivable, or accounts receivable should be reduced. So, for example, if the 2021 changes in accounts receivable is $250, then we have collected $250 in receivables. So, the 2020 receivables balance of $1,000 should be reduced by $250 to $750.

Cash Flow	2021
Changes in Accounts Receivable	250.0

Balance Sheet	2020	2021
Receivables	1,000.0	750.0

Or:

2021 Balance Sheet Inventories = 2020 Balance Sheet Inventories –
2021 Cash Flow Changes in Inventory

Notice the formula structure is similar to the inventory formula structure. Also, note the "−" being used.

2021 Accounts Receivable (Balance Sheet Cell F11)

Excel Keystrokes	Description
type "="	Begins the formula
select E11	2020 Accounts Receivable
type "-"	Subtracts
select Cash Flow cell G17	2021 Changes in Accounts Receivable
hit "Enter"	End
Formula Result	=E11-'Cash Flow Statement'!G17

This gives us $28,802.3. We can copy this formula to the right through 2025.

It is important to note that, for all assets (except for cash), the formula structure will *always* be:

2021 Balance Sheet Line Item = 2020 Balance Sheet Line Item –
2021 Related Cash Flow Statement Line Item

The one exception, cash, will be:

2021 Balance Sheet Line Item = 2020 Balance Sheet Line Item +
2021 Related Cash Flow Statement Line Item

This should make logical sense, because next year's balance sheet item is last year's balance increased or decreased by the related cash impact. For assets, cash flow cash has the opposite effect (increasing the asset if cash is negative, or decreasing the asset if cash is positive), hence the need for the "–." The exception is the balance sheet cash asset, where positive cash increases the cash balance, and negative cash decreases the cash balance, hence the "+." This pattern in formula structure is part of the key to a well-built model. Although there are other ways to project some of these line items, we encourage you to keep this consistent structure throughout the model. The more straightforward and consistent your model is, the better it is to read, the higher the chances are that the model will be error free, and the simpler it will be to error check the model if there are mistakes. These formulas should also make conceptual sense, as it's the better understanding of such concepts that can help an analyst think through where errors in models can possibly be.

We can continue this process throughout the asset section of the income statement, matching the following balance sheet items to the related cash flow statement items. (See Table 6.2.)

We can copy each of these line items to the right through 2025. We can copy the total current assets (row 12) and total assets (row 17), which we had calculated when inputting the historical values to the right. We have now completed the assets side of the balance sheet. (See Table 6.3.)

TABLE 6.2   Balance Sheet Asset Projections

Balance Sheet Item	Cash Flow Statement Item(s)	Formula
Marketable Securities (cell F9)	Sales and maturities in marketable securities (G28), Purchases of marketable securities (G29)	=E9-'Cash Flow Statement'!G28-'Cash Flow Statement'!G29
Property, plant, and equipment, net (cell F13)	CAPEX (cell G24), Depreciation and Amortization (cell G8), Proceeds from property and equipment sales and incentives (cell G26), Business acquisitions, net of cash acquired (cell G27). Note: As shown here, there may be more than one cash flow item that can relate to the balance sheet line item. Also, investments and business acquisitions could have some effects on goodwill. But we will keep the assumptions simple for now.	=E13-'Cash Flow Statement'!G24-'Cash Flow Statement'! G8-'Cash Flow Statement'!G26-'Cash Flow Statement'!G27
Operating Leases (cell F14)	0. We couldn't find any cash flow line item directly related to operating leases so we will leave this flat. *Note:* If there is no cash flow item impacting the balance sheet, this means the balance sheet item will stay flat, i.e., zero change. A common mistake is to hardcode "0" in the balance sheet.	=E14
Goodwill (cell F15)	0. Note: Again, we could have assumed a portion of "Business acquisitions" could be related to goodwill but we had made the simplifying assumption that it affects our PP&E. Nothing else affects goodwill here.	=E15
Other assets and (cell F16)	Other operating expense (cell G11), Other expense (cell G13). Note: This is a best guess. It is often vague where the "other" line items should be linked to. Further research could give some more clues. But as a default, we obviously assumed both "other" cash flow line items from the operating activities section would go into the current "other assets" line item.	=E16-'Cash Flow Statement'!G11-'Cash Flow Statement'!G13

TABLE 6.3 Amazon Projected Assets

Consolidated Balance Sheets (in US$ millions except per share amounts)

On December 31	2019A	2020A	2021E	2022E	Estimates 2023E	2024E	2025E
Assets							
Current Assets							
Cash and cash equivalents	36,092.0	42,122.0	54,989.9	74,019.7	103,903.2	122,195.8	151,430.0
Marketable securities	18,929.0	42,274.0	41,134.0	50,265.0	49,125.0	58,256.0	57,116.0
Inventories	20,497.0	23,795.0	28,125.4	33,356.7	37,630.9	40,952.5	43,442.8
Accounts receivable, net and other	20,816.0	24,542.0	28,802.3	34,159.6	38,536.5	41,938.1	44,488.3
Total Current Assets	**96,334.0**	**132,733.0**	**153,051.6**	**191,801.0**	**229,195.6**	**263,342.5**	**296,477.1**
Property, plant and equipment, net	72,705.0	113,114.0	138,867.6	167,572.1	196,456.5	222,963.4	244,948.7
Operating leases	25,141.0	37,553.0	37,553.0	37,553.0	37,553.0	37,553.0	37,553.0
Goodwill	14,754.0	15,017.0	15,017.0	15,017.0	15,017.0	15,017.0	15,017.0
Other assets	16,314.0	22,778.0	22,649.2	23,005.1	22,906.8	23,287.0	23,207.3
Total Assets	**225,248.0**	**321,195.0**	**367,138.4**	**434,948.3**	**501,128.9**	**562,162.9**	**617,203.1**

Liabilities

Let's look at the first line, "Accounts payable," and assume the 2020 accounts payable balance sheet balance was $1,000.

Cash Flow	2021
?	?

Balance Sheet	2020	2021
Accounts Payable	1,000.0	?

To answer the first question from the two discussed earlier, it's the 2021 changes in accounts payable line item in the working capital section of the cash flow statement that drives this item. Now remember the relationship between accounts payable on the cash flow statement and the balance sheet as discussed in the Working Capital chapter (Chapter 5). If the cash change is positive, then we have increased our accounts payable. So, for example, if the 2021 changes in accounts payable is $500, then we have increased our payables by $500.

Cash Flow	2021
Changes in Accounts Payable	500.0

Balance Sheet	2020	2021
Accounts Payable	1,000.0	1,500.0

Or:

2021 Balance Sheet Accounts Payable = 2020 Balance Sheet Accounts Payable + 2021 Cash Flow Changes in Accounts Payable

Notice here, the formula structure is similar to the formula for the assets, but we are using a "+" instead of a "−." This is due to the direct relationship between liabilities and cash (i.e., cash increasing results in liabilities increasing and cash decreasing results in liabilities decreasing).

So in the same way, we can project the 2021 accounts payable for Amazon.

2021 Accounts Payable (Balance Sheet Cell F20)

Excel Keystrokes	Description
type "="	Begins the formula
select E20	2020 Accounts Payable
type "+"	Adds
select Cash Flow cell G18	2021 Changes in Accounts Payable
hit "Enter"	End
Formula Result	=E20+'Cash Flow Statement'!G18

This gives us $76,023.5, and we can copy this formula to the right.

We can continue this process throughout the liabilities section of the income statement, matching the following balance sheet items to the related cash flow statement items. (See Table 6.4.)

TABLE 6.4 Balance Sheet Liabilities Projections

Balance Sheet Item	Cash Flow Statement Item(s)	Formula
Accrued expenses and other (cell F21)	Changes accrued expenses (cell G19)	=E21+'Cash Flow Statement'!G19
Short-term debt (cell F22)	Short-term debt borrowings (repayments) (cell G32). Note that Amazon did not report short-term debt on its balance sheet, which we felt was highly unusual since it does have indication of it on the cash flow. So we added a line item in the balance sheet with a zero balance for now.	=E22+'Cash Flow Statement'!G32
Unearned revenue (cell F23)	Changes in unearned revenue (cell G20)	=E23+'Cash Flow Statement'!G20
Long-term lease liabilities (cell F25)	Principal repayments of finance leases (cell G34)	=E25+'Cash Flow Statement'!G34
Long-term debt (cell F26)	Long-term borrowings (repayments) (cell G33)	=E26+'Cash Flow Statement'!G33
Other long-term liabilities (cell F27)	Principal repayments of finance obligations (G35), Deferred income taxes (cell G14). *Note:* It's hard to define what goes into an "other" category. However, we did realize principal repayments of finance obligations must be connected with some liability (we will later change this), and this is the only one left. Deferred taxes *could* have been an asset, but since we have already completed the asset side, we linked it into this only other liability line; also, deferred taxes is more likely a liability than an asset.	=E27+'Cash Flow Statement'!G35+ 'Cash Flow Statement'!G14

We can copy each of these line items to the right through 2025. We can copy the total current liabilities (row 24) and the total liabilities (row 28), which we had calculated inputting the historical values to the right. We have now completed the current liabilities side of the balance sheet. (See Table 6.5.)

TABLE 6.5 Amazon Projected Liabilities

Consolidated Balance Sheets (in US$ millions except per share amounts)

On December 31	2019A	2020A	2021E	Estimates 2022E	2023E	2024E	2025E
Liabilities							
Current Liabilities:							
Accounts payable	47,183.0	72,539.0	76,023.5	90,163.8	101,716.8	110,695.3	117,426.5
Accrued expenses and other	32,439.0	44,138.0	48,626.4	57,670.9	65,060.5	70,803.3	75,108.7
Short-term debt	0.0	0.0	0.0	0.0	0.0	0.0	0.0
Unearned revenue	8,190.0	9,708.0	11,365.2	13,479.2	15,206.3	16,548.5	17,554.8
Total Current Liabilities	87,812.0	126,385.0	136,015.1	161,313.9	181,983.6	198,047.2	210,090.1
Long-term lease liabilities	39,791.0	52,573.0	52,573.0	52,573.0	52,573.0	52,573.0	52,573.0
Long-term debt	23,414.0	31,816.0	31,816.0	31,816.0	31,816.0	31,816.0	31,816.0
Other long-term liabilities	12,171.0	17,017.0	16,463.0	15,909.0	15,355.0	14,801.0	14,247.0
Total Liabilities	163,188.0	227,791.0	236,867.1	261,611.9	281,727.6	297,237.2	308,726.1

Shareholders' Equity

Shareholders' equity line items act the same way as a liability. Cash is generated; that could mean equity was raised. Or, if cash is spent, a company could have purchased shares in a share buyback. So the general formula for a shareholders' equity balance sheet line item is:

$$2021 \text{ Shareholders' Equity Line Item} = 2020 \text{ Shareholders' Equity}$$
$$\text{Line Item} + 2021 \text{ Cash Flow Net change}$$

We always use a "+" so we can proceed using the same method as before. (See Table 6.6.)

TABLE 6.6   Balance Sheet Shareholders' Equity Projections

Balance Sheet Item	Cash Flow Statement Item(s)	Formula
Preferred Stock (cell F30)	0. Although the company lists Preferred Stock on its balance sheet, it is listed at 0 and there are no cash flow statement line items referencing this.	=E30
Common stock + APIC (cell G31)	0. Note: There is no line item on the cash flow statement relating to proceeds from a common stock equity raise, which would be the major driver of this balance sheet item.	=E31
Treasury stock (cell F32)	0. There are no line items on the cash flow referring to the repurchase of stock at this time.	=E32
Accumulated other comprehensive income (cell F33)	Effect of exchange rate on cash (cell G37).	=E33+'Cash Flow Statement'!G37
Retained earnings (cell F34)	Net income (cell G7) + Stock-based compensation (cell G9). Note: Retained earnings is always driven by net income. We are linking stock-based compensation here as we are assuming this is stock that has been *granted* and not yet *vested*. Once the stock has actually been vested, then the value would impact the "common stock + APIC."	=E34+'Cash Flow Statement'!G7+ 'Cash Flow Statement'!G9

So we are done! Copy each of these line items to the right through 2025. We can also copy the total shareholders' equity (row 35) and the total liabilities and equity (row 36), which we had calculated when inputting the historical values to the right. (See Table 6.7.)

After completing this process we should have a balancing balance sheet. You may notice another match line at the bottom of the balance sheet in row 38. This match checks to be sure the balance sheet is in balance, or if:

$$\text{Assets} = \text{Liabilities} + \text{Shareholders' Equity}$$

If the model does not balance, then we need to take the appropriate steps to identify where the problem could be. This is the daunting task we were referring to earlier. However, with our methodology, there are several simple steps to find a balance sheet error without the need to pull an all-nighter.

BALANCING AN UNBALANCED BALANCE SHEET

With the proper understanding that balance sheet line items increase or decrease based on how cash is sourced or spent, it is easy to understand that an unbalanced balance sheet occurs when there is a mismatch between the cash flow statement and the balance sheet. More specifically, there are four major reasons why a balance sheet may not be in balance:

1. *There is a line item in the cash flow statement that has not been linked to the balance sheet.* This happens quite often, especially when cash flow statements have a lot of nonstandard line items. It is often the case that they are accidentally left out and forgotten about.
2. *There is a line item in the cash flow statement that has been used more than once in the balance sheet.* Again, this happens often in cash flow statements that have a lot of nonstandard line items. But in this case it has accidentally been included in more than one place in the balance sheet. Remember: A balance sheet stays in balance when each cash flow statement item drives one of the asset, liability, or shareholders' equity line items – *only* one. If you link one cash flow statement item in two places, the model will be out of balance.

TABLE 6.7 Amazon Projected Balance Sheet

Consolidated Balance Sheets (in US$ millions except per share amounts)

On December 31	2019A	2020A	2021E	2022E	Estimates 2023E	2024E	2025E
Assets							
Current Assets							
Cash and cash equivalents	36,092.0	42,122.0	54,989.9	74,019.7	103,903.2	122,195.8	151,430.0
Marketable securities	18,929.0	42,274.0	41,134.0	50,265.0	49,125.0	58,256.0	57,116.0
Inventories	20,497.0	23,795.0	28,125.4	33,356.7	37,630.9	40,952.5	43,442.8
Accounts receivable, net and other	20,816.0	24,542.0	28,802.3	34,159.6	38,536.5	41,938.1	44,488.3
Total current assets	**96,334.0**	**132,733.0**	**153,051.6**	**191,801.0**	**229,195.6**	**263,342.5**	**296,477.1**
Property, plant and equipment, net	72,705.0	113,114.0	138,867.6	167,572.1	196,456.5	222,963.4	244,948.7
Operating leases	25,141.0	37,553.0	37,553.0	37,553.0	37,553.0	37,553.0	37,553.0
Goodwill	14,754.0	15,017.0	15,017.0	15,017.0	15,017.0	15,017.0	15,017.0
Other assets	16,314.0	22,778.0	22,649.2	23,005.1	22,906.8	23,287.0	23,207.3
Total Assets	**225,248.0**	**321,195.0**	**367,138.4**	**434,948.3**	**501,128.9**	**562,162.9**	**617,203.1**
Liabilities							
Current Liabilities							
Accounts payable	47,183.0	72,539.0	76,023.5	90,163.8	101,716.8	110,695.3	117,426.5
Accrued expenses and other	32,439.0	44,138.0	48,626.4	57,670.9	65,060.5	70,803.3	75,108.7
Short-term debt	0.0	0.0	0.0	0.0	0.0	0.0	0.0

(Continued)

TABLE 6.7 (*Continued*)

Consolidated Balance Sheets (in US$ millions except per share amounts)

On December 31	2019A	2020A	2021E	2022E	Estimates 2023E	2024E	2025E
Unearned revenue	8,190.0	9,708.0	11,365.2	13,479.2	15,206.3	16,548.5	17,554.8
Total Current Liabilities	87,812.0	126,385.0	136,015.1	161,313.9	181,983.6	198,047.2	210,090.1
Long-term lease liabilities	39,791.0	52,573.0	52,573.0	52,573.0	52,573.0	52,573.0	52,573.0
Long-term debt	23,414.0	31,816.0	31,816.0	31,816.0	31,816.0	31,816.0	31,816.0
Other long-term liabilities	12,171.0	17,017.0	16,463.0	15,909.0	15,355.0	14,801.0	14,247.0
Total Liabilities	163,188.0	227,791.0	236,867.1	261,611.9	281,727.6	297,237.2	308,726.1
Stockholders' Equity							
Preferred stock	0.0	0.0	0.0	0.0	0.0	0.0	0.0
Common stock par value + additional paid-in-capital	33,663.0	42,870.0	42,870.0	42,870.0	42,870.0	42,870.0	42,870.0
Treasury stock	(1,837.0)	(1,837.0)	(1,837.0)	(1,837.0)	(1,837.0)	(1,837.0)	(1,837.0)
Accumulated other comprehensive income (loss)	(986.0)	(180.0)	(531.0)	(461.0)	157.0	(194.0)	(124.0)
Retained earnings	31,220.0	52,551.0	89,769.3	132,764.4	178,211.3	224,086.7	267,568.0
Total Stockholders' Equity	62,060.0	93,404.0	130,271.3	173,336.4	219,401.3	264,925.7	308,477.0
Total Liabilities & Stockholders' Equity	225,248.0	321,195.0	367,138.4	434,948.3	501,128.9	562,162.9	617,203.1
SUPPLEMENTAL DATA:							
Balance? (Y/N)	Y	Y	Y	Y	Y	Y	Y

3. *A line item in the cash flow statement is linked to the correct balance sheet item, but it is moving the balance sheet item in the wrong direction, or the line item is pulling from the wrong year.* This is where having a common structure of formulas as described earlier can be of great help. As you notice in the projected balance sheet we have built together, every formula has the following structure:

$$= \text{Balance Sheet Item } 2020 + / - \text{Cash Flow Item } 2021$$

So we know that every formula in this model should have an "E" in the first term, representing the 2020 balance sheet line item, and a "G" in the second term (and subsequent terms if applicable), representing the 2021 cash flow statement line item. We also know that every asset except cash should have a "–" between the first and second terms, and every liability and shareholders' equity line item should have a "+" between the first and second terms. Knowing all of this, we can easily scan each balance sheet formula to ensure that the structure is correct. If that first term is not pointing to Column E and if that second term is not pointing to column G, then one of those items is pulling from the wrong year. We also know that if there is a "–" where there should be a "+" or vice versa, then the projected balance sheet line item is moving in the wrong direction.

4. The totals are not calculating properly in the cash flow statement or balance sheet. It is possible that a balance sheet is out of balance simply because the total assets, for example, are not adding up properly or, more commonly, the total change in cash and cash equivalents is not properly including all line items in the total.

Here is an example of a simple balanced balance sheet. Each cash flow statement line item is properly driving each balance sheet line item, and the balance sheet is in balance.

Cash Flow	2021
Net Income	1,000.0
Changes in Accounts Receivable	(100.0)
Changes in Inventory	250.0
Total Changes in Cash	**1,150.0**

Balance Sheet	2020	2021
Cash	1,000.0	2,150.0
Accounts Receivable	500.0	600.0
Inventory	250.0	0.0
Liabilities	0.0	0.0
Retained Earnings (Net Income)	1,750.0	2,750.0
Balance?	Y	Y

If there happens to be a cash flow line item that was not included in the balance sheet, then we have detected a problem of type 1, as identified previously. We had left a cash flow line item out and need to link it to the balance sheet. In the following example, we had forgotten to link inventory into the balance sheet. This creates a total of $3,000 ($2,150 + $600 + $250) in assets, which, less $0 in liabilities, no longer matches the shareholders' equity of $2,750. If we had linked in the inventory properly, as we had done previously, the balance sheet would balance.

Cash Flow	2021
Net Income	1,000.0
Changes in Accounts Receivable	(100.0)
Changes in Inventory	250.0
Total Changes in Cash	**1,150.0**

Balance Sheet	2020	2021
Cash	1,000.0	2,150.0
Accounts Receivable	500.0	600.0
Inventory	250.0	250.0
Liabilities	0.0	0.0
Retained Earnings (Net Income)	1,750.0	2,750.0
Balance?	Y	N

If a cash flow statement line item was linked into the balance sheet more than one time, then we have detected a problem of type 2. We have used the same cash flow line item two times. We can only use a cash flow statement line item once. In the following example, we accidentally linked inventory into two separate places in the balance sheet. So there is $250 less assets (inventory cash inflow reduces our asset balance) than we should have in the balance sheet, as we have double-counted the inventory. This creates a total of $2,500 ($2,150 + $350) in assets, less $0 liabilities, versus $2,750 in shareholders' equity.

Cash Flow	2021
Net Income	1,000.0
Changes in Accounts Receivable	(100.0)
Changes in Inventory	250.0
Total Changes in Cash	**1,150.0**

Balance Sheet	2020	2021
Cash	1,000.0	2,150.0
Accounts Receivable	500.0	350.0
Inventory	250.0	0.0
Liabilities	0.0	0.0
Retained Earnings (Net Income)	1,750.0	2,750.0
Balance?	Y	N

If we have added the cash flow statement item into the balance sheet when we should have subtracted or vice versa, we have detected a problem of type 3. In the following example, the inventory is linked into the balance sheet but has increased the asset from $250 to $500, when it should have decreased the asset from $250 to $0. A type 3 problem can also occur if the balance sheet item is linking from the wrong cash flow statement column, which meant it is linking in from the wrong year.

Cash Flow	2021
Net Income	1,000.0
Changes in Accounts Receivable	(100.0)
Changes in Inventory	250.0
Total Changes in Cash	**1,150.0**

Balance Sheet	2020	2021
Cash	1,000.0	2,150.0
Accounts Receivable	500.0	600.0
Inventory	250.0	500.0
Liabilities	0.0	0.0
Retained Earnings (Net Income)	1,750.0	2,750.0
Balance?	Y	N

If there is a problem with a total item either in the cash flow or the balance sheet, this is a problem of type 4. In this example, each cash flow item is properly linked to the balance sheet. However, the total changes in cash is totaling wrong; it should be $1,150. This creates a mismatch because we have linked a total of $1,150 in individual cash flow items into balance sheet line items, but are showing only $900 in total changes in cash affecting our cash balance.

Cash Flow	2021
Net Income	1,000.0
Changes in Accounts Receivable	(100.0)
Changes in Inventory	250.0
Total Changes in Cash	**900.0**

Balance Sheet	2020	2021
Cash	1,000.0	1,900.0
Accounts Receivable	500.0	600.0
Inventory	250.0	0.0
Liabilities	0.0	0.0
Retained Earnings (Net Income)	1,750.0	2,750.0
Balance?	Y	N

There is a foolproof method for detecting where and why a balance sheet is out of balance. Even if the model you are working with is not structured as our model is, this method can still detect the error. We have proven this method time and time again with the most complex of models on Wall Street. We assure you, if you can get a handle on this process, balancing an unbalanced balance sheet will no longer be a daunting task.

NYSF Balance Sheet Balancing Method

We strongly recommend printing out the cash flow statement and the balance sheet, and performing this method on paper. Going through this method on paper with a pencil and calculator is the surest way to find the balance sheet errors the first time through. But, proofing the balance sheet in Excel can work as well. Whether using paper or Excel, the first step is to create a differences column on the balance sheet. The differences column will subtract the first year the model is not balancing from the previous balancing year. So, if 2020 is balancing but 2021 is not, the differences column will subtract 2020 from 2021 for each line item. It doesn't really matter which way you are subtracting, because we will just be matching the values. We should now have a column listing the differences for each balance sheet line item, as shown in Table 6.8.

These differences are essentially cash flows. So, we now need to match each of these differences to the cash flow statement. For each balance sheet line item, we ask ourselves two balance sheet balancing questions:

1. Does this difference number match the appropriate cash flows?
2. Is this balance sheet line item moving in the right direction?

Let's take Inventories, for example. The difference in Inventories is $4,330.4. So for question 1, this difference should match the "Changes in Inventory" line item from the cash flow statement. (See Table 6.9.)

TABLE 6.8 Balance Sheet Differences

Consolidated Balance Sheets (in US$ millions except per share amounts)

On December 31	2019A	2020A	Estimates 2021E	Differences
Assets				
Current Assets				
Cash and cash equivalents	36,092.0	42,122.0	54,989.9	12,867.9
Marketable securities	18,929.0	42,274.0	41,134.0	(1,140.0)
Inventories	20,497.0	23,795.0	28,125.4	4,330.4
Accounts receivable, net and other	20,816.0	24,542.0	28,802.3	4,260.3
Total Current Assets	96,334.0	132,733.0	153,051.6	
Property, plant and equipment, net	72,705.0	113,114.0	138,867.6	25,753.6
Operating leases	25,141.0	37,553.0	37,553.0	0.0
Goodwill	14,754.0	15,017.0	15,017.0	0.0
Other assets	16,314.0	22,778.0	22,649.2	(128.8)
Total Assets	225,248.0	321,195.0	367,138.4	

2021 "Changes in Inventory" is $4,330.4; the value is the same. So, for the second question, we notice the "Changes in Inventory" on the cash flow statement is negative. That should be increasing the asset on the balance sheet. Going back to the balance sheet, we notice the inventories are in fact increasing from $23,795.0 in 2020 to $28,125.4 in 2021. So the inventories check out. It is crucial that we cross off the "Changes in Inventory" line item on the cash flow statement to indicate that we have already used this line item. Remember that one of the more common errors is accidentally including the cash flow line items into the balance sheet more than once or leaving it out altogether. Marking each cash flow line item as we go through this process helps make sure we are using every cash flow line item, but only one time. So, we can continue this process moving to the next line item, answering the same two questions and crossing off the cash flow line items accordingly. We should do this for every balance sheet line item, including cash; by the time we get to the end of the balance sheet, we should have crossed off every line item in the cash flow statement, but only one time.

If the process is completed and there are cash flow line items not crossed off, then you know the problem is type 1 and you need to link that cash flow item into the balance sheet. If you find an item crossed off but used twice,

TABLE 6.9 Cash Flow from Operating Activities

Consolidated Statements of Cash Flows (in US$ millions except per share amounts)

Period Ending December 31	Actuals			Estimates
	2018A	2019A	2020A	2021E
Cash flows from operating activities				
Net income	10,073.0	11,588.0	21,331.0	25,524.1
Depreciation and amortization	15,341.0	21,879.0	25,251.0	28,669.8
Stock-based compensation	5,418.0	6,864.0	9,208.0	11,694.2
% of Total Operating Expenses	*8.2%*	*8.7%*	*8.8%*	*8.8%*
Other operating expense (income), net	274.0	164.0	(71.0)	(90.2)
% of Total Net Sales	*0.1%*	*0.1%*	*0.0%*	*0.0%*
Other expense (income), net	219.0	(249.0)	(2,582.0)	219.0
Deferred income taxes	441.0	796.0	(554.0)	(554.0)
Changes in operating operating working capital				
Changes in inventory	(1,314.0)	(3,278.0)	(2,849.0)	(4,330.4)
Changes in accounts receivable	(4,615.0)	(7,681.0)	(8,169.0)	(4,260.3)
Changes in accounts payable	3,263.0	8,193.0	17,480.0	3,484.5
Changes in accrued expenses	472.0	(1,383.0)	5,754.0	4,488.4
Changes in unearned revenue	1,151.0	1,711.0	1,265.0	1,657.2
Net changes in working capital	**(1,043.0)**	**(2,438.0)**	**13,481.0**	**1,039.3**

then the problem is type 2, and you need to choose only one balance sheet item to link the cash flow item to. If the value in the differences column does not match the cash flow statement, then this is a problem of type 3. A type 3 problem also exists if the balance sheet item is moving the wrong way— that is, increasing when the cash flow item indicates it should be decreasing, or vice versa.

There is a possibility that, when after going through this method everything checks out but the balance sheet still does not balance. If that is the case, then this is a problem of type 4. There must be a totaling error in either the cash flow statement or balance sheet.

We encourage you to take the time and think through the relationship between the cash flow statement and balance sheet. Over much time this method should make conceptual sense. With a complete understanding of the relationship between the cash flow statement and balance sheet, it should be clear that outside of the four potential balance sheet problems mentioned previously, there is no other way a balance sheet can be out of balance.

With our completed balance sheet we can now move on to the final schedule: the debt schedule.

CHAPTER 7

The Debt Schedule, Circular References, and Finalizing the Model

The debt schedule is designed to track every major type of debt a company has, and the associated interest and payment schedules for each. It also helps track the cash available that could be used to pay down those debts and any interest income that could be generated from cash or cash equivalents available. Simply put, a debt schedule helps us better track the debt and interest. There is also a very important "circular reference" that is created once the debt schedule is complete and properly linked through the rest of the model. This circular reference is crucial in helping us determine various debt situations, such as the absolute maximum amount of debt a company can raise, making sure there is still enough cash to meet the interest payments.

Note: Once the circular reference is created, you may receive an Excel error message. Please refer to the "Circular References" section of this chapter on how to resolve circular reference errors.

It is important to note that the debt schedule should be the very last statement to build due to this circular reference. Make sure you have a properly balancing balance sheet before beginning the debt schedule. If you do not have a balancing balance sheet, moving on to the debt schedule will only complicate things further.

DEBT SCHEDULE STRUCTURE

Please refer to the "Debt Schedule" tab in the model.

The "Cash available to pay down debt" section, rows 6 through 10, will help us track the amount of cash we have available to pay down debts.

The next sections are grouped by types of debt. Here we will calculate each balance of debt from year to year, track the potential debt paydowns or issuances, and calculate the interest.

At the bottom of the debt schedule we will total all issuances and payments ("total issuances/(retirements)") and all interests ("total interest expense"). We will then calculate cash at the end of the year and interest income associated with that cash, if any exist.

Notice that there is a final match, which will make sure the cash at the end of the year we are calculating in the debt schedule matches the cash found on the balance sheet.

MODELING THE DEBT SCHEDULE

The very first step to modeling the debt schedule is to pull in the last reported cash and debt balances from the balance sheet. We can begin with pulling the cash balance from Amazon's 2020 balance sheet into the 2020 "Cash at the end of the year" line on the debt schedule. So cell F34 on the debt schedule should be "='Balance Sheet'!E8." We can now start pulling in the last reported debt balances. However, before doing so, it is important to make sure the debt schedule has properly included each debt item reported on the balance sheet, including long-term debt, short-term borrowings, and capital leases. So when looking at the balance sheet we notice we have:

- Short-term debt
- Long-term lease liabilities
- Long-term debt

It is ideal to create a separate debt section for each debt listed. So, we will have three sections, and we can pull in the respective ending debt balances of each debt from the balance sheet into the debt schedule.

Cell F15, "Short-term debt (end of year)," will be "='Balance Sheet'!E22" and so on, as per Table 7.1.

Short-Term Debt

Once we have the ending balances linked in, we can build out each debt balance, starting with the short-term debt.

TABLE 7.1 Debt Schedule Last Reported Balances

Debt Schedule Item	Balance Sheet Item	Formula
Short-term debt (end of year) (Cell F15)	Short-term debt (Cell E22)	='Balance Sheet'!E22
Long-term debt (end of year)(Cell F22)	Long-term debt (Cell E26)	='Balance Sheet'!E26
Long-term lease liabilities (end of year) (Cell F29)	Long-term lease liabilities (Cell E25)	='Balance Sheet'!E25

Notice the short-term debt balance is 0. If you recall, Amazon did not identify its short-term debt separately on the balance sheet. Now we can dig deeper into the company's debt balances. Performing a quick word search on "debt" reveals the table and notes on page 56 of the 10-K. (See Figure 7.1.)

We will use this table throughout the chapter to analyze Amazon's debts. Here you can see the last line before the total is titled "Less current portion of long-term debt." This implies the company does record a short-term debt balance even though it does not separately report the balance on its balance sheet. It is important for us to separate this out as best we can to show a more accurate debt schedule. So the values of "$1,305" and "$1,155" for 2019 and 2020, respectively, can be considered a part of our short-term debt. However, we are not done. When further researching the company's debt balances, specifically its finance leases, we uncovered the following table on page 54 of the 10-K. (See Figure 7.2.) At this point, you may feel lost about how one would know to search for these items. If it at all helps, we also had to search for "debts" to research interest rates for the long-term debt. We later had to search for "long-term lease" when analyzing interest rates for the debt that comes later in the schedule. It was at that point that we uncovered Figure 7.2 relevant to this discussion.

In this figure, the top table is related to interest rates; we will save that for later. The next table contains 2019 balances, and the last table contains 2020 balances. The second-to-last lines of the bottom two tables are titled "Less: current portion of lease liabilities." Again, current portion implies the amount of the total balance that comes due in the current year – implying "sort term." So the 2019 current portion of $13,023 and the 2020 current portion of $14,960 can be added to the balances already found in Figure 7.1. In other words, we can hardcode directly into the balance sheet cell D22 "=1305+13023" and E22 "=1155+14960." If hardcoded directly into the balance sheet, it will automatically flow into the debt schedule.

Now we can't just add values to a balance sheet – it will now be out of balance. These identified short-term debt values must have been buried in the balance sheet somewhere else; we now need to figure out where. As we are

Note 6 — DEBT

As of December 31, 2020, we had $32.2 billion of unsecured senior notes outstanding (the "Notes"), including $10.0 billion issued in June 2020 for general corporate purposes. We also have other long-term debt and borrowings under our credit facility of $1.6 billion and $924 million as of December 31, 2019 and 2020. Our total long-term debt obligations are as follows (in millions):

	Maturities (1)	Stated Interest Rates	Effective Interest Rates	December 31, 2019	December 31, 2020
2012 Notes issuance of $3.0 billion	2022	2.50%	2.66%	1,250	1,250
2014 Notes issuance of $6.0 billion	2021 - 2044	3.30% - 4.95%	3.43% - 5.11%	5,000	5,000
2017 Notes issuance of $17.0 billion	2023 - 2057	2.40% - 5.20%	2.56% - 4.33%	17,000	16,000
2020 Notes issuance of $10.0 billion	2023 - 2060	0.40% - 2.70%	0.56% - 2.77%	—	10,000
Credit Facility				740	338
Other long-term debt				830	586
Total face value of long-term debt				24,820	33,174
Unamortized discount and issuance costs, net				(101)	(203)
Less current portion of long-term debt				(1,305)	(1,155)
Long-term debt				$ 23,414	$ 31,816

(1) The weighted average remaining lives of the 2012, 2014, 2017, and 2020 Notes were 1.9, 11.8, 16.2, and 18.7 years as of December 31, 2020. The combined weighted average remaining life of the Notes was 15.8 years as of December 31, 2020.

Interest on the Notes is payable semi-annually in arrears. We may redeem the Notes at any time in whole, or from time to time, in part at specified redemption prices. We are not subject to any financial covenants under the Notes. The estimated fair value of the Notes was approximately $26.2 billion and $37.7 billion as of December 31, 2019 and 2020, which is based on quoted prices for our debt as of those dates.

In October 2016, we entered into a $500 million secured revolving credit facility with a lender that is secured by certain seller receivables, which we subsequently increased to $740 million and may from time to time increase in the future subject to lender approval (the "Credit Facility"). The Credit Facility is available until October 2022, bears interest at the London interbank offered rate ("LIBOR") plus 1.40%, and has a commitment fee of 0.50% on the undrawn portion. There were $740 million and $338 million of borrowings outstanding under the Credit Facility as of December 31, 2019 and 2020, which had a weighted-average interest rate of 3.4% and 3.0%, respectively. As of December 31, 2019 and 2020, we have pledged $852 million and $398 million of our cash and seller receivables as collateral for debt related to our Credit Facility. The estimated fair value of the Credit Facility, which is based on Level 2 inputs, approximated its carrying value as of December 31, 2019 and 2020.

Other long-term debt, including the current portion, had a weighted-average interest rate of 4.1% and 2.9% as of December 31, 2019 and 2020. We used the net proceeds from the issuance of this debt primarily to fund certain business operations. The estimated fair value of other long-term debt, which is based on Level 2 inputs, approximated its carrying value as of December 31, 2019 and 2020.

FIGURE 7.1   Amazon's Debts

Other information about lease amounts recognized in our consolidated financial statements is as follows:

	December 31, 2019	December 31, 2020
Weighted-average remaining lease term – operating leases	11.5	11.3
Weighted-average remaining lease term – finance leases	5.5	6.2
Weighted-average discount rate – operating leases	3.1 %	2.5 %
Weighted-average discount rate – finance leases	2.7 %	2.1 %

Our lease liabilities were as follows (in millions):

	December 31, 2019		
	Operating Leases	Finance Leases	Total
Gross lease liabilities	$ 31,963	$ 28,875	$ 60,838
Less: imputed interest	(6,128)	(1,896)	(8,024)
Present value of lease liabilities	25,835	26,979	52,814
Less: current portion of lease liabilities	(3,139)	(9,884)	(13,023)
Total long-term lease liabilities	$ 22,696	$ 17,095	$ 39,791

	December 31, 2020		
	Operating Leases	Finance Leases	Total
Gross lease liabilities	$ 46,164	$ 30,437	$ 76,601
Less: imputed interest	(7,065)	(2,003)	(9,068)
Present value of lease liabilities	39,099	28,434	67,533
Less: current portion of lease liabilities	(4,586)	(10,374)	(14,960)
Total long-term lease liabilities	$ 34,513	$ 18,060	$ 52,573

FIGURE 7.2 Amazon's Leases

referring to short-term debt, this must be buried in a current liability line item. There are only three current liability line items, so we immediately jump to the "Accrued expenses *and other*" line items, as the ". . .and other" maybe an indicator that several various items have been grouped together. Sure enough, a word search on "accrued expenses and other" reveals the following note:

> *Included in "Accrued expenses and other" on our consolidated balance sheets are liabilities primarily related to leases and asset retirement obligations, payroll and related expenses, tax-related liabilities, unredeemed gift cards, customer liabilities, current debt, acquired digital media content, and other operating expenses.*

You can see in this note, they do in fact not only include "Current debt" but they even mention "leases," which is why we also added the current portion of leases into the short-term debt cell.

So we have to reduce the current "Accrued expenses and other" line item by the value of current portion of debts and leases we have identified. So cell D21 now reads "=32439-14328" and D22 now reads "=44138-16115." And in case you were wondering, the new working capital balances automatically flow into the working capital schedule and cash flow statement. (See Table 7.2.)

Now we can continue building out the short-term debt section of the debt schedule. Let's go back to the Debt Schedule. The 2021 short-term debt (beginning of year) is the beginning balance of debt for that year. We assume this is the same value as the ending balance of debt from the year before. In other words, we assume the balance of debt as of 1/1/2021 is the exact same as the balance of debt from 12/31/2020. So we will have:

$$2021 \text{ Short-Term Debt (Beginning of Year)} =$$
$$2020 \text{ Short-Term Debt (End of Year)}$$

Or, in cell G12, we will have "=F15, " and we can copy this to the right.

Mandatory Issuances/(Retirements) and Non-Mandatory Issuances/(Retirements)

An issuance represents a debt raise and a retirement represents a debt paydown. In modeling, we separate issuances and retirements into two categories: mandatory and non-mandatory. Mandatory issuances or retirements are those that have been planned or scheduled. For example, a yearly principal payment would be considered a mandatory payment, as a principal

TABLE 7.2 Updated Current Liabilities

Debt Schedule (in US$ millions except per share amounts)

Period Ending December 31	Actuals				Estimates		
	2019A	2020A	2021E	2022E	2023E	2024E	2025E
Current liabilities:							
Accounts payable	47,183.0	72,539.0	76,023.5	90,163.8	101,716.8	110,695.3	117,426.5
Accrued expenses and other	18,111.0	28,023.0	29,295.1	34,744.0	39,195.8	42,655.6	45,249.4
Short-term debt	14,328.0	16,115.0	16,115.0	16,115.0	16,115.0	16,115.0	16,115.0
Unearned revenue	8,190.0	9,708.0	11,365.2	13,479.2	15,206.3	16,548.5	17,554.8
Total current liabilities	**87,812.0**	**126,385.0**	**132,798.8**	**154,502.0**	**172,234.0**	**186,014.5**	**196,345.8**

payment must be paid down as per the debt contract. A non-mandatory issuance or retirement is a payment or issuance made that is beyond the contractual requirements of the debt. In other words, let's say we happen to have a cash surplus at the end of one particular year. And, although it is not necessary, and assuming we are allowed to, we have decided to pay down some more debt beyond what has been required to pay down so we can save on interest payments. This is non-mandatory. Non-mandatory payments are often used in revolving lines of credit, where one would pay down debt if there is a cash surplus. In modeling, as the mandatory payments are planned, we typically hardcode them in based on the debt contract terms. And, typically, non-mandatory payments are based on a formula created that compares the cash available to our outstanding debt balance. If we have excess cash available, we will automatically pay down our debt. So in modeling it is important to separate our mandatory issuances and retirements from our non-mandatory, so we can have a place for our scheduled payments, and also be able to create this "automatic" formula and not have one disturb the other.

For now, we can keep them both as "0," and we will create these formulas once the debt schedule is complete. So let's hardcode G13 and G14 as "0," and we can copy this formula to the right.

In order to calculate short-term debt at the end of the year, we simply start with the debt at the beginning of the year and add our issuances and retirements. If we want to raise $1MM in debt, for example, we would hardcode $1MM into mandatory issuances, and our debt at the end of the year would be the beginning debt plus the $1MM. Conversely, if we wanted to pay down debt, we would hardcode –$1MM into mandatory issuances, and our debt at the end of the year would be the beginning debt minus the $1MM.

2021 Short-Term Borrowings (End of Year) = 2021 Short-Term Borrowings (Beginning of Year) + Mandatory Issuances/(Retirements) + Non-Mandatory Issuances/(Retirements)

Or, cell G15 would be "=SUM(G12:G14)."

We can copy this formula to the right and move on to the interest expense calculation.

We need to first do some research to determine what Amazon's short-term borrowings interest rate is. If you recall, the Amazon debt table in Figure 7.1 also contains information on interest rates.

This table is going to be very helpful in estimating the interest Amazon is paying on the various debts. Underneath the table we find the following reference:

Other long-term debt, including the current portion, *had a weighted-average interest rate of 4.1% and 2.9% as of December 31, 2019 and 2020.*

"Current portion" typically implies "short-term." This is the only reference we see to current portion or short-term debt here, so we will take the 2020 noted 2.9% as the short-term debt interest rate.

We can type 2.9% into cell G17 and we can copy this rate to the right.

To calculate interest expense, it is better to take an average balance of the beginning of year and end of year debt balances. This is important if we do not know exactly when during the year potential issuances or retirements occur. For example, let's say we have $1MM of short-term borrowings outstanding and we have a mandatory retirement of $1MM, in 2021. So, the ending balance of debt will be $0. Since we have paid down debt sometime during 2021, technically the interest on that debt will only be incurred during the time the debt has been outstanding. If we had paid that $1MM down on the very first day of the year, we should technically not incur any interest (or very little interest) for the year. On the other hand, if we had not paid down that debt until the very last day of the year, we should have incurred a full year of interest. Of course, if we know exactly when the debt is paid down, we can adjust accordingly, but assuming we do not have that information readily available, we take an average as a simplifying assumption.

So 2021 interest expense on the short-term borrowings is:

Average (2021 Short-Term Borrowings (Beginning of Year), 2021 Short-Term Borrowings (End of Year)) × 2021 Interest Rate

2021 Short-Term Debt Interest Expense (Cell G16)

Excel Keystrokes	Description
type "="	Enters into "formula" mode
type "average("	Creates the "Average" formula
select cell G12	2021 Short-Term Debt (Beginning of Year)
type ","	Separates the two values we want to average
select cell G15	2021 Short-Term Debt (End of Year)
type ")"	Closes the "Average" formula
type "*"	Multiplies
select cell G17	2021 Interest Rate
type "Enter"	End
Formula Result	= AVERAGE(G12, G15)*G17

This gives us 467.3. We can copy this formula to the right. (See Table 7.3)

Long-Term Debt

We can now move on to the next debt: the long-term debt. In order to build this out, we need to repeat the exact same process as what we have done with the short-term borrowings.

The 2021 long-term debt (beginning of year) is the same value as the ending balance of debt from the year before. So:

2021 Long-Term Debt Due within One Year (Beginning of Year) = 2020 Long-Term Debt Due within One Year (End of Year)

Or, in cell G19, we will have "=F22." We can copy this to the right.

We can make the mandatory and non-mandatory issuances "0" for now, and we can calculate the long-term debt due within one year (end of year), which will be:

2020 Long-Term Debt Due within One Year (End of Year) = 2020 Long-Term Debt Due within One Year (Beginning of Year) + Mandatory Issuances/(Retirements) + Non-Mandatory Issuances/(Retirements)

Or,

Cell G22 would be "=SUM(G19:G21)."

Debt Interest   Before calculating the interest expense, we need to estimate the interest rate. Notice in Figure 7.1 that there is a table of "effective interest rates" for various notes with various securities. Although not ideal, we could use this table along with the posted December 2020 values, to calculate a weighted average interest rate. So you'll note, for example, the first line shows "2012 Notes issuance of $3.0 billion" with a 2.66% effective interest rate and a $1,250 December 31, 2020, estimated value. Next, we have a "2014 Notes issuance of $6.0 billion." However, here we have been given an effective interest rate range of 3.43–5.11%. So the question is, what percentage should we utilize to calculate our weighted average? For now, let's take the maximum rate in each note, as I prefer conservative estimates. Note that this may produce interest values that are too high, and if so, we can shift our estimates down later. We will know once we have calculated our values and compared them to the prior years. In order to estimate the overall interest, we can first calculate the interest on each individual note. (See Table 7.4.)

TABLE 7.3 Projected Short-Term Borrowings

Debt Schedule (in US$ millions except per share amounts)

Period Ending December 31	Actuals			Estimates				
	2018A	2019A	2020A	2021E	2022E	2023E	2024E	2025E
Cash Available to Pay Down Debt								
Cash at beginning of year								
Cash flow before debt paydown								
Minimum cash cushion								
Total Cash Available to Pay Down Debt								
Short-term Debt / Revolver								
Short-term debt (beginning of year)				16,115.0	16,115.0	16,115.0	16,115.0	16,115.0
Mandatory issuances / (retirements)				0.0	0.0	0.0	0.0	0.0
Non-mandatory issuances / (retirements)				0.0	0.0	0.0	0.0	0.0
Short-term Debt (End of Year)			16,115.0	16,115.0	16,115.0	16,115.0	16,115.0	16,115.0
Short-term interest expense				467.3	467.3	467.3	467.3	467.3
Short-term interest rate				2.9%	2.9%	2.9%	2.9%	2.9%

TABLE 7.4 Estimated Interest Calculation

Note Value ($MM)	Interest (%)	Interest ($MM)
1,250	2.66%	33.25
5,000	5.11%	255.50
16,000	4.33%	692.80
10,000	2.77%	277.00
338	3.00%	10.14
586	2.90%	16.99
33,174		1,285.68

Looking at the notes in Figure 7.1, we were able to find the 3.0% rate on the "Credit Facility" of 338 and the 2.9% rate on the "Other long-term debt" of 586.

In Table 7.4, we simply multiplied the note value by the interest rate to get the implied interest. We then totaled the note value ($33,174) and the interest expense ($1,285.68). If we divide these totals, we will get the implied interest rate of 3.88% (1,285.68/33,174). We can hardcode 3.88% into cell G24 and copy to the right. Now we can calculate the interest expense in 2021.

2021 Long-Term Debt Interest Expense (Cell G23)

Excel Keystrokes	Description
type "="	Enters into "formula" mode
type "average("	Creates the "Average" formula
select cell G19	2021 Long-Term Debt (Beginning of Year)
type "," "	Separates the two values we want to average
select cell G22	2021 Long-Term Debt (End of Year)
type ")"	Closes the "average" formula
type "*"	Multiplies
select cell G24	2021 Interest Rate
type "Enter"	End
Formula Result	=AVERAGE(G19, G22)*G24

We can copy this formula to the right. (See Table 7.5.)

Long-Term Lease Liabilities

We can now move on to the long-term lease liabilities. We can again have cell G26 link to cell F29. Cell G27 and cell G28 will remain "0." Cell G29 will be "=SUM(G26:G28)" and we can now calculate the interest expense.

TABLE 7.5 Projected Long-Term Debt

Debt Schedule (in US$ millions except per share amounts)

Period Ending December 31	Actuals			Estimates				
	2018A	2019A	2020A	2021E	2022E	2023E	2024E	2025E
Long-Term Debt								
Long-term debt (beginning of year)				31,816.0	31,816.0	31,816.0	31,816.0	31,816.0
Mandatory issuances / (retirements)				0.0	0.0	0.0	0.0	0.0
Non-mandatory issuances / (retirements)				0.0	0.0	0.0	0.0	0.0
Long-Term Debt (End of Year)			31,816.0	31,816.0	31,816.0	31,816.0	31,816.0	31,816.0
Long-term interest expense				1,234.5	1,234.5	1,234.5	1,234.5	1,234.5
Long-term interest rate				*3.88%*	*3.88%*	*3.88%*	*3.88%*	*3.88%*

TABLE 7.6 Projected Long-Term Lease Liabilities

Debt Schedule (in US$ millions except per share amounts)

Period Ending December 31	Actuals			Estimates				
	2018A	2019A	2020A	2021E	2022E	2023E	2024E	2025E
Long-term Lease Liabilities								
Long-term lease liabilities (beginning of year)				52,573.0	52,573.0	52,573.0	52,573.0	52,573.0
Mandatory issuances / (retirements)				0.0	0.0	0.0	0.0	0.0
Non-mandatory issuances / (retirements)				0.0	0.0	0.0	0.0	0.0
Long-term Lease Liabilities (End of Year)			52,573.0	52,573.0	52,573.0	52,573.0	52,573.0	52,573.0
Long-term lease liabilities interest expense				1,104.0	1,104.0	1,104.0	1,104.0	1,104.0
Long-term lease liabilities interest rate				2.10%	2.10%	2.10%	2.10%	2.10%

We can refer back to Figure 7.2, which contains the lease rates. Here we can see the stated rate for finance leases as of December 31, 2020, is 2.1%. So we can use this rate as a proxy to calculate our interest, hardcoding 2.1% into cell G31.

We can now calculate the interest expense in cell G30.

2021 Long-Term Lease Liabilities Interest Expense (Cell G30)

Excel Keystrokes	Description
type "="	Enters into "formula" mode
type "average("	Creates the "Average" formula
select cell G26	2021 Long-term lease liabilities (Beginning of Year)
type ," "	Separates the two values we want to average
select cell G29	2021 Long-term lease liabilities (end of year)
type ")"	Closes the "average" formula
type " * "	Multiplies
select cell G31	2021 Interest Rate
type "Enter"	End
Formula Result	=AVERAGE(G26, G29)*G31

We can copy the complete section from cell G26 through cell G31 to the right. (See Table 7.6.)

If you notice, there is a pattern in the formulae for each debt, containing six rows from the beginning balance of debt through to the interest rate. As a shortcut, we can copy the formulae of these six rows from the previous debt down to the next debts, and all we would have to do from there is make minor adjustments to the interest rate and the issuances rows.

Total Issuances/(Retirements)

We can now move on to "Total issuances/(retirements)" (row 32). As stated, this is a sum of all of the mandatory and non-mandatory issuances and retirements from the debts already mentioned. So, cell G32 is "=G13+G14 +G20+G21+G27+G28." The value will be zero for now. We can copy this to the right.

Total Interest Expense

Row 33 ("Total interest expense") is the sum of the interests. Cell G33 is "=G16+G23+G30." This gives us $2,805.8.

Cash Available to Pay Down Debt

We can now consider the cash. Note the ending balance of cash that we had pulled in to cell F34. As we had done with the debts, this will link into the cash at the beginning of the year (Cell G7). Cell G7 will read "=F34." We can copy this to the right.

Cash flow before debt paydown is a measure of all cash generated or paid, excluding cash raised or paid for debts. It is important for us to get a proper measure of cash, excluding cash related to debts, because in the debt schedule we want to determine how much cash we can use to pay down debts. At the bottom of the cash flow statement, in row 40, is the line item "Cash flow before debt paydown." In order to calculate this, we need to sum everything in the cash flow statement that is not related to debts. We exclude:

- Short-term borrowings (repayments)
- Long-term borrowings (repayments)
- Principal repayments of finance leases
- Principal repayments of financing obligations

The formula in cell G40 of the cash flow statement will be "=G22+G30+G37."

We are only concerned with the projected years, so we begin with 2021 and we can copy to the right. Take care to include the "Effect of exchange rate on cash," which is easy to accidentally leave out.

Note: It may seem like we simply excluded the entire Cash flow from financing activities section but oftentimes there are other line items within the financing activities section that are not related to debts. In such cases, we would also add in those financing activities line items that are not related to debts. Also, some believe we can simply take the total change in cash and cash equivalents and subtract the previously mentioned debts. Although that is mathematically correct, doing so in the model would create a second circular reference. It is better to sum as before and exclude them from the formula altogether. (See Table 7.7.)

We can now link this into the row 8 of debt schedule. G8 in the debt schedule is "='Cash Flow Statement'!G40" and we can copy this to the right.

Minimum cash is the minimum cash balance a company maintains at the end of the year. There could be several reasons why a company would want to maintain a minimum cash balance. First, it is a safety cushion in order to avoid a potential cash shortfall. Second, lenders often require a company to maintain a minimum balance in order to ensure principal and interest payments are made. Projecting the minimum cash balance can vary from company to company. Minimum cash balances might be calculated as a percentage of sales, operating capital, or total cash, or it can be the

TABLE 7.7 Projected Cash Flow before Debt Paydown

Consolidated Statements of Cash Flows (in US$ millions except per share amounts)

| Period Ending December 31 | Actuals | | | Estimates | | | | |
	2018A	2019A	2020A	2021E	2022E	2023E	2024E	2025E
SUPPLEMENTAL DATA:								
Cash flow before debt paydown				9,651.6	15,434.2	26,945.8	16,009.5	27,522.6

collateral stated in the company's debt contracts that a company must maintain. It is not the most significant of projections, but we do recommend researching how the company has come up with its minimum cash balance for clues. Notice that Amazon had $42.12Bn of cash on its balance sheet in 2020, so it is unlikely facing a cash shortfall unless there has been a major company event. So we are not surprised that further research on minimum cash does not reveal much information. The company's cash balance the prior year was $36.0Bn; so the cash balance is increasing. We can for now assume the company does not want a drop in cash balance, so let's put the minimum cash balance at $40Bn. This is a safe assumption but this suggests that if we want to start running scenarios on the model, we do not want the balance of cash to drop below its current levels, which is a plausible truth. We can always change this if needed. So, we can enter –40,000 into cell G9 of the debt schedule. We enter the value as a negative number because we want to remove the minimum cash balance from the cash we can use to pay down debts. So the total cash available to pay down debt is a sum of the cash at the beginning of the year and the cash flow before debt paydown, less the minimum cushion, or "=SUM(G7:G9)."

The total cash available to pay down debt is the amount of cash that's arguably free to utilize. Should a company decide to manage its business as such, it can conceivably utilize all those funds to pay down debts in order to save on interest payments. However, it is important to note that not all debts can be paid at will without penalty.

We can now calculate "Cash at the end of the year" at the bottom of the debt schedule in row 34. We calculate cash at the end of the year by first starting with "Cash at the beginning of the year" and then adding to it "Cash flow before debt paydown" and "Total issuances and retirements." This confuses many, but think about the fact that we want to capture a complete measure of cash from the beginning of the period to the end of the period, including capturing cash payments or issuances from debt paydowns. We first want to begin with "Cash at the beginning of the year, " as we have done with any continuous balance, such as the debts. We then want to add all of the cash generated during the year. The "Cash flow before debt paydown" is the closest measure of that on this particular sheet. So we have all cash except for cash raised or paid for debts. This is located in total issuances/retirements. It is often confused that we need to subtract interest here, but once linked in properly, interest will already be included in this calculation. We will discuss this next. So the formula for "Cash at the end of the year" is:

Cash at the Beginning of the Year + Cash Flow before Debt Paydown
+ Total Issuances and Retirements

Or, in cell G34, "=G7+G8+G32."
We can copy this to the right. See Table 7.8.

TABLE 7.8 Projected Total Cash Available to Pay Down Debt

Debt Schedule (in US$ millions except per share amounts)

Period Ending December 31	Actuals			Estimates				
	2018A	2019A	2020A	2021E	2022E	2023E	2024E	2025E
Cash Available to Pay Down Debt								
Cash at beginning of year				42,122.0	51,773.6	67,207.8	94,153.6	110,163.1
Cash flow before debt paydown				9,651.6	15,434.2	26,945.8	16,009.5	27,522.6
Minimum cash cushion				(40,000.0)	(40,000.0)	(40,000.0)	(40,000.0)	(40,000.0)
Total Cash Available to Pay Down Debt				11,773.6	27,207.8	54,153.6	70,163.1	97,685.7

Interest Income

Now that we have a value of cash at the end of the year, we can calculate interest income. Interest income is commonly the income received from cash held in savings accounts, certificates of deposits, and other investments.

As done with interest expense, we can take the average balance of the cash at the beginning of the year and the cash at the end of the year and multiply by some interest rate. So, interest income is:

$$\text{Average (Cash at the beginning of the year,}$$
$$\text{Cash at the end of the year)} \times \text{Interest Rate}$$

Before calculating the actual value, we need an interest income rate. A word search on "interest rate" reveals Figure 7.3 from page 33 of the 10K.

Figure 7.3 lists all of the company's investments made with "Cash equivalents and marketable fixed income securities." We can utilize this table to create a weighted average interest rate by first multiplying the fair values of each security by the respective interest rate as we had done with the debt. (See Table 7.9).

This gives us 362.08. We divide these totals we to get a new implied interest rate of 0.49% (362.08/73,933).

We can hardcode "0.49%" into cell G36 and copy to the right. We can now proceed with calculating the interest income.

2021 Interest Income (Cell G35)

Excel Keystrokes	Description
Type "="	Enters into "formula" mode
Type "average("	Creates the "Average" formula
Select cell G7	2021 Cash at Beginning of Year
Type ","	Separates the two values we want to average
Select cell G34	2021 Cash at the End of Year
Type ")"	Closes the "Average" formula
Type "*"	Multiplies
Select cell G36	2021 Interest Rate
Type "Enter"	End
Formula Result	=AVERAGE(G7, G34)*G36

	2021	2022	2023	2024	2025	Thereafter	Total	Estimated Fair Value as of December 31, 2020
Money market funds	$ 27,430	$ —	$ —	$ —	$ —	$ —	$ 27,430	$ 27,430
Weighted average interest rate	(0.16)%	— %	— %	— %	— %	— %	(0.16)%	
Corporate debt securities	16,505	4,459	5,531	1,990	886	—	29,371	29,988
Weighted average interest rate	0.42 %	1.65 %	1.32 %	1.86 %	1.84 %	—	0.92 %	
U.S. government and agency securities	5,439	587	899	298	67	71	7,361	7,439
Weighted average interest rate	0.30 %	1.38 %	1.12 %	1.74 %	1.13 %	2.97 %	0.58 %	
Asset-backed securities	870	773	472	763	243	46	3,167	3,235
Weighted average interest rate	2.08 %	2.00 %	1.53 %	2.13 %	1.57 %	1.25 %	1.94 %	
Foreign government and agency securities	4,932	147	45	3	—	—	5,127	5,131
Weighted average interest rate	0.25 %	0.74 %	1.28 %	1.76 %	— %	— %	0.28 %	
Other fixed income securities	109	156	230	160	43	—	698	710
Weighted average interest rate	2.10 %	1.85 %	1.10 %	0.84 %	1.31 %	— %	1.38 %	
Cash equivalents and marketable fixed income securities	$ 55,285	$ 6,122	$ 7,177	$ 3,214	$ 1,239	$ 117	$ 73,154	$ 73,933

FIGURE 7.3 Interest Rates

TABLE 7.9   Estimated Interest Income Rate Calculation

Note Value ($MM)	Interest(%)	Interest ($MM)
27,430	(0.16)%	(43.89)
29,988	0.92%	275.89
7,439	0.58%	43.15
3,235	1.94%	62.76
5,131	0.28%	14.37
710	1.38%	9.80
73,933		362.08

We can now link the interest expense and interest income into the income statement. Rows 38 and 39 in the income statement still have yet to be properly linked. So, G38 on the income statement will be

"='Debt Schedule'!G33."

We can copy this to the right.

Finally we can link the interest income in from the debt schedule. We will, however, link the interest income in as a negative value. Although a little confusing, Amazon lists its interest income as a negative value, as the income nets against interest expenses to create a total net value. In other words:

Net Interest Expense = Interest Expense + – Interest Income
(plus negative interest income)

Some companies will show interest income as a positive value, but then we would need to have the net interest expense line be Interest Expense – Interest Income. It is important to double-check how these items are flowing in the historical numbers to make sure our projections are correct. So we can link interest income into the income statement in cell G39:

"=-'Debt Schedule'!G35."

We can copy this to the right.

We finally have a complete representation of the income statement. (See Table 7.10.)

TABLE 7.10 Amazon Projected Income Statement with Interest

Consolidated Income Statements (in US$ millions except per share amounts)

Period Ending December 31	Actuals			Estimates				
	2018A	2019A	2020A	2021E	2022E	2023E	2024E	2025E
Revenue								
Net product sales	141,915.0	160,408.0	215,915.0					
Y/Y growth (%)		13.0%	34.6%					
Net service sales	90,972.0	120,114.0	170,149.0					
Y/Y growth (%)		32.0%	41.7%					
Total Net Sales	232,887.0	280,522.0	386,064.0	490,301.3	581,497.3	656,006.5	713,912.0	757,323.5
Y/Y net sales growth (%)		20.5%	37.6%	27.0%	18.6%	12.8%	8.8%	6.1%
Y/Y growth (%) decline				*(28.2%)*	*(31.1%)*	*(31.1%)*	*(31.1%)*	*(31.1%)*
Cost of Goods Sold								
Cost of Goods Sold	139,156.0	165,536.0	233,307.0	296,299.9	351,411.7	396,439.2	431,432.8	457,667.3
COGS as a % of net sales	59.8%	59.0%	60.4%	60.4%	60.4%	60.4%	60.4%	60.4%
Gross Profit	93,731.0	114,986.0	152,757.0	194,001.4	230,085.6	259,567.3	282,479.2	299,656.2
Gross profit margin (%)	40%	41%	40%	40%	40%	40%	40%	40%
Operating Expenses								
Fulfillment	34,027.0	40,232.0	58,517.0	74,316.6	88,139.5	99,433.1	108,210.0	114,790.0
Fulfillment as a % of net sales	14.6%	14.3%	15.2%	15.2%	15.2%	15.2%	15.2%	15.2%
Technology and content	13,496.0	14,142.0	17,489.0	22,211.0	26,342.3	29,717.6	32,340.8	34,307.3

(Continued)

TABLE 7.10 (Continued)

Consolidated Income Statements (in US$ millions except per share amounts)

Period Ending December 31	Actuals			Estimates				
	2018A	2019A	2020A	2021E	2022E	2023E	2024E	2025E
Technology and content as a % of net sales	*5.8%*	*5.0%*	*4.5%*	*4.5%*	*4.5%*	*4.5%*	*4.5%*	*4.5%*
Marketing	13,814.0	18,878.0	22,008.0	27,950.2	33,148.9	37,396.4	40,697.3	43,172.1
Marketing as a % of net sales	*5.9%*	*6.7%*	*5.7%*	*5.7%*	*5.7%*	*5.7%*	*5.7%*	*5.7%*
General and administrative	4,336.0	5,203.0	6,668.0	8,468.4	10,043.5	11,330.4	12,330.5	13,080.3
General and administrative as a % of net sales	*1.9%*	*1.9%*	*1.7%*	*1.7%*	*1.7%*	*1.7%*	*1.7%*	*1.7%*
Other operating expense (income), net	296.0	201.0	(75.0)	(95.3)	(113.0)	(127.4)	(138.7)	(147.1)
Other operating expense as a % of net sales	*0.1%*	*0.1%*	*0.0%*	*0.0%*	*0.0%*	*0.0%*	*0.0%*	*0.0%*
Total Operating Expenses	65,969.0	78,656.0	104,607.0	132,850.9	157,561.2	177,750.0	193,439.9	205,202.6
EBITDA	27,762.0	36,330.0	48,150.0	61,150.5	72,524.5	81,817.3	89,039.3	94,453.6
EBITDA margin (%)	*11.9%*	*13.0%*	*12.5%*	*12.5%*	*12.5%*	*12.5%*	*12.5%*	*12.5%*
Depreciation and amortization	15,341.0	21,789.0	25,251.0	28,669.8	35,841.6	43,932.4	52,737.3	62,077.6
EBIT	12,421.0	14,541.0	22,899.0	32,480.7	36,682.8	37,884.9	36,302.0	32,375.9
EBIT margin (%)	*5.3%*	*5.2%*	*5.9%*	*6.6%*	*6.3%*	*5.8%*	*5.1%*	*4.3%*
Other Income	183.0	(203.0)	(2,371.0)	183.0	(203.0)	183.0	(203.0)	183.0

Interest

Interest expense	1,417.0	1,600.0	1,647.0	2,805.8	2,805.8	2,805.8	2,805.8	2,805.8
Interest income	(440.0)	(832.0)	(555.0)	(225.0)	(276.6)	(370.8)	(466.8)	(564.6)
Net Interest Expense	977.0	768.0	1,092.0	2,580.8	2,529.2	2,435.0	2,339.0	2,241.2
Earnings before Tax (EBT)	11,261.0	13,976.0	24,178.0	29,716.9	34,356.6	35,266.9	34,166.0	29,951.7
EBT margin (%)	*4.8%*	*5.0%*	*6.3%*	*6.1%*	*5.9%*	*5.4%*	*4.8%*	*4.0%*
Income tax expense	1,197.0	2,374.0	2,863.0	6,240.5	7,214.9	7,406.1	7,174.9	6,289.9
All-in effective tax rate (%)	*10.6%*	*17.0%*	*11.8%*	*21.0%*	*21.0%*	*21.0%*	*21.0%*	*21.0%*
Net Income from Continuing Operations	10,064.0	11,602.0	21,315.0	23,476.3	27,141.7	27,860.9	26,991.1	23,661.9
Non-Recurring Events								
Discontinued operations	0.0	0.0	0.0	0.0	0.0	0.0	0.0	0.0
Extraordinary items	0.0	0.0	0.0	0.0	0.0	0.0	0.0	0.0
Effect of accounting changes	0.0	0.0	0.0	0.0	0.0	0.0	0.0	0.0
Other items	0.0	0.0	0.0	0.0	0.0	0.0	0.0	0.0
Total Non-Recurring Events	0.0	0.0	0.0	0.0	0.0	0.0	0.0	0.0
Net Income (after Non-Recurring Events)	10,064.0	11,602.0	21,315.0	23,476.3	27,141.7	27,860.9	26,991.1	23,661.9
Income attributable to equity method investments	(9.0)	14.0	(16.0)	(9.0)	14.0	(16.0)	(9.0)	14.0
Dividends paid on common stock	0.0	0.0	0.0	0.0	0.0	0.0	0.0	0.0

(Continued)

229

TABLE 7.10 (*Continued*)

Consolidated Income Statements (in US$ millions except per share amounts)

Period Ending December 31	Actuals			Estimates				
	2018A	2019A	2020A	2021E	2022E	2023E	2024E	2025E
Net Income (As Reported)	10,073.0	11,588.0	21,331.0	23,485.3	27,127.7	27,876.9	27,000.1	23,647.9
Earnings per Share (EPS)								
Basic	20.68	23.46	42.66	46.57	53.79	55.28	53.54	46.89
Diluted	20.15	22.99	41.83	45.22	52.24	53.68	51.99	45.54
Average Common Shares Outstanding								
Basic	487	494	500	504	504	504	504	504
Diluted	500	504	510	519	519	519	519	519

Notice that once the interest expense and interest income are linked in, the values have changed. Interest income, for example, has lowered to $225. This is normal and due to the circular reference created when linking these items through. (We will discuss this in the next section.)

We have one final set of links left before the model is complete. We still need to link the debt payments and issuances into the financing activities of the cash flow statement from the debt schedule. Each debt in the debt schedule contains rows reflecting any issuance or payments made. These should be reflected in the financing activities in the cash flow statement. For example, row 32 of the cash flow statement contains "Short-term borrowings (repayments)." This should be linked in from the issuances/(retirements) line items in the short-term debt section of the debt schedule, both the mandatory and non-mandatory. So, cell G32 in the cash flow statement should be

"='Debt Schedule'!G13 + 'Debt Schedule'!G14"

We can copy this formula to the right.

Similarly the next line on the cash flow statement, "Long-term borrowings (repayments)," should be linked in from the issuances/(retirements) line items in the long-term debt section of the debt schedule, both the mandatory and non-mandatory. So, cell G33 should be

"='Debt Schedule'!G20 + 'Debt Schedule'!G21"

We can copy this formula to the right and continue with "Principal repayments of finance leases," cell G34. This should be "='Debt Schedule'!G27+'Debt Schedule'!G28." We can copy this to the right. Notice that there is one more item in the cash flow statement, "Principal repayments of financing obligations." We had originally linked this line item into the "Other liabilities" as there was no better place that fit. But now as we are discussing the debt schedule, we can create a more accurate "home" for this item. We should first add a line item to the balance sheet called "Financing obligations," then add a respective section to the debt schedule.

So let's go to the "Balance sheet" tab and add a row underneath the "Long-term debt." So in cell D27 we can hit "Shift" + "Space Bar" to highlight the entire row, then hit "Ctrl" + "+" (or "Ctrl" + "Shift" + "=") to add a row. We can now label row 27 as "Financing obligations." We can hardcode "0" for the historical years, D27 and E27; the projected years will build

TABLE 7.11 Amazon Updated Liabilities

Consolidated Balance Sheets (in US$ millions except per share amounts)

On December 31	2019A	2020A	2021E	2022E	2023E	2024E	2025E
Liabilities				Estimates			
Current Liabilities							
Accounts payable	47,183.0	72,539.0	76,023.5	90,163.8	101,716.8	110,695.3	117,426.5
Accrued expenses and other	18,111.0	28,023.0	29,295.1	34,744.0	39,195.8	42,655.6	45,249.4
Short-term debt	14,328.0	16,115.0	16,115.0	16,115.0	16,115.0	16,115.0	16,115.0
Unearned revenue	8,190.0	9,708.0	11,365.2	13,479.2	15,206.3	16,548.5	17,554.8
Total Current Liabilities	**87,812.0**	**126,385.0**	**132,798.8**	**154,502.0**	**172,234.0**	**186,014.5**	**196,345.8**
Long-term lease liabilities	39,791.0	52,573.0	52,573.0	52,573.0	52,573.0	52,573.0	52,573.0
Long-term debt	23,414.0	31,816.0	31,816.0	31,816.0	31,816.0	31,816.0	31,816.0
Financing obligations	0.0	0.0	0.0	0.0	0.0	0.0	0.0
Other long-term liabilities	12,171.0	17,017.0	16,463.0	15,909.0	15,355.0	14,801.0	14,247.0
Total Liabilities	**163,188.0**	**227,791.0**	**233,650.8**	**254,800.0**	**271,978.0**	**285,204.5**	**294,981.8**

off of the cash flow statement. So, F27 will read "=E27+'Cash Flow Statement'!G35." We now need to remove the reference to cell G35 from the Other Liabilites line item to avoid any double counting. So Balance Sheet Cell F26 will now read "=E26+'Cash Flow Statement'!G33". This can be copied to the right.

Since we added this new row, it's important to make sure all of the totals below this row include this new line item, so double check that "Total liabilities" includes this new row in the total. (See Table 7.11.)

Note: Ideally we would be able to dig up a historical value for the financing obligations. Like with the short-term debt, we assume it must be buried in another long-term liability line item, likely "*Other* long-term liabilities." Sure enough, a word search on "Financing obligations" reveals the following note from page 50 of the 10K:

Included in "Other long-term liabilities" on our consolidated balance sheets are liabilities primarily related to financing obligations, asset retirement obligations, deferred tax liabilities, unearned revenue, tax contingencies, and digital video and music content.

This note proves financing obligations has in fact been consolidated into the "Other long-term liabilities" line item, but it doesn't reveal the value. So, we will have to leave this at zero for now until we obtain more information.

We can now add a "Financing obligations" section to the debt schedule. Toggling over to the "Debt schedule" tab, we first need to add an entire section, seven rows, below the "Long-term lease liabilities" section. So in row 32 we can hit "shift" + "space bar" to highlight the entire row, then hit "Ctrl" + "+" (or "Ctrl" + "Shift" + "="), seven times to add a placeholder for the section.

For efficiency, we can copy the entire "Long-term lease liabilities" section into here and change the label to "Financing obligations." We can go up to row 25, hit "shift" + "space bar" to highlight the entire row, then while holding down "shift" tap the down arrow six times to highlight the entire section. Copy this section by using "Ctrl" + "c." Move down to row 32, then hit "Ctrl" + "v" to paste. We now have copied the entire "Long-term lease liabilities" section. Now change every instance of "Long-term lease liabilities" in this section to "Financing obligations."

We need to make some adjustments to the balances, starting with cell F36, the end-of-year financing obligations balance. This should come from the balance sheet, so cell F36 should be "='Balance Sheet'!E27." Because the structure of each debt section is relatively identical, nothing else needs to be

TABLE 7.12 Amazon Updated Cash Flow from Financing Activities

Consolidated Statements of Cash Flows (in US$ millions except per share amounts)

Period Ending December 31	Actuals			Estimates				
	2018A	2019A	2020A	2021E	2022E	2023E	2024E	2025E
Cash Flows from Financing Activities								
Short-term borrowings (repayments)	73.0	(116.0)	619.0	0.0	0.0	0.0	0.0	0.0
Long-term borrowings (repayments)	27.0	(295.0)	8,972.0	0.0	0.0	0.0	0.0	0.0
Principal repayments of finance leases	(7,449.0)	(9,628.0)	(10,642.0)	0.0	0.0	0.0	0.0	0.0
Principal repayments of financing obligations	(337.0)	(27.0)	(53.0)	0.0	0.0	0.0	0.0	0.0
Total Cash from Financing Activities	(7,686.0)	(10,066.0)	(1,104.0)	0.0	0.0	0.0	0.0	0.0
Foreign Currency Effect on Cash, Cash Equivalents, and Restricted Cash	(351.0)	70.0	618.0	(351.0)	70.0	618.0	(351.0)	70.0
Total Change in Cash and Cash Equivalents	10,317.0	4,327.0	5,967.0	7,612.8	13,436.1	25,022.2	14,161.7	25,752.1

changed; we must now just be sure the interest expense and total issuance and retirements totals include the respective items from this section. So, we need to add the two new "issuances / (retirements)" lines from this new section into the "Total issuances / (retirements)" row 39. So G39 will now read "=G13+G14+G20+G21+G27+G28+G34+G35." Copy this to the right. We also need to be sure the new interest expense (even though it's "0") totals into the "Total interest expense" line. So G40 will now read "=G16+G23+ G30+G37."

We can now go back to the cash flow statement and finalize linking all of our debt issuances / (retirements) in from the debt schedule. Since we now have financing obligations, we can link the financing obligations issuances / (retirements) into cell G35 from the debt schedule. So, Cash flow statement cell G35 will read "='Debt Schedule'!G34+'Debt Schedule'!G35." We can copy this to the right. (See Table 7.12.)

Now that the debt schedule is fully linked, we can make sure our final "match" checks out. Row 44 in the debt schedule checks to make sure the cash at the end of the year matches the cash at the top of the balance sheet. This match is important because we are effectively calculating cash two different ways in the model. The balance sheet cash is calculated from the prior year's balance sheet cash balance plus changes in cash from the cash flow statement. However, the cash at the end of the year on the debt schedule is calculated from the cash balance at the beginning of the year at top of the debt schedule, then adding in cash flow before debt paydown and issuances and retirements. The point of this is to ensure we have the debt issuances/ (retirements), interest expense, and interest income wired in correctly. (See Table 7.13.)

CIRCULAR REFERENCES

In a fully linked model, there is one major, yet important circular reference flowing through the statements. This circular reference is related to the debt and interest. Specifically, if debt is raised in the debt schedule, cash at the end of the year will increase and therefore interest income will increase. As interest income links to the income statement, net income is increased. That net income increase flows to the top of the cash flow statement, and increases cash and, more importantly, "Cash flow before debt paydown" at the bottom of the cash flow statement. This cash flow before debt paydown links to the debt schedule and increases the cash available to pay down debt, and therefore increases the cash at the end of the year, which increases the interest income, and so on.

TABLE 7.18 Projected Debt Schedule

Debt Schedule (in US$ millions except per share amounts)

	Actuals			Estimates				
Period Ending December 31	2018A	2019A	2020A	2021E	2022E	2023E	2024E	2025E
Cash Available to Pay Down Debt								
Cash at beginning of year				42,122.0	49,734.8	63,170.9	88,193.1	102,354.8
Cash flow before debt paydown				7,612.8	13,436.1	25,022.2	14,161.7	25,752.1
Minimum cash cushion				(40,000.0)	(40,000.0)	(40,000.0)	(40,000.0)	(40,000.0)
Total Cash Available to Pay Down Debt				9,734.8	23,170.9	48,193.1	62,354.8	88,106.8
Short-term Debt / Revolver								
Short-term debt (beginning of year)				16,115.0	16,115.0	16,115.0	16,115.0	16,115.0
Mandatory issuances / (retirements)				0.0	0.0	0.0	0.0	0.0
Non-mandatory issuances / (retirements)				0.0	0.0	0.0	0.0	0.0
Short-term Debt (End of Year)			16,115.0	16,115.0	16,115.0	16,115.0	16,115.0	16,115.0
Short-term interest expense				467.3	467.3	467.3	467.3	467.3
Short-term interest rate				*2.9%*	*2.9%*	*2.9%*	*2.9%*	*2.9%*
Long-term Debt								
Long-term debt (beginning of year)				31,816.0	31,816.0	31,816.0	31,816.0	31,816.0
Mandatory issuances / (retirements)				0.0	0.0	0.0	0.0	0.0
Non-mandatory issuances / (retirements)				0.0	0.0	0.0	0.0	0.0

Long-term Debt (End of Year)	31,816.0	31,816.0	31,816.0	31,816.0	31,816.0	31,816.0
Long-term interest expense		1,234.5	1,234.5	1,234.5	1,234.5	1,234.5
Long-term interest rate		*3.88%*	*3.88%*	*3.88%*	*3.88%*	*3.88%*
Long-term Lease Liabilities						
Long-term lease liabilities (beginning of year)		52,573.0	52,573.0	52,573.0	52,573.0	52,573.0
Mandatory issuances / (retirements)		0.0	0.0	0.0	0.0	0.0
Non-mandatory issuances / (retirements)		0.0	0.0	0.0	0.0	0.0
Long-term Lease Liabilities (End of Year)	52,573.0	52,573.0	52,573.0	52,573.0	52,573.0	52,573.0
Long-term lease liabilities interest expense		1,104.0	1,104.0	1,104.0	1,104.0	1,104.0
Long-term lease liabilities interest rate		*2.10%*	*2.10%*	*2.10%*	*2.10%*	*2.10%*
Financing Obligations						
Financing obligations (beginning of year)		0.0	0.0	0.0	0.0	0.0
Mandatory issuances / (retirements)		0.0	0.0	0.0	0.0	0.0

(Continued)

TABLE 7.13 (*Continued*)

Debt Schedule (in US$ millions except per share amounts)

Period Ending December 31	Actuals			Estimates				
	2018A	2019A	2020A	2021E	2022E	2023E	2024E	2025E
Non-mandatory issuances / (retirements)				0.0	0.0	0.0	0.0	0.0
Financing Obligations (End of Year)			0.0		0.0	0.0	0.0	0.0
Financing obligations interest expense				0.0	0.0	0.0	0.0	0.0
Financing obligations interest rate				*2.10%*	*2.10%*	*2.10%*	*2.10%*	*2.10%*
Total Issuances / (Retirements)				0.0	0.0	0.0	0.0	0.0
Total Interest Expense				2,805.8	2,805.8	2,805.8	2,805.8	2,805.8
Cash at the End of the Year			42,122.0	49,734.8	63,170.9	88,193.1	102,354.8	128,106.8
Interest income				225.0	276.6	370.8	466.8	564.6
Interest rate				*0.49%*	*0.49%*	*0.49%*	*0.49%*	*0.49%*
Match? (Y/N)				Y	Y	Y	Y	Y

When this circular reference is created, an error message may pop up in Excel. Excel automatically assumes circular references in a model are errors. We need to adjust a setting in Excel to explain that we want the circular reference in the model. When doing so, we need to tell Excel how many of these circular iterations we want it to go through before stopping, as, theoretically, this loop can go on forever. If you go to "File," then "Options," an "Excel Options" box will open. (See Figure 7.4.)

You may have an older version of Excel where the menu options may look slightly different than what we have. If so, just search for "Excel Options" in the help section and you will be directed to the location of the pop-up box in Figure 7.4.

Once the setting box pops open, select "Formulas," which should reveal a "Calculation options" section. Within this section there should be a selection box titled "Enable iterative calculations." Checking this box allows circular references. Once the box is checked, we can tell Excel how many iterations we want Excel to cycle through. One hundred iterations are enough.

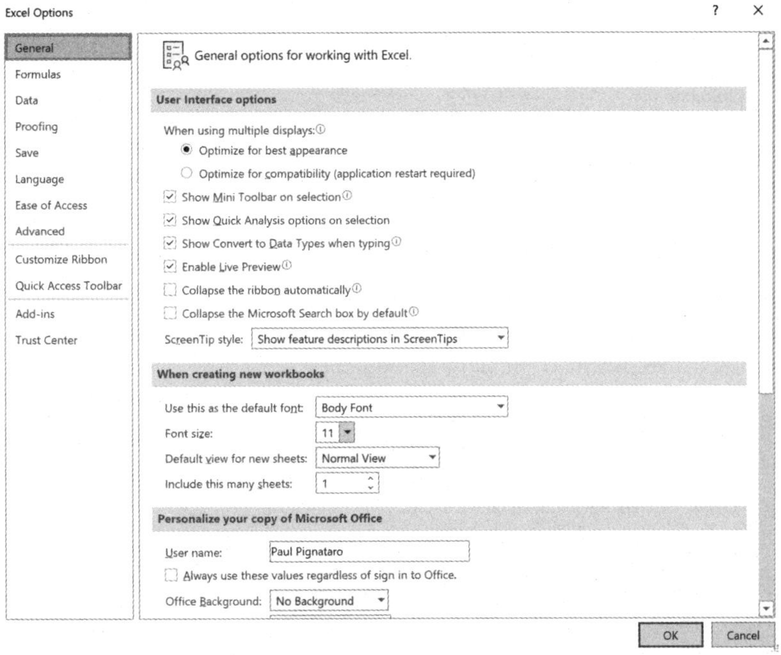

FIGURE 7.4   Excel Options

See the following example of raising $1,000 in debt. For purposes of explaining the circular reference, let's just focus on what happens to interest income.

Debt Schedule	
Cash beginning of year	0.0
Cash flow before debt paydown	0.0
Minimum cash	0.0
Long-term debt	
Beginning of year	0.0
Issuances	1,000.0
Interest (@10%)*	100.0
End of year	1,000.0
Cash at the end of the year	1,000.0
Interest income (@1%)*	10.0

*Note that we are trying to illustrate only the interest income flow, so let's ignore the interest expense for now. In order to keep this simple, we did not take the average of beginning and end of year.

Income Statement	
Interest income	10.0
Taxes (@ 40%)	(4.0)
Net Income	6.0

Cash Flow	
Net Income	6.0
Long-term debt issuance	1,000.0
Total Changes in Cash	1,006.0
Cash Flow before Debt Paydown	6.0

So, the interest income flows into the income statement and increases net income (after tax) by $6. Net income flows into the cash flow statement. With the $1,000 debt issuance, cash increases by $1,006. However, cash flow before debt paydown excludes the cash from debt issuance, so it only increases by $6. Back to the debt schedule:

Debt Schedule	
Cash beginning of year	0.0
Cash flow before debt paydown	6.0
Minimum cash	0.0
Long-term debt	
Beginning of year	0.0
Issuances	1,000.0
Interest (@10%)*	100.0

End of year	1,000.0
Cash at the end of the year	1,006.0
Interest income (@1%)*	10.1

*Again, we are trying to illustrate only the interest income flow so let's ignore the interest expense for now. In order to keep this simple, we did not take the average of beginning and end of year.

So because the cash flow before debt paydown has increased by an additional $6, the interest income has increased by $0.1 (really $0.06, but we rounded up to $0.1), and will flow back through the income statement and continue the cycle.

Let's take another example, but this time illustrating with interest expense on the debt.

If debt is paid down in the debt schedule, interest expense will decrease. As interest expense links to the income statement, a reduction in interest expense increases net income. That net income increase flows to the top of the cash flow statement, and increases cash and, more importantly, "Cash flow before debt paydown" at the bottom of the cash flow statement. This cash flow before debt paydown links to the debt schedule and increases the cash available to pay down debt. Based on the interest savings from paying down debt, we now have a little more cash we can use to pay down more debt. If we do so, interest expense will reduce further, which will reduce net income further, and the cycle will repeat.

See the following example of paying down $1,000 in debt. For purposes of explaining the circular reference, let's just focus on what happens to interest expense. We will also have to assume we had $1,000 of cash at the beginning of the year in order to pay down that $1,000 of debt:

Debt Schedule	
Cash beginning of year	1,000.0
Cash flow before debt paydown	0.0
Minimum cash	0.0
Long-term debt	
Beginning of year	1,000.0
Issuances	(1,000.0)
Interest (@10%)*	(100.0)
End of year	0.0
Cash at the end of the year	0.0
Interest Income (@1%)*	0.0

*We are illustrating the idea that interest expense has reduced by $100. In order to keep this simple, we did not take the average of beginning and end of year. We are also assuming no interest income to illustrate just the interest expense movements.

Income Statement			Cash Flow	
Interest Expense*	(100.0)	→	Net Income	60.0
Taxes (@ 40%)	40.0		Long-Term Debt Issuance	(1,000.0)
Net Income	**60.0**		**Total Changes in Cash**	**(940.0)**
			Cash Flow before Debt Paydown	60.0

*We are illustrating the idea that interest expense has reduced by $100. In order to keep this simple, we did not take the average of beginning and end of year. We are also assuming no interest income to illustrate just the interest expense movements.

So, the reduction in interest expense flows into the income statement and increases net income (after tax) by $60. Net income flows into the cash flow statement. With the $1,000 debt retirement, cash decreases by $940. However, cash flow before debt paydown excludes the cash from debt issuance, so it increases by $60. Now back to the debt schedule.

Debt Schedule	
Cash beginning of year	1,000.0
Cash flow before debt paydown	60.0
Minimum cash	0.0
Long-term debt	
Beginning of year	1,000.0
Issuances	(1,000.0)
Interest (@10%)*	(100.0)
End of year	0.0
Cash at the end of the year	**60.0**
Interest income (@1%)*	0.0

*Again, we are illustrating the idea that interest expense has reduced by $100. In order to keep this simple, we did not take the average of beginning and end of year. We are also assuming no interest income to illustrate just the interest expense movements.

We now have $60 more that we could use to pay down more debt. We can choose to pay down more debt if we had more debt, reduce interest expense further, which will flow back into the income statement, and repeat the cycle.

Technically, since the issuing and paying down of debt is hardcoded in the model, this particular loop is not an endless one. In other words, we have to manually adjust the paydown after each iteration. But we will later look at automatic paydown formulas, which will create an endless loop. Having the Excel iteration setting set to a number such as 100 will limit the iterations.

Circular Reference #Value! Errors

It can often happen at this point in the model that the whole model becomes riddled with #Value! or other errors. This is because of the circular reference and happens when a formula is accidentally mistyped in a cell that is connected to the circular loop. If a particular formula is mistyped in such a way that Excel thinks it is a string as opposed to a number, an error message is produced because Excel cannot make the calculation. If such an error message is produced in the circular reference loop, that error message is caught in the loop, and every cell in its path is affected.

You can try this (don't worry, we have a quick fix) by forcing a cell within the loop to be a string. We can type "test," for example, in one of the debt issuances cells, let's say G13 in the debt schedule. The model should now be filled with #Value! error messages. If you don't see the error messages right away, try hitting the "F9" key, which is a shortcut to recalculate the Excel model cells. (See Table 7.14.)

To repair this, we first need to identify where the error is and fix it. So let's change "test" back to "0." Although this fixes the original mistake, the errors still exist because that #Value! message is caught in the infinite loop. To repair this, we need to break the loop, allow Excel to recalculate as normal, and relink the loop. An easy way to do this is to look to the interest expense and interest income on the income statement (Income Statement tab rows 38, 39). (See Table 7.15.)

We can easily highlight and delete these rows, starting in cell G38, selecting the first row by holding down "Shift," tapping the space bar once, then selecting the other row by holding down "Shift" and tapping the arrow key down. We can now hit the "Delete" button to erase the row. Excel should recalculate as normal. At this point, instead of rebuilding the entire row, we can simply put those links back in by "undoing" the deletion or typing "Ctrl" + "Z." Everything should be back to normal. (See Table 7.16.)

AUTOMATIC DEBT PAYDOWNS

Earlier we discussed the reason for a "Non-mandatory issuances/(retirement)" line item is to automatically pay down debt if there happens to be excess cash, or to raise debt if there is some cash need. Not all businesses choose to or are allowed to pay down debt at will, but let's walk through how to enter such a formula into the model. First, it is important to explain the particular conditions we want such a formula to handle. We want to set up a series of logical conditions that essentially compares a debt balance with cash available to paydown debt. If we have more cash than debt, then we can pay down all of the debt; if we have less cash than debt, then we can only pay down as much cash as we have; if our cash balance is negative, then we need to raise debt to fulfill the cash need. Let's list these into a more formal set of logical conditions:

1. If cash available is negative, then we need to raise cash.
2. If cash available is positive, then:
   a. If cash available is greater than debt, then we can pay down the debt.
   b. If cash available is less than the debt, then we can only pay down as much cash as we have.

TABLE 7.14 Debt Schedule #Value! Error

Debt Schedule (in US$ millions except per share amounts)

Period Ending December 31	Actuals			Estimates				
	2018A	2019A	2020A	2021E	2022E	2023E	2024E	2025E
Cash Available to Pay Down Debt								
Cash at beginning of year				42,122.0	#VALUE!	#VALUE!	#VALUE!	#VALUE!
Cash flow before debt paydown				#VALUE!	#VALUE!	#VALUE!	#VALUE!	#VALUE!
Minimum cash cushion				(40,000.0)	(40,000.0)	(40,000.0)	(40,000.0)	(40,000.0)
Total Cash Available to Pay Down Debt				#VALUE!	#VALUE!	#VALUE!	#VALUE!	#VALUE!
Short-term Debt / Revolver								
Short-term debt (beginning of year)				16,115.0	16,115.0	16,115.0	16,115.0	16,115.0
Mandatory issuances / (retirements)				test	0.0	0.0	0.0	0.0
Non-mandatory issuances / (retirements)				0.0	0.0	0.0	0.0	0.0
Short-term Debt (End of Year)			16,115.0	16,115.0	16,115.0	16,115.0	16,115.0	16,115.0
Short-term interest expense				467.3	467.3	467.3	467.3	467.3
Short-term interest rate				*2.9%*	*2.9%*	*2.9%*	*2.9%*	*2.9%*

Long-term Debt

Long-term debt (beginning of year)	31,816.0	31,816.0	31,816.0	31,816.0	31,816.0
Mandatory issuances / (retirements)	0.0	0.0	0.0	0.0	0.0
Non-mandatory issuances / (retirements)	0.0	0.0	0.0	0.0	0.0
Long-term Debt (End of Year)	31,816.0	31,816.0	31,816.0	31,816.0	31,816.0
Long-term interest expense	1,234.5	1,234.5	1,234.5	1,234.5	1,234.5
Long-term interest rate	3.88%	3.88%	3.88%	3.88%	3.88%

Long-term Lease Liabilities

Long-term lease liabilities (beginning of year)	52,573.0	52,573.0	52,573.0	52,573.0	52,573.0
Mandatory issuances / (retirements)	0.0	0.0	0.0	0.0	0.0
Non-mandatory issuances / (retirements)	0.0	0.0	0.0	0.0	0.0
Long-term Lease Liabilities (End of Year)	52,573.0	52,573.0	52,573.0	52,573.0	52,573.0
Long-term lease liabilities interest expense	1,104.0	1,104.0	1,104.0	1,104.0	1,104.0
Long-term lease liabilities interest rate	2.10%	2.10%	2.10%	2.10%	2.10%

(Continued)

TABLE 7.14 (*Continued*)

Debt Schedule (in US$ millions except per share amounts)

Period Ending December 31	Actuals			Estimates				
	2018A	2019A	2020A	2021E	2022E	2023E	2024E	2025E
Financing Obligations								
Financing obligations (beginning of year)				0.0	0.0	0.0	0.0	0.0
Mandatory issuances / (retirements)				0.0	0.0	0.0	0.0	0.0
Non-mandatory issuances / (retirements)				0.0	0.0	0.0	0.0	0.0
Financing Obligations (End of Year)			0.0	0.0	0.0	0.0	0.0	0.0
Financing obligations interest expense				0.0	0.0	0.0	0.0	0.0
Financing obligations interest rate				*2.10%*	*2.10%*	*2.10%*	*2.10%*	*2.10%*
Total Issuances / Retirements)				#VALUE!	0.0	0.0	0.0	0.0
Total Interest Expense				2,805.8	2,805.8	2,805.8	2,805.8	2,805.8
Cash at the End of the Year			42,122.0	#VALUE!	#VALUE!	#VALUE!	#VALUE!	#VALUE!
Interest income				#VALUE!	#VALUE!	#VALUE!	#VALUE!	#VALUE!
Interest rate				*0.49%*	*0.49%*	*0.49%*	*0.49%*	*0.49%*
Match? (Y/N)				#VALUE!	#VALUE!	#VALUE!	#VALUE!	#VALUE!

TABLE 7.15 Income Statement #Value! Error

Consolidated Income Statements (in US$ millions except per share amounts)

Period Ending December 31	Actuals			Estimates				
	2018A	2019A	2020A	2021E	2022E	2023E	2024E	2025E
Interest								
Interest expense	1,417.0	1,600.0	1,647.0	#VALUE!	#VALUE!	#VALUE!	#VALUE!	#VALUE!
Interest income	(440.0)	(832.0)	(555.0)	#VALUE!	#VALUE!	#VALUE!	#VALUE!	#VALUE!
Net Interest Expense	977.0	768.0	1,092.0	#VALUE!	#VALUE!	#VALUE!	#VALUE!	#VALUE!
Earnings before Tax (EBT)	11,261.0	13,976.0	24,178.0	#VALUE!	#VALUE!	#VALUE!	#VALUE!	#VALUE!
EBT margin (%)	*4.8%*	*5.0%*	*6.3%*	*#VALUE!*	*#VALUE!*	*#VALUE!*	*#VALUE!*	*#VALUE!*
Income tax expense	1,197.0	2,374.0	2,863.0	#VALUE!	#VALUE!	#VALUE!	#VALUE!	#VALUE!
All-in effective tax rate (%)	*10.6%*	*17.0%*	*11.8%*	*21.0%*	*21.0%*	*21.0%*	*21.0%*	*21.0%*
Net Income from Continuing Operations	10,064.0	11,602.0	21,315.0	#VALUE!	#VALUE!	#VALUE!	#VALUE!	#VALUE!
Non-Recurring Events								
Discontinued operations	0.0	0.0	0.0	0.0	0.0	0.0	0.0	0.0
Extraordinary items	0.0	0.0	0.0	0.0	0.0	0.0	0.0	0.0
Effect of accounting changes	0.0	0.0	0.0	0.0	0.0	0.0	0.0	0.0

(Continued)

TABLE 7.15 (*Continued*)

Consolidated Income Statements (in US$ millions except per share amounts)

Period Ending December 31	Actuals			Estimates				
	2018A	2019A	2020A	2021E	2022E	2023E	2024E	2025E
Other items	0.0	0.0	0.0	0.0	0.0	0.0	0.0	0.0
Total Non-Recurring Events	0.0	0.0	0.0	0.0	0.0	0.0	0.0	0.0
Net Income (after Non-Recurring Events)	10,064.0	11,602.0	21,315.0	#VALUE!	#VALUE!	#VALUE!	#VALUE!	#VALUE!
Income attributable to equity method investments	(9.0)	14.0	(16.0)	(9.0)	14.0	(16.0)	(9.0)	14.0
Dividends paid on common stock	0.0	0.0	0.0	0.0	0.0	0.0	0.0	0.0
Net Income (as Reported)	10,073.0	11,588.0	21,331.0	#VALUE!	#VALUE!	#VALUE!	#VALUE!	#VALUE!
Earnings per Share (EPS)								
Basic	20.68	23.46	42.66	#VALUE!	#VALUE!	#VALUE!	#VALUE!	#VALUE!
Diluted	20.15	22.99	41.83	#VALUE!	#VALUE!	#VALUE!	#VALUE!	#VALUE!
Average Common Shares Outstanding								
Basic	487	494	500	504	504	504	504	504
Diluted	500	504	510	519	519	519	519	519

TABLE 7.16 Fixed Income Statement

Consolidated Income Statements (in US$ millions except per share amounts)

| | Actuals | | | | Estimates | | | | |
Period Ending December 31	2018A	2019A	2020A	2021E	2022E	2023E	2024E	2025E
Interest								
Interest expense	1,417.0	1,600.0	1,647.0	2,805.8	2,805.8	2,805.8	2,805.8	2,805.8
Interest income	(440.0)	(832.0)	(555.0)	(225.0)	(276.6)	(370.8)	(466.8)	(564.6)
Net Interest Expense	977.0	768.0	1,092.0	2,580.8	2,529.2	2,435.0	2,339.0	2,241.2
Earnings before Tax (EBT)	11,261.0	13,976.0	24,178.0	29,716.9	34,356.6	35,266.9	34,166.0	29,951.7
EBT margin (%)	*4.8%*	*5.0%*	*6.3%*	*6.1%*	*5.9%*	*5.4%*	*4.8%*	*4.0%*
Income tax expense	1,197.0	2,374.0	2,863.0	6,240.5	7,214.9	7,406.1	7,174.9	6,289.9
All-in effective tax rate (%)	*10.6%*	*17.0%*	*11.8%*	*21.0%*	*21.0%*	*21.0%*	*21.0%*	*21.0%*
Net Income from Continuing Operations	10,064.0	11,602.0	21,315.0	23,476.3	27,141.7	27,860.9	26,991.1	23,661.9
Non-Recurring Events								
Discontinued operations	0.0	0.0	0.0	0.0	0.0	0.0	0.0	0.0
Extraordinary items	0.0	0.0	0.0	0.0	0.0	0.0	0.0	0.0
Effect of accounting changes	0.0	0.0	0.0	0.0	0.0	0.0	0.0	0.0
Other items	0.0	0.0	0.0	0.0	0.0	0.0	0.0	0.0

(Continued)

TABLE 7.16 (*Continued*)

Consolidated Income Statements (in US$ millions except per share amounts)

Period Ending December 31	Actuals				Estimates					
	2018A	2019A	2020A	2021E	2022E	2023E	2024E	2025E		
Total Non-Recurring Events	0.0	0.0	0.0	0.0	0.0	0.0	0.0	0.0		
Net Income (after Non-Recurring Events)	10,064.0	11,602.0	21,315.0	23,476.3	27,141.7	27,860.9	26,991.1	23,661.9		
Income attributable to equity method investments	(9.0)	14.0	(16.0)	(9.0)	14.0	(16.0)	(9.0)	14.0		
Dividends paid on common stock	0.0	0.0	0.0	0.0	0.0	0.0	0.0	0.0		
Net Income (as Reported)	10,073.0	11,588.0	21,331.0	23,485.3	27,127.7	27,876.9	27,000.1	23,647.9		
Earnings per Share (EPS)										
Basic	20.68	23.46	42.66	46.57	53.79	55.28	53.54	46.89		
Diluted	20.15	22.99	41.83	45.22	52.24	53.68	51.99	45.54		
Average Common Shares Outstanding										
Basic	487	494	500	504	504	504	504	504		
Diluted	500	504	510	519	519	519	519	519		

We can then rewrite these conditions as "if . . . then" statements. Taking condition 1, for example: If the cash is negative, we clearly have a cash need and we need to raise càsh to fulfill that cash need. So the condition would be:

1. If Cash < 0, then return –Cash.

So the "–cash" at the end of the formula literally means to have the output be the negative value of the cash. In other words, if we have –$500 in cash available to pay down debt, then we need to issue $500 to fill that cash need. So the formula would read ––$500 (yes, a double negative), or $500.

2a. If Cash > 0, then if Cash Available > Debt, return – Debt.

Or if cash is positive, and if we have more cash than debt, then we can pay down the debt. A debt paydown is represented by –Debt, the negative balance of debt.

2b. If Cash > 0, then if Cash Available < Debt, return – Cash.

Or if cash is positive, and if we have less cash than debt, then we can only pay down as much cash as we have. This is represented by the negative cash balance.

Notice that conditions 2a and 2b can be satisfied in another way: by taking the minimum balance of cash and debt. Let's take an example for 2a and say cash is $1,000 and debt is $500. In this case, cash is positive and is also greater than debt, so we can certainly pay down all of the debt. So the output will be –$500, or –Debt. Let's now take an example for 2b and say cash is $1,000 and debt is $2,500. In this case, cash is positive but is less than debt, so we can only pay down as much cash as we have, –$1,000, or –Cash. In either case we are taking the minimum of the two, cash or debt. And notice in both cases the output is negative of the respective value. So the formula "-Min (Cash, Debt)" will satisfy both of the conditions. What about condition 1, where cash is negative? In this case, "-Min (Cash, Debt)" also satisfies this case. We know that debt can never be negative, so if this is the case where the cash is negative, the negative value (cash) will always be smaller than the positive value (debt). If cash is negative, the formula "-Min (Cash, Debt)" will always give us –Cash, the desired result.

We can now enter this formula into the model if we choose to. In cell G14 of the debt schedule, we can enter:

$$=-min(G10,G12)$$

You can also copy this formula to the right.

It is important to understand the details of the formula and how it works so one can adjust the formula to handle different tasks. For example, adding an additional "min" function to the formula can cap how much debt can be raised. This would be helpful if one is modeling a revolver that only has a capacity of $500, for example. So the formula will look like this:

$$=min(-min(cash, debt),500)$$

Whatever the negative output is (which will always be a debt paydown) won't be affected, but if a debt issuance becomes greater than $500, that outer "min" function will prevent it from going beyond the 500.

BASIC SWITCHES

It is also helpful to put in a simple "switch" to be able to turn on or off the use of this "min" formula. We can do this by simply multiplying the formula by a "1" or "0." Multiplying any formula by "0" will always produce "0," so the formula will be turned off; multiplying any formula by "1" will not change the output of the formula, so it will be turned on. So, for example, we can type a "1" in cell F14. We can also append the formula in G14 to add "*$F$14," making sure to add dollar signs around the reference to F14, so that we can copy the formula to the right without affecting the reference to F14. The formula in G14 should read "=-min(G10, G12)*$F$14." Now, if we type "0" into cell F14, the formula will read "0" and be turned off. If we type "1" into cell F14, the formula will read "1" and be turned on. Let's keep the formula switched off. Remember to copy the adjusted formula to the right.

FINALIZING THE MODEL

Now that the core model is complete, it is important to step back and take a high-level look at the output. Let's start with earnings per share (EPS). In the early stages of the modeling process, we took a look at the "Analyst

Estimates" section in Yahoo! Finance, which gave us an average of revenue and EPS estimates across the Street (shown in Figure 7.5). Although we used this to ensure our revenue estimates were in line with the street, we mentioned that, without a complete income statement (depreciation and interest were not complete), we could not yet look at a final EPS number.

Here are some basic steps to determine if our numbers are in line with the Street:

1. *Revenue.* See Table 7.17. The basic rule for determining if the projections are in line with the Street is to first make sure revenue is similar to Street estimates. As discussed, when projecting revenue, our Amazon projection in 2021 of $490,301.3 looks very close to the $490.35Bn average suggested in the Street average. Our 2022 revenue of $581,497.3 is also close to the average of $581.65Bn. Going from there we estimated scaling down the revenue growth each year. Again, it is always recommended to do more extensive research to better home in on these projections.

2. *EPS.* See Table 7.18. We then look at EPS. If the EPS is much lower or much higher than the Street even though revenue is in line, then there must be a difference in our cost assumptions. Our 2021 Projected EPS is 46.57, within the low and high range of 42.68 to 71.13 provided in Figure 7.5. Notice that we are more toward the lower end of that range, but the average of 46 analysts on the Street estimate is 55.74, not too far off from our assumption. If we wanted our EPS to be lower or higher, we may want to consider further researching and adjusting some of the major variables and assumptions driving the EPS estimates.

For example:

a. *Taxes.* See Table 7.19. Looking up from EPS, comparing our projected metrics with the historical metrics is a good way to see where major shifts could be. This could serve as a clue for what may be different. Unless the company has had very unusual tax activity, there should not be any major shift to the future tax levels versus the historical. Notice our Amazon tax rate is considerably higher than the prior year's. As discussed in Chapter 1, we had assumed the 2020 rate of 11.8% was unusually low, so we found a note in Amazon's 10-K suggesting a tax rate of 21%. Notice if we change our 2021 tax rate assumption down to 11.8%, our EPS increases to 52.00, much closer to the EPS estimated average. Could it be possible that the Wall Street analysts estimating a higher EPS are using this lower tax rate? Or, could other analysts have projected a high EPS because

TABLE 7.17 Amazon Projected Revenue

Consolidated Income Statements (in US$ millions except per share amounts)

Period Ending December 31	Actuals			Estimates				
	2018A	2019A	2020A	2021E	2022E	2023E	2024E	2025E
Revenue								
Net product sales	141,915.0	160,408.0	215,915.0					
Y/Y growth (%)		*13.0%*	*34.6%*					
Net service sales	90,972.0	120,114.0	170,149.0					
Y/Y growth (%)		*32.0%*	*41.7%*					
Total Net Sales	232,887.0	280,522.0	386,064.0	490,301.3	581,497.3	656,006.5	713,912.0	757,323.5
Y/Y net sales growth (%)		20.5%	37.6%	27.0%	18.6%	12.8%	8.8%	6.1%
Y/Y growth (%) decline				(28.2%)	(31.1%)	(31.1%)	(31.1%)	(31.1%)

TABLE 7.18 Amazon Projected Revenue

Consolidated Income Statements (in US$ millions except per share amounts)

Period Ending December 31	Actuals			Estimates				
	2018A	2019A	2020A	2021E	2022E	2023E	2024E	2025E
Earnings per Share (EPS)								
Basic	20.68	23.46	42.66	46.57	53.79	55.28	53.54	46.89
Diluted	20.15	22.99	41.83	45.22	52.24	53.68	51.99	45.54

yahoo! finance

Search for news, symbols or companies

Summary | Company Outlook ➕ | Chart | Conversations | Statistics | Historical Data | Profile | Financials | **Analysis** | Options

Currency in USD

Earnings Estimate	Current Qtr. (Jun 2021)	Next Qtr. (Sep 2021)	Current Year (2021)	Next Year (2022)
No. of Analysts	36	36	46	46
Avg. Estimate	12.21	12.92	55.74	72.09
Low Estimate	9.77	6.84	42.68	45.11
High Estimate	15.18	17.7	71.13	96.53
Year Ago EPS	10.3	12.37	41.83	55.74

Revenue Estimate	Current Qtr. (Jun 2021)	Next Qtr. (Sep 2021)	Current Year (2021)	Next Year (2022)
No. of Analysts	36	36	45	45
Avg. Estimate	115.17B	118.7B	490.35B	581.65B
Low Estimate	112.15B	110.97B	473.77B	547.19B
High Estimate	120.76B	123.56B	508.88B	612.25B
Year Ago Sales	88.91B	96.14B	386.06B	490.35B
Sales Growth (year/est)	29.50%	23.50%	27.00%	18.60%

FIGURE 7.5   Yahoo! Finance AMZN Estimates

of lowering some other cost assumptions? This is where significant further research could be of value. Let's stick with the 21% as noted in the 10-K and move on.

b. *Net interest.* See Table 7.20. The net interest has been historically increasing and we have projected an increase as well. The major driver here is the interest rates. If you notice, there is an increase in the interest expense, but a drop in the interest income. It could be considered that the interest rate is too high. If you recall, we based the interest rate off of a given table (Figure 7.1) that contained a range of interest rates. We chose the highest end of the range to be conservative – were we perhaps too conservative? If we recalculated the interest rates using the low end of the ranges, we would have a 2.1% rate. This would reduce our total interest expense to $2,239.5 and would increase our EPS to 47.46. Although this is an increase, it is not very significant. So, let's move on.

c. *Depreciation.* See Table 7.21. As discussed in the depreciation schedule, unless the company has made major announcements, there should not be a significant drop in or increase to the depreciation expense.

TABLE 7.19 Amazon Projected Taxes

Consolidated Income Statements (in US$ millions except per share amounts)

Period Ending December 31	Actuals			Estimates				
	2018A	2019A	2020A	2021E	2022E	2023E	2024E	2025E
Income tax expense	1,197.0	2,374.0	2,863.0	6,240.5	7,214.9	7,406.1	7,174.9	6,289.9
All-in effective tax rate (%)	*10.6%*	*17.0%*	*11.8%*	*21.0%*	*21.0%*	*21.0%*	*21.0%*	*21.0%*
Net Income from Continuing Operations	10,064.0	11,602.0	21,315.0	23,476.3	27,141.7	27,860.9	26,991.1	23,661.9

TABLE 7.20 Amazon Projected Net Interest Expense

Consolidated Income Statements (in US$ millions except per share amounts)

Period Ending December 31	Actuals			Estimates				
	2018A	2019A	2020A	2021E	2022E	2023E	2024E	2025E
Interest								
Interest expense	1,417.0	1,600.0	1,647.0	2,805.8	2,805.8	2,805.8	2,805.8	2,805.8
Interest income	(440.0)	(832.0)	(555.0)	(225.0)	(276.6)	(370.8)	(466.8)	(564.6)
Net Interest Expense	977.0	768.0	1,092.0	2,580.8	2,529.2	2,435.0	2,339.0	2,241.2
Earnings before Tax (EBT)	11,261.0	13,976.0	24,178.0	29,716.9	34,356.6	35,266.9	34,166.0	29,951.7
EBT margin (%)	4.8%	5.0%	6.3%	6.1%	5.9%	5.4%	4.8%	4.0%

TABLE 7.21 Amazon Projected Taxes

Consolidated Income Statements (in US$ millions except per share amounts)

Period Ending December 31	Actuals				Estimates				
	2018A	2019A	2020A	2021E	2022E	2023E	2024E	2025E
EBITDA	27,762.0	36,330.0	48,150.0	61,150.5	72,524.5	81,817.3	89,039.3	94,453.6
EBITDA margin (%)	11.9%	13.0%	12.5%	12.5%	12.5%	12.5%	12.5%	12.5%
Depreciation and amortization	15,341.0	21,789.0	25,251.0	28,669.8	35,841.6	43,932.4	52,737.3	62,077.6
EBIT	12,421.0	14,541.0	22,899.0	32,480.7	36,682.8	37,884.9	36,302.0	32,375.9
EBIT margin (%)	5.3%	5.2%	5.9%	6.6%	6.3%	5.8%	5.1%	4.3%

d. *COGS and operating expenses.* See Table 7.22. This is where there can be major variability in assumptions. If everything else is in line, yet the EPS is still slightly off, then the Street may be suggesting some increase or decrease to the COGS or operating expenses. Notice if we lower the 2021 "COGS as a % of revenue" from 60.4% to 59%, the EPS increases dramatically from $46.57 to $57.58. That's a huge jump. This is where we would again recommend some significant research to determine if the company is taking any initiatives to reduce future costs.

In summary, as our EPS is in line with the estimate range and close to the average, I would not recommend making many adjustments here; some small tweaks could get us closer to the average, but I would not suggest doing this until we have done significant research. Remember that projections are always a "guesstimate"; just noting from the wide low to high Street estimates from 42.61 to 71.13, even the best of analysts can have very different perspectives. This is your model and your tool to adjust and home in on as you learn more and more about the company. Please also note that Yahoo! Finance is by no means a standard benchmark, and its data can change quite often. It is, however, a good "sanity" check.

We have the complete model in the following pages for reference. (See Tables 7.22 to 7.27.)

We are done with the model and can move on to valuing the business.

TABLE 7.22 Amazon Consolidated Income Statements

Consolidated Income Statements (in US$ millions except per share amounts)

Period Ending December 31	Actuals			Estimates				
	2018A	2019A	2020A	2021E	2022E	2023E	2024E	2025E
Revenue								
Net product sales	141,915.0	160,408.0	215,915.0					
Y/Y growth (%)		13.0%	34.6%					
Net service sales	90,972.0	120,114.0	170,149.0					
Y/Y growth (%)		32.0%	41.7%					
Total Net Sales	232,887.0	280,522.0	386,064.0	490,301.3	581,497.3	656,006.5	713,912.0	757,323.5
Y/Y net sales growth (%)		20.5%	37.6%	27.0%	18.6%	12.8%	8.8%	6.1%
Y/Y growth (%) decline				(28.2%)	(31.1%)	(31.1%)	(31.1%)	(31.1%)
Cost of Goods Sold								
Cost of Goods Sold	139,156.0	165,536.0	233,307.0	296,299.9	351,411.7	396,439.2	431,432.8	457,667.3
COGS as a % of net sales	59.8%	59.0%	60.4%	60.4%	60.4%	60.4%	60.4%	60.4%
Gross Profit	93,731.0	114,986.0	152,757.0	194,001.4	230,085.6	259,567.3	282,479.2	299,656.2
Gross profit margin (%)	40%	41%	40%	40%	40%	40%	40%	40%

(Continued)

TABLE 7.22 (Continued)

Consolidated Income Statements (in US$ millions except per share amounts)

Period Ending December 31	Actuals		Estimates					
	2018A	2019A	2020A	2021E	2022E	2023E	2024E	2025E
Operating Expenses								
Fulfillment	34,027.0	40,232.0	58,517.0	74,316.6	88,139.5	99,433.1	108,210.0	114,790.0
Fulfillment as a % of net sales	*14.6%*	*14.3%*	*15.2%*	*15.2%*	*15.2%*	*15.2%*	*15.2%*	*15.2%*
Technology and content	13,496.0	14,142.0	17,489.0	22,211.0	26,342.3	29,717.6	32,340.8	34,307.3
Technology and content as a % of net sales	*5.8%*	*5.0%*	*4.5%*	*4.5%*	*4.5%*	*4.5%*	*4.5%*	*4.5%*
Marketing	13,814.0	18,878.0	22,008.0	27,950.2	33,148.9	37,396.4	40,697.3	43,172.1
Marketing as a % of net sales	*5.9%*	*6.7%*	*5.7%*	*5.7%*	*5.7%*	*5.7%*	*5.7%*	*5.7%*
General and administrative	4,336.0	5,203.0	6,668.0	8,468.4	10,043.5	11,330.4	12,330.5	13,080.3
General and administrative as a % of net sales	*1.9%*	*1.9%*	*1.7%*	*1.7%*	*1.7%*	*1.7%*	*1.7%*	*1.7%*
Other operating expense (income), net	296.0	201.0	(75.0)	(95.3)	(113.0)	(127.4)	(138.7)	(147.1)

Other operating expense as a % of net sales	0.1%	0.1%	0.0%	0.0%	0.0%	0.0%	0.0%	0.0%
Total Operating Expenses	65,969.0	78,656.0	104,607.0	132,850.9	157,561.2	177,750.0	193,439.9	205,202.6
EBITDA	27,762.0	36,330.0	48,150.0	61,150.5	72,524.5	81,817.3	89,039.3	94,453.6
EBITDA margin (%)	*11.9%*	*13.0%*	*12.5%*	*12.5%*	*12.5%*	*12.5%*	*12.5%*	*12.5%*
Depreciation and amortization	15,341.0	21,789.0	25,251.0	28,669.8	35,841.6	43,932.4	52,737.3	62,077.6
EBIT	**12,421.0**	**14,541.0**	**22,899.0**	**32,480.7**	**36,682.8**	**37,884.9**	**36,302.0**	**32,375.9**
EBIT margin (%)	*5.3%*	*5.2%*	*5.9%*	*6.6%*	*6.3%*	*5.8%*	*5.1%*	*4.3%*
Other Income	183.0	(203.0)	(2,371.0)	183.0	(203.0)	183.0	(203.0)	183.0
Interest								
Interest expense	1,417.0	1,600.0	1,647.0	2,805.8	2,805.8	2,805.8	2,805.8	2,805.8
Interest income	(440.0)	(832.0)	(555.0)	(225.0)	(276.6)	(370.8)	(466.8)	(564.6)
Net Interest Expense	977.0	768.0	1,092.0	2,580.8	2,529.2	2,435.0	2,339.0	2,241.2
Earnings before Tax (EBT)	**11,261.0**	**13,976.0**	**24,178.0**	**29,716.9**	**34,356.6**	**35,266.9**	**34,166.0**	**29,951.7**
EBT margin (%)	*4.8%*	*5.0%*	*6.3%*	*6.1%*	*5.9%*	*5.4%*	*4.8%*	*4.0%*
Income tax expense	1,197.0	2,374.0	2,863.0	6,240.5	7,214.9	7,406.1	7,174.9	6,289.9
All-in effective tax rate (%)	*10.6%*	*17.0%*	*11.8%*	*21.0%*	*21.0%*	*21.0%*	*21.0%*	*21.0%*

(Continued)

TABLE 7.22 (*Continued*)

Consolidated Income Statements (in US$ millions except per share amounts)

Period Ending December 31	Actuals			Estimates				
	2018A	2019A	2020A	2021E	2022E	2023E	2024E	2025E
Net Income from Continuing Operations	10,064.0	11,602.0	21,315.0	23,476.3	27,141.7	27,860.9	26,991.1	23,661.9
Non-Recurring Events								
Discontinued operations	0.0	0.0	0.0	0.0	0.0	0.0	0.0	0.0
Extraordinary items	0.0	0.0	0.0	0.0	0.0	0.0	0.0	0.0
Effect of accounting changes	0.0	0.0	0.0	0.0	0.0	0.0	0.0	0.0
Other items	0.0	0.0	0.0	0.0	0.0	0.0	0.0	0.0
Total Non-Recurring Events	0.0	0.0	0.0	0.0	0.0	0.0	0.0	0.0
Net Income (after Non-Recurring Events)	10,064.0	11,602.0	21,315.0	23,476.3	27,141.7	27,860.9	26,991.1	23,661.9
Income attributable to equity method investments	(9.0)	14.0	(16.0)	(9.0)	14.0	(16.0)	(9.0)	14.0

Dividends paid on common stock	0.0	0.0	0.0	0.0	0.0	0.0	0.0	0.0
Net Income (as Reported)	10,073.0	11,588.0	21,331.0	23,485.3	27,127.7	27,876.9	27,000.1	23,647.9
Earnings per Share (EPS)								
Basic	20.68	23.46	42.66	46.57	53.79	55.28	53.54	46.89
Diluted	20.15	22.99	41.83	45.22	52.24	53.68	51.99	45.54
Average Common Shares Outstanding								
Basic	487	494	500	504	504	504	504	504
Diluted	500	504	510	519	519	519	519	519

TABLE 7.23 Amazon Consolidated Statement of Cash Flows

Consolidated Statements of Cash Flows (in US$ millions except per share amounts)

Period Ending December 31	Actuals			Estimates				
	2018A	2019A	2020A	2021E	2022E	2023E	2024E	2025E
Cash Flows from Operating Activities								
Net income	10,073.0	11,588.0	21,331.0	23,485.3	27,127.7	27,876.9	27,000.1	23,647.9
Depreciation and amortization	15,341.0	21,789.0	25,251.0	28,669.8	35,841.6	43,932.4	52,737.3	62,077.6
Stock-based compensation	5,418.0	6,864.0	9,208.0	11,694.2	13,869.3	15,646.4	17,027.5	18,062.9
% of total operating expenses	*8.2%*	*8.7%*	*8.8%*	*8.8%*	*8.8%*	*8.8%*	*8.8%*	*8.8%*
Other operating expense (income), net	274.0	164.0	(71.0)	(90.2)	(106.9)	(120.6)	(131.3)	(139.3)
% of total net sales	*0.1%*	*0.1%*	*0.0%*	*0.0%*	*0.0%*	*0.0%*	*0.0%*	*0.0%*
Other expense (income), net	219.0	(249.0)	(2,582.0)	219.0	(249.0)	219.0	(249.0)	219.0
Deferred income taxes	441.0	796.0	(554.0)	(554.0)	(554.0)	(554.0)	(554.0)	(554.0)
Changes in Operating Working Capital								
Changes in inventory	(1,314.0)	(3,278.0)	(2,849.0)	(4,330.4)	(5,231.3)	(4,274.1)	(3,321.7)	(2,490.2)
Changes in accounts receivable	(4,615.0)	(7,681.0)	(8,169.0)	(4,260.3)	(5,357.2)	(4,377.0)	(3,401.6)	(2,550.2)

Changes in accounts payable	3,263.0	8,193.0	17,480.0	3,484.5	14,140.4	11,553.0	8,978.5	6,731.2

Changes in accounts payable	3,263.0	8,193.0	17,480.0	3,484.5	14,140.4	11,553.0	8,978.5	6,731.2
Changes in accrued expenses	472.0	(1,383.0)	5,754.0	1,272.1	5,448.9	4,451.9	3,459.8	2,593.8
Changes in unearned revenue	1,151.0	1,711.0	1,265.0	1,657.2	2,113.9	1,727.1	1,342.3	1,006.3
Net Changes in Working Capital	(1,043.0)	(2,438.0)	13,481.0	(2,177.0)	11,114.6	9,080.9	7,057.3	5,290.8
Total Cash from Operating Activities	30,723.0	38,514.0	66,064.0	61,247.2	87,043.3	96,080.9	102,887.9	108,605.0
Cash Flows from Investing Activities								
CAPEX [Purchase of property and equipment]	(13,427.0)	(16,861.0)	(40,140.0)	(54,423.4)	(64,546.2)	(72,816.7)	(79,244.2)	(84,062.9)
% of Revenue	*5.8%*	*6.0%*	*10.4%*	*11.1%*	*11.1%*	*11.1%*	*11.1%*	*11.1%*
Proceeds from property and equipment sales and incentives	2,104.0	4,172.0	5,096.0	0.0	0.0	0.0	0.0	0.0
Business acquisitions, net of cash acquired	(2,186.0)	(2,461.0)	(2,325.0)	0.0	0.0	0.0	0.0	0.0
Sales and maturities in marketable securities	8,240.0	22,681.0	50,237.0	8,240.0	22,681.0	8,240.0	22,681.0	8,240.0
Purchases of marketable securities	(7,100.0)	(31,812.0)	(72,479.0)	(7,100.0)	(31,812.0)	(7,100.0)	(31,812.0)	(7,100.0)

(Continued)

TABLE 7.23 (*Continued*)

Consolidated Statements of Cash Flows (in US$ millions except per share amounts)

Period Ending December 31	Actuals			Estimates				
	2018A	2019A	2020A	2021E	2022E	2023E	2024E	2025E
Total Cash Flows from Investing Activities	(12,369.0)	(24,281.0)	(59,611.0)	(53,283.4)	(73,677.2)	(71,676.7)	(88,375.2)	(82,922.9)
Cash Flows from Financing Activities								
Short-term borrowings (repayments)	73.0	(116.0)	619.0	0.0	0.0	0.0	0.0	0.0
Long-term borrowings (repayments)	27.0	(295.0)	8,972.0	0.0	0.0	0.0	0.0	0.0
Principal repayments of finance leases	(7,449.0)	(9,628.0)	(10,642.0)	0.0	0.0	0.0	0.0	0.0
Principal repayments of financing obligations	(337.0)	(27.0)	(53.0)	0.0	0.0	0.0	0.0	0.0
Total Cash Flows from Financing Activities	(7,686.0)	(10,066.0)	(1,104.0)	0.0	0.0	0.0	0.0	0.0
Foreign Currency Effect on Cash, Cash Equivalents, and Restricted Cash	(351.0)	70.0	618.0	(351.0)	70.0	618.0	(351.0)	70.0
Total Change in Cash and Cash Equivalents	10,317.0	4,237.0	5,967.0	7,612.8	13,436.1	25,022.2	14,161.7	25,752.1
SUPPLEMENTAL DATA:								
Cash flow before debt paydown				7,612.8	13,436.1	25,022.2	14,161.7	25,752.1

TABLE 7.24 Amazon Consolidated Balance Sheets

Consolidated Balance Sheets (in US$ millions except per share amounts)

On December 31	2019A	2020A	2021E	2022E	2023E	2024E	2025E
				Estimates			
Assets							
Current Assets							
Cash and cash equivalents	36,092.0	42,122.0	49,734.8	63,170.9	88,193.1	102,354.8	128,106.8
Marketable securities	18,929.0	42,274.0	41,134.0	50,265.0	49,125.0	58,256.0	57,116.0
Inventories	20,497.0	23,795.0	28,125.4	33,356.7	37,630.9	40,952.5	43,442.8
Accounts receivable, net and other	20,816.0	24,542.0	28,802.3	34,159.6	38,536.5	41,938.1	44,488.3
Total Current Assets	**96,334.0**	**132,733.0**	**147,796.5**	**180,952.2**	**213,485.5**	**243,501.5**	**273,153.9**
Property, plant and equipment, net	72,705.0	113,114.0	138,867.6	167,572.1	196,456.5	222,963.4	244,948.7
Operating leases	25,141.0	37,553.0	37,553.0	37,553.0	37,553.0	37,553.0	37,553.0
Goodwill	14,754.0	15,017.0	15,017.0	15,017.0	15,017.0	15,017.0	15,017.0
Other assets	16,314.0	22,778.0	22,649.2	23,005.1	22,906.8	23,287.0	23,207.3
Total Assets	**225,248.0**	**321,195.0**	**361,883.3**	**424,099.5**	**485,418.7**	**542,321.9**	**593,879.9**
Liabilities							
Current Liabilities							
Accounts payable	47,183.0	72,539.0	76,023.5	90,163.8	101,716.8	110,695.3	117,426.5
Accrued expenses and other	18,111.0	28,023.0	29,295.1	34,744.0	39,195.8	42,655.6	45,249.4
Short-term debt	14,328.0	16,115.0	16,115.0	16,115.0	16,115.0	16,115.0	16,115.0

(Continued)

TABLE 7.24 (*Continued*)

Consolidated Balance Sheets (in US$ millions except per share amounts)

On December 31	2019A	2020A	2021E	2022E	2023E	2024E	2025E
				Estimates			
Unearned revenue	8,190.0	9,708.0	11,365.2	13,479.2	15,206.3	16,548.5	17,554.8
Total Current Liabilities	87,812.0	126,385.0	132,798.8	154,502.0	172,234.0	186,014.5	196,345.8
Long-term lease liabilities	39,791.0	52,573.0	52,573.0	52,573.0	52,573.0	52,573.0	52,573.0
Long-term debt	23,414.0	31,816.0	31,816.0	31,816.0	31,816.0	31,816.0	31,816.0
Financing obligations	0.0	0.0	0.0	0.0	0.0	0.0	0.0
Other long-term liabilities	12,171.0	17,017.0	16,463.0	15,909.0	15,355.0	14,801.0	14,247.0
Total Liabilities	163,188.0	227,791.0	233,650.8	254,800.0	271,978.0	285,204.5	294,981.8
Stockholders' Equity							
Preferred stock	0.0	0.0	0.0	0.0	0.0	0.0	0.0
Common stock par value + additional paid-in-capital	33,663.0	42,870.0	42,870.0	42,870.0	42,870.0	42,870.0	42,870.0
Treasury stock	(1,837.0)	(1,837.0)	(1,837.0)	(1,837.0)	(1,837.0)	(1,837.0)	(1,837.0)
Accumulated other comprehensive income (loss)	(986.0)	(180.0)	(531.0)	(461.0)	157.0	(194.0)	(124.0)
Retained earnings	31,220.0	52,551.0	87,730.5	128,727.5	172,250.8	216,278.4	257,989.2
Total Stockholders' Equity	62,060.0	93,404.0	128,232.5	169,299.5	213,440.8	257,117.4	298,898.2
Total Liabilities & Stockholders' Equity	225,248.0	321,195.0	361,883.3	424,099.5	485,418.7	542,321.9	593,879.9
SUPPLEMENTAL DATA:							
Balance? (Y/N)	Y	Y	Y	Y	Y	Y	Y

TABLE 7.25 Amazon Depreciation Schedule

Depreciation (in US$ millions except per share amounts)

Period Ending December 31	Actuals			Estimates				
	2018A	2019A	2020A	2021E	2022E	2023E	2024E	2025E
Property, Plant & Equipment on Jan 1 2021				113,114.0				
Capital Expenditures as of Jan 1 of each year				54,423.4	64,546.2	72,816.7	79,244.2	84,062.9
Straight-line Depreciation								
Years								
Existing PP&E				5				
CAPEX				9	9	9	9	9
Depreciation ($)								
Existing PP&E				22,622.8	22,622.8	22,622.8	22,622.8	22,622.8
2021 CAPEX				6,047.0	6,047.0	6,047.0	6,047.0	6,047.0
2022 CAPEX					7,171.8	7,171.8	7,171.8	7,171.8
2023 CAPEX						8,090.7	8,090.7	8,090.7
2024 CAPEX							8,804.9	8,804.9
2025 CAPEX								9,340.3
Total Book Depreciation	15,341.0	21,879.0	25,251.0	28,669.8	35,841.6	43,932.4	52,737.3	62,077.6

TABLE 7.26 Amazon Operating Working Capital Schedule

Operating Working Capital Schedule (OWC) (in US$ millions except per share amounts)

On December 31	Actuals			Estimates				
	2018A	2019A	2020A	2021E	2022E	2023E	2024E	2025E
Current Assets								
Inventories		20,497.0	23,795.0	28,125.4	33,356.7	37,630.9	40,952.5	43,442.8
Inventory turnover days				*34.2*	*34.2*	*34.2*	*34.2*	*34.2*
Accounts receivable, net and other		20,816.0	24,542.0	28,802.3	34,159.6	38,536.5	41,938.1	44,488.3
Days receivable			*21.1*	*21.1*	*21.1*	*21.1*	*21.1*	*21.1*
Total Current Assets		41,313.0	48,337.0	56,927.8	67,516.3	76,167.4	82,890.7	87,931.1
Current Liabilities								
Accounts payable		47,183.0	72,539.0	76,023.5	90,163.8	101,716.8	110,695.3	117,426.5
Days payable			*92.4*	*92.4*	*92.4*	*92.4*	*92.4*	*92.4*
Accrued expenses and other		18,111.0	28,023.0	29,295.1	34,744.0	39,195.8	42,655.6	45,249.4
Days payable			*79.4*	*79.4*	*79.4*	*79.4*	*79.4*	*79.4*
Unearned revenue		8,190.0	9,708.0	11,365.2	13,479.2	15,206.3	16,548.5	17,554.8
Unearned revenue days			*8.3*	*8.3*	*8.3*	*8.3*	*8.3*	*8.3*
Total Current Liabilities		73,484.0	110,270.0	116,683.8	138,387.0	156,119.0	169,899.5	180,230.8
Total Operating Working Capital		(32,171.0)	(61,933.0)	(59,756.0)	(70,870.7)	(79,951.6)	(87,008.9)	(92,299.7)
Change in total operating working capital				2,177.0	(11,114.6)	(9,080.9)	(7,057.3)	(5,290.8)
Match? (Y/N)				Y	Y	Y	Y	Y

TABLE 7.27 Amazon Debt Schedule

Debt Schedule (in US$ millions except per share amounts)

Period Ending December 31	Actuals				Estimates				
	2018A	2019A	2020A	2021E	2022E	2023E	2024E	2025E
Cash Available to Pay Down Debt								
Cash at beginning of year				42,122.0	49,734.8	63,170.9	88,193.1	102,354.8
Cash flow before debt paydown				7,612.8	13,436.1	25,022.2	14,161.7	25,752.1
Minimum cash cushion				(40,000.0)	(40,000.0)	(40,000.0)	(40,000.0)	(40,000.0)
Total Cash Available to Pay Down Debt				9,734.8	23,170.9	48,193.1	62,354.8	88,106.8
Short-term Debt / Revolver								
Short-term debt (beginning of year)				16,115.0	16,115.0	16,115.0	16,115.0	16,115.0
Mandatory issuances / (retirements)				0.0	0.0	0.0	0.0	0.0
Non-mandatory issuances / (retirements)				0.0	0.0	0.0	0.0	0.0
Short-term debt (end of year)			16,115.0	16,115.0	16,115.0	16,115.0	16,115.0	16,115.0
Short-term interest expense				467.3	467.3	467.3	467.3	467.3
Short-term interest rate				*2.9%*	*2.9%*	*2.9%*	*2.9%*	*2.9%*

(Continued)

TABLE 7.27 (*Continued*)

Debt Schedule (in US$ millions except per share amounts)

	Actuals			Estimates				
Period Ending December 31	2018A	2019A	2020A	2021E	2022E	2023E	2024E	2025E
Long-term Debt								
Long-term debt (beginning of year)				31,816.0	31,816.0	31,816.0	31,816.0	31,816.0
Mandatory issuances / (retirements)				0.0	0.0	0.0	0.0	0.0
Non-mandatory issuances / (retirements)				0.0	0.0	0.0	0.0	0.0
Long-term Debt (End of Year)			31,816.0	31,816.0	31,816.0	31,816.0	31,816.0	31,816.0
Long-term interest expense				1,234.5	1,234.5	1,234.5	1,234.5	1,234.5
Long-term interest rate				3.88%	3.88%	3.88%	3.88%	3.88%
Long-term Lease Liabilities								
Long-term lease liabilities (beginning of year)				52,573.0	52,573.0	52,573.0	52,573.0	52,573.0
Mandatory issuances / (retirements)				0.0	0.0	0.0	0.0	0.0
Non-mandatory issuances / (retirements)				0.0	0.0	0.0	0.0	0.0
Long-term Lease Liabilities (End of Year)			52,573.0	52,573.0	52,573.0	52,573.0	52,573.0	52,573.0

Long-term lease liabilities interest expense		1,104.0	1,104.0	1,104.0	1,104.0	1,104.0
Long-term lease liabilities interest rate		2.10%	2.10%	2.10%	2.10%	2.10%
Financing Obligations						
Financing obligations (beginning of year)		0.0	0.0	0.0	0.0	0.0
Mandatory issuances / (retirements)		0.0	0.0	0.0	0.0	0.0
Non-mandatory issuances / (retirements)		0.0	0.0	0.0	0.0	0.0
Financing Obligations (End of Year)	0.0	0.0	0.0	0.0	0.0	0.0
Financing obligations interest expense		0.0	0.0	0.0	0.0	0.0
Financing obligations interest rate		2.10%	2.10%	2.10%	2.10%	2.10%
Total Issuances / (Retirements)		0.0	0.0	0.0	0.0	0.0
Total Interest Expense		2,805.8	2,805.8	2,805.8	2,805.8	2,805.8
Cash at the End of the Year	42,122.0	49,734.8	63,170.9	88,193.1	102,354.8	128,106.8
Interest income		225.0	276.6	370.8	466.8	564.6
Interest rate		0.49%	0.49%	0.49%	0.49%	0.49%
Match? (Y/N)		Y	Y	Y	Y	Y

Valuation

Valuation is crucial in investment banking. How much is this entity worth? What is the appropriate price of this stock? We will take a look at Amazon, analyze its financial standing, and determine if the stock is overvalued or undervalued, as done by Wall Street analysts.

The goals of this section are:

1. Understanding valuation
   a. Multiples
   b. Comparable company analysis
   c. Precedent transactions analysis
   d. Discounted cash flow analysis
2. Developing the ability to build a complete valuation of Amazon

As a disclaimer, there are a lot of excellent valuation books. This section does not set out to be a complete and thorough explanation of valuation. Rather, it is meant to be a practical methodology toward utilizing valuation. We will go through a basic understanding of valuation and the concepts, but a deep discussion of the ever-changing theories and the proofs of such is beyond the scope of this book.

CHAPTER 8

What Is Value?

The most important question before even getting into valuation techniques is this: What is value? To help answer this question, we note there are two major categories of value:

1. *Book value.* Book value is the value of an asset or entire business entity as determined by its books, or the financials.
2. *Market value.* Market value is the value as determined by the market.

BOOK VALUE

The book value can be determined by the balance sheet. The total book value of a company's property, for example, can be found under the net PP&E in the assets section of the balance sheet. The book value of the shareholders' interest in the company (not including the non-controlling interest holder) can be found under shareholders' equity. Amazon's shareholders' equity value of $93,404MM (as per the 2020 financials) is the book value of its equity to the shareholders.

MARKET VALUE

The market value can be defined by its market capitalization, or shares outstanding times share price. Amazon, which is trading at $3,432.97 per share and has 519.3MM diluted shares outstanding at the time of this writing, has a market capitalization of $1.78TN. This is Amazon's market value.

These values represent the equity value of a business, the value of the business attributable to just equity holders, that is, the value of the business excluding debt lenders, and other obligations.

Shareholders' equity, for example, is a value of the company's assets less the value of the company's liabilities. So this shareholders' equity value (making sure non-controlling interest is not included in shareholders' equity) is the value of the business excluding lenders and other obligations; an equity value. The market value, or market capitalization, is based on the stock price, which is inherently an equity value, as equity investors value a company's stock, excluding debt lenders and other obligations.

ENTERPRISE VALUE

Enterprise value (also known as firm value) is defined as the value of the entire business including debt lenders and other obligations. We will see why – the importance of enterprise value is that it approaches an approximate value of the operating assets of an entity. To be more specific, "Debt Lenders and Other Obligations" can include short-term debts, long-term debts, current portion of long-term debts, capital lease obligations, preferred securities, non-controlling interests, and other nonoperating liabilities (e.g., unallocated pension funds). So, for complete reference, enterprise value can be calculated as:

Equity value
+ Short-term debts
+ Long-term debts
+ Current portion of long-term debts
+ Capital lease obligations
+ Preferred securities
+ Non-controlling interests
+ Other non-operating liabilities (e.g., unallocated pension funds)
– Cash and cash equivalents

We will explain why subtracting cash and cash equivalents is significant. To arrive at enterprise value on a book value basis, we take the shareholders' equity and add back any potential debts and obligations less cash and cash equivalents. Similarly, if we add to market capitalization any potential debts and obligations less cash and cash equivalents, we approach the enterprise value of a company on a market value basis.

Here is a quick recap:

Valuation Categories	Book Value	Market Value
Equity Value	Shareholders' Equity	Market Capitalization
Enterprise Value	Shareholders' Equity + Any Potential Debts and Obligations* – Cash and Cash Equivalents	Market Capitalization + Any Potential Debts and Obligations* – Cash and Cash Equivalents

*Note: This can include short-term debts, long-term debts, current portion of long-term debts, capital lease obligations, preferred securities, non-controlling interests, other non-operating liabilities (e.g., unallocated pension funds).

Let's take the example of a company that has a shareholders' equity of $10MM as per its balance sheet. Let's also say it has $5MM in total liabilities. We will assume no non-controlling interest holders in these examples to better illustrate the main idea. As per the balance sheet formula (where Assets = Liabilities + Shareholders' Equity), the total value of the company's assets is $15MM. So $10MM is the book equity value of the company.

Book Value

Let's now say the company trades in the market at a premium to its book equity value; the market capitalization of the company is $12MM. The market capitalization of a company is an important value, because it is current; it is the value of a business as determined by the investor (Share price × Shares outstanding). When we take the market capitalization and add the total liabilities of $5MM, we get a value that represents the value of the company's total assets as determined by the market.

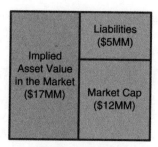

Market Value

However, in valuation, we typically take market capitalization or book value and add back not the total liabilities but just debts and obligations, as noted above, to get to enterprise value. The balance sheet formula can help us explain why:

$$\text{Shareholders' Equity} + \text{Liabilities} = \text{Assets}$$

Using this equation, let's list the actual balance sheet items:

$$\text{Shareholders' Equity [or Market Capitalization]} + \text{Accounts}$$
$$\text{Payable} + \text{Accrued Expenses} + \text{Short-Term Debt} + \text{Long-Term Debt} =$$
$$\text{Cash} + \text{Accounts Receivable} + \text{Inventory} + \text{Property, Plant, and Equipment}$$

To better illustrate the theory, in this example we assume the company has no non-controlling interests, no preferred securities, and no other non-operating liabilities such as unallocated pension funds – just short-term debt, long-term debt, and cash.

We will abbreviate some line items so the formula is easier to read:

$$\text{S.E. [or Mkt. Cap.]} + \text{AP} + \text{AE} + \text{STD} + \text{LTD} = \text{Cash} + \text{AR} + \text{Inv.} + \text{PP \& E}$$

Now we need to move everything that's not related to debt to the other side of the equation, or the accounts payable (AP) and accrued expenses (AE). We can simply subtract AP and AE from both sides of the equation to get:

$$\text{S.E. [or Mkt. Cap.]} + \text{STD} + \text{LTD} = \text{Cash} + \text{AR} + \text{Inv.} + \text{PP \& E} - [\text{AP} + \text{AE}]$$

And we can regroup the terms on the right to get:

$$\text{S.E. [or Mkt. Cap.]} + \text{STD} + \text{LTD} = \text{Cash} + \text{PP \& E} + \text{AR} + \text{Inv.} - \text{AP} - \text{AE}$$

Notice that AR + Inv. – AP – AE, or current assets less current liabilities is working capital, so:

$$\text{S.E. [or Mkt. Cap.]} + \text{STD} + \text{LTD} = \text{Cash} + \text{PP \& E} + \text{W.C.}$$

Now remember enterprise value is shareholders' equity (or market capitalization) plus debt *less cash*, so we need to subtract cash from both sides of the equation:

$$\text{S.E. [or Mkt. Cap.]} + \text{STD} + \text{LTD} - \text{Cash} = \text{PP \& E} + \text{W.C.}$$

Short-term debt plus long-term debt less cash and cash equivalents is also known as Net Debt. So, this gives us:

$$\text{S.E. [or Mkt. Cap.]} + \text{Net Debt} = \text{PP \& E} + \text{W.C.}$$

This is a very important formula. So, when adding net debt to shareholders' equity or market capitalization, we are backing into the value of the company's PP&E and working capital in the previous example, or more generally, the core operating assets of the business. So, enterprise value is a way of determining the implied value of a company's core operating assets. Further, enterprise value based on market capitalization, or

$$(\text{Enterprise Value} = \text{Market Capitalization} + \text{Net Debt})$$

is a way to approach the value of the operating assets as determined by the market.

	Net Debt ($3MM)		Implied Value of	Net Debt ($3MM)
W.C. and PP&E ($13MM)			Operating Assets in the Market ($15MM)	
	Shareholders' Equity ($10MM)			Market Cap ($12MM)

Book Value   **Market Value**

Note that we have simplified the example for illustration. If the company had non-controlling interests, preferred securities, or other non-operating liabilities such as unallocated pension funds in addition to debts, the formula would read:

Enterprise Value = Market Capitalization + Net Debt + Non-Controlling Interests + Preferred Securities + Capital Lease Obligations (+ Other Non-Operating Liabilities)

Quite often, people wonder why cash needs to be removed from net debt in this equation. This is also a very common investment banking interview question. And, as illustrated here, cash is not considered an operating asset; it is not an asset that will be generating future income for the business (arguably). And so, true value of a company to an investor is the value of just those assets that will continue to produce profit and growth in the future. This is one of the reasons why, in a discounted cash flow analysis, we are only concerned about the cash being produced from the operating assets of the business. (We will discuss this further later.) It is also crucial to understand this core valuation concept, because the definition of an operating asset, or the interpretation of which portions of the company will provide future value, can differ from company to market to industry. Rather than depending on simple formulas, it is important to understand the reason behind them in this rapidly changing environment so you can be equipped with the proper tools to create your own formulas. For example, do internet businesses rely on PP&E as the core operating assets? If not, would the current enterprise value formula have meaning? How about in emerging markets? Subsequent books will dive into each industry in more detail.

MULTIPLES

Multiples are metrics that compare the value of a business relative to its operations. A company could have a market capitalization of $100MM, but what does that mean in relation to their operating performance? If that company is producing $10MM in net income, then its value is 10× the net income it produces. "10× net income" is a market value multiple. These multiples are used to compare the performance of one company to another. Let's say I wanted to compare this business to another business that also has $100MM in market cap. How would I know which business is the better investment? The value itself is arbitrary in this case unless it is compared to the actual performance of the business. So if the other company is producing $5MM in net income, its multiple is 20×; its value is 20× the net income it produces. As an investor, I would prefer to invest in the lower multiple, as it is the "cheaper" investment. It is more net income for lower value. So, multiples help us compare relative values to a business's operations.

Other multiples exist, depending on what underlying operating metric one would like to use as the basis of comparison. Instead of net income, for example, EBIT, EBITDA, and revenue can be used. But how do we determine which are better metrics to compare? Let's compare two companies with similar operations. (See Table 7.1.)

Let's say we want to consider investing in either Company A or Company B. Company A is a small distribution business, a package delivery business that has generated $10,000 in revenue in a given period. This is a startup company run and operated by one person. It has a cost structure that has netted $5,000 in EBITDA. Company B is also a small delivery business operating in a different region, also producing $5,000 in EBITDA. However, the current owner of Company A has decided to operate his business out of his home. He parks the delivery truck in his garage, so he has minimal depreciation costs and no interest expense. The owner of Company B, however, has decided to operate his business differently. He has built a warehouse to store the packages and park the truck. This has increased the depreciation expense and has created additional interest expense, bringing net income to zero. If we were to compare both businesses based on net income, Company A is clearly performing better than Company B. But, what if we are only concerned about the core operations? That is, what if we are only concerned about the volume of packages being delivered, number of customers, and the direct costs associated to the deliveries? What if we were looking to acquire Company A or B, for example? In that case, let's say we don't care

TABLE 7.1 Business Comparison

Business Comparison	Company A	Company B
Revenue	10,000.0	10,000.0
COGS	3,500.0	3,500.0
Operating Expenses	1,500.0	1,500.0
EBITDA	5,000.0	5,000.0
Depreciation	500.0	3,000.0
EBIT	4,500.0	2,000.0
Interest	0.0	2,000.0
EBT	4,500.0	0.0
Taxes (@ 35%)	1,575.0	0.0
Net Income	2,925.0	0.0

about the debt, the warehouse, or the trucks, as we would sell the warehouse and trucks and pay down the debt. Here, EBITDA would be a better underlying comparable measure. From an operations perspective, looking at EBITDA, both companies are performing well, and we could have been misled in that case by looking at net income.

So, although Market Capitalization / Net Income is a common multiple, there are other multiples using metrics, such as EBIT or EBITDA. However, since EBIT and EBITDA are values before interest is taken into effect, we cannot compare them to market capitalization. Remember: Market capitalization, based on the share price, is the value of a business after lenders are paid; EBITDA (before interest) is before lenders have been paid. So, adding net debt (plus potentially other items as discussed in the enterprise value section) back to market capitalization gives us a numerator (enterprise value) that we can use with EBIT or EBITDA as a multiple:

$$\text{Enterprise Value} / \text{EBIT}$$

Or:

$$\text{Enterprise Value} / \text{EBITDA}$$

So, in short, if a financial metric you want to use as the comparable metric is after debt or interest, it must be related to market capitalization – this is a market value multiple. If the financial metric is before debt or interest, it is related to enterprise value – an enterprise value multiple.

Market Value Multiples	Enterprise Value Multiples
Market Capitalization / Net Income	Enterprise Value / Sales
Price ($/share) / EPS	Enterprise Value / EBITDA
Market Capitalization / Book Value	Enterprise Value / EBIT

THREE CORE METHODS OF VALUATION

The value definitions and multiples from earlier in the chapter are applied in several ways to best approach how much an entity could be worth. There are three major methods utilized to approach this value:

1. Comparable company analysis
2. Precedent transactions analysis
3. Discounted cash flow analysis

Each method is based on wide-ranging variables and could be considered quite subjective. However, each method approaches value from a very different perspective. So we can have relatively strong support of value from a financial perspective if all three methods fall along a similar valuation range.

Note that there is often considered a fourth method based on a leveraged buyout analysis. Leveraged buyouts are a much larger subject, and will be covered in subsequent books.

Comparable Company Analysis

The comparable company analysis compares our company with companies that are similar in size, product, and geography. The comparable company analysis utilizes multiples as a measure of comparison. If the peers' multiples are consistently higher than the multiples of the company we are valuing, it could mean that our company is undervalued. Conversely, if the peers' multiples are consistently lower than the multiples of the company we are valuing, it could mean that our company is overvalued. The comparable company analysis has one major advantage over the other three:

- It is the most current of all three analyses. It gives a market perspective. The comparable company analysis is based on the most recent stock prices and financials of the company.

However, the comparable company analysis has the following drawbacks:

- It may be difficult to find companies to compare. If the company has a unique business model, is in a very "niche" industry, or is not the size of a public company, it may be difficult to find the right peer group.
- The markets may be undervalued or overvalued. We could be in a market environment in which the entire industry is overvalued or undervalued. If so, our analysis will be flawed.

Precedent Transactions Analysis

The precedent transactions analysis assesses relative value by looking at multiples of historical transactions. The value of our company is relative to the price others have paid for similar companies. So, if we look for other companies, similar to ours, that have been acquired, we can compare their purchase multiples to assess approximate value of our business.

Purchase Multiples Purchase multiples are similar to market multiples (described previously), except the numerator in a purchase multiple is based on the price paid for an entity as opposed to the current market value.

Enterprise Value/Net Income, for example, is based on (Market Capitalization + Net Debt[a])/Net Income in a market multiple. But in a purchase multiple, Enterprise Value/Net Income is based on (Purchase Price + Net Debt[a])/Net Income.

A precedent transactions analysis has this major advantage over the other three:

- *Purchase price includes a premium.* This could be advantageous if we were looking to acquire a company. It would help us determine how much of a premium we would need to consider to convince the owner or shareholders to hand over the company to us.

There are several major drawbacks to the analysis:

- *Historical analysis.* Precedent transactions by definition are historical transactions. The analysis may be irrelevant if we are in a completely different economic environment.
- *Difficult-to-find relevant transactions.* Especially in an environment where there are not many acquisitions, it may not be possible to find acquisitions similar to the one we are analyzing.

TABLE 7.2 Multiples

	Market Value	**Enterprise Value (E.V.)**
Market Multiples	Market Cap/Net Income Price / E.P.S (P/E)	E.V. / EBIT E.V. / EBITDA E.V. / Sales (where E.V. is Market Cap. + Net Debt[a])
Purchase Multiples	Purchase Price/Net Income	E.V. / EBIT E.V. / EBITDA E.V. / Sales (where E.V. is Purchase Price + Net Debt[a])

[a]Plus potentially non-controlling interests, preferred securities, unallocated pension funds (and arguably other non-operating liabilities) as discussed in the enterprise value section earlier in this chapter.

- *Difficult-to-get data.* Even if we do find relevant transactions, it is not always easy to find the data to create the multiples.

Discounted Cash Flow Analysis

The discounted cash flow (DCF) analysis is known as the most "technical" of the three major methods, as it is based on the company's cash flows. The discounted cash flow takes the company's projected unlevered free cash flow (UFCF) and discounts it back to present value (PV). We typically project the company's cash flows out five to seven years. We then create a terminal value, which is the value of the business from the last projected year into perpetuity. The enterprise value of the business is the sum of the PV of all the projected cash flows and the PV of the terminal value.

DCF Enterprise Value = Present Value (PV) of UFCF Year 1 + ... + PV of UFCF Year n + PV of Terminal Value

The DCF analysis has this major advantage over the other three:

- *It is the most technical.* It is based on the company's cash flows from model projections, as opposed to the comparable company analysis, for example, which is mainly driven by market data.

The analysis also has several disadvantages:

- *Terminal value.* Although the first projected years are based on modeled cash flows, the terminal value accounts for a very significant portion of the overall valuation. That terminal value is based on a multiple or a perpetuity.
- *Model projections.* The model projections could be inaccurate; they could be overstated or understated, depending on what is driving the projections.
- *Discount rate.* The discount rate may be difficult to estimate. We will go through standard techniques, but these standards do not apply in all situations.

Again, just as all three valuation methodologies have significant drawbacks, they do have strengths. In the next few chapters, we will see how to play the strengths of each off of the others to come up with an approximate value for Amazon.

CHAPTER 9

Discounted Cash Flow Analysis

As discussed in Chapter 8, in order to properly value a business based on cash flows, we need to first establish the appropriate cash flows to value – the unlevered free cash flow (UFCF). Once we have properly calculated UFCF we can project and discount the cash flows to present value (PV). We then estimate a terminal value, which is a representation of the value of the business after the last projected year. The sum of the present values of each cash flow is added to the PV of the terminal value to give us the total value of the business.

DCF Enterprise Value = Present Value (PV) of UFCF Year 1 + ... +
PV of UFC Year n + PV of Terminal Value

MIDYEAR VS. END-OF-YEAR CONVENTION

The formula to calculate PV is UFCF/$(1 + DiscountRate)^{period}$. When discounting cash flows in valuation, there are two methods to determine the period: the midyear convention and the end-of-year convention.

The end-of-year convention assumes each cash flow is discounted at a full year. Year 1 is discounted by one full year, Year 2 by two full years, and so on.

The midyear-convention discounts each cash flow by half a year. Year 1 is discounted by half a year (0.5), Year 2 by 1.5 years, and so on. The concept here is that we don't know exactly when these cash flows come in. Technically, if the end-of-year convention is used where we discount the cash flows by one year in full, we are assuming the cash flow has come in one lump sum at the end of the year. The midyear convention slightly adjusts for this by discounting half a year.

UNLEVERED FREE CASH FLOW

Unlevered free cash flow (UFCF) is cash that is available to all capital providers, including equity holders and lenders. In other words, it is a measure of cash flow before equity holders and lenders have been paid. Further, as valuation is a measure of a company's core operating assets of a business, UFCF should represent the cash generated or lost based on the core operations of the business. To clarify, let's take a look at Amazon's complete cash flow statement. (See Table 9.1.)

To get to an unlevered cash flow amount, we want to remove all cash flows related to the capital structure. So we eliminate anything related to dividend payouts, non-controlling interests, share issuances, share buybacks, debt raises, and debt paydowns; the entire financing activities section is removed.

Further, we want a measure of cash that approaches everyday activity, so non-recurring and extraordinary items such as business acquisitions, purchases and sales of marketable securities, and proceeds from property and equipment sales will be removed. In the investing activities section, we are left with capital expenditures. (See Table 9.2.)

Simplifying the leftover cash flows gives us:

Unlevered Free Cash Flow
Net income
+ Depreciation & amortization
+ Deferred taxes
+ Other non-cash items
+ Working capital changes
– Capital expenditures

Finally, since we are trying to capture a complete measure of cash before lenders have been paid, we also need to adjust the net income for interest expense. So we need to add one more line item: after-tax net interest expense.

Unlevered Free Cash Flow
Net income
+ Depreciation & amortization
+ Deferred taxes
+ Other non-cash items
+ Working capital changes
– Capital expenditures
+ A/T Net interest expense
= Total unlevered free cash flow

TABLE 9.1 Consolidated Statements of Cash Flows

Consolidated Statements of Cash Flows (in US$ millions except per share amounts)

Period Ending December 31	Actuals			Estimates				
	2018A	2019A	2020A	2021E	2022E	2023E	2024E	2025E
Cash Flows from Operating Activities								
Net income	10,073.0	11,588.0	21,331.0	23,485.3	27,127.7	27,876.9	27,000.1	23,647.9
Depreciation and amortization	15,341.0	21,789.0	25,251.0	28,669.8	35,841.6	43,932.4	52,737.3	62,077.6
Stock-based compensation	5,418.0	6,864.0	9,208.0	11,694.2	13,869.3	15,646.4	17,027.5	18,062.9
% of total operating expenses	8.2%	8.7%	8.8%	8.8%	8.8%	8.8%	8.8%	8.8%
Other operating expense (income), net	274.0	164.0	(71.0)	(90.2)	(106.9)	(120.6)	(131.3)	(139.3)
% of total net sales	0.1%	0.1%	0.0%	0.0%	0.0%	0.0%	0.0%	0.0%
Other expense (income), net	219.0	(249.0)	(2,582.0)	219.0	(249.0)	219.0	(249.0)	219.0
Deferred income taxes	441.0	796.0	(554.0)	(554.0)	(554.0)	(554.0)	(554.0)	(554.0)
Changes in Operating Working Capital								
Changes in inventory	(1,314.0)	(3,278.0)	(2,849.0)	(4,330.4)	(5,231.3)	(4,274.1)	(3,321.7)	(2,490.2)
Changes in accounts receivable	(4,615.0)	(7,681.0)	(8,169.0)	(4,260.3)	(5,357.2)	(4,377.0)	(3,401.6)	(2,550.2)

(Continued)

TABLE 9.1 (*Continued*)

Consolidated Statements of Cash Flows (in US$ millions except per share amounts)

Period Ending December 31	Actuals			Estimates				
	2018A	2019A	2020A	2021E	2022E	2023E	2024E	2025E
Changes in accounts payable	3,263.0	8,193.0	17,480.0	3,484.5	14,140.4	11,553.0	8,978.5	6,731.2
Changes in accrued expenses	472.0	(1,383.0)	5,754.0	1,272.1	5,448.9	4,451.9	3,459.8	2,593.8
Changes in unearned revenue	1,151.0	1,711.0	1,265.0	1,657.2	2,113.9	1,727.1	1,342.3	1,006.3
Net Changes in Working Capital	(1,043.0)	(2,438.0)	13,481.0	(2,177.0)	11,114.6	9,080.9	7,057.3	5,290.8
Total Cash from Operating Activities	30,723.0	38,514.0	66,064.0	61,247.2	87,043.3	96,080.9	102,887.9	108,605.0
Cash Flows from Investing Activities								
CAPEX [Purchase of property and equipment]	(13,427.0)	(16,861.0)	(40,140.0)	(54,423.4)	(64,546.2)	(72,816.7)	(79,244.2)	(84,062.9)
% of Revenue	5.8%	6.0%	10.4%	11.1%	11.1%	11.1%	11.1%	11.1%
Proceeds from property and equipment sales and incentives	2,104.0	4,172.0	5,096.0	0.0	0.0	0.0	0.0	0.0
Business acquisitions, net of cash acquired	(2,186.0)	(2,461.0)	(2,325.0)	0.0	0.0	0.0	0.0	0.0

Sales and maturities in marketable securities	8,240.0	22,681.0	50,237.0	8,240.0	22,681.0	8,240.0	22,681.0	8,240.0
Purchases of marketable securities	(7,100.0)	(31,812.0)	(72,479.0)	(7,100.0)	(31,812.0)	(7,100.0)	(31,812.0)	(7,100.0)
Total Cash Flows from Investing Activities	**(12,369.0)**	**(24,281.0)**	**(59,611.0)**	**(53,283.4)**	**(73,677.2)**	**(71,676.7)**	**(88,375.2)**	**(82,922.9)**
Cash Flows from Financing Activities								
Short-term borrowings (repayments)	73.0	(116.0)	619.0	0.0	0.0	0.0	0.0	0.0
Long-term borrowings (repayments)	27.0	(295.0)	8,972.0	0.0	0.0	0.0	0.0	0.0
Principal repayments of finance leases	(7,449.0)	(9,628.0)	(10,642.0)	0.0	0.0	0.0	0.0	0.0
Principal repayments of financing obligations	(337.0)	(27.0)	(53.0)	0.0	0.0	0.0	0.0	0.0
Total Cash Flows from Financing Activities	**(7,686.0)**	**(10,066.0)**	**(1,104.0)**	**0.0**	**0.0**	**0.0**	**0.0**	**0.0**
Foreign Currency Effect on Cash, Cash Equivalents, and Restricted Cash	(351.0)	70.0	618.0	(351.0)	70.0	618.0	(351.0)	70.0
Total Change in Cash and Cash Equivalents	**10,317.0**	**4,237.0**	**5,967.0**	**7,612.8**	**13,436.1**	**25,022.2**	**14,161.7**	**25,752.1**
SUPPLEMENTAL DATA:								
Cash flow before debt paydown				7,612.8	13,436.1	25,022.2	14,161.7	25,752.1

TABLE 9.2 Simplified Statements of Cash Flows

Consolidated Statements of Cash Flows (in US$ millions except per share amounts)

Period Ending December 31	Actuals			Estimates				
	2018A	2019A	2020A	2021E	2022E	2023E	2024E	2025E
Cash Flows from Operating Activities								
Net income	10,073.0	11,588.0	21,331.0	23,485.3	27,127.7	27,876.9	27,000.1	23,647.9
Depreciation and amortization	15,341.0	21,789.0	25,251.0	28,669.8	35,841.6	43,932.4	52,737.3	62,077.6
Stock-based compensation	5,418.0	6,864.0	9,208.0	11,694.2	13,869.3	15,646.4	17,027.5	18,062.9
% of total operating expenses	*8.2%*	*8.7%*	*8.8%*	*8.8%*	*8.8%*	*8.8%*	*8.8%*	*8.8%*
Other operating expense (income), net	274.0	164.0	(71.0)	(90.2)	(106.9)	(120.6)	(131.3)	(139.3)
% of total net sales	*0.1%*	*0.1%*	*0.0%*	*0.0%*	*0.0%*	*0.0%*	*0.0%*	*0.0%*
Other expense (income), net	219.0	(249.0)	(2,582.0)	219.0	(249.0)	219.0	(249.0)	219.0
Deferred income taxes	441.0	796.0	(554.0)	(554.0)	(554.0)	(554.0)	(554.0)	(554.0)

Changes in Operating Working Capital								
Changes in inventory	(1,314.0)	(3,278.0)	(2,849.0)	(4,330.4)	(5,231.3)	(4,274.1)	(3,321.7)	(2,490.2)
Changes in accounts receivable	(4,615.0)	(7,681.0)	(8,169.0)	(4,260.3)	(5,357.2)	(4,377.0)	(3,401.6)	(2,550.2)
Changes in accounts payable	3,263.0	8,193.0	17,480.0	3,484.5	14,140.4	11,553.0	8,978.5	6,731.2
Changes in accrued expenses	472.0	(1,383.0)	5,754.0	1,272.1	5,448.9	4,451.9	3,459.8	2,593.8
Changes in unearned revenue	1,151.0	1,711.0	1,265.0	1,657.2	2,113.9	1,727.1	1,342.3	1,006.3
Net Changes in Working Capital	(1,043.0)	(2,438.0)	13,481.0	(2,177.0)	11,114.6	9,080.9	7,057.3	5,290.8
Total Cash Flows from Operating Activities	30,723.0	38,514.0	66,064.0	61,247.2	87,043.3	96,080.9	102,887.9	108,605.0
Cash Flows from Investing Activities								
CAPEX [Purchase of property and equipment]	(13,427.0)	(16,861.0)	(40,140.0)	(54,423.4)	(64,546.2)	(72,816.7)	(79,244.2)	(84,062.9)
% of revenue	*5.8%*	*6.0%*	*10.4%*	*11.1%*	*11.1%*	*11.1%*	*11.1%*	*11.1%*

There's often a lot of confusion as to whether these line items should be added or subtracted. The best rule of thumb is to follow how the cash flow statement is making these adjustments. We are trying to replicate a form of cash flow, so if the cash flow statement is adding the item, we should also add it; if the cash flow statement is subtracting the item, we should subtract. According to a standard cash flow statement, the flow should be:

Net Income + D & A + Deferred Taxes + Other Non-Cash Items + Working Capital Changes – CAPEX + A/T Net Interest Expense

Yes, it is plus working capital, because the cash flow statement adds working capital to the net income to get to cash from operations. We get confused here a lot because many textbooks suggest subtracting working capital. They are actually referring to subtracting the balance sheet working capital changes. In other words, if accounts receivable increased from $0 to $1,000, or if the change is $1,000, then we know the cash flow change is –$1,000, because an increase in an asset reflects a cash outflow. However, if we take the actual working capital number directly from the cash flow statement, which is already represented as a negative (–$1,000), we just add it.

It is crucial to note that there can be other items in the investing activities other than CAPEX that could arguably be attributable to everyday operations. Although it's not explicitly defined in the UFCF formula, the point of the entire analysis is to get to a number that reflects the cash we expect to be generated from the future operations of the business. Further, in the operating activities, there may be other adjustments that are not categorized within the standard UFCF definition. It is important to step back and think about how these line items are affecting net income to decide if they should also be adjusted in the UFCF. In other words, if these line items are actually non-cash items that need to be adjusted to net income in order to get to a closer measure of cash from net income, then they should be included in the analysis. However, if these are truly non-recurring events, and if we have already pulled them out of net income on the income statement, adjusting them here may not be correct. This is one example of how important it is to fully understand where UFCF is coming from and why it is being used, as opposed to just taking and using the formula as printed.

Now, the previous definition is not the most standard definition of UFCF. Typically, we use EBIT as a starting point, not net income. It is easier to project an income statement from revenue down to EBIT only, rather than all the way down to net income, especially since we are adding back so many items anyway. However, either way will get you the same results. So if we had EBIT as a starting point, we still have to make the same core adjustments:

Unlevered Free Cash Flow
Net income
+Depreciation and amortization
+Deferred taxes
+Other non-cash items
+Working capital changes
− Capital expenditures
+ A/T net interest expense
= Total unlevered free cash flow

Unlevered Free Cash Flow
EBIT
+Depreciation and amortization
+Deferred taxes
+Other non-cash items
+Working capital changes
− Capital expenditures

Note here we have to double-check once again which line items we are (or are not) including as other non-cash items, and for different reasons: If the particular non-cash item was a net income adjustment for a line item that was below the EBIT line, which we didn't even include anyway, adjusting it here would be incorrect.

We still have to make one more adjustment: taxes. We do not need to adjust for interest expense as EBIT is already before interest expense. But, EBIT is also before taxes. So in order to adjust for taxes we need to take EBIT × Tax%. It is important to note we do not take the exact number of taxes from the income statement as that number includes the effects of interest.

Unlevered Free Cash Flow
Net income
+Depreciation and amortization
+Deferred taxes
+Other non-cash items
+Working capital changes
− Capital expenditures
+A/T net interest expense
= Total unlevered free cash flow

Unlevered Free Cash Flow
EBIT
+Depreciation and amortization
+Deferred taxes
+Other non-cash items
+Working capital changes
− Capital expenditures
− Taxes (EBIT × Tax%)
= Total unlevered free cash flow

Note here the importance of understanding the derivation of UFCF. In this ever-changing market environment with new and evolving business models, the standard "textbook" definition of UFCF may need to be adjusted to be a true measure of value for a particular entity. Understanding the purpose of UFCF as a measure of value will help one to create his or her own adjustments to get to the true value of an entity.

WEIGHTED AVERAGE COST OF CAPITAL (WACC)

Note: We will knowingly take an oversimplistic view of WACC in this book. Again, there are many great books out there that focus solely on this topic, and although important to valuation, the purpose of this book is not to focus solely on WACC but to understand it just enough to use it as a tool for analysis.

Now that we have UFCF, we need to discount the flows to PV. The rate at which we discount them is determined by how much an investor expects to be returned for his or her particular investment. For a company with both debt and equity in its capital structure, we would calculate a weighted average of the returns the equity investors would expect and the returns the lenders would expect weighted by the amount of equity versus debt in the business.

For example, if our company had both equity investors and debt lenders, and if the equity investors expect a 25% rate of return and the debt lenders expect a 10% rate of return, our WACC would be a weighted average of the equity investors' and lenders' required rate of returns to the actual amount of debt and equity invested in the business. So if the business contains $100 of equity and $200 of debt, the equity investors expect a $25 ($100 × 25%) annual return, and the lenders expect a $20 ($200 × 10%) annual return, or, we would need to return $45 ($25+ $20) each year. This represents a combined 15% ($45 / $300) expected rate of return. We have ignored tax here for simplicity.

This is the weighted average cost of capital. More specifically, the formula is:

$$\text{WACC} = \frac{\text{Debt}}{(\text{Debt} + \text{Equity})} \times \text{Cost of Debt} \times (1 - \text{Tax\%}) + \frac{\text{Equity}}{(\text{Debt} + \text{Equity})} \times \text{Cost of Equity}$$

Note that we apply (1 – Tax%) to the cost of debt as those interest payments are tax deductible.

We can apply this to the previous example:

$$\text{WACC} = \frac{\$200}{(\$100 + \$200)} \times 10\% \times (1 - 0\%) + \frac{\$100}{(\$100 + \$200)} \times 25\%$$

Note that we assumed 0% taxes in this simple example.

This gives us 15%.

Although this is the fundamental definition of WACC, true WACC would take into account all types of debts and equity a company may have in the following way. Let's say a company has long-term debt, mezzanine debt, common equity, and preferred capital. And, let's call total capital the sum of the long-term debt, mezzanine debt, common equity, and preferred capital. So, the WACC would be:

$$WACC = \frac{Long\text{-}Term\ Debt}{Total\ Capital} \times Cost\ of\ Long\text{-}Term\ Debt \times (1 - Tax\%)$$

$$+ \frac{Mezzanine}{Total\ Capital} \times Cost\ of\ Mezzanine \times (1 - Tax\%) + \frac{Preferred}{Total\ Capital}$$

$$\times Cost\ of\ Preferred + \frac{Common\ Equity}{Total\ Capital} \times Cost\ of\ Common\ Equity$$

We assume here the interest payments on the long-term and mezzanine debts are tax deductible, and we also assume there are no tax-deductible payments made on the preferred securities.

WACC should be a current value based on market trends, so it is appropriate to take the market value of equity, and the market value of debts and interests (when available) to calculate the most current WACC.

Cost of Debt

The cost of debt is the expected return to the debt lenders, or the interest rate. It is important to use the most current interest rates if available.

Cost of Equity

The cost of equity is the expected return to the equity investors. To estimate the cost of equity, we must determine the expected rate of return of a company. Since the expected rate of return is not directly obtainable, especially for a public company, we must rely on an asset-pricing model. Asset-pricing models base expected return on the risk of an entity. There are several different asset-pricing models; each differs in the way risk is defined and interpreted into an appropriate return. The most common used in investment banking is the Capital Asset Pricing Model (CAPM).

The general idea of the CAPM is based on the graph in Figure 9.1.

Here the x-axis represents the risk and the y-axis represents return. This graph can represent any investment within the universe of investments from playing poker to investing in the S&P 500. In such an environment, given that it is a rational environment, where we assume all investors are making

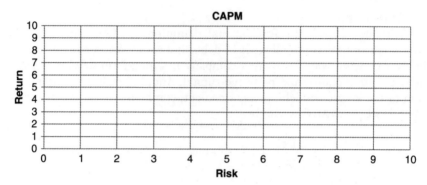

FIGURE 9.1   Capital Asset Pricing Model

rational investment decisions, we assume there is always some investment with zero risk. This investment could have a 0% return or a negative return, but we assume if that was the case, no investors would be interested. So, we assume there exists some riskless investment with some minimal return. We understand that many investments do not work out, but we are making assumptions in an environment of expected returns. In the US markets, we can take the US Treasury bonds as an example of an arguably riskless investment at a 2.07% return as of July 1, 2021. CAPM states if such an investment exists, no rational investor would make an investment that would bring about the same return but would contain risk. (See Figure 9.2.)

Why would we take additional risk for the exact same return when we can get that return with zero risk? CAPM goes further to state that an investor would accept greater risk in a particular investment if there is an equivalent potential to receive a greater rate of return. (See Figure 9.3.)

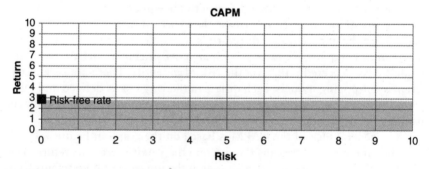

FIGURE 9.2   Capital Asset Pricing Model: Risk-Free Rate
We would never invest in the shaded area, which is less return for additional risk.

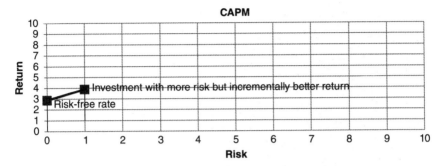

FIGURE 9.3   Capital Asset Pricing Model: Risky Investment

This can go on with an investment of even greater risk. A rational investor would only consider an investment of greater risk than the previous investment if there is an equivalently greater return. This would continue out to the line in Figure 9.4, below where all rational investments should center on.

It is important to note that although there are investments that have poor results, there will never be a rational investor making continuous poor-return investments with great risk. For that reason, there should not be a majority of investments made below the drawn line.

Further, if there exist investments that produce a higher return, or investments above the line, then all rational investors would eventually gravitate to that investment and would form a new basis of what levels of returns an investor would expect for the associated risk. Therefore, if that were the case, then there would be a new line drawn, a new basis. (See the dotted line in Figure 9.5, which would replace the solid line.)

Given the fact that that line would exist if it could exist, and further given the fact that it does not exist, implies that it cannot exist.

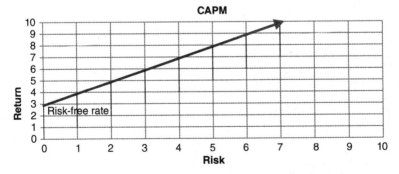

FIGURE 9.4   Capital Asset Pricing Model: Average Risk/Return

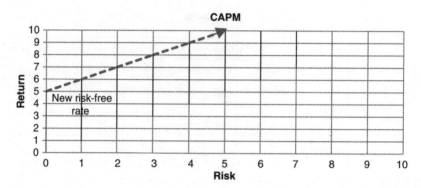

FIGURE 9.5 Capital Asset Pricing Model: Theoretical New Average Line

This line is expected to be an average, and in reality there are investments that can fall anywhere in the box, but the main idea is that on average they should hover around the line. (See Figure 9.6.)

In order to find the cost of equity of our investment, we need to locate the dot representing the expected risk/return of Amazon.

Market Risk Premium

Before locating the risk/return of Amazon, it is important to find the estimated expected return of the entire market. Based on the logic of the previous section, the average return of an index, such as the S&P 500, should be somewhere on the line drawn in Figure 9.6 as this is an indicator of where one would hope rational investors would gravitate toward, at least in theory. There are several ways to estimate this return. One is by taking the

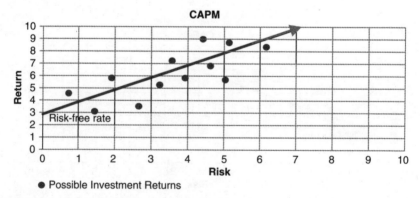

FIGURE 9.6 Capital Asset Pricing Model: Average Line with Additional Investments

historical average of the index or portfolio over the last 10, 20, 30 years through the last 100 years, and then taking a median of those averages.

Ibbotson Associates is an expert consulting firm that provides great data on market risk premiums; however, it is not a free resource. We strongly recommend Mr. Aswath Damodaran's website, which can be found at http://pages.stern.nyu.edu/~adamodar/.

Another method is based on the dividend model. The dividend model states the expected return is equal to the dividend yield plus the growth in dividends of the stocks that make up a particular index.

For CAPM, we are concerned about the spread between the expected return of the market and the risk-free rate – the premium. This is called the market risk premium. Ibbotson also has research on the spread between the historical returns of the market and the historical risk-free rates to calculate the market risk premium. (*Note:* This valuation section is designed to be light on the theory and cut to the practical methods. For a more thorough and complete theoretical understanding of CAPM, I highly recommend Aswath Damodaran's books on valuation.)

The market risk premium answers this: How much above the risk-free rate can I expect to return from my investment? Let's say the expected return of the S&P 500 is shown in Figure 9.7.

This implies that the components of the S&P 500 index, the individual stocks that make up the index, should hover somewhere around the S&P 500 index. Although there will be exceptions, there should be a radius from where all investments that make up the index should lie. (See Figure 9.8.)

So, if we find a way to pinpoint where Amazon can be within this radius, we can estimate its expected return. This is where beta helps us.

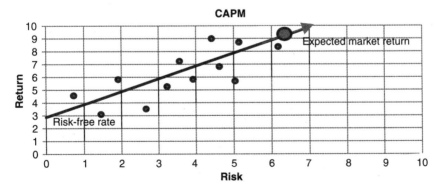

FIGURE 9.7 Capital Asset Pricing Model: Expected Market Return

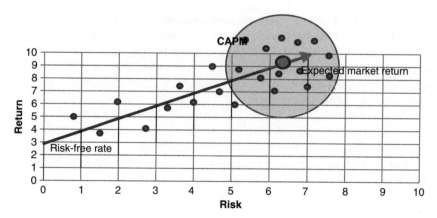

FIGURE 9.8 Capital Asset Pricing Model: Expected Return of S&P 500 Companies

BETA

Beta is a correlation coefficient that represents how closely one set of historical returns correlates or moves with another. In other words, if we compare the historical returns of Amazon with the S&P 500, and if Amazon has a beta of 1, this means that Amazon is perfectly correlated with the S&P 500. Or, if the S&P 500 is expected to return 5%, then Amazon will be expected to return 5%. If, however, beta is 0.5, then if the S&P 500 is expected to return 5%, Amazon will be expected to return 2.5%. Further, if beta is –1, then if the S&P 500 is expected to return 5%, the Amazon will be expected to return –5%.

Amazon's beta is achieved by comparing the last x years of its historical returns to the S&P 500, where x can be 10 years, 30 years, up to 100 years, or more.

The formula for the beta of an asset is

$$\beta_a = \frac{\text{Cov}(r_a, r_p)}{\text{Var}(r_p)}$$

where r_a measures the rate of return of the asset, r_p measures the rate of return of the index or portfolio, $\text{Cov}(r_a, r_p)$ is the covariance between the rates of return of the asset and the index, and $\text{Var}(r_p)$ is the variance between the rates of return of the index.

Many resources have beta data. Barra (www.mscibarra.com) is a research firm known to accurately calculate betas over many different time periods. Unfortunately, this data is not free, but if one has Bloomberg,

Thompson, Capital IQ, or a similar data resource, many of them either pull in Barra betas or calculate their own betas. Yahoo! Finance is a good free resource that also contains beta information.

Levering and Unlevering Beta

Since beta as defined previously is based on market value returns, it is often believed that removing the leverage from such betas would give a closer estimate of the beta directly related to the operating assets of the business. This concept of *unlevering* and *levering* the beta can be achieved by the following formula:

$$\text{Unlevered Beta} = \frac{\text{Levered Beta}}{1 + (1 - \text{Tax}\%) \times \dfrac{\text{Debt}}{\text{Equity}}}$$

$$\text{Re-Levered Beta} = \text{Unlevered Beta} \times \left\{ 1 + (1 - \text{Tax}\%) \times \frac{\text{Debt}}{\text{Equity}} \right\}$$

In practice, this can be used for purposes of valuation. In addition to calculating a company's beta in relation to the market, or looking up a calculated beta, one can take an average of the comparable company's betas. However, since companies have varying capital structures, one can first "unlever" each beta, take the average, then relever the beta using the target company's (Amazon's) capital structure. This can be helpful when trying to assess the beta of a private company or if the company you are trying to assess has for some reason a very unusual beta. It may also be useful to try several methods and compare. Also, the concept of utilizing an unlevered beta can be a useful approximation of the beta directly related to the operating assets of the business.

So in terms of CAPM, the beta of a particular stock can help us identify what its expected return can be. So beta times the market risk premium (MRP) is the effective expected return of our investment. But note the MRP, and effectively the beta times MRP (beta × MRP) is just the expected premium above the risk-free rate. So in order to get the estimated total equity return of a particular investment, we need to add back the risk-free rate of return (rf). So:

$$\text{Cost of Equity} = \text{rf} + \text{Beta}(\beta) \times \text{MRP}$$

When calculating this formula for a particular investment, it is crucial to understand the drivers, even at this most basic level, as they may change in different markets or for unique investments. First, timing is an important consideration. One must consider whether to use a 10-year Treasury rate for the risk-free rate, or a 30-year rate. One must also consider using 10-year calculated betas or 30-year calculated betas. The first rule of thumb is to be consistent. If using a 30-year risk-free rate of return, then one should use 30-year betas and an MRP based on 30-year average returns. Some investors prefer to calculate shorter-term betas based on 10-year metrics; we prefer longer-term betas, as a discounted cash flow (DCF) analysis is a representation of a business far into maturity and perpetuity. But we respect the 10-year argument as well.

It is also important to consider the relative markets. If one is valuing a German company, for example, one would not use the S&P 500 and the US Treasury rates as basis, but rather a German index and German risk-free rate of return.

TERMINAL VALUE

Once we have the discount rate, we will use that rate to discount the projected cash flows. This only gives us the value of the company over the first few projected years. What about the value of the company after the last projected year? In other words, if we have built a five-year model, discounting the UFCFs gives us the implied value of the company for just the first five years.

The terminal value of a company estimates the value of the business after the last estimated year. There are two major methods for calculating the terminal value of a company:

- Multiple method
- Perpetuity method

Multiple Method

The multiple method applies a multiple to the final projected year's financials. Typically, an EBITDA multiple is applied to the company's final-year EBITDA. The value of the company in year 2025, for example, is the value we can sell the company for in 2025. So if we are using a 5× EBITDA multiple, and if the company's 2025 EBITDA is 100,000, then we believe we can sell the company for 500,000. The multiple to use can come from comparable companies, or we can take the company's current market EBITDA multiple. Taking the company's current market multiple can be considered a conservative approach (unless the company is extremely overvalued).

In other words, if we sell the company in five years for at least what it is worth today (on a multiple basis), and we assume EBITDA is growing, then the total sale value should be higher.

Once we have the terminal value, we then discount that value back to PV.

Perpetuity Method

The perpetuity method is based on a typical perpetuity, which is a steady stream of cash flows with no end. The formula for a perpetuity terminal value is:

$$\frac{UFCF \times (1 + g)}{r - g}$$

where r is the discount rate (the WACC) and g should represent the perpetual rate of cash flow growth. g is not easy to estimate. Some people suggest using the GDP growth rate (currently 2–3%) or the rate of inflation (1–2%), but remember this is supposed to represent the growth rate for many years, even if the current environment is sluggish.

Once a terminal value is established, this is also discounted to PV.

It is important to understand the differences between the terminal value of a business based on the multiple and the terminal value based on perpetuity. The perpetuity is based on cash flow and some low growth. The terminal value based on a multiple is driven by the market. It is good practice to run both methods and compare the two. If the multiple method is much higher than the perpetuity, maybe the markets are overvalued, or maybe the cash flow projections are too low (low perpetuity value). Or if the multiple method is much lower than the perpetuity method, maybe our projections are too aggressive, or maybe the markets are undervaluing the business (low multiple). Or, in the best case, both methods produce similar results, which can imply the cash projections are in line with market expectations. These are meant to just be a few of the many ways to interpret the terminal value.

It is interesting to note that in 2008 and 2009, during the recession, we saw many companies whose terminal values utilizing the multiple method were significantly lower than the perpetuity method. This implies the companies' cash flows were strong, but the market was undervaluing the businesses, potentially a rare and good investment opportunity. Today, most of those stocks have increased back to normal levels.

Once we have a terminal value, we would add the terminal value to the sum of the PV of the company's projected cash flows to get a total enterprise value for the business. Let's run the analysis for Amazon to get a better picture of the process.

AMAZON DCF ANALYSIS

We will build a five-year DCF analysis for Amazon. We could have done a 7-year or 10-year, but we felt anything beyond five years would be too uncertain. This is more a matter of preference than rule. We will utilize the DCF tab in the spreadsheet for this analysis. As per the UFCF formula, we need to first locate Amazon's projected 2021 EBIT. This can be found on the income statement in cell G24. So, we can have G7 on the DCF tab be

"= 'Income Statement'!G34"

The rest of the line items in the UFCF analysis should come from the cash flow statement. Remember: The goal is to get an accurate measure of cash produced from the company's operations. However, we take EBIT as opposed to net income, as EBIT already has interest and potentially some other items adjusted, so in that respect it is a closer measure of cash and a better starting point.

Depreciation and amortization will come from row 8 in the cash flow statement. Or, G8 will read

"= 'Cash Flow Statement'!G8"

Deferred taxes, row 9 on the DCF tab, will be linked in from row 14 in the cash flow statement. Or, G9 on the DCF tab equals

"= 'Cash Flow Statement'!G14"

"Other" is a tricky "catch-all" row. This reflects any non-cash items that are not standard to the unlevered cash flow formula for which we may need to adjust. (Please refer to the "Unlevered Free Cash Flow" section earlier in this chapter for a more detailed description.) We should look to the cash flow statement for any other possible adjustments to be considered. Row 9 in the cash flow statement, for example, titled "Stock-based compensation," should be considered.

We need to analyze whether we should be adjusting for this line item. The reason being the cash flow statement makes adjustments on *Net Income*; the DCF makes adjustments to *EBIT*. So, if there is a non-cash adjustment on the cash flow statement that was adjusting out an expense from *below* the EBIT line, and if we make the adjustment here, we would be double counting. This is because, if that expense was *below* the EBIT line, then it is already out of the EBIT formula. Since we are building our DCF analysis from EBIT, before those income statement adjustments are made, it would not make sense to add back that line item in the cash flow statement.

In this case, the "Stock-based compensation" is an adjustment to an SG&A line item. This is above the EBIT line, so we would most likely adjust out this line item by adding it into the "Other" section of the DCF.

We also have row 11 in the cash flow statement titled "Other operating expenses (income)." We have analyzed in Chapters 1 and 2 that this is related to operating expenses that are above the EBIT line. ("Operating" in the line item is a key clue.) So, we will also add this into the "Other" line item in the DCF. Row 13 in the cash flow statement "Other expense (income)" we identified in Chapter 2 as being related to "Other Income," which is *below* the EBIT line item. So, our EBIT number already excludes this item; adding this to the "Other" line item in the DCF would be adding back an expense (or income) that has not yet been accounted for. So, we will *not* include this in our "Other" line item in the DCF.

G10 of our DCF tab should be

"= 'Cash Flow Statement'!G9 + 'Cash Flow Statement'!G11"

"Changes in working capital," row 11 of our DCF tab, will come from the changes in working capital section of our cash flow statement. So, in cell G11 we will have

"= 'Cash Flow Statement'!G21"

Remember the rule here on keeping the working capital flowing exactly as it is flowing in the cash flow statement. Often people get confused, as definitions of UFCF suggest working capital should be subtracted. While, yes, we are adding working capital here, we are effectively subtracting the year-to-year working capital changes from the balance sheet. Please refer to the "Unlevered Free Cash Flow" section earlier in this chapter for more clarification.

Capital expenditures will come from the investing activities section of the cash flow statement. So cell G12 will be

"= 'Cash Flow Statement'!G24"

Finally, taxes will be recalculated here. Don't make the mistake of taking taxes from the income statement. The income statement taxes take into account the effects of interest, which we do not want; EBIT does not do that (as it is *before* interest). So we need to recalculate taxes based on EBIT. Or, Taxes = EBIT × Tax%, so cell G13 should be

"= -G7 * 'Income Statement'!G44"

Remember to put a "-" before this formula, as we want to subtract the taxes from the cash flows.

Now we can sum up the unlevered free cash flow in row 14. G14 is

$$\text{"= SUM(G7 : G13)"}$$

We can highlight every cell from G7 through G14 and copy every formula to the right to get the projected cash flows shown in Table 9.3.

Now that we have calculated UFCFs, we need to calculate the PV of each. Notice there is a "period" row (row 16), where we list the discount period for each year. We will use end-of-year convention. So, since 2021 is one year away, we will have a discount period of 1. In 2022, we will have a discount period of 2, and so on, through 5. So, we will simply hardcode 1 in cell G16, 2 and H16, and so on.

Before we can actually discount each cash flow we need to calculate the weighted average cost of capital (WACC).

WACC

$$\text{WACC} = \frac{\text{Debt}}{(\text{Debt} + \text{Equity})} \times \text{Cost of Debt} \times (1 - \text{Tax\%}) + \frac{\text{Equity}}{(\text{Debt} + \text{Equity})} \times \text{Cost of Equity}$$

There is a box beginning in cell J20 that can help us lay out the inputs for this calculation. Before beginning it is important to consider the time frame and geographic scope of our analysis. Should we create a 10-year WACC or a 30-year WACC? Please refer to the "Weighted Average Cost of Capital" section earlier in this chapter for more detail on the thought process and the differences. Let's create a 30-year WACC, as we like the theory that we are creating a value of the business through perpetuity, a long-term value. In terms of geography, even though Amazon is a global business, they are US–based and a component of the S&P 500. So we need to be sure to use a 30-year US Treasury rate and 30-year beta. We also need to use an MRP based on the S&P 500.

Cost of Equity   Cost of Equity = rf + beta (β) × MRP, where rf is the risk-free rate and MRP is the market risk premium. The best place to get the US Treasury rate is from the Department of Treasury (www.treasury .gov). Googling "US Treasury Rate" will lead you to the page shown in Figure 9.9.

As of July 1, 2021, it looks like the 30-year US Treasury rate is 2.07%. So we can enter 2.07% into cell L21.

TABLE 9.3 Amazon Unlevered Free Cash Flow

Discounted Cash Flow Analysis Consolidated Statements of Cash Flows

Period Ending January 31	Actuals			Estimates				
	2018A	2019A	2020A	2021E	2022E	2023E	2024E	2025E
Unlevered Free Cash Flow								
EBIT				32,480.7	36,682.8	37,884.9	36,302.0	32,375.9
Depreciation & amortization				28,669.8	35,841.6	43,932.4	52,737.3	62,077.6
Deferred taxes				(554.0)	(554.0)	(554.0)	(554.0)	(554.0)
Other				11,604.0	13,762.3	15,525.7	16,896.2	17,923.6
Changes in working capital				(2,177.0)	11,114.6	9,080.9	7,057.3	5,290.8
Capital expenditures				(54,423.4)	(64,546.2)	(72,816.7)	(79,244.2)	(84,062.9)
Taxes				(6,820.9)	(7,703.4)	(7,955.8)	(7,623.4)	(6,798.9)
Total Unlevered Free Cash Flow				8,779.2	24,597.8	25,097.4	25,571.1	26,252.2

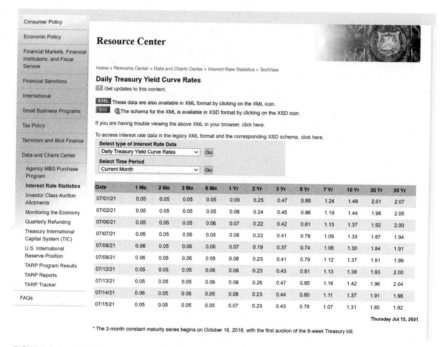

FIGURE 9.9 US Department of the Treasury Resource Center

Now we need to find the market risk premium. We can find MRP data on Mr. Aswath Damodaran's website, which can be found at http://pages .stern.nyu.edu/~adamodar/.

Once arriving at Damodaran's website, selecting "Data" on the top will bring up a section of the site containing very valuable data, including market statistics and multiples for the United States and worldwide. This site is a great reference, and can be utilized to cross-check various market and statistical data. Here, selecting "Current data" will open a dropbox where you should select "Risk/Discount Rate." About four rows down on this page you will find the line to "Risk premiums for Other Markets." This will bring up a file of market risk premiums for the United States and other markets throughout the world. (See Figure 9.10.)

In Figure 9.10, it can be seen that the current market risk premium for the United States is 4.72%. Let's use this. We can hardcode 4.72% into cell L22.

We now need beta to calculate the cost of equity. As mentioned earlier in this chapter, there are many resources that have beta data. A good public

Senegal	Africa	Ba3	3.18%	8.21%	3.49%
Serbia	Eastern Europe & Russia	Ba3	3.18%	8.21%	3.49%
Sharjah	Middle East	Baa2	1.68%	6.56%	1.84%
Singapore	Asia	Aaa	0.00%	4.72%	0.00%
Slovakia	Eastern Europe & Russia	A2	0.75%	5.54%	0.82%
Slovenia	Eastern Europe & Russia	A3	1.06%	5.88%	1.16%
Solomon Islands	Asia	B3	5.75%	11.02%	6.30%
South Africa	Africa	Ba2	2.65%	7.63%	2.91%
Spain	Western Europe	Baa1	1.41%	6.27%	1.55%
Sri Lanka	Asia	Caa1	6.63%	11.98%	7.26%
St. Maarten	Caribbean	Baa3	1.95%	6.85%	2.13%
St. Vincent & the Grenadines	Caribbean	B3	5.75%	11.02%	6.30%
Suriname	Central and South America	Caa3	8.83%	14.40%	9.68%
Swaziland	Africa	B3	5.75%	11.02%	6.30%
Sweden	Western Europe	Aaa	0.00%	4.72%	0.00%
Switzerland	Western Europe	Aaa	0.00%	4.72%	0.00%
Taiwan	Asia	Aa3	0.53%	5.31%	0.59%
Tajikistan	Eastern Europe & Russia	B3	5.75%	11.02%	6.30%
Tanzania	Africa	B2	4.86%	10.05%	5.33%
Thailand	Asia	Baa1	1.41%	6.27%	1.55%
Togo	Africa	B3	5.75%	11.02%	6.30%
Trinidad and Tobago	Caribbean	Ba1	2.21%	7.14%	2.42%
Tunisia	Africa	B2	4.86%	10.05%	5.33%
Turkey	Western Europe	B2	4.86%	10.05%	5.33%
Turks and Caicos Islands	Caribbean	Baa1	1.41%	6.27%	1.55%
Uganda	Africa	B2	4.86%	10.05%	5.33%
Ukraine	Eastern Europe & Russia	B3	5.75%	11.02%	6.30%
United Arab Emirates	Middle East	Aa2	0.44%	5.20%	0.48%
United Kingdom	Western Europe	Aa3	0.53%	5.31%	0.59%
United States	North America	Aaa	0.00%	4.72%	0.00%
Uruguay	Central and South America	Baa2	1.27%	6.56%	1.68%
Uzbekistan	Eastern Europe & Russia	B1	3.98%	9.08%	4.36%
Venezuela	Central and South America	C	17.50%	23.90%	19.18%
Vietnam	Asia	Ba3	3.18%	8.21%	3.49%
Zambia	Africa	Ca	10.60%	16.34%	11.62%

FIGURE 9.10　Country Risk Premiums

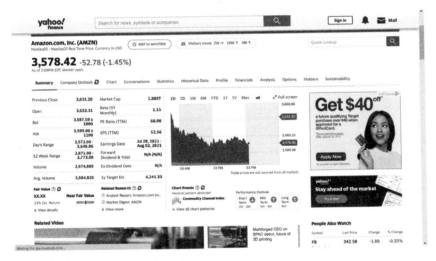

FIGURE 9.11　Amazon Key Statistics

and free resource is Yahoo! Finance. If we go to finance.yahoo.com, and type in AMZN in the "Quote Lookup" section of the site, a company description for Amazon will come up. (See Figure 9.11.)

We can see on the right side of the page in Figure 9.11 "beta" is listed at 1.15. Let's type 1.15 into cell L23. We can now calculate the cost of equity by multiplying the beta times the market risk premium, and then adding the risk-free rate of return. Or, in cell L24:

$$\text{"= L23 * L22 + L21"}$$

This gives us a 7.50% cost of equity.

The cost of debt of a company should be based on the interest rate of debt raised today. It is important to note that the cost of debt should not represent the interest rate on past debts. If the company has a current corporate debt rating, that would be preferred. If not, one would need to estimate the current rate by taking the rate of the most recent debt raised. One can also estimate the rate by looking at similar debts from competitors, but one must make sure that the competitor's capital structure and other factors that may affect the rating are similar.

There are several sites known for establishing current debt rates such as Morningstar, but unfortunately one would often need a business account for access. If you cannot find current market debt information, we can turn to the financials. If we go back the Debt Note 6 from page 56 of the 10-K (Figure 9.12), we can see the latest note issued had an effective interest rate

Note 6 — DEBT

As of December 31, 2020, we had $32.2 billion of unsecured senior notes outstanding (the "Notes"), including $10.0 billion issued in June 2020 for general corporate purposes. We also have other long-term debt and borrowings under our credit facility of $1.6 billion and $924 million as of December 31, 2019 and 2020. Our total long-term debt obligations are as follows (in millions):

	Maturities (1)	Stated Interest Rates	Effective Interest Rates	December 31, 2019	December 31, 2020
2012 Notes issuance of $3.0 billion	2022	2.50%	2.66%	1,250	1,250
2014 Notes issuance of $6.0 billion	2021 - 2044	3.30% - 4.95%	3.43% - 5.11%	5,000	5,000
2017 Notes issuance of $17.0 billion	2023 - 2057	2.40% - 5.20%	2.56% - 4.33%	17,000	16,000
2020 Notes issuance of $10.0 billion	2023 - 2060	0.40% - 2.70%	0.56% - 2.77%	—	10,000
Credit Facility				740	338
Other long-term debt				830	586
Total face value of long-term debt				24,820	33,174
Unamortized discount and issuance costs, net				(101)	(203)
Less current portion of long-term debt				(1,305)	(1,155)
Long-term debt				$ 23,414	$ 31,816

(1) The weighted average remaining lives of the 2012, 2014, 2017, and 2020 Notes were 1.9, 11.8, 16.2, and 18.7 years as of December 31, 2020. The combined weighted average remaining life of the Notes was 15.8 years as of December 31, 2020.

Interest on the Notes is payable semi-annually in arrears. We may redeem the Notes at any time in whole, or from time to time, in part at specified redemption prices. We are not subject to any financial covenants under the Notes. The estimated fair value of the Notes was approximately $26.2 billion and $37.7 billion as of December 31, 2019 and 2020, which is based on quoted prices for our debt as of those dates.

In October 2016, we entered into a $500 million secured revolving credit facility with a lender that is secured by certain seller receivables, which we subsequently increased to $740 million and may from time to time increase in the future subject to lender approval (the "Credit Facility"). The Credit Facility is available until October 2022, bears interest at the London interbank offered rate ("LIBOR") plus 1.40%, and has a commitment fee of 0.50% on the undrawn portion. There were $740 million and $338 million of borrowings outstanding under the Credit Facility as of December 31, 2019 and 2020, which had a weighted-average interest rate of 3.4% and 3.0%, respectively. As of December 31, 2019 and 2020, we have pledged $852 million and $398 million of our cash and seller receivables as collateral for debt related to our Credit Facility. The estimated fair value of the Credit Facility, which is based on Level 2 inputs, approximated its carrying value as of December 31, 2019 and 2020.

Other long-term debt, including the current portion, had a weighted-average interest rate of 4.1% and 2.9% as of December 31, 2019 and 2020. We used the net proceeds from the issuance of this debt primarily to fund certain business operations. The estimated fair value of other long-term debt, which is based on Level 2 inputs, approximated its carrying value as of December 31, 2019 and 2020.

FIGURE 9.12 Amazon's Debts

range from 0.56% to 2.77%. Let's for now use the maximum rate of 2.77 and we can consider this an adjustable variable.

We can hardcode 2.77% into cell L25. We can now use these rates to calculate the WACC.

As WACC is the weighted average cost of capital, we need to weight the cost of equity and cost of debt by the amount of equity in the business versus debt. It is important to note we should take the most current value of the business's equity (market capitalization) and the most current value of the business's debt (if available). Taking Amazon's most current stock price of $3,432.97 (as of 7/1/2021), and 2021 diluted shares outstanding of 519,323,736, gives us a market capitalization of $1,782,822.8MM (after dividing the shares by 1,000,000 so we can continue reporting in $MM). We can hardcode the most current Amazon stock price into cell O22. We can link in the shares outstanding from the income statement. So cell O23 will be "='Income Statement'!G61." The equity value in cell O24 will just be the product of the two:

$$= O22 * O23$$

For total Amazon debt, we can add the latest value of short-term debts, long-term debts, and capital leases as per the latest balance sheet. This gives us in cell O21,

$$= \text{'Balance Sheet'!E22} + \text{'Balance Sheet'!E25} + \text{'Balance Sheet'!E26}$$

As a reminder, the WACC analysis should be a *current* analysis. We pulled the diluted share count from 2021 because we had sourced that number from more current research. To stay in line with timing, we could technically have pulled 2021 debt numbers instead of 2020, but given the mechanics of the model, if we were to capture 2021, we might also be capturing a projected debt issuance or paydowns that would greatly impact the WACC if an extreme debt issuance or paydown scenario would be run. So I feel it best to take the latest reported debt numbers (2020). One could have utilized the Q1 debt numbers for this analysis as well.

We can apply all these inputs to the WACC formula:

$$\text{WACC} = \frac{\text{Debt}}{(\text{Debt} + \text{Equity})} \times \text{Cost of Debt} \times (1 - \text{Tax\%}) + \frac{\text{Equity}}{(\text{Debt} + \text{Equity})} \times \text{Cost of Equity}$$

Or, in cell L27,

$$= O21 / (O21 + O24) * L25 * (1 - \text{'Income Statement'!F44}) + O24 / (O21 + O24) * L24$$

The WACC is 7.23%. (See Table 9.4.)

TABLE 9.4   Walmart WACC

WACC			
Risk-Free Rate	2.07%	**Debt YE 2020**	100,504
Market Risk Premium	4.72%	Stock Price	3,432.97
Beta	1.15	Shares Outstanding	519
Cost of Equity	7.50%	**Equity Value**	1,782,822.8
Cost of Debt	2.77%		
WACC	7.23%		

We can now discount each cash flow using the formula:

$$UFCF/(1 + \text{Discount Rate})^{\text{period}}$$

where the discount rate is the WACC.

Let's first link the WACC calculated in cell L27 into cell F17 to discount the cash flows. So, in cell F17,

$$= L27$$

And in cell G17, we will discount the 2021 UFCF using the discount rate (WACC) in cell F17 and the period of one year from cell G16. Or, in cell G17,

$$= G14/(1 + \$F\$17)^{\wedge}G16$$

Notice that we have put dollar signs in the reference to cell F17. We can copy this formula to the right and all references will shift except for the reference to the discount rate, which we want to be fixed.

Finally, in cell G18 we can sum up all of the discounted cash flows so cell G18 will be,

$$= SUM(G17:K17)$$

(See Table 9.5.)

TABLE 9.5 Discounted Cash Flow Analysis

Discounted Cash Flow Analysis (in US$ millions)

Period Ending January 31	Actuals			Estimates				
	2018A	2019A	2020A	2021E	2022E	2023E	2024E	2025E
Unlevered Free Cash Flow								
EBIT				32,480.7	36,682.8	37,884.9	36,302.0	32,375.9
Depreciation and amortization				28,669.8	35,841.6	43,932.4	52,737.3	62,077.6
Deferred taxes				(554.0)	(554.0)	(554.0)	(554.0)	(554.0)
Other				11,604.0	13,762.3	15,525.7	16,896.2	17,923.6
Changes in working capital				(2,177.0)	11,114.6	9,080.9	7,057.3	5,290.8
Capital expenditures				(54,423.4)	(64,546.2)	(72,816.7)	(79,244.2)	(84,062.9)
Taxes				(6,820.9)	(7,703.4)	(7,955.8)	(7,623.4)	(6,798.9)
Total Unlevered Free Cash Flow				8,779.2	24,597.8	25,097.4	25,571.1	26,252.2
Net Present Value Calculation			7.23%					
Period				1.0	2.0	3.0	4.0	5.0
Discounted Cash Flow				8,187.4	21,393.4	20,356.4	19,342.6	18,519.1
Total Net Present Value				87,798.8				

So $87,798.8MM is the expected present value of Amazon's cash flows for the next five years.

Now, to complete the total value of the business we need to calculate the terminal value, which is the implied value of the business after Year 5. As previously discussed, we will calculate it two ways and compare.

EBITDA Method

For this method, we will take the 2025E EBITDA and multiply it by some EBITDA multiple. It is most common to take an average or median multiple from the comparable company analyses. We also recommend, as another conservative approach, to calculate Amazon's current EBITDA multiple. Let's take the latter approach, and upon conclusion we will cross-check with the comparable company analysis multiples.

In cell F21, we can pull in the company's 2025E EBITDA:

$$= K7 + K8$$

We can now calculate Amazon's current 2020 EBITDA multiple in cell F22. The formula is:

$$\frac{\text{Enterprise Value}}{2020\,\text{EBITDA}}$$

where enterprise value is the market capitalization plus debts, capital leases, non-controlling interests, preferred securities, less cash and cash equivalents. We already have calculated the market capitalization in cell O24 and the total debt in cell O21. We have already included leases in the total debt value; the financing obligations and preferred securities are zero but we should technically include them in the formula. We also need to remove cash to get to enterprise value. So we will take total debt plus financing obligations and preferred securities less cash plus the market capitalization for enterprise value. And we can then divide that enterprise value by the 2020 EBITDA on the income statement to get the multiple. So cell F22 will look like this: =(O24+O21+'Balance Sheet'!E27+'Balance Sheet'!E31-'Balance Sheet'!E8)/'Income Statement'!F31. This gives us 38.2×. Again, we will later compare this with the EBITDA multiples in the comparable company analysis. It's a tough judgment call to determine which are the most appropriate multiples to use. Once the analysis is done we can play around with a few different multiples to see if it has a major effect on the overall analysis.

So for the terminal value in cell F23, we multiply the multiple by the Exit EBITDA, or

$$= F21 * F22$$

We then need to discount this value back to PV. As this EBITDA is based on a 2025 metric, we will discount this back five years. So, in F24 we will have

$$= F23/(1 + F17)\wedge K16$$

So the PV of Amazon's terminal value is $2,547,882.7MM. (See Table 9.6.)

In order to get the total enterprise value for Amazon based on the EBITDA method, we would add this to the PV of UFCF calculated in cell G18. We have a place for this calculation in cell E34, and we can calculate this now. First, we can pull in the total of PV of cash flows into cell E32; that would be "=G18." We can then pull in the PV of terminal value into cell E33, or "=F24." Now we can just add those two cells together into cell E34: "=E32+ E33."

This gives us $2,635,681.6. (See Table 9.7.)

TABLE 9.6   EBITDA Method Terminal Value

EBITDA Method	
Exit Year EBITDA	94,453.6
Multiple	38.2×
Terminal Value	3,611,804.4
Net Present Value	2,547,882.7

TABLE 9.7   Enterprise Value Based on the EBITDA Method

Discounted Cash Flow Total Valuation	EBITDA Method
Total of Present Value of Cash Flows	87,798.8
Present Value of Terminal Value	2,547,882.7
Total Enterprise Value	**2,635,681.6**
Net Debt, Non-controlling Interests, Preferred Securities	
Equity Value	
Share Count (millions)	
Estimated Equity Value per Share	

Let's now take a look at the equity value. Directly below cell E34 is a place for net debt, non-controlling interests, and preferred securities. Let's calculate this using the total debt we have already calculated in cell O21, adding the financing obligations and preferred securities, and subtracting cash from the balance sheet. So in E35 we have:

= O21 + 'Balance Sheet'!E27 + 'Balance Sheet'!E31 − 'Balance Sheet'!E8

We can subtract this from the enterprise value. So cell E36 will read "=E34-E35," which gives us $2,577,299.6MM.

We can now divide the equity value by the number of shares outstanding calculated in O23. So, E37 can read "=O23." And we can divide, so cell E38 will be "=E36/E37." This will give us $4,962.80 based on the EBITDA method. (See Table 9.8.)

We can compare this to the company's current stock price of $3,432.97. This may suggest that the company is still slightly undervalued. Or maybe we had chosen a multiple that is too high. However, this is the multiple at which the company is currently trading. This is the thought process one should be going through. We need to continue with the analysis and compare with other methods before we can truly formulate an opinion. Let's compare this to the enterprise and equity value we get from the perpetuity method for more input.

Perpetuity Method

The perpetuity method takes the company's final projected UFCF and applies the perpetuity formula:

$$\frac{UFCF \times (1 + g)}{r - g}$$

TABLE 9.8 Equity Value per Share Based on the EBITDA Method

Discounted Cash Flow Total Valuation	EBITDA Method
Total of Present Value of Cash Flows	87,798.8
Present Value of Terminal Value	2,547,882.7
Total Enterprise Value	**2,635,681.6**
Net Debt, Non-Controlling Interests, Preferred Securities	58,382.0
Equity Value	**2,577,299.6**
Share Count (millions)	519.3
Estimated Equity Value per Share	**$4,962.80**

where *r* is the WACC and *g* is some growth rate. We recommend in this market environment using something low (from 1% to 4%). Remember that this percentage represents the annual growth of cash for the entire life of the business. Even though the growth rate of cash now is higher, we assume as the business approaches maturity, the growth would be quite low.

In cell F26, we can pull in the 2025 UFCF, from cell K14, or

$$= K14$$

In cell F27, let's for now hardcode 3% in for our growth assumption. As with the multiple in the EBITDA method, we reserve the ability to adjust these assumptions once the valuation is complete.

In cell F28, we can calculate the perpetuity formula:

$$= F26 * (1 + F27)/(F17 - F27)$$

And we can discount this to PV in cell F29:

$$= F28/(1 + F17)\text{^}K16$$

This gives us $451,132.0MM. (See Table 9.9.)

It is interesting to note that this value is significantly lower than the net PV based on the EBITDA terminal value. Remember: The perpetuity method is more fundamentally based on the financials (cash flow) than the EBITDA method, as the EBITDA method is highly dependent on the market multiple. So, for fast-growing companies multiple in the EBITDA method can capture growth impact while the perpetuity method may not; *especially* since we decided to construct a very conservative model. If you notice, the unlevered free cash flow is not only quite conservative, but it's not growing significantly fast in relation to the revenue or EBITDA. This is where running multiple model scenarios can help. Again, the purpose of this book is to be able to build the tools to manipulate the model as you see fit. What's important is not only knowing the output but also interpreting that output. So seeing the results of a perpetuity method significantly lower than the

TABLE 9.9 Perpetuity Method Terminal Value

Perpetuity Method	
Unlevered Free Cash Flow	26,252.2
Growth Rate	3%
Terminal Value	639,511.7
Net Present Value	451,132.0

EBITDA method is okay if you can rationalize it's because we were very conservative on cash flow estimates.

I'd also like to note that although I'm providing the most standard and traditional methods of calculating cash flow for analysis purses, other methods do exist and may be interpreted as more appropriate for Amazon.

For example, it has been highly debated whether stock-based compensation should be added back to the unlevered free cash flow. We included it in the "Other" line item as it is a non-cash operating expense as per the definition of Unlevered Free Cash Flow.

I defer to Aswath Damodoran's article on the subject.[1]

> *"The stock-based compensation may not represent cash but it is so only because the company has used a barter system to evade the cash flow effect. Put differently, if the company had issued the options and restricted stock (that it was planning to give employees) to the market and then used the cash proceeds to pay employees, we would have treated it as a cash expense. . . We have to hold equity compensation to a different standard than we do non-cash expenses like depreciation, and be less cavalier about adding them back."*

Mr. Damodoran implies stock-based compensation should not be added back, and while I do agree with the theory, removing this add-back will significantly drop the cash flow. So, I will leave it in for purposes of this book.

There are other analysts who simply take operating cash flow and discount it back (i.e., not including CAPEX). Again, there are multiple theories; all may be plausible. My goal of the book is to provide the most traditional taught at the top business schools and Wall Street firms for fundamental grounding. It's up to you to adjust from here.

Let's calculate on.

We can now calculate total enterprise value based on the perpetuity method. First, we can pull in the total PV of cash flows into cell F32, so that would be "=G18." We can then pull in the PV of terminal value into cell F33, or "=F29." Now we can just add those two rows together into cell F34: "=F32+F33," which gives us $538,930.9MM.

We have already calculated net debt, non-controlling interests, and preferred securities in cell E35, so we can just use that number cell F35, or cell F35 will be "=E35." We can subtract this from the enterprise value. So cell F36 will read "= F34-F35," which gives us $480,548.9MM.

[1]Aswath Damodaran, "Stock-based Employee Compensation: Value and Pricing Effects," *Musings on Markets,* February 13, 2014, https://aswathdamodaran.blogspot .com/2014/02/stock-based-employee-compensation-value.html.

TABLE 9.10 Discounted Cash Flow Total Valuation

Discounted Cash Flow Total Valuation	EBITDA Method	Perpetuity Method
Total of Present Value of Cash Flows	87,798.8	87,798.8
Present Value of Terminal Value	2,547,882.7	451,132.0
Total Enterprise Value	**2,635,681.6**	**538,930.9**
Net Debt, Non-Controlling Interests, Preferred Securities	58,382.0	58,382.0
Equity Value	**2,577,299.6**	**480,548.9**
Share Count (millions)	519.3	519.3
Estimated Equity Value per Share	**$4,962.80**	**$925.34**

We can now divide the equity value by the number of shares outstanding calculated in cell O23. So, cell F37 can read "=O23." And we can divide into cell F38, which will be "=F36/F37." This will give us $983.91 based on the perpetuity method. (See Table 9.10.)

Is this an appropriate value range for Amazon? What does the Street say? How about adjusting the variables? We will first consider the other two valuation methods and utilize all to discuss possible answers to these questions in the final chapter.

CHAPTER 10

Comparable Company Analysis

As we discussed earlier, the comparable company analysis ("comps") compares companies that are similar in size, product, and geography to the company we are valuing. It is not always easy to find good comparable companies, but we have some recommended sources:

■ *Company financials.* Often, the company lists who it believes its competitors are in the market. Performing a quick word search on "competitors" or "competition" in the 2020 Amazon 10-K, for example, reveals the following note in Figure 10.1.

Unfortunately, Amazon does not name its exact competitors, but it does explain its business segments and the *types* of companies that would compete with each segment. Based on Figure 10.1, we could suggest Amazon's competitors fall into these categories:

■ *Online retailers.* Etsy, eBay, Overstock.com, and Wayfair are good examples.
■ *Physical stores.* Walmart, Target, Best Buy, Costco.
■ *Subscription (streaming) services.* Netflix, Apple (iTunes), Google (Play Store).
■ *Amazon web services.* Google (again), Microsoft, IBM, Alibaba.

Because Amazon doesn't outright name its competitors, these are just examples and suggestions. Remember: The purpose of the comparable company analysis is to get a general range of valuation based on how its competitors are trading. Because Amazon is such a large company, and because the business is divided into various segments, it's beneficial to look at competitors in each segment in addition to analyzing the company as a whole. Note the real purpose of this book is to instruct *how* a comparable company

Competition

Our businesses encompass a large variety of product types, service offerings, and delivery channels. The worldwide marketplace in which we compete is evolving rapidly and intensely competitive, and we face a broad array of competitors from many different industry sectors around the world. Our current and potential competitors include: (1) physical, e-commerce, and omnichannel retailers, publishers, vendors, distributors, manufacturers, and producers of the products we offer and sell to consumers and businesses; (2) publishers, producers, and distributors of physical, digital, and interactive media of all types and all distribution channels; (3) web search engines, comparison shopping websites, social networks, web portals, and other online and app-based means of discovering, using, or acquiring goods and services, either directly or in collaboration with other retailers; (4) companies that provide e-commerce services, including website development and hosting, omnichannel sales, inventory and supply chain management, advertising, fulfillment, customer service, and payment processing; (5) companies that provide fulfillment and logistics services for themselves or for third parties, whether online or offline; (6) companies that provide information technology services or products, including on-premises or cloud-based infrastructure and other services; (7) companies that design, manufacture, market, or sell consumer electronics, telecommunication, and electronic devices; (8) companies that sell grocery products online and in physical stores; and (9) companies that provide advertising services, whether in digital or other formats. We believe that the principal competitive factors in our retail businesses include selection, price, and convenience, including fast and reliable fulfillment. Additional competitive factors for our seller and enterprise services include the quality, speed, and reliability of our services and tools, as well as customers' ability and willingness to change business practices. Some of our current and potential competitors have greater resources, longer histories, more customers, greater brand recognition, and greater control over inputs critical to our various businesses. They may secure better terms from suppliers, adopt more aggressive pricing, pursue restrictive distribution agreements that restrict our access to supply, direct consumers to their own offerings instead of ours, lock-in potential customers with restrictive terms, and devote more resources to technology, infrastructure, fulfillment, and marketing. The Internet facilitates competitive entry and comparison shopping, which enhances the ability of new, smaller, or lesser-known businesses to compete against us. Each of our businesses is also subject to rapid change and the development of new business models and the entry of new and well-funded competitors. Other companies also may enter into business combinations or alliances that strengthen their competitive positions.

FIGURE 10.1 Note on Amazon Competitors

analysis is done, so we are going to focus more on the overall method rather than digging deep into each segment. So, for our analysis, we will focus Amazon into two groups: Retail (online and offline) and Web (both subscription and services). This will give you an idea as to how the analysis is done, and with these tools you can break out further as you see fit.

LAST TWELVE MONTHS (LTM)

Before calculating the comparable metrics, it is important to understand *last 12 months* (LTM) calculations. The LTM is a method to calculate the most recent financials based on combining annual reports (10-Ks) with quarterly reports (10-Qs). Let's look at Amazon, for example. Although we constructed the Amazon model on an annual basis, for purposes of the comps, it is important to look at Amazon's LTM metrics. Comps are meant to be a "current" analysis, so we would like to incorporate the most up-to-date financials regardless of whether they are quarterly or annual financials. We could have done this in the full-scale model, but our goal in the model constructed in Part One was to get an accurate annual representation of Amazon. Depending on the requirements of the model, one could have created a quarterly representation of Amazon – a quarterly model – but we decided that was unnecessary for our valuation.

When we go back to the "Amazon Investor Relations" section of its website, we notice it has produced a quarterly report after its annual report. So, it not only has financial data from January 1, 2020, to December 31, 2020, but it has a "Q1" report showing financial results from January 1, 2021, to March 31, 2021. So, technically, we can get Amazon financial results for the LTM up to March 31, 2021, or April 1, 2020, to March 31, 2021. (See Table 10.1.)

In order to use this information to get 12 months of financials through March 31, 2021, we can first add the Q1 financials to the annual report financials. When we say "add," we literally mean adding each line item. For example, we can add the 2020 revenue from the annual report to the Q1 revenue. This gives us 15 months of financials from January 1, 2020, to March 31, 2021. So, we now need to subtract three months of financials or one quarter, from January 1, 2020, to March 31, 2020, to get a representation

TABLE 10.1 LTM Example

Annual 2020	Q1 2021
1/1/2020 – 12/31/2020	1/1/2021 – 3/31/2021

TABLE 10.2   LTM Example

Annual 2020	Q1 2021
1/1/2020 – 12/31/2020	1/1/2021 – 3/31/2021

Q1 2020	
1/1/2020 – 3/31/2020	

TABLE 10.3   Calendarization Example

Annual 2020	Q1 2021
11/1/2019 – 10/31/2020	11/1/2020 – 1/31/2021

Q1 2020	
11/1/2019 – 1/31/2020	

of 12 months of revenue from April 1, 2020, through March 31, 2021. (See Table 10.2.)

So, in other words, if we take the 2020 annual report numbers, add the Q1 2021, and subtract the Q1 2020 numbers, we will get financials from April 1, 2020, to March 31, 2021:

$$LTM = \text{Annual } 2020 + Q1\ 2021 - Q1\ 2020$$

CALENDARIZATION

Another important method to note before calculating comps is calendarization. A comps analysis should not only be current but should also be adjusted so that the financial ending dates are the same for each company compared in the comps analysis. So, for example, Amazon's annual financials are reported from January 1, 2020, to December 31, 2020. Now what if an Amazon comparable company is reported on a slightly different cycle? Let's take an example of a company that produced an annual report ending on October 31, 2020. Now, we can add that company's Q1 report, presumably ending three months later, on January 31, 2021, to the annual report, and subtract the prior year's Q1 report. (See Table 10.3.)

This should give us 12 months' financials from February 1, 2020, through January 31, 2021 – close, but not exactly in line with Amazon's annual financials of January 1, 2020, to December 31, 2020. To resolve this,

TABLE 10.4 Calendarization Example

Annual 2020	2/3 × Q1 2021
11/1/2019 – 10/31/2020	11/1/2020 – 12/31/2021

TABLE 10.5 Calendarization Example

Annual 2020	2/3 × Q1 2021
11/1/2019 – 10/31/2020	11/1/2020 – 12/31/2021
2/3 × Q1 2020	
11/1/2019 – 12/31/2020	

we can adjust the Q1 financials to give us an equivalent of two months' financials from November 1, 2020 to December 31, 2020, by simply taking two-thirds of the Q1 data. So, 2/3 × Q1 2021 would give us an estimate of data from November 1, 2020, to December 31, 2020. (See Table 10.4.)

Now, this gives us 14 months of days (12 months of annual data plus 2 quarterly), so we need to remove two months from November 1, 2019, through December 31, 2019, in order to get annual data from January 1, 2020, through December 31, 2020. So, we can subtract 2/3 of the 2020 Q1. (See Table 10.5.)

In other words, if we take the 2020 annual report numbers, add 2/3 × Q1 2021, and subtract 2/3 × Q1 2020 numbers, we will get financials from January 1, 2020, to December 31, 2020:

$$LTM = Annual\ 2020 + 2/3 \times Q1\ 2021 - 2/3 \times Q1\ 2020$$

NETFLIX AS A COMPARABLE COMPANY

We will not step through creating comparable metrics for every company, as it is quite redundant. However, we will take one example: Netflix. Although Netflix is not a retail company, it is comparable as a streaming service to Amazon Prime. Note after going through this analysis, you may find it helpful to review the comp done in my original book on Costco, as that company had different issues and adjustments that needed to be made.

The Netflix financials can be found in the Netflix Investor Relations site, either by googling for "Netflix Investor Relations" or going directly to

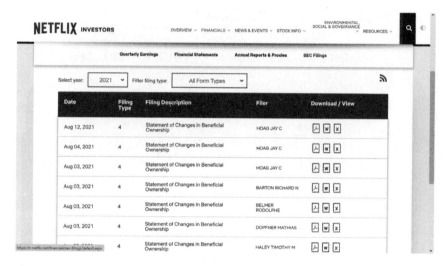

FIGURE 10.2 Netflix Investor Relations

"ir.netflix.net." If you select "Financials" in the menu bar, a drop-down box opens, revealing several helpful options containing company financials. "Sec Filings" takes you directly to a log of *all* company filings. (See Figure 10.2.)

It is important to note: When creating a comps output page, we are most often interested in generating at least one year historical data (2020 YE), LTM data, and one year projected data (2021 E), each of which dates should be in line with the target company's (in our case, Amazon's) data. So we will in the least need Netflix's 2020 10-K and their latest quarterly report.

Netflix 2020 Year End

While in the SEC section of the Netflix investor relations site, we can select "Annual Filings" in the "Filter Filing Type" drop box. This brings up Netflix 10-K reports. (See Figure 10.3.) If you click the "pdf" icon, you can open and download the Annual Report in pdf format.

Upon opening the 10-K, we first want to look at the report date found on the first page. We want to be sure it falls in line with Amazon's; if it does not, we would have to make calendarization adjustments. Right on the first page of the report we see "For the fiscal year ended December 31, 2020."

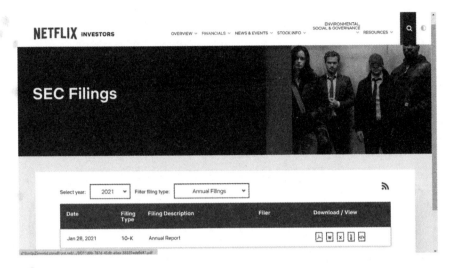

FIGURE 10.3   Netflix Investor Relations – Annual Report

This falls in line with Amazon, so we can use this report as is to lay out 2020 financials.

Revenue   As we have already learned the nuances of an income statement and making projections, we will not go into stepping through linking Netflix's income statement cell by cell. Rather, we will focus on illustrating just the new and complex situations as they arise. That being said, the first step is to lay out a simple income statement, which will be a basis for our comparable metrics. In the Excel file template, there is a Netflix tab, "NFLX Comp," already set up to support the annual and quarterly data.

We will first input the annual data from the 2020 10-K, then we will go back and assess quarterly data for an LTM analysis. (See Figure 10.4, from page 42 of the Netflix 10-K.)

We first notice Netflix financials are reported in "thousands," while we built the Amazon model in "millions." It's ideal to keep comparable units, so when inputting this data we want to adjust to "millions." The company reports Revenue and "Cost of revenue" (which is COGS), so we can start listing the 2020 values as they have, except we will adjust to millions. We can also calculate the COGS as a % of Revenue, Gross Profit, and Gross Profit Margin. (See Table 10.6.)

NETFLIX, INC.

CONSOLIDATED STATEMENTS OF OPERATIONS
(in thousands, except per share data)

		Year ended December 31,		
		2020	2019	2018
Revenues	$	24,996,056	$	20,156,447	$	15,794,341
Cost of revenues		15,276,319	12,440,213	9,967,538
Marketing		2,228,362	2,652,462	2,369,469
Technology and development		1,829,600	1,545,149	1,221,814
General and administrative		1,076,486	914,369	630,294
Operating income		4,585,289	2,604,254	1,605,226
Other income (expense):				
Interest expense		(767,499)	(626,023)	(420,493)
Interest and other income (expense)		(618,441)	84,000	41,725
Income before income taxes		3,199,349	2,062,231	1,226,458
Provision for income taxes		(437,954)	(195,315)	(15,216)
Net income	$	2,761,395	$	1,866,916	$	1,211,242
Earnings per share:				
Basic	$	6.26	$	4.26	$	2.78
Diluted	$	6.08	$	4.13	$	2.68
Weighted-average common shares outstanding:				
Basic		440,922	437,799	435,374
Diluted		454,208	451,765	451,244

FIGURE 10.4 Netflix Annual Report Income Statement

Operating Expenses   Next, there are three separate cost items, "Marketing," "Technology and development," and "General and administrative." We are going to total these three into one general "Operating Expenses" line item. You may want to break out further at your discretion, but our view is for purposes of comparable companies; each company will have different line items detailing "Operating Expenses." What's most important is that we have identified "Operating Expenses" as a whole to build to EBITDA. (See Table 10.6.)

Depreciation   You may have noticed there is no line for depreciation, so we need to find out where it could be by conducting further research. Assuming Netflix does depreciate assets, we can usually look to the cash flow statement. (See Figure 10.5.)

Here we see not only depreciation but also "Amortization of Content Assets." This amortization is significantly larger than the depreciation. Regardless if we add this to the company's operations, we need to remove them from one of the expense items we have already laid out in the company analysis. A quick word search on "Amortization of Content Assets" reveals the following note from Page 24 of the Netflix 10-K.

TABLE 10.6   Netflix EBITDA

	Q1 2020A	2020A	Q1 2021A	LTM 2021	2021E
Revenue		24,996.1			
Y/Y revenue growth (%)					
Cost of Goods Sold		15,276.3			
COGS as a % of revenue		61%			
Gross Profit		9,719.7			
Gross profit margin (%)		39%			
Operating Expenses		5,134.4			
OpEx as a % of revenue		21%			
EBITDA		4,585.3			
EBITDA margin (%)		18%			

NETFLIX, INC.

CONSOLIDATED STATEMENTS OF CASH FLOWS
(in thousands)

	Year Ended December 31,		
	2020	2019	2018
Cash flows from operating activities:			
Net income	$ 2,761,395	$ 1,866,916	$ 1,211,242
Adjustments to reconcile net income to net cash provided by (used in) operating activities:			
Additions to content assets	(11,779,284)	(13,916,683)	(13,043,437)
Change in content liabilities	(757,433)	(694,011)	999,880
Amortization of content assets	10,806,912	9,216,247	7,532,088
Depreciation and amortization of property, equipment and intangibles	115,710	103,579	83,157
Stock-based compensation expense	415,180	405,376	320,657
Foreign currency remeasurement loss (gain) on debt	533,278	(45,576)	(73,953)
Other non-cash items	293,126	228,230	81,640
Deferred income taxes	70,066	(94,443)	(85,520)
Changes in operating assets and liabilities:			
Other current assets	(187,623)	(252,113)	(200,192)
Accounts payable	(41,605)	96,063	199,198
Accrued expenses and other liabilities	198,183	157,778	150,422
Deferred revenue	193,247	163,846	142,277
Other non-current assets and liabilities	(194,075)	(122,531)	2,062
Net cash provided by (used in) operating activities	2,427,077	(2,887,322)	(2,680,479)
Cash flows from investing activities:			
Purchases of property and equipment	(497,923)	(253,035)	(173,946)
Change in other assets	(7,431)	(134,029)	(165,174)
Net cash used in investing activities	(505,354)	(387,064)	(339,120)
Cash flows from financing activities:			
Proceeds from issuance of debt	1,009,464	4,469,306	3,961,852
Debt issuance costs	(7,559)	(36,134)	(35,871)
Proceeds from issuance of common stock	235,406	72,490	124,502
Other financing activities	—	—	(1,956)
Net cash provided by financing activities	1,237,311	4,505,662	4,048,527
Effect of exchange rate changes on cash, cash equivalents and restricted cash	36,050	469	(39,682)
Net increase in cash, cash equivalents and restricted cash	3,195,084	1,231,745	989,246
Cash, cash equivalents and restricted cash, beginning of year	5,043,786	3,812,041	2,822,795
Cash, cash equivalents and restricted cash, end of year	$ 8,238,870	$ 5,043,786	$ 3,812,041
Supplemental disclosure:			
Income taxes paid	$ 291,582	$ 400,658	$ 131,069
Interest paid	762,904	599,132	375,831

FIGURE 10.5   Netflix Cash Flow Statement

Cost of Revenues

Amortization of content assets makes up the majority of cost of revenues. Expenses associated with the acquisition, licensing and production of content (such as payroll and related personnel expenses, costs associated with obtaining rights to music included in our content, overall deals with talent, miscellaneous production related costs and participations and residuals), streaming delivery costs and other operations costs make up the remainder of cost of revenues. . .

So, from that first line, we know the Amortization comes from Costs of Revenue. What about depreciation? Depreciation isn't mentioned much in relation to the operating expenses, so it's not easy to determine which specific cost it should be pulled out of, so I would recommend to just pull everything out of the costs of revenue, as we already know the majority of the expenses in question (namely, the amortization) is in costs of revenue.

Remember, although we try to be as accurate as possible, as long as depreciation is removed from EBITDA we have achieved our primary goal.

So, we need to add the 2020 10,806.912 to the 115.710 directly into the depreciation cell. We then need to remove these values from the "Cost of Goods Sold" line item so we do not double count them. We can also then calculate EBIT and EBIT margin. (See Table 10.7.)

Interest The company clearly lists interest expense. However, the line after interest expense is labeled "Interest and other income (expense)." As discussed in Chapter 1, we ideally need to identify and separate the interest

TABLE 10.7 Depreciation and Updated EBITDA

Netflix Income Statement

	Actuals				Estimates
	Q1 2020A	2020A	Q1 2021A	LTM 2021	2021E
Revenue		24,996.1			
Y/Y revenue growth (%)					
Cost of Goods Sold		4,353.7			
COGS as a % of revenue		17%			
Gross Profit		20,642.4			
Gross profit margin (%)		83%			
Operating Expenses		5,134.4			
OpEx as a % of revenue		21%			
EBITDA		15,507.9			
EBITDA margin (%)		62%			
Depreciation and amortization		10,922.6			
D&A % of revenue		44%			
EBIT		4,585.3			
EBIT margin (%)		18%			

income from the other income. Researching the 10-K reveals a note on page 26:

> Interest and other income (expense) decreased primarily due to foreign exchange losses of $660 million for the year ended December 31, 2020 as compared to a gain of $7 million for the year ended December 31, 2019.

So of the 618,441 of 2020 Interest and other income (expense), a 660,000 was due to foreign exchange losses. The difference, or 41,559, is a net gain. We can assume this is the interest income. Remember, we enter this value as a negative even though it's income; as in Chapter 1, we mentioned having all expenses shown as a positive number and income as a negative. So we enter the 41.559 as interest income. The 660 will be placed in the non-recurring events section as an extraordinary item and we need to adjust this value for taxes because we are moving a line from above the EBT line to below. We will discuss this later.

Taxes In 2020, we see that Netflix paid $437,954 in taxes as per its annual report. But because we had removed an expense (foreign exchange (gains) losses) from the income statement, we need to adjust this tax number. If we effectively move an expense from above the net income line to below, the taxes associated with that expense should go with it. We suggest handling this by calculating the effective tax rate paid in a given period, then using that tax rate to calculate adjusted taxes. So, if the company had paid $437,954 in 2020 taxes, based on a $3,199,349 EBT (see "Income Before Income Taxes" in Figure 10.4), the company had an implied tax rate of 13.7% (437,954 / 3,199,349) (see Table 10.8). So we recommend directly in the "Tax%" row to hardcode in the calculation behind the 13.7% tax rate and to footnote it.

TABLE 10.8   Interest

Netflix Income Statement

		Actuals			Estimates
	Q1 2020A	2020A	Q1 2021A	LTM 2021	2021E
Interest					
Interest expense		767.5			
Interest income		(41.6)			
Net interest expense		725.9			
Earnings before Tax (EBT)		3,859.3			
IBT margin (%)		*15%*			

TABLE 10.9 Netflix Taxes

Netflix Income Statement

		Actuals			Estimates
	Q1 2020A	2020A	Q1 2021A	LTM 2021	2021E
Income Tax Expense		528.3			
Effective tax rate (%)		13.7%			
Net income from continuing operations		3,331.0			

Once that is done, for "Income tax expense," we can simply multiply the EBT we have calculated times the new rate to get the implied taxes incurred if the non-recurring expense was not included above the net income. We can now calculate Net Income from Continuing Operations. (See Table 10.9.)

Non-Recurring Events There are a host of various non-recurring events listed in the model template, basically examples from the other comparable companies. The one we will focus on is the foreign exchange loss (gain). This line item was not explicitly laid out in the Netflix operations, but we uncovered this when digging into the "Interest and Other Income" line.

Once non-recurring events have been identified and removed from the income statement (if any exist) we need to place them in this section. Be sure you have read the section prior to this ("Taxes") to be sure you have not only removed the expenses but have readjusted the reported taxes. Once that is complete, each expense you have moved from above EBT to below, must be tax affected. (There may be several advanced exceptions.) So the $660 in foreign exchange losses should be moved down to the section; however, it must also be tax affected. We need to include $660 × (1 – Tax%) in order to be sure we have properly moved the tax savings associated with that expense from the tax line to the non-recurring events line. The tax rate we use is the same tax rate calculated in the "Effective tax rate" line of that period, so it is best if we just link up to that exact tax cell. This should give you $569.7. (See Table 10.10.)

It is good to note that despite our adjustments along the way, our net income (as reported) line matches the "Net income" reported on the Netflix financials.

Earnings per Share (EPS) We can now calculate our EPS metric for use in our comps analysis. Notice we have two versions of our EPS, one based on "Net income (adjusted)" and the other based on "net income (as reported)." This is so we can tie the "Net income (as reported)" metric to the financials to be

TABLE 10.10 Netflix Annual Net Income (as Reported)

Netflix Income Statement

		Actuals			Estimates
	Q1 2020A	2020A	Q1 2021A	LTM 2021	2021E
Net Income from Continuing Operations		3,331.0			
Foreign currency exchange (gain) loss, net		569.7			
(Gain) loss on debt securities, net		0.0			
(Gain) loss on equity securities		0.0			
Performance fees		0.0			
Income and impairment from equity method investments, net		0.0			
Other		0.0			
Net Income (as reported)	0.0	2,761.4	0.0	0.0	0.0

sure we are using all of the numbers as reported, but we really want to use the "clean" "Net income (adjusted)" numbers for our comps.

The formula for calculating EPS is Net Income/Shares. The shares are found at the bottom of the income statement, and we have listed both the basic and diluted, just as we did with Amazon. The earnings per share (as reported) takes the net income (as reported) and divides by the basic and diluted shares, respectively. We now see that the EPS (as reported) matches the Netflix income statement. The EPS (adjusted) takes the net income from continuing operations as the numerator. This earnings number is our "cleaned" net income; it has the non-recurring and extraordinary items removed and the taxes accordingly adjusted. We can divide this by the basic and diluted shares, respectively, to get earnings per share (adjusted). This "cleaned" number we will use for our comps analysis.

(See Table 10.11 and Figure 10.4.)

Netflix Quarterly Income Statement

We can now repeat the exact same process for the quarterly reports. We will not step through building the quarters line by line, as it is too repetitive. You should have the skills by now to lay out an income statement. (It may be helpful to reread Chapter 1.) Make sure you are typing in the numbers correctly, and be careful of the signs and totals. Always check for typos and make sure the formulas are calculating properly. Also be sure you are lining up the correct columns, i.e., March 31, 2021, as the Q1 2021 data. (See Figure 10.6 from page 3 of the Quarterly report.)

TABLE 10.11 Netflix Annual Income Statement

Netflix Income Statement

		Actuals			Estimates
	Q1 2020A	2020A	Q1 2021A	LTM 2021	2021E
Revenue		24,996.1			
Y/Y revenue growth (%)					
Cost of Goods Sold		4,353.7			
COGS as a % of revenue		17%			
Gross Profit		20,642.4			
Gross profit margin (%)		83%			
Operating Expenses		5,134.4			
OpEx as a % of revenue		21%			
EBITDA		15,507.9			
EBITDA margin (%)		62%			
Depreciation and amortization		10,922.6			
D&A % of revenue		44%			
EBIT		4,585.3			
EBIT margin (%)		18%			
Other Income		0.0			
Interest					
Interest expense		767.5			
Interest income		(41.6)			
Net Interest Expense		725.9			
Earnings before Tax (EBT)		3,859.3			

(continued)

TABLE 10.11 (*Continued*)

Netflix Income Statement

| | Actuals | | | | Estimates |
	Q1 2020A	2020A	Q1 2021A	LTM 2021	2021E
IBT margin (%)		15%			
Income tax expense		528.3			
Effective tax rate (%)		14%			
Net Income from Continuing Operations		3,331.0			
Foreign currency exchange (gain) loss, net		569.7			
(Gain) loss on debt securities, net		0.0			
(Gain) loss on equity securities		0.0			
Performance fees		0.0			
Income and impairment from equity method investments, net		0.0			
Other		0.0			
Net Income (as reported)		**2,761.4**			
Earnings per Share (as reported)					
Basic		6.26			
Diluted		6.08			
Earnings per Share (adjusted)					
Basic		7.55			
Diluted		7.33			
Average Common Shares Outstanding					
Basic		441			
Diluted		454			

NETFLIX, INC.

Consolidated Statements of Operations

(unaudited)

(in thousands, except per share data)

	Three Months Ended	
	March 31, 2021	March 31, 2020
Revenues	$ 7,163,282	$ 5,767,691
Cost of revenues	3,868,511	3,599,701
Marketing	512,512	503,830
Technology and development	525,207	453,817
General and administrative	297,196	252,087
Operating income	1,959,856	958,256
Other income (expense):		
Interest expense	(194,440)	(184,083)
Interest and other income	269,086	21,697
Income before income taxes	2,034,502	795,870
Provision for income taxes	(327,787)	(86,803)
Net income	$ 1,706,715	$ 709,067
Earnings per share:		
Basic	$ 3.85	$ 1.61
Diluted	$ 3.75	$ 1.57
Weighted-average common shares outstanding:		
Basic	443,224	439,352
Diluted	455,641	452,494

FIGURE 10.6 Netflix Quarterly Income Statement

A couple of additional items to remember in the Netflix quarterly reports:

■ *Depreciation and amortization.* Make sure to add both the "Depreciation and amortization" line *and* the "Amortization of content assets" together, as we had done in the 2020 report. See the cash flow statement for depreciation and amortization numbers. Let's continue to remove these expenses from the COGS line. (See Figure 10.7 from page 5 of the quarterly report.)

■ *Interest and other income.* A note on page 24 of the quarterly report discussed the portion of "interest and other income" attributed to "Foreign exchange loss (gains)."

Interest and other income increased in the three months ended March 31, 2021 primarily due to foreign exchange gains of $258 million, compared to gains of $9 million for the corresponding period in 2020.

Let's continue to treat this as an extraordinary item and move it down to the non-recurring events section. Make sure that as you move it into the non-recurring section, it is multiplied by 1 – Tax%.

NETFLIX, INC.

Consolidated Statements of Cash Flows
(unaudited)
(in thousands)

	Three Months Ended	
	March 31, 2021	March 31, 2020
Cash flows from operating activities:		
Net income	$ 1,706,715	$ 709,067
Adjustments to reconcile net income to net cash provided by operating activities:		
Additions to content assets	(3,284,576)	(3,294,275)
Change in content liabilities	(266,040)	258,945
Amortization of content assets	2,719,196	2,483,385
Depreciation and amortization of property, equipment and intangibles	35,741	28,517
Stock-based compensation expense	107,230	97,019
Foreign currency remeasurement gain on debt	(253,330)	(93,060)
Other non-cash items	72,657	65,448
Deferred income taxes	159,733	46,619
Changes in operating assets and liabilities:		
Other current assets	(221,555)	(127,353)
Accounts payable	(137,313)	(149,153)
Accrued expenses and other liabilities	177,897	214,191
Deferred revenue	22,279	62,008
Other non-current assets and liabilities	(61,368)	(41,446)
Net cash provided by operating activities	777,266	259,912
Cash flows from investing activities:		
Purchases of property and equipment	(81,001)	(98,015)
Change in other assets	(4,615)	(288)
Net cash used in investing activities	(85,616)	(98,303)
Cash flows from financing activities:		
Repayments of debt	(500,000)	—
Proceeds from issuance of common stock	48,071	43,694
Net cash provided by (used in) financing activities	(451,929)	43,694
Effect of exchange rate changes on cash, cash equivalents and restricted cash	(42,138)	(70,902)
Net increase in cash, cash equivalents and restricted cash	197,583	134,401
Cash, cash equivalents and restricted cash at beginning of period	8,238,870	5,043,786
Cash, cash equivalents and restricted cash at end of period	$ 8,436,453	$ 5,178,187

FIGURE 10.7 Netflix Quarterly Cash Flow Statement

We will assume that the remaining balance is interest. Make sure the signs are all moving in the right direction. Try it yourself and use the final model as a guide.

When all inputs are completed, you should have what is shown in Table 10.12.

Netflix LTM Adjustments

We can now make appropriate adjustments to calculate the year-end and LTM data.

We discussed earlier in this chapter that the adjustment to get to an LTM that's in line with Amazon's for our comps analysis is achieved with the following formula:

$$LTM\ 2021 = Annual\ 2020 + Q1\ 2021 - Q1\ 2020$$

So, in cell G6 for Netflix, we can have "=E6+F6-D6." This should give you $26,391.6 in sales. We can use this same formula for every LTM line item, but not the totals and metrics. Although COGS, for example, will be using this LTM formula, "Gross Profit" will still be calculated as Revenue – COGS. (See Table 10.13.)

In addition, you should note the following adjustments:

- The income tax expense line item should be calculated like revenue, COGS, or any other expense line item using the LTM formula. We can then back into the implied tax rate by dividing the income tax calculated into the EBT. For 2020, you should get $728.7 in taxes and 15% for the implied tax rate.
- Apply the LTM formula to the "Foreign Currency (Gain) Loss" line item. You do not need to adjust again for taxes as the individual line items (Q1, Annual) have already been adjusted for taxes.
- The shares outstanding is an outstanding balance item. In other words, this is not an item that is reported over a period, where the sum of the quarters would equal the year end. So do not apply the LTM formula here. We can just take the latest Q1 balance of shares for LTM.

Netflix Projections

We can now make 2021 estimated projections for Netflix. We have already discussed making projections in Chapter 1 and we do not want to be too redundant; we just want to give high-level suggestions with the understanding that one can get into as much detail as possible.

TABLE 10.12 Netflix Historical Income Statement

Netflix Income Statement

	Actuals				Estimates
	Q1 2020A	2020A	Q1 2021A	LTM 2021	2021E
Revenue	5,767.7	24,996.1	7,163.3		
Y/Y revenue growth (%)					
Cost of Goods Sold	1,087.8	4,353.7	1,113.6		
COGS as a % of revenue	19%	17%	16%		
Gross Profit	4,679.9	20,642.4	6,049.7		
Gross profit margin (%)	81%	83%	84%		
Operating Expenses	1,209.7	5,134.4	1,334.9		
OpEx as a % of revenue	21%	21%	19%		
EBITDA	3,470.2	15,507.9	4,714.8		
EBITDA margin (%)	60%	62%	66%		
Depreciation and amortization	2,511.9	10,922.6	2,754.9		
D&A % of revenue	44%	44%	38%		
EBIT	958.3	4,585.3	1,959.9		
EBIT margin (%)	17%	18%	27%		
Other income	0.0	0.0	0.0		
Interest					
Interest expense	184.1	767.5	194.4		

Interest income	(12.7)	(41.6)	(11.1)
Net Interest Expense	171.4	725.9	183.4
Earnings before Tax (EBT)	786.9	3,859.3	1,776.5
IBT margin (%)	14%	15%	25%
Income tax expense	85.8	528.3	286.2
Effective tax rate (%)	11%	14%	16%
Net Income from Continuing Operations	701.0	3,331.0	1,490.3
Foreign currency exchange (gain) loss, net	(8.0)	569.7	(216.4)
(Gain) loss on debt securities, net	0.0	0.0	0.0
(Gain) loss on equity securities	0.0	0.0	0.0
Performance fees	0.0	0.0	0.0
Income and impairment from equity method investments, net	0.0	0.0	0.0
Other	0.0	0.0	0.0
Net Income (as Reported)	709.1	2,761.4	1,706.7
Earnings per Share (as Reported)			
Basic	1.61	6.26	3.85
Diluted	1.57	6.08	3.75
Earnings per Share (Adjusted)			
Basic	1.60	7.55	3.36
Diluted	1.55	7.33	3.27
Average Common Shares Outstanding			
Basic	439	441	443
Diluted	452	454	456

TABLE 10.13 Netflix Income Statement

Netflix Income Statement

	Actuals				Estimates
	Q1 2020A	2020A	Q1 2021A	LTM 2021	2021E
Revenue	5,767.7	24,996.1	7,163.3	26,391.6	
Y/Y revenue growth (%)	*19%*	*17%*	*16%*	*17%*	
Cost of Goods Sold	1,087.8	4,353.7	1,113.6	4,379.5	
COGS as a % of revenue	*19%*	*17%*	*16%*	*17%*	
Gross Profit	4,679.9	20,642.4	6,049.7	22,012.2	
Gross profit margin (%)	*81%*	*83%*	*84%*	*83%*	
Operating Expenses	1,209.7	5,134.4	1,334.9	5,259.6	
OpEx as a % of revenue	*21%*	*21%*	*19%*	*20%*	
EBITDA	3,470.2	15,507.9	4,714.8	16,752.5	
EBITDA margin (%)	*60%*	*62%*	*66%*	*63%*	
Depreciation and amortization	2,511.9	10,922.6	2,754.9	11,165.7	
D&A % of Revenue	*44%*	*44%*	*38%*	*42%*	
EBIT	958.3	4,585.3	1,959.9	5,586.9	
EBIT margin (%)	*17%*	*18%*	*27%*	*21%*	
Other Income	0.0	0.0	0.0	0.0	
Interest					
Interest expense	184.1	767.5	194.4	777.9	

	(12.7)	(41.6)	(11.1)	(40.0)
Interest income				
Net Interest Expense	171.4	725.9	183.4	737.9
Earnings before Tax (EBT)	786.9	3,859.3	1,776.5	4,849.0
IBT margin (%)	14%	15%	25%	18%
Income tax expense	85.8	528.3	286.2	728.7
Effective tax rate (%)	11%	14%	16%	15%
Net Income from Continuing Operations	701.0	3,331.0	1,490.3	4,120.3
Foreign currency exchange (gain) loss, net	(8.0)	569.7	(216.4)	361.2
(Gain) loss on debt securities, net	0.0	0.0	0.0	0.0
(Gain) loss on equity securities	0.0	0.0	0.0	0.0
Performance fees	0.0	0.0	0.0	0.0
Income and impairment from equity method investments, net	0.0	0.0	0.0	0.0
Other	0.0	0.0	0.0	0.0
Net Income (as Reported)	709.1	2,761.4	1,706.7	3,759.0
Earnings per Share (as Reported)				
Basic	1.61	6.26	3.85	8.48
Diluted	1.57	6.08	3.75	8.25
Earnings per Share (Adjusted)				
Basic	1.60	7.55	3.36	9.30
Diluted	1.55	7.33	3.27	9.04
Average Common Shares Outstanding				
Basic	439	441	443	443
Diluted	452	454	456	456

The first item to consider is: From which date do we project our 2021 data? The most common suggestion is to project one year off of the last reported year. So, we would project 2021E off of 2020A. This fairly standard and much of the financial analyst projections we will see and use as a guide will be based off of year-end data. Another suggestion is to project off the most current information we have (but annualized), which would be the LTM data. Although this does make logical sense, it will really depend on where we are getting our future guidance. If it's from Wall Street research, for example, which is making their projections off of year-end data, we may not want to use those projections on LTM data. Note that the projections we create will be tweaked and honed to stay in line with Street estimates, so our argument is it wouldn't make a huge difference either way. So, let's project off of the 2020, as we will use Wall Street analyst guidance.

Revenue   We will conduct our research and look to Street estimates to project revenue as we had done with Amazon. (See Figure 10.8.)

Finance Home	Watchlists	My Portfolio	Screeners	Yahoo Finance Plus ♦	Markets	News	Pe

Summary	Company Outlook ♦	Chart	Conversations	Statistics	Historical Data	Profile	Financials

Earnings Estimate	Current Qtr. (Sep 2021)	Next Qtr. (Dec 2021)	Current Year (2021)
No. of Analysts	33	32	42
Avg. Estimate	2.56	1.1	10.45
Low Estimate	2.5	0.63	9.94
High Estimate	2.67	2.3	11.61
Year Ago EPS	1.74	1.19	6.08

Revenue Estimate	Current Qtr. (Sep 2021)	Next Qtr. (Dec 2021)	Current Year (2021)
No. of Analysts	33	31	41
Avg. Estimate	7.48B	7.67B	29.61B
Low Estimate	7.36B	7.47B	27.59B
High Estimate	7.53B	7.8B	29.85B
Year Ago Sales	6.38B	6.64B	25B
for sb.scorecardresearch.com...		15.50%	18.50%

FIGURE 10.8   Netflix Analyst Estimates

According to the Yahoo! Financials Analyst Estimates, the Street is averaging an 18.5% estimated revenue growth. So we will use that. As done in the Amazon income statement, we can hardcode 18.5 into cell H7, and project revenue using the following formula:

$$2021E \text{ Revenue} = 2020 \text{ Revenue} \times \left(1 + 2021E \text{ Revenue} (\%)\right)$$

Or cell H6 will read "=E6*(1+H7)." (See Table 10.14.)

COGS We will then project each cost as the percentage of the revenue we calculated in 2020. For example, we had calculated Netflix's 2020 "COGS as a % of Revenue" to be 17%. We will use 17% in 2021, and back into the implied COGS by multiplying 2021 revenue by that percentage. However, it is important to note that decimals can make a large difference. So in the previous example, rather than hardcoding 17, we should link that assumption into the 2020 "COGS as a % of revenue" line. So, for example, have cell H10 read "=E10." This way, we are linking the exact metric. We can then back calculate into the projected COGS. We should do this for every expense down through EBITDA. (See Table 10.15.)

Depreciation We can continue with this same approach. Notice with depreciation we assumed a metric of depreciation as a percentage of sales. For now, we can project depreciation as we did for the COGS and other expenses. If one chooses to add more detail, a full-scale depreciation schedule could be created, as illustrated with Amazon.

We can also calculate EBIT. (See Table 10.16.)

Interest Although we could create a full debt schedule as we had done with Amazon to get accurate interest projections, we are trying to avoid having to build a full model for each comp. Also, remember many major valuation metrics are based off of EBITDA, which we now have. With the exception of net income leading to EPS, the interest doesn't play too significant a role here, and the interest values should not change too dramatically unless there

TABLE 10.14 Netflix Projected Revenue

Netflix Income Statement					
		Actuals			Estimates
	Q1 2020A	2020A	Q1 2021A	LTM 2021	2021E
Revenue	5,767.7	24,996.1	7,163.3	26,391.6	29,620.3
Y/Y revenue growth (%)					*18.5%*

TABLE 10.15 Netflix Projected Expenses

	Actuals				Estimates
	Q1 2020A	2020A	Q1 2021A	LTM 2021	2021E
Revenue	5,767.7	24,996.1	7,163.3	26,391.6	29,620.3
Y/Y revenue growth (%)					*18.5%*
Cost of Goods Sold	1,087.8	4,353.7	1,113.6	4,379.5	5,159.1
COGS as a % of revenue	*19%*	*17%*	*16%*	*17%*	*17%*
Gross Profit	4,679.9	20,642.4	6,049.7	22,012.2	24,461.2
Gross profit margin (%)	*81%*	*83%*	*84%*	*83%*	*83%*
Operating Expenses	1,209.7	5,134.4	1,334.9	5,259.6	6,084.3
OpEx as a % of revenue	*21%*	*21%*	*19%*	*20%*	*21%*
EBITDA	3,470.2	15,507.9	4,714.8	16,752.5	18,376.9
EBITDA margin (%)	*60%*	*62%*	*66%*	*63%*	*62%*

TABLE 10.16 Netflix Projected Depreciation and EBIT

Netflix Income Statement

	Actuals				Estimates
	Q1 2020A	2020A	Q1 2021A	LTM 2021	2021E
Depreciation and amortization	2,511.9	10,922.6	2,754.9	11,165.7	12,943.3
D&A % of revenue	*44%*	*44%*	*38%*	*42%*	*44%*
EBIT	958.3	4,585.3	1,959.9	5,586.9	5,433.6
EBIT margin (%)	*17%*	*18%*	*27%*	*21%*	*18%*

was a major debt paydown, issuance, or reassessment. So, for these reasons, we will simply take the last year's interest values.

We can also calculate EBT. (See Table 10.17.)

Taxes We took the 2020 tax rate in order to calculate projected 2021 taxes. (See Table 10.18.) Note that we did not hardcode the tax rate in; rather, we linked in the 2020 exact rate.

We can now calculate "Net Income from Continuing Operations."

TABLE 10.17 Netflix Projected Interest and EBT

Netflix Income Statement

	Actuals				Estimates
	Q1 2020A	2020A	Q1 2021A	LTM 2021	2021E
Other Income	0.0	0.0	0.0	0.0	0.0
Interest					
Interest expense	184.1	767.5	194.4	777.9	767.5
Interest income	(12.7)	(41.6)	(11.1)	(40.0)	(41.6)
Net Interest Expense	171.4	725.9	183.4	737.9	725.9
Earnings before Tax (EBT)	786.9	3,859.3	1,776.5	4,849.0	4,707.6
IBT margin (%)	*14%*	*15%*	*25%*	*18%*	*16%*

TABLE 10.18 Netflix Projected Taxes and Net Income from Continuing Operations

Netflix Income Statement

	Actuals				Estimates
	Q1 2020A	2020A	Q1 2021A	LTM 2021	2021E
Income tax expense	85.8	528.3	286.2	728.7	644.4
Effective tax rate (%)	*11%*	*14%*	*16%*	*15%*	*14%*
Net income from Continuing Operations	701.0	3,331.0	1,490.3	4,120.3	4,063.2

Non-Recurring Events We typically leave any projected non-recurring events or extraordinary items at 0 as for projections, we want an estimate of everyday or recurring costs.

Shares and Earnings per Share In order to get a projected 2021 share count, as we had done with Amazon, we should dilute the share count.

There are several resources we can use to obtain the total number of Netflix diluted shares outstanding, but the best way to obtain that diluted share count is to calculate the number ourselves. The best starting point is to pull the most recently reported financial SEC filing. In this case, it is Netflix's 2021 10Q report, shown in Figure 10.9. Each financial filing should have posted on the front page the most current count of basic shares outstanding as of filing date.

This is found on the front page of the Netflix filing. At the bottom is a line that reads "As of March 31, 2021, there were 443,383,732 shares of the registrant's common stock, par value $0.001, outstanding." We will use this

---

UNITED STATES
SECURITIES AND EXCHANGE COMMISSION
Washington, D.C. 20549

FORM 10-Q

(Mark One)

☒   QUARTERLY REPORT PURSUANT TO SECTION 13 OR 15(d) OF THE SECURITIES EXCHANGE ACT OF 1934

For the quarterly period ended March 31, 2021

OR

☐   TRANSITION REPORT PURSUANT TO SECTION 13 OR 15(d) OF THE SECURITIES EXCHANGE ACT OF 1934

For the transition period from   to

Commission File Number: 001-35727

Netflix, Inc.
(Exact name of Registrant as specified in its charter)

Delaware	77-0467272
(State or other jurisdiction of incorporation or organization)	(I.R.S. Employer Identification Number)
100 Winchester Circle, Los Gatos, California	95032
(Address of principal executive offices)	(Zip Code)

(408) 540-3700
(Registrant's telephone number, including area code)

Securities registered pursuant to Section 12(b) of the Act:

Title of each class	Trading Symbol(s)	Name of each exchange on which registered
Common stock, par value $0.001 per share	NFLX	NASDAQ Global Select Market

Indicate by check mark whether the registrant (1) has filed all reports required to be filed by Section 13 or 15(d) of the Securities Exchange Act of 1934 during the preceding 12 months (or for such shorter period that the registrant was required to file such reports) and (2) has been subject to such filing requirements for the past 90 days.   Yes ☒   No ☐

Indicate by check mark whether the registrant has submitted electronically every Interactive Data File required to be submitted pursuant to Rule 405 of Regulation S-T (§232.405 of this chapter) during the preceding 12 months (or for such shorter period that the registrant was required to submit such files).   Yes ☒   No ☐

Indicate by check mark whether the registrant is a large accelerated filer, an accelerated filer, a non-accelerated filer, a smaller reporting company, or an emerging growth company. See the definitions of "large accelerated filer," "accelerated filer," "smaller reporting company," and "emerging growth company" in Rule 12b-2 of the Exchange Act.

Large Accelerated Filer	☒	Accelerated filer	☐
Non-accelerated filer	☐	Smaller reporting company	☐
		Emerging growth company	☐

If an emerging growth company, indicate by check mark if the registrant has elected not to use the extended transition period for complying with any new or revised financial accounting standards provided pursuant to Section 13(a) of the Exchange Act. ☐

Indicate by check mark whether the registrant is a shell company (as defined by Rule 12b-2 of the Exchange Act).   Yes ☐   No ☒

As of March 31, 2021, there were 443,383,732 shares of the registrant's common stock, par value $0.001, outstanding.

FIGURE 10.9   Netflix's 2021 10-Q

Stock Option Plan

In June 2020, the Company's stockholders approved the 2020 Stock Plan, which was adopted by the Company's Board of Directors in March 2020 subject to stockholder approval. The 2020 Stock Plan is the successor to the 2011 Stock Plan and provides for the grant of incentive stock options to employees and for the grant of non-statutory stock options, stock appreciation rights, restricted stock and restricted stock units to employees, directors and consultants.

A summary of the activities related to the Company's stock option plans is as follows:

| | Shares Available for Grant | Options Outstanding | |
		Number of Shares	Weighted-Average Exercise Price (per share)
Balances as of December 31, 2020	21,702,085	18,676,810 $	170.23
Granted	(400,126)	400,126	537.47
Exercised	—	(488,471)	92.45
Expired	—	(4,648)	30.30
Balances as of March 31, 2021	21,301,959	18,583,817 $	180.22
Vested and exercisable as of March 31, 2021		18,583,817 $	180.22

FIGURE 10.10 Options Outstanding and Exercisable

number as the basic share count. Now, in order to get a count of diluted shares, we need to find all notes regarding options and warrants that may be held end exercisable by the company. Performing a quick word search on "Options" reveals the following note. (See Figure 10.10.)

Figure 10.10 represents outstanding options within the company's stock option plan and their respective exercise price. If the options are in-the-money, meaning the options are exercisable, or the current stock price is above the exercise price, then technically these options could be exercised and should be included into our diluted share count. The column on the far right estimates the average exercise price of the options as $180.22, which is far below the current stock price of $533.54. So, all 18,583,817 options are currently in-the-money. This means that the options holder can technically exercise these options at (on average) $180.22 per option. Or, if all options were exercised, they would all total a value of $3,349,175,499.74 ($180.22 × 18,583,817). There is a common method called the Treasury method that states that if these options are exercised at 180.22, they would most likely be bought back at the current stock price. So, if we divide the total value of options exercised by the current stock price ($3,349,175,499.74 /$533.54), we get 6,277,271.62 shares bought back. In other words, 18,583,817 options have been exercised, but effectively 6,277,271.62 bought back, giving us 12,306,545 (18,583,817 – 6,277,271.62) new shares outstanding. We add this number to the basic shares outstanding to get 455,690,277. This can all be laid out in the table found in rows 48–56 in "NFLX Comp" tab. We won't go through every cell calculation here, so use the example here and the model solution as a guide.

(See Table 10.19.)

TABLE 10.19 Netflix Diluted Share Count

	Netflix Diluted Shares
Share price	$533.54
Number of basic shares outstanding	443,383,732
Number of outstanding options (in the money)	18,583,817
Average option strike price	$180.22
Total option proceeds	$3,349,175,499.74
Treasury stock method shares repurchased	6,277,271.62
Additional shares outstanding	12,306,545
Total diluted shares outstanding	**455,690,277**

In order to get a complete diluted share count, it is crucial to be thorough in making sure you have found all stock options, employee stock options, and warrants that may be exercisable. There could have been more options than what was found in Figure 10.10, so thorough research is recommended. It is also recommended to see if there are any additional filings posted announcing the issuance of options or warrants that would not have been captured in the annual or quarterly filings.

We can now use these basic and diluted share counts as our 2021E projected numbers. *Note:* The share counts on the Netflix income statement is reported in millions, so we can pull in these numbers into the basic and diluted share count cells dividing by 1,000,000. Or, H45 would be "=D50/1000000" and H46 would be "=D56/1000000."

Now we can use these share counts as the denominator for our basic and diluted EPS calculations. These formulas can easily be copied across from the left columns. (See Table 10.20.)

This is a "first cut" approach to making basic projections. We can now adjust and compare the EPS we have with the Street's EPS. If you look back to Figure 10.8, you may notice 42 analysts on the Street estimate the EPS to be somewhere between 9.94 and 11.61. The average EPS projection on the Street is 10.45. So our EPS is slightly lower than the Street estimates. If we are using Street revenue estimates, and if our revenue is in line with the Street, yet the EPS is lower than the Street estimates, this could mean we have overstated our cost assumptions. Or, it is likely possible that Wall Street has not pulled out the "Foreign currency" line as we have done. I will note, looking at the Q3 and LTM costs as a % of revenue compared

TABLE 10.20   Netflix Projected EPS

Netflix Income Statement

	Actuals				Estimates
	Q1 2020A	2020A	Q1 2021A	LTM 2021	2021E
Net Income (as reported)	709.1	2,761.4	1,706.7	3,759.0	4,063.2
Earnings per Share (as Reported)					
Basic	1.61	6.26	3.85	8.48	9.16
Diluted	1.57	6.08	3.75	8.25	8.92
Earnings per Share (Adjusted)					
Basic	1.60	7.55	3.36	9.30	9.16
Diluted	1.55	7.33	3.27	9.04	8.92
Average Common Shares Outstanding					
Basic	439	441	443	443	443
Diluted	452	454	456	456	456

to 2020, the COGS, OpEx, and depreciation numbers do slightly decrease. If we were to reduce those estimates lower to tie with the Q3 and LTM trends, our EPS does increase enough to fall right in line with Street estimates. This is where you, as an analyst, a manager, a director, would take ownership of these assumptions and understand how to best interpret them for your individual purpose. The major question here is: Is the company really expecting costs to decrease in the future, or are the Street's assumptions too aggressive? Although these is some indication that costs are reducing, I like to keep things conservative for purposes of this book, so we will keep our EPS as is. The complete Netflix analysis is shown in Table 10.21.

Calculating Comparable Metrics

We now have our core underlying data we will use to calculate our comparable metrics. But first we need to properly calculate the market capitalization

TABLE 10.21   Netflix Comparable Analysis

Netflix Income Statement

	Actuals				Estimates
	Q1 2020A	2020A	Q1 2021A	LTM 2021	2021E
Revenue	5,767.7	24,996.1	7,163.3	26,391.6	29,620.3
Y/Y revenue growth (%)	*19%*	*17%*	*16%*	*17%*	*18.5%*
Cost of Goods Sold	1,087.8	4,353.7	1,113.6	4,379.5	5,159.1
COGS as a % of revenue	*19%*	*17%*	*16%*	*17%*	*17%*
Gross Profit	4,679.9	20,642.4	6,049.7	22,012.2	24,461.2
Gross profit margin (%)	*81%*	*83%*	*84%*	*83%*	*83%*
Operating Expenses	1,209.7	5,134.4	1,334.9	5,259.6	6,084.3
OpEx as a % of revenue	*21%*	*21%*	*19%*	*20%*	*21%*
EBITDA	3,470.2	15,507.9	4,714.8	16,752.5	18,376.9
EBITDA margin (%)	*60%*	*62%*	*66%*	*63%*	*62%*
Depreciation and amortization	2,511.9	10,922.6	2,754.9	11,165.7	12,943.3
D&A % of revenue	*44%*	*44%*	*38%*	*42%*	*44%*
EBIT	958.3	4,585.3	1,959.9	5,586.9	5,433.6
EBIT margin (%)	*17%*	*18%*	*27%*	*21%*	*18%*
Other Income	0.0	0.0	0.0	0.0	0.0
Interest					
Interest expense	184.1	767.5	194.4	777.9	767.5
Interest income	(12.7)	(41.6)	(11.1)	(40.0)	(41.6)

Net Interest Expense	171.4	725.9	183.4	737.9	725.9
Earnings before Tax (EBT)	786.9	3,859.3	1,776.5	4,849.0	4,707.7
IBT margin (%)	14%	15%	25%	18%	16%
Income tax expense	85.8	528.3	286.2	728.7	644.4
Effective tax rate (%)	11%	14%	16%	15%	14%
Net Income from Continuing Operations	701.0	3,331.0	1,490.3	4,120.3	4,063.2
Foreign currency exchange (gain) loss, net	(8.0)	569.7	(216.4)	361.2	0.0
(Gain) loss on debt securities, net	0.0	0.0	0.0	0.0	0.0
(Gain) loss on equity securities	0.0	0.0	0.0	0.0	0.0
Performance fees	0.0	0.0	0.0	0.0	0.0
Income and impairment from equity method investments, net	0.0	0.0	0.0	0.0	0.0
Other	0.0	0.0	0.0	0.0	0.0
Net Income (as Reported)	709.1	2,761.4	1,706.7	3,759.0	4,063.2
Earnings per Share (as Reported)					
Basic	1.61	6.26	3.85	8.48	9.16
Diluted	1.57	6.08	3.75	8.25	8.92
Earnings per Share (Adjusted)					
Basic	1.60	7.55	3.36	9.30	9.16
Diluted	1.55	7.33	3.27	9.04	8.92
Average Common Shares Outstanding					
Basic	439	441	443	443	443
Diluted	452	454	456	456	456

and enterprise value of Netflix. We need the current stock price and the number of shares outstanding. Netflix's stock price can be found at Yahoo! Finance or any online stock resource.

As of this writing (July 1, 2021), its current price is $533.54. We can use this along with the projected diluted share count to calculate market value and enterprise value.

Market Value and Enterprise Value   With our total diluted share count, we can easily calculate Netflix's market value by multiplying diluted shares by the current share price, giving us $243,128,990,593.7. We will divide this number by $1,000,000 to continue reporting in millions. Use rows 59–67 in the "NFLX Comp" tab. (See Table 10.22.)

We can now look to the balance sheet to calculate enterprise value. To be completely thorough, one should perform extensive research to see if there are any "off balance sheet" obligations that may need to be considered at part of enterprise value. To get as current information as possible, we will use the latest quarterly report. (See Figure 10.11.)

Netflix reports short-term debt and long-term debt. We don't see any preferred securities or non-controlling interests. Note we list the cash as a negative because this will net against the debt balance to get enterprise value. (See Table 10.22.)

TABLE 10.22   Netflix Market Value and Enterprise Value

	Netflix Enterprise Value
Market value	243,129.0
Short-term debt	698.8
Long-term debt (includes current portions)	14,860.6
Capital lease obligations	0.0
Convertible debt	0.0
Preferred securities	0.0
Non-controlling interest	0.0
Less: Cash & equivalents	(8,403.7)
Enterprise value	$250,284.6

NETFLIX, INC.

Consolidated Balance Sheets
(in thousands, except share and par value data)

	As of	
	March 31, 2021	December 31, 2020
	(unaudited)	
Assets		
Current assets:		
Cash and cash equivalents	$ 8,403,705	$ 8,205,550
Other current assets	1,703,803	1,556,030
Total current assets	10,107,508	9,761,580
Content assets, net	26,043,991	25,383,950
Property and equipment, net	1,015,419	960,183
Other non-current assets	2,956,096	3,174,646
Total assets	$ 40,123,014	$ 39,280,359
Liabilities and Stockholders' Equity		
Current liabilities:		
Current content liabilities	$ 4,297,957	$ 4,429,536
Accounts payable	532,942	656,183
Accrued expenses and other liabilities	1,291,812	1,102,196
Deferred revenue	1,140,271	1,117,992
Short-term debt	698,788	499,878
Total current liabilities	7,961,770	7,805,785
Non-current content liabilities	2,465,626	2,618,084
Long-term debt	14,860,552	15,809,095
Other non-current liabilities	1,950,986	1,982,155
Total liabilities	27,238,934	28,215,119
Commitments and contingencies (Note 7)		
Stockholders' equity:		
Common stock, $0.001 par value; 4,990,000,000 shares authorized at March 31, 2021 and December 31, 2020; 443,383,732 and 442,895,261 issued and outstanding at March 31, 2021 and December 31, 2020, respectively	3,600,084	3,447,698
Accumulated other comprehensive income	4,137	44,398
Retained earnings	9,279,859	7,573,144
Total stockholders' equity	12,884,080	11,065,240
Total liabilities and stockholders' equity	$ 40,123,014	$ 39,280,359

FIGURE 10.11   Netflix Quarterly Balance Sheet

Multiples   We can now use the market value, the enterprise value, and the Netflix estimated and adjusted income statement to create comparable metrics. Please refer to the "Comparable Companies Analysis" tab in the Excel file. This is where we will calculate all of our multiples. First, we recommend pulling in key statistics from each individual company tab into the "Operating Statistics" section starting in row 22. If all of the statistics necessary to calculate the multiples are on one page, this helps avoid common linking errors made when calculating the multiples by pulling data in from several sheets. This is literally just pulling data in one by one, so use the provided models and Table 10.23 as a guide.

Once we have the core data linked in, we can move to the "Comparable Company Analysis" section shown in Table 10.24. Here we can first pull in the share price, market value, and enterprise value metrics calculated in each individual comp tab. We can then simply divide to calculate the

TABLE 10.23 Netflix Summary Operating Statistics

Operating Statistics

Company	Sales			EBIT			EBITDA			EPS		
	20A $MM	LTM $MM	21E $MM	20A $MM	LTM $MM	21E $MM	20A $MM	LTM $MM	21E $MM	20A $/share	LTM $/share	21E $/share
Amazon	386,064.0	419,130.0	490,301.3	22,899.0	27,775.0	32,480.7	48,150.0	58,126.0	61,150.5	$41.79	$52.22	$45.21
eBay	10,271.0	11,165.0	12,037.6	2,711.0	2,988.0	3,177.3	3,320.0	3,596.0	3,891.0	$2.53	$2.82	$3.12
Etsy	1,725.6	2,048.2	2,286.5	424.0	549.3	561.8	492	615	652	$2.72	$3.34	$3.46
Walmart	556,218.8	561,609.7	710,121.8	22,383.0	23,671.3	28,636.0	33,521	34,737	42,799	$4.77	$5.06	$6.26
Target	92,273.6	96,615.7	102,075.1	6,382.2	7,809.7	7,134.0	8,623	10,054	9,567	$8.48	$10.71	$9.79
Best Buy	46,960.0	49,312.0	49,294.3	2,595.4	2,976.3	2,758.7	3,432	3,821	3,634	$7.43	$8.79	$8.28
Google	182,527.0	196,682.0	250,609.6	41,224.0	49,684.0	56,600.6	54,129	62,234	74,319	$49.06	$58.41	$67.40
Netflix	24,996.1	26,391.6	29,620.3	4,585.3	5,586.9	5,433.6	15,508	16,753	18,377	$7.33	$9.04	$8.92
IBM	73,620.0	73,779.0	75,166.0	6,785.0	7,875.0	6,927.5	13,480	14,608	13,763	$7.46	NM	$7.57

TABLE 10.24 Comparable Company Analysis

Comparable Companies Analysis (in US$ millions)

Company	Current Stock Price$	Market Capitalization (Value)$	Enterprise Value $MM	Price / Earnings 20A	Price / Earnings LTM	Price / Earnings 21E	E.V. / Revenue 20A	E.V. / Revenue LTM	E.V. / Revenue 21E	E.V. / EBIT 20A	E.V. / EBIT LTM	E.V. / EBIT 21E	E.V. / EBITDA 20A	E.V. / EBITDA LTM	E.V. / EBITDA 21E
Amazon	$3,432.97	1,782,822.8	1,835,282.8	82.1x	65.7x	75.9x	4.8x	4.4x	3.7x	80.1x	66.1x	56.5x	38.1x	31.6x	30.0x
Group 1: Retail / E-Commerce															
eBay	$69.80	48,389.7	53,749.7	27.6x	24.7x	22.4x	5.2x	4.8x	4.5x	19.8x	18.0x	16.9x	16.2x	14.9x	13.8x
Etsy	$199.51	29,049.2	29,239.5	73.2x	59.7x	57.7x	16.9x	14.3x	12.8x	69.0x	53.2x	52.0x	59.4x	47.5x	44.8x
Walmart	$138.81	390,909.2	437,142.2	29.1x	27.4x	22.2x	0.8x	0.8x	0.6x	19.5x	18.5x	15.3x	13.0x	12.6x	10.2x
Target	$243.47	120,538.0	125,404.0	28.7x	22.7x	24.9x	1.4x	1.3x	1.2x	19.6x	16.1x	17.6x	14.5x	12.5x	13.1x
Best Buy	$116.37	29,176.8	28,889.8	15.7x	13.2x	14.1x	0.6x	0.6x	0.6x	11.1x	9.7x	10.5x	8.4x	7.6x	8.0x
Group 2: Subscription / Web Services															
Google	$2,527.37	1,831,976.3	1,710,759.3	51.5x	43.3x	37.5x	9.4x	8.7x	6.8x	41.5x	34.4x	30.2x	31.6x	27.5x	23.0x
Netflix	$533.54	243,129.0	250,284.6	72.8x	59.0x	59.8x	10.0x	9.5x	8.4x	54.6x	44.8x	46.1x	16.1x	14.9x	13.6x
IBM	$145.17	130,614.0	176,469.0	19.4x	NM	19.2x	2.4x	2.4x	2.3x	26.0x	22.4x	25.5x	13.1x	12.1x	12.8x
Median				28.9x	27.4x	23.6x	3.8x	3.6x	3.4x	22.9x	20.4x	21.5x	15.3x	13.8x	13.4x
High				73.2x	59.7x	59.8x	16.9x	14.3x	12.8x	69.0x	53.2x	52.0x	59.4x	47.5x	44.8x
Low				15.7x	13.2x	14.1x	0.6x	0.6x	0.6x	11.1x	9.7x	10.5x	8.4x	7.6x	8.0x

respective metrics. (Please refer to Chapter 8 for a review of the multiples and the respective formulas.)

We can now repeat this whole process for other companies comparable to Amazon. We will not go through the others, as it is too redundant and we have discussed all key lessons learned when we built the Amazon model and the Netflix comp. You can view the solution file found on the companion website (www.wiley.com/go/pignataro) for a fully completed comp analysis. In Chapter 12, we will analyze these multiples for use in Amazon's valuation.

CHAPTER 11

Precedent Transactions Analysis

As we discussed earlier, the precedent transactions analysis assesses relative value by looking at multiples of historical transactions. The value of our company is relative to the price others have paid for similar companies. So, if we look for other companies similar to ours that have been acquired, we can compare their purchase multiples to assess approximate value.

Purchase multiples are similar to market multiples, except the numerator in a purchase multiple is based on the price paid for an entity as opposed to the current market value.

IDENTIFYING PRECEDENT TRANSACTIONS

The greatest difficulty in obtaining precedent transactions is identifying relevant transactions. It is important to consider transactions that are similar in industry to the company we are valuing. In other words, to use precedent transactions as a valuation methodology for Amazon, we would have to find acquisitions of other corporations similar to Amazon. We also need to consider transactions that are relatively similar financially. Now, this becomes the major problem when the target is Amazon, as the company is so large and so diverse, not only do similar companies not exist, but it is very unlikely that similar transactions exist. Finally, timing is an important factor. We need to consider recent transactions; transactions that have happened many years ago may have happened in a market environment that is no longer relevant today.

There are several major sources that can provide historical transactions. Securities Data Corporation (SDC) is a leading provider of mergers and acquisitions data. Always double-check the data from such sources; do not assume it is accurate. Use this information as a guide and try to research to back into the relevant statistics using government filings if available. SEC filings can be the best resource for financial data on the company being acquired.

A merger proxy contains an "Opinion of Financial Advisor" section, also known as a "Fairness Opinion," where the financial advisors detail the valuation supporting the merger. The SEC Form S-4 and an 8-K are other examples of filings that may contain financial details on a merger. The company's annual report can also contain a paragraph discussing the merger. Finally, other information such as tender offers, news releases, and research reports are good resources that may contain financial information on a merger.

AMAZON PRECEDENT TRANSACTION ANALYSIS

As mentioned above, Amazon is a truly unique company. Finding acquisitions similar to Amazon in order to prove value is nearly impossible. However, for purposes of demonstrating how such an analysis is put together, we can do some research to see what companies Amazon has recently purchased by googling "Amazon acquisitions," for example. Here we find that in May, Amazon announced the acquisition of MGM Studios:

> Amazon said Wednesday it will acquire MGM
> Studios for $8.45 billion, marking its boldest
> move yet into the entertainment industry and
> turbocharging its streaming ambitions.

Unfortunately, since this acquisition was only announced May 26, 2021, at the time of writing this book there were no readily available transaction-related documents with enough relevant information to calculate multiples. So, we go to the next, and probably most notable, Amazon acquisition – Whole Foods. Whole Foods, a grocery chain, is very different from Amazon. So, the theory of analyzing the acquisition of Whole Foods to help determine the value of Amazon itself falls apart a bit here. Regardless, there is still value in analyzing such acquisitions for other purposes, so we will continue to step through this analysis.

The first pieces of data we need to analyze this acquisition are the purchase price, equity value, and enterprise value. We then need to find some financial statistics on Whole Foods in order to calculate multiples.

If you google "Amazon acquisition of Whole Foods," a host of articles come up, most referring to the original announcement. An article referring to the original announcement is ideal because it will provide for us the announcement date and most likely purchase price. (See Figure 11.1.)

This gives us two valuable pieces of information: the announcement date and purchase price. The article references the deal was announced on

Amazon.com Inc. said on Friday it would buy Whole Foods Market Inc. for $13.7 billion, including debt, instantly transforming the online giant into a major player in the bricks-and-mortar retail sector it has spent years upending.

FIGURE 11.1 Amazon Whole Foods Acquisition Press Release

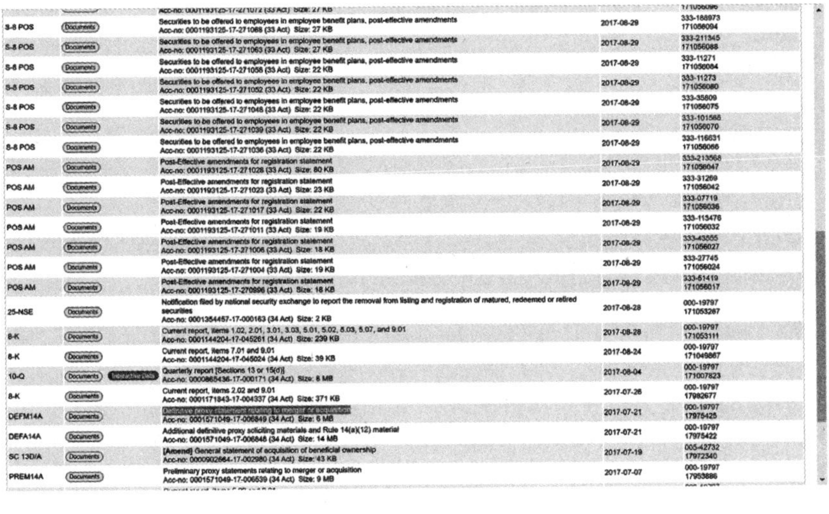

	Documents	Acc-no: 0001193125-17-271072 (33 Act) Size: 27 KB		171056096
S-8 POS	Documents	Securities to be offered to employees in employee benefit plans, post-effective amendments Acc-no: 0001193125-17-271068 (33 Act) Size: 27 KB	2017-08-29	333-188973 171056094
S-8 POS	Documents	Securities to be offered to employees in employee benefit plans, post-effective amendments Acc-no: 0001193125-17-271063 (33 Act) Size: 27 KB	2017-08-29	333-211345 171056088
S-8 POS	Documents	Securities to be offered to employees in employee benefit plans, post-effective amendments Acc-no: 0001193125-17-271058 (33 Act) Size: 22 KB	2017-08-29	333-11271 171056084
S-8 POS	Documents	Securities to be offered to employees in employee benefit plans, post-effective amendments Acc-no: 0001193125-17-271052 (33 Act) Size: 22 KB	2017-08-29	333-11273 171056080
S-8 POS	Documents	Securities to be offered to employees in employee benefit plans, post-effective amendments Acc-no: 0001193125-17-271048 (33 Act) Size: 22 KB	2017-08-29	333-35809 171056075
S-8 POS	Documents	Securities to be offered to employees in employee benefit plans, post-effective amendments Acc-no: 0001193125-17-271039 (33 Act) Size: 22 KB	2017-08-29	333-101568 171056070
S-8 POS	Documents	Securities to be offered to employees in employee benefit plans, post-effective amendments Acc-no: 0001193125-17-271036 (33 Act) Size: 22 KB	2017-08-29	333-116631 171056066
POS AM	Documents	Post-Effective amendments for registration statement Acc-no: 0001193125-17-271028 (33 Act) Size: 80 KB	2017-08-29	333-213568 171056047
POS AM	Documents	Post-Effective amendments for registration statement Acc-no: 0001193125-17-271023 (33 Act) Size: 23 KB	2017-08-29	333-31269 171056042
POS AM	Documents	Post-Effective amendments for registration statement Acc-no: 0001193125-17-271017 (33 Act) Size: 22 KB	2017-08-29	333-07719 171056036
POS AM	Documents	Post-Effective amendments for registration statement Acc-no: 0001193125-17-271011 (33 Act) Size: 19 KB	2017-08-29	333-113476 171056032
POS AM	Documents	Post-Effective amendments for registration statement Acc-no: 0001193125-17-271006 (33 Act) Size: 18 KB	2017-08-29	333-43555 171056027
POS AM	Documents	Post-Effective amendments for registration statement Acc-no: 0001193125-17-271004 (33 Act) Size: 19 KB	2017-08-29	333-27745 171056024
POS AM	Documents	Post-Effective amendments for registration statement Acc-no: 0001193125-17-270896 (33 Act) Size: 18 KB	2017-08-29	333-51419 171056017
25-NSE	Documents	Notification filed by national security exchange to report the removal from listing and registration of matured, redeemed or retired securities Acc-no: 0001354457-17-000163 (34 Act) Size: 2 KB	2017-08-28	000-19797 171053267
8-K	Documents	Current report, items 1.02, 2.01, 3.01, 3.03, 5.01, 5.02, 5.03, 5.07, and 9.01 Acc-no: 0001144204-17-045261 (34 Act) Size: 239 KB	2017-08-28	000-19797 171053111
8-K	Documents	Current report, items 7.01 and 9.01 Acc-no: 0001144204-17-045024 (34 Act) Size: 39 KB	2017-08-24	000-19797 171049867
10-Q	Documents Interactive Data	Quarterly report [Sections 13 or 15(d)] Acc-no: 0000865436-17-000171 (34 Act) Size: 8 MB	2017-08-04	000-19797 171007823
8-K	Documents	Current report, items 2.02 and 9.01 Acc-no: 0001171843-17-004337 (34 Act) Size: 371 KB	2017-07-26	000-19797 17982677
DEFM14A	Documents	Definitive proxy statement relating to merger or acquisition Acc-no: 0001571049-17-006849 (34 Act) Size: 6 MB	2017-07-21	000-19797 17975425
DEFA14A	Documents	Additional definitive proxy soliciting materials and Rule 14(a)(12) material Acc-no: 0001571049-17-006848 (34 Act) Size: 14 MB	2017-07-21	000-19797 17975422
SC 13D/A	Documents	[Amend] General statement of acquisition of beneficial ownership Acc-no: 0000902664-17-002980 (34 Act) Size: 43 KB	2017-07-19	005-42732 17972340
PREM14A	Documents	Preliminary proxy statements relating to merger or acquisition Acc-no: 0001571049-17-006539 (34 Act) Size: 9 MB	2017-07-07	000-19797 17953886

FIGURE 11.2 US Securities and Exchange Commission

June 16, 2017, and will be acquired at $13.7Bn. This is the deal's purchase price. In order to calculate multiples, we need to dig deeper to find more underlying data: debt for enterprise value, revenue, EBIT, and EBITDA.

At www.sec.gov, we were able to find the proxy statement reflecting the acquisition of Whole Foods. Typing in "Whole Foods" in the SEC website "Company Search" box will produce a list of the company's last filings before it was fully acquired. The most beneficial document here will be the company's Proxy statement, the description of which clearly states "Definitive proxy statement relating to merger or acquisition." (See Figure 11.2.)

Scrolling down to page 36 of the report, we find very helpful projections we can use for calculating the multiples. (See Figure 11.3.)

Summary of the Whole Foods Market Projections[1]
(dollars in millions)

	2017	2018[4]	2019	2020	2021
Revenue	$15,887	$16,490	$17,339	$18,217	$19,238
EBITDA[2]	$ 1,216	$ 1,331	$ 1,656	$ 1,815	$ 1,949
Free Cash Flow[3]	$ 324	$ 422	$ 639	$ 738	$ 814

FIGURE 11.3 Whole Foods Revenue and EBITDA Projections

Reconciliation of Projected EBITDA to Projected Net Income
(dollars in millions)

	2017[1]	2018[2]	2019	2020	2021
EBITDA					
Net income	$ 409	$ 470	$ 658	$ 739	$ 794
Provision for income taxes	$ 262	$ 300	$ 420	$ 473	$ 507
Interest expense	$ 47	$ 47	$ 47	$ 47	$ 47
Investment and other income	$ (8)	$ (14)	$ (20)	$ (29)	$ (33)
Operating income	$ 710	$ 803	$1,105	$1,230	$1,315
Depreciation and amortization	$ 506	$ 528	$ 551	$ 585	$ 634
EBITDA	$1,216	$1,331	$1,656	$1,815	$1,949

(1) EBITDA in 2017 excludes charges incurred for a severance payment and store and facility closures.

(2) Estimates in 2018, a 53-week fiscal year, are presented on a 52-week basis.

FIGURE 11.4 Whole Foods Net Income and EBIT Projections

We can use the 2017 Revenue and EBITDA for our Enterprise Value / Revenue and Enterprise Value/EBITDA multiples, respectively. However, we also need Depreciation to back into EBIT, and Net Income for our Equity Value / Net Income multiples. Further, to calculate Enterprise Value, we still need to find how much of Whole Food's debt will be assumed by the acquisition. (See Figure 11.4.)

Here we can use the Net Income and Depreciation to back into EBIT from our EBITDA projections above. Now we just need debt.

When searching for "debt" in the Proxy, we don't find much explicit information on Whole Foods' outstanding debt upon acquisition announcement. So, we need to turn to the Whole Foods' filing (10-K or 10-Q) closest to the transaction announcement date. Going back to www.sec.gov, we find a 10-Q report that's dated July 2, 2017, very close to the June 16, 2017, announcement date. So, we can use this balance sheet to calculate net debt for our Enterprise Value. (See Figure 11.5.)

Here we can calculate the net debt as $1,046 (Long-term debt) plus $2 (Short-term debt) and less $279 (Cash), or $769MM.

So we now have enough information to calculate our multiples. Please refer to the "Precedent transactions" tab in the model template. Here we can

Assets		July 2, 2017		September 25, 2016
Current assets:				
Cash and cash equivalents	$	279	$	351
Short-term investments - available-for-sale securities		720		379
Restricted cash		124		122
Accounts receivable		246		242
Merchandise inventories		483		517
Prepaid expenses and other current assets		117		167
Deferred income taxes		222		197
Total current assets		2,191		1,975
Property and equipment, net of accumulated depreciation and amortization		3,482		3,442
Long-term investments - available-for-sale securities		24		—
Goodwill		710		710
Intangible assets, net of accumulated amortization		70		74
Deferred income taxes		87		100
Other assets		46		40
Total assets	$	6,610	$	6,341

Liabilities and Shareholders' Equity

Current liabilities:				
Current installments of long-term debt and capital lease obligations	$	2	$	3
Accounts payable		305		307
Accrued payroll, bonus and other benefits due team members		391		407
Dividends payable		58		43
Other current liabilities		568		581
Total current liabilities		1,324		1,341
Long-term debt and capital lease obligations, less current installments		1,046		1,048
Deferred lease liabilities		678		640
Other long-term liabilities		104		88
Total liabilities		3,152		3,117

Commitments and contingencies

Shareholders' equity:				
Common stock, no par value, 1,200 shares authorized; 376.8 and 377.0 shares issued; 320.1 and 318.3 shares outstanding at 2017 and 2016, respectively		2,946		2,933
Common stock in treasury, at cost, 56.7 and 58.7 shares at 2017 and 2016, respectively		(1,959)		(2,026)
Accumulated other comprehensive loss		(30)		(32)
Retained earnings		2,501		2,349

FIGURE 11.5 Whole Foods 10-Q Balance Sheet

see two tables; one contains the precedent metrics, and underneath we lay out the underlying date for these metrics. The stated market value (purchase price) of $13,700MM can be hardcoded into C21. Next we have the components of net debt for our Enterprise value. We've just mentioned these components above, so use Table 11.1 as a guide. We can then lay out the revenue, EBIT, and EBITDA, also identified above.

We can now use this underlying data to create multiples, just as we've done in the comps section, as shown in Table 11.2.

TABLE 11.1 Amazon / Whole Foods Statistics

Operating Statistics (in US$ millions)

Transaction	Market Value	Cash	Short Term Debt	Long Term Debt	Other	Enterprise Value	Earnings	Revenue	EBIT	EBITDA
Amazon / MGM	8,450.0	NA	NA	NA	NA	8,450.0	NA	NA	NA	NA
Amazon / Whole Foods	13,700.0	279	2	1046	0	14,469.0	409.0	15,887.0	710.0	1,216.0

TABLE 11.2 Precedent Transactions

Precedent Transactions (in US$ millions)

| Transaction | Announcement Date | Purchase Price | | Equity Value / | Enterprise Value / | | |
| | | Market Value | Enterprise Value | Earnings | Revenue | EBIT | EBITDA |
		$MM	$MM	x	x	x	x
Amazon / MGM	5/26/2021	8,450.0	8,450.0	N/A	N/A	N/A	N/A
Amazon / Whole Foods	6/16/2017	13,700.0	14,469.0	33.5x	0.9x	20.4x	11.9x

Date Announced	Target	Acquiror	TEV/LTM Adjusted EBITDA:
04/10/17	Unified Grocers, Inc.	Supervalu Inc.	10.0x
10/17/16	Save-A-Lot (subsidiary of Supervalu Inc.)	Onex Corp.	6.4x
03/14/16	The Fresh Market, Inc.	Apollo Global Management, LLC	7.1x
11/11/15	Roundy's, Inc.	The Kroger Co.	7.1x
06/24/15	Delhaize Group	Koninklijke Ahold N.V	8.1x
08/27/14	Demoulas Super Markets, Inc. (50.5% stake)	Arthur T. Demoulas	*
03/06/14	Safeway Inc.	Cerberus Capital Management, L.P., Kimco Realty Corporation, Klaff Realty, LP, Lubert-Adler Partners LP, Schottenstein Stores Corporation	5.0x
12/20/13	Arden Group, Inc.	TPG	10.0x
07/22/13	Nash Finch Company	Spartan Stores, Inc.	6.7x
07/09/13	Harris Teeter Supermarkets, Inc.	The Kroger Co.	7.3x
01/10/13	Supervalu (five retail grocery banners)	Cerberus Capital Management L.P.	4.0x
10/11/12	Smart & Final Holdings Corp.	Ares Management	7.5x
12/19/11	Winn-Dixie Stores, Inc.	Lone Star Funds	5.4x

FIGURE 11.6   Amazon Transactions

Now that we have this transaction down, for a more complete analysis, we need to find more precedent acquisitions. Like in the comps, if we find more like acquisitions we can calculate average, maximum, and minimum multiple ranges for analysis. In the fairness opinion section of the Proxy, we find the following table (Figure 11.6) from page 41.

This lists other acquisitions of grocers that were used to help justify the value of a Whole Foods acquisition. Unfortunately, these are only grocers, and as discussed in Chapter 10, Amazon has many other business segments. Ideally, we would find acquisitions that also match Amazon's other business segments, as we had done with the comps analysis to get ranges of multiples across all business segments. Likewise, we would hope to be able to dig for acquisition of other online retail companies, physical stores, and subscription service companies, to correlate with all Amazon business segments. Regardless, the precedents transaction analysis does have its major flaws, and in the case of Amazon, due to its size and varied scope, looking at target acquisitions may not be the best indicator of Amazon's value. So we will lean to the DCF and comps as more appropriate measures of value.

But for purposes of instruction, we will just pull a few of these more recent acquisitions. We went ahead and completed the analysis. Take a look at the final model as a guide. I would also recommend looking at the precedent transaction analysis in my first book for another perspective. (See Table 11.3.)

In the next chapter, we will combine the results of this analysis with the DCF and comparable companies to draw a final conclusion on the valuation of Amazon.

TABLE 11.3 Precedent Transactions Analysis

Precedent Transactions (in US$ millions)

| Transaction | Announcement Date | Purchase Price | | Equity Value / | Enterprise Value / | | |
		Market Value $MM	Enterprise Value $MM	Earnings x	Revenue x	EBIT x	EBITDA x
Amazon / MGM	5/26/2021	8,450.0	8,450.0	N/A	N/A	N/A	N/A
Amazon / Whole Foods	6/16/2017	13,700.0	14,469.0	33.5x	0.9x	20.4x	11.9x
Supervalu Inc. / Unified Grocers, Inc.	7/23/2017	114.0	398.0	N/A	0.1x	N/A	9.7x
Onex Corp. / Save-A-Lot	10/17/2016	655.0	1,365.0	N/A	N/A	N/A	6.8x
Apollo Global Management, LLC / The Fresh Market, Inc	3/14/2016	1,360.0	1,299.2	20.8x	0.7x	12.0x	7.3x
The Kroger Co. / Roundy's Inc.	11/11/2015	800.0	1,384.1	NM	0.4x	27.3x	11.6x
Median		1,080.0	1,374.5	27.1x	0.5x	20.4x	9.7x
High		13,700.0	14,469.0	33.5x	0.9x	27.3x	11.8x
Low		114.0	398.0	20.8x	0.1x	12.0x	6.8x

CHAPTER 12

Conclusion

Now we can do our best to assess all three valuation methods and draw some conclusions as to Amazon's current valuation. Of course, we caution that this is just one of several possible points of view. It is most important that you gain the ability to understand the tools used so that you can make your own judgments to value businesses and investments. The best next step is to lay out a summary page consisting of estimates resulting from each of the three valuation methods. As each method depends on a wide range of variables, many of which change with market swings, we expand each output across a range, as opposed to centering on one specific number. Even a range can hopefully suggest proper direction of a particular investment. The summary page should consist of a range of equity value, enterprise value, implied stock price, and an implied multiple. Let's assess each valuation method, come up with a relative range, and then create the summary tab, which we will analyze to approximate Amazon's value.

In addition to a summary output, we will create what is commonly known as a "football field" chart. This is a floating bar chart – a visual representation of the summary page. For many, it's easier for both analysis and presentation purposes to establish an appropriate company value by drawing conclusions from the bar chart.

Please refer to the tab in the template titled "Football Field." Notice the summary output table contains four categories: the three core valuation methods, plus "52-week high/low." For each of these categories, we want to assess value.

52-WEEK HIGH/LOW

It is useful to compare the value results with the company's equity value based on where its stock has peaked and troughed within the last 52-week period. We can easily find the 52-week high and low from Yahoo! Finance, by searching

TABLE 12.1 Amazon Value Based on 52-Week High/Low

	Low	—	High
		52-week high / low	
Share price	$2,878.70	—	$3,531.45
Shares outstanding	519.32	—	519.32
Equity value	$1,494,977	—	$1,833,966
Net debt & other	$58,382	—	$58,382
Enterprise value	$1,553,359	—	$1,892,348
LTM EBITDA	58,126.0		58,126.0
Multiple	26.7x	—	32.6x

under the ticker "AMZN." As of this writing, Amazon is showing a 52-week low of $2,878.70 and a 52-week high of $3,531.4. So to be able to convert this into comparable value, we need to multiply the 52-week high and low by the number of Amazon shares outstanding. We can pull in the diluted share count calculated in the discounted cash flow analysis (DCF). Multiplying the diluted shares by the respective low and high stock prices gives an equity value range of $1,494,977–$1,833,966. We can then *add* Amazon's net debt and non-controlling interest (also from the DCF analysis) to convert the equity value into enterprise value. Notice in the DCF we *subtracted* net debt because we had enterprise value and were trying to obtain equity value. Going the other way, we need to add to get to enterprise value from equity value. We divide the enterprise value (EV) by Amazon's LTM earnings before interest, taxes, depreciation, and amortization (EBITDA from the comps analysis) to get an EV/EBITDA multiple range of 26.7x to 32.6x. We could have also multiplied by Amazon's 2020 EBITDA or 2021 EBITDA. We are choosing LTM because it is the most current. The rule of thumb is to pick one underlying metric and stay consistent with this throughout the analysis. So, this is the effective value of Amazon over the past 52 weeks. Let's compare this with the other valuation methods. (See Table 12.1.)

COMPARABLE COMPANY ANALYSIS

Recall the discussion in Chapter 8 regarding what multiples are most comparable. Although this can differ from situation to industry, we can look at the comparable company output table (Chapter 10, Table 10.24) to help establish what ranges of multiples are best to help assess value for Amazon. Looking at Table 10.24, we see the price-to-earnings (P/E) multiples in

Group 1 have a pretty wide range. For example, the eBay multiple is around 20–30× while Best Buy is 13–16×. This is not surprising, as P/E multiples include effects of capital structure. Given that information, let's look at the EBITDA multiples. It is arguable whether we should utilize the 2020YE, last 12 months (LTM), or 2021E multiple. Let's use the LTM multiple for consistency, as we have already decided to use the LTM EBITDA. Looking at any of these multiples, or all together, suggests a range from around 7.5× to 15.0×, and even as high as 47.5×, taking Etsy into account. And yes, Etsy's numbers seem extremely high (out of the range of the others), but I would recommend keeping it in for now. Your individual judgment can have an effect here, so you may have a different opinion on this. Given this estimated range, we can interpret multiple ranges into value ranges by multiplying 7.5× and 47.5× by Amazon's LTM EBITDA. This gives us an enterprise value range of $434,945–$2,760,985. We can now subtract from this the Amazon net debt, and divide by the number of shares outstanding to get an implied equity value and stock price based on our valuation range. (See Table 12.2.)

So we can look at this for every group of comparables we create. Based on Group 1, maybe Amazon should be trading anywhere between $727.03 and **$5,204.08**. This is quite a wide range and could suggest that Amazon is either overvalued or still undervalued. But remember, Group 1 is composed of retailers and so assumes the market is basing Amazon's value solely on their retail business, which may or may not be true. We need to run this analysis on Group 2, which appears to have a multiple range of 12–27.5×, a bit narrower than the Group 1 range. This results in a value of $1,230.70–$2,965.55. (See Table 12.3.) We need to compare all of this with the other analyses before making a full assessment.

TABLE 12.2 Amazon Value Based on Comparable Company Analysis, Group 1: Retail / E-commerce

	Comparable company analysis Group 1: Retail / E-Commerce		
	Low	—	High
Share Price	$727.03	—	$5,204.08
Shares outstanding	519.3		519.3
Equity Value	$377,563		$2,702,603
Net debt & other	$58,382		$58,382
Enterprise Value	$435,945	—	$2,760,985
LTM EBITDA	58,126.0		58,126.0
Multiple	7.5×	—	47.5×

TABLE 12.3 Amazon Value Based on Comparable Company Analysis, Group 2: Subscription / Web Services

| | Comparable company analysis | | |
| | Group 2: Subscription / Web Services | | |
	Low	—	High
Share price	$1,230.70	—	$2,965.55
Shares outstanding	519.3		519.3
Equity value	$639,130		$1,540,083
Net debt & other	$58,382		$58,382
Enterprise value	$697,512	—	$1,598,465
LTM EBITDA	58,126.0		58,126.0
Multiple	12.0x	—	27.5x

PRECEDENT TRANSACTIONS

Let's now take a look at the precedent transactions. Looking at the precedent transaction table (Chapter 11, Table 11.3), we see the EBITDA multiples are ranging from 6.8x to 11.9x. Let's use the EBITDA multiples as we have used them for the comps, and they don't include capital structure effects. We can use the same process as we did with the comps to back into implied value and stock price ranges, resulting in a range of **$648.68** to **$1,219.50**. As you may recall, we focused only on grocers because we had limited data, so this analysis will not be as valuable to us as the other two. Let's move on to the DCF analysis. (See Table 12.4.)

TABLE 12.4 Amazon Value Based on Precedent Transactions

| | Precedent transactions | | |
	Low	—	High
Share Price	$648.68	—	$1,219.50
Shares outstanding	519.3		519.3
Equity Value	$336,875		$633,317
Net debt & other	$58,382		$58,382
Enterprise Value	$395,257	—	$691,699
LTM EBITDA	58,126.0		58,126.0
Multiple	6.8x	—	11.9x

DISCOUNTED CASH FLOW

For the DCF, we have already estimated $4,962.80 based on the EBITDA method and $925.34 based on the perpetuity method; two very different values. As we discussed, the EBITDA method is based on market multiples, and since Amazon can be seen as a growth company, the value based on this method is higher and more in line with the current stock price. The perpetuity method is more fundamentally based on the underlying cash flow of the business, which would not normally include market premium; hence the much lower valuation. So with a company like Amazon, where there is such a significant gap between the resulting values in the methods, we need to look at each method individually and dig a bit deeper into the variables. To recap, the major variables in this analysis are:

- *Model projections.* First and foremost, the underlying projections of the model can make a difference here. If the revenue growth is reduced to 1%, for example, both the EBITDA and perpetuity values will decrease. Let's assume that we will keep the model projections where they are for this analysis, but it is important to not overlook the importance of the model projections here.
- *Weighted average cost of capital (WACC).* Our 7.23% WACC could be considered quite low for a growth company. The underlying drivers for this are beta and the market risk premium. A small adjustment to one of the WACC formula drivers (e.g., increasing the beta to 2) will increase the WACC to 11.03%. Notice how, as the WACC increases, the EVs based on the EBITDA and perpetuity methods decrease.
- *EBITDA exit multiple.* In our DCF, we took Amazon's current EBITDA multiple as the terminal value multiple. If we now used the comps range of multiples, starting with the lowest 7.5× for example, the total value would drop significantly down to $1,018.91. We do this by temporarily hardcoding 7.5 over the 38.2 multiple (Cell F22 in the DCF tab). So, we can create a range from the lowest to the highest price based on adjusting the EBITDA exit multiples, from 7.5× (the lowest in the comps ranges) to 47.5× (the highest in the comps ranges) for the football field. Like in the 52-week high / low table, we will use the high and low share price estimates and then back into Equity value and Enterprise value. (See Table 12.5.)
- *Perpetuity growth rate.* Even a 1% change to the perpetuity growth rate can make a significant change to the value of the business based on the perpetuity. This does not affect the EBITDA value, however. The 3% currently in the model was just a guesstimate, so we can create a range

based on the traditional market range of 2–4%, for example, and see where that puts the overall value of the company. So, as with the EBITDA method, we can hardcode 2% over the 3% in Cell F27 on the DCF tab. This gives us an estimated price of $752.36. Hardcoding 4% gives us $1,205.48. We can now use this range for the football field. (See Table 12.6.)

We have now completed all necessary underlying data to assess Amazon's value.

TABLE 12.5 Amazon Value Based on DCF: EBITDA Method

	Discounted cash flow analysis		
	EBITDA Method		
	Low	—	High
Share Price	$1,018.91	—	$6,151.02
Shares outstanding	519.3		519.3
Equity Value	$529,146.2	—	$3,194,371
Net debt & other	$58,382	—	$58,382
Enterprise Value	$587,526	—	$3,252,753
LTM EBITDA	58,126.0		58,126.0
Multiple	10.1×	—	56.0×

TABLE 12.6 Amazon Value Based on DCF: Perpetuity Method

	Discounted cash flow analysis		
	Perpetuity Method		
	Low	—	High
Share Price	$752.36	—	$1,205.48
Shares outstanding	519.3		519.3
Equity Value	$390,718	—	$626,034
Net debt & other	$58,382	—	$58,382
Enterprise Value	$449,100	—	$684,416
LTM EBITDA	58,126.0		58,126.0
Multiple	7.7×	—	11.8×

FOOTBALL FIELD

Let's create the "football field" chart, which will lay out all of our valuation results in floating bars for comparison and analysis. I will step through the creation of this chart.

We first need to decide what output data we want the football field to represent. It could be equity value, enterprise value, multiples, or share prices. Let's create a football field of share prices based on each valuation method. So, we need to create a table with each valuation method, the low share price based on our range, the high price, and then the difference between the two. It is this difference that will be the floating bar. You can see the table template starting on row 14. We are simply pulling in the respective low and high values. The "variance" column is the high minus the low. (See Table 12.7.)

Notice that we started with the rightmost valuation method (DCF perpetuity). You will see as we create the bar chart, the first row of the table will actually become the bottom bar in the bar chart.

Now we can highlight the entire table (including the header row) and create the bar chart. We will be creating a "Stacked bar chart." The location of this button may vary, depending on the version of Microsoft Excel that you have, but it's commonly under "Insert," then "Chart," then "Bar," and "Stacked bar." If you can't find it, you can always type "Stacked bar" in the help box. This should create a chart that looks something like Figure 12.1.

So here we see the valuation methods, and each method has three bars. The leftmost bar is actually representing the low value. We don't want to see this bar, but it is important to have in order to properly position the middle bar. The middle bar is the actual data we want to see represented. This bar is actually plotting the variance, but the leftmost border of this bar represents the "low" value, and the rightmost border, the "high" value.

TABLE 12.7 Valuation Data Table

Table Data	Low	Variance	High
DCF Perpetuity	$752.36	$453.12	$1,205.48
DCF EBITDA	$1018.91	$5,132.11	$6,151.02
Precedent Transactions	$648.68	$570.82	$1,219.50
Comps Group 2	$1,230.70	$1,734.86	$2,965.55
Comps Group 1	$727.03	$4,477.05	$5,204.08
52-Week High / Low	$2,878.70	$652.75	$3,531.45

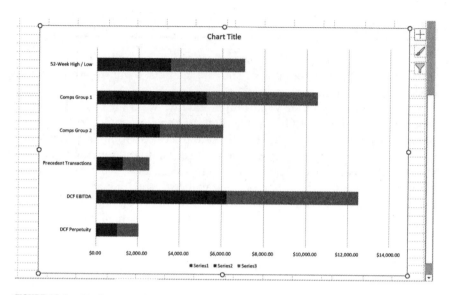

FIGURE 12.1 Unformatted Bar Chart

So, we want to first be sure the data *values* are displayed for the low and high (leftmost and rightmost) bars. So, if we click on one of the leftmost bars, it should highlight *all* of the bars in that series. Now, in order to add the data labels, right-click and select "Add data labels."

You may instead see "Format data label. . ." – if so, you will next need to select the box for "Value." Again, the location of this may vary based on your version of Excel, and if you cannot find it, try searching help for "Display data labels."

Now we don't need the middle set of data labels; we only want to show the leftmost and rightmost labels in each bar, representing the high and low. So, if we next click on one of the rightmost bars, we can add labels there as well. (See Figure 12.2.)

Next, we only want to display the middle bar, so in order to make the other bars invisible, first click the leftmost bar. This should highlight *all* of the left bars. Once highlighted, you can right-click and select "Format data series. . .". This will open up a box on the right. You want to select the paint bucket or "Fill" options. Within these options, select "No Fill." This will keep the bar data intact, but will make the bar invisible. We want to repeat this for the rightmost bar. (See Figure 12.3.)

I'd like to narrow down the y-axis so you can right-click on this axis and select "Format axis. . .". This will open a box on the right; under "Axis option," there are minimum and maximum bounds. The maximum has been set quite high and is causing a large empty space to the right of the chart.

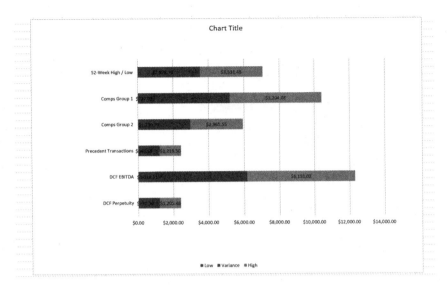

FIGURE 12.2 Bar Chart with Labels

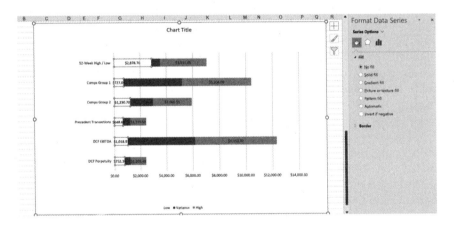

FIGURE 12.3 Bar Chart with Labels

Change this down to 10,000, to reduce that empty space. Be careful not to go too low or you will lose some of the data or data values.

Now you can add some manual formatting. Select the chart title to rename; move some of the data labels around to better organize. I changed the color of my bars to blue. I also added a dotted line to represent the current

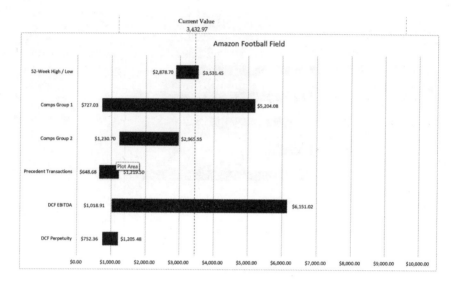

FIGURE 12.4 Amazon Football Field Chart

stock price. I think that's helpful to see in order to compare to the value ranges. This was manual addition created by selecting "Insert," then "Shapes," then "Line." And I just used the cursor to draw a dotted line and manually placed it on the chart. We now have the final chart in Figure 12.4.

So when looking at each of these bars, we first see Amazon is currently trading at the higher end of the 52-week high / low range. One year earlier, on July 1, 2020, the stock was at $2,878.70, so although there was some volatility over the past year, the stock is trending up.

The comps show a very wide range. Now, we do know the comparable set of companies widely vary in industry sector and size. And, we have determined that Amazon is an outlier as being not only very large but having several different business segments. Notice the Comps Group 2 is a subset of the Comp Group 1 range. Looking at all of these multiples as a whole can possibly suggest there is room for the multiple to expand and for the company to grow.

The precedents are showing a very low and tight range compared to the comps. But remember, we have only identified one type of acquisition target of companies that are much smaller than Amazon, and this analysis is a historical analysis. So, I don't think this analysis is going to be very useful here.

The discounted cash flow analysis is showing us two very different results, depending on whether you analyze the EBITDA method or the Perpetuity method. This is actually quite interesting, as the Perpetuity method, which is based more on the company's model (primarily the cash flow), is showing a considerably low valuation compared to the EBITDA method, which is showing much wider and higher valuation results. As mentioned before, this is not surprising for growth companies where the valuations based on market multiples (EBITDA method, DCF, and Comps) are higher that those based on the core financials (Perpetuity method DCF).

So, in conclusion, it appears there is still a lot of support suggesting the potential for the stock to rise above its current value of $3,432.97, given continued strong guidance. Again, this depends on the company's performance in the next quarters and assumes no other extraordinary or unplanned events will happen. Once the company provides new financials, we can update the model and get a stronger assessment.

Amazon is a very difficult and unusual company to value. It is one of the largest companies (by market cap) in the world, with many varied business segments. It is a high-growth company, but some business segments don't suggest high growth; it is in a business segment (retail) that has flourished given the pandemic. This opens the door to many variables that are difficult to nail down at this time. Nevertheless, the most important goal is that you understand each and every variable to be able to use this model as a tool. As the environment changes and (hopefully) slowly shifts out of a pandemic, we can adjust these variables accordingly and continue to assess how that will impact Amazon's value. We also need to take into consideration the decisions Amazon will make to its business structure (i.e., acquisitions, change in management).

Remember: The goal of this book is to give you all the tools necessary to analyze not only Amazon but *any* company with a robust set of financials. The results of any valuation analysis are up for interpretation, and the key is that you have stronger understanding to not only build your own valuation analysis but also draw your own conclusions and make rational judgments based on a multitude of variables. I hope this book has achieved that for you.

Model Quick Steps

I. Income Statement
1. Input Historical Income Statement Data
2. Project revenue
3. Project all expenses
   a. Leave Depreciation empty (to come from Depreciation Schedule; III.1.a)
   b. Leave Interest Expense and Interest Income empty (to come from Debt Schedule; VI.8 and VI.9)
4. Build to Net Income

II. Cash Flow
1. Input Historical Cash Flow Data
2. Cash Flow from Operations Projections
   a. Pull in Net Income before Dividends from Income Statement
   b. Leave Depreciation empty (to come from Depreciation schedule; III.1.b.)
   c. Leave Deferred Taxes empty (to come from Depreciation schedule; III.3.a)
   d. Leave Changes in Operating Working Capital empty (to come from Operating Working Capital schedule; IV.1.a. and IV.2.a)
   e. Project "Other" items
3. Cash Flow from Investing
   a. Project CAPEX
   b. Project "Other" Items
4. Cash Flow from Financing
   a. Leave Short-Term Debt Borrowings / (Retirements) empty (to come from Debt Schedule VI.3.b)
   b. Leave Long-Term Debt Borrowings / (Retirements) empty (to come from Debt Schedule VI.4.b)
   c. Pull in Dividends from Income Statement
   d. Project "Other" items
5. Sum Total Cash Flow

III. Balance Sheet
    1. Input Historical Balance Sheet data
IV. Depreciation Schedule
    1. Project GAAP Depreciation
        a. GAAP Depreciation links to Income Statement (I.3.a.)
        b. GAAP Depreciation will link to Cash Flow (II.2.b)
    2. Project Tax Deprecation
    3. Calculate Deferred Taxes
        a. Deferred Taxes will link to Cash Flow (II.2.c)
V. Operating Working Capital
    1. Project each Current Asset line item
        a. Each Change in Current Asset line item will link to Cash Flow (II.2.d)
    2. Project each Current Liability line item
        a. Each Change in Current Liability line item will link to Cash Flow (II.2.d)
    3. Calculate Changes in Operating Working Capital
VI. Balance Sheet Projections
    1. Build Balance Future Sheet balances using the Cash Flow Statement movements
VII. Debt Schedule
    1. Pull in year-end debt and cash balances from Balance Sheet
    2. Calculate Cash Available to Pay Down Debt
    3. Build Short-Term Debt Balance
        a. Calculate Interest Expense
        b. Create Mandatory + Automatic issuances / (retirements)
    4. Build Long-Term Debt Balance
        a. Calculate Interest Expense
        b. Create Mandatory + Automatic issuances (retirements)
    5. Calculate Total Interest Expense
    6. Calculate Total Mandatory + Automatic Issuances
    7. Calculate Cash at the end of Year
        a. Calculate Interest Income
    8. Link total Interest Expense to Income Statement (I.3.b)
    9. Link total Interest Income to Income Statement (I.3.b)
    10. Short-Term Mandatory + Automatic issuances links to Cash Flow Statement (II.4.a)
    11. Long-Term Mandatory + Automatic issuances links to Cash Flow Statement (II.4.b)

Model is complete.

Financial Statement Flows

INCOME STATEMENT TO CASH FLOW

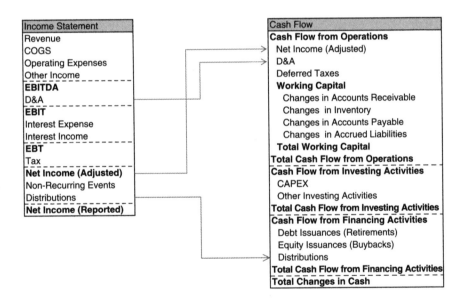

CASH FLOW TO BALANCE SHEET

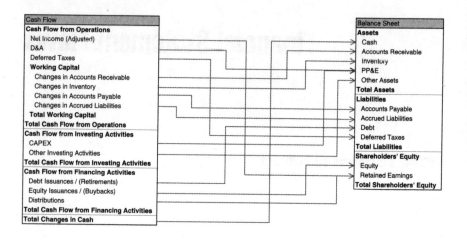

Excel Hotkeys

File Operation	Shortcut Key	Cell Formatting	Shortcut Key
New file	Ctrl + N	Format cells	Ctrl + 1
Open file	Ctrl + O	Format as currency	Ctrl + Shift + 4
Save file	Ctrl + S	Format as date	Ctrl + Shift + 3
Close file	Ctrl + F4	Format as percentage	Ctrl + Shift + 5
Save as	F12	Format as number	Ctrl + Shift + 1
Exit Excel	Alt + F4	Bold	Ctrl + B
Print	Ctrl + P	Italicize	Ctrl + I
Cell Operations	**Shortcut Key**	Underline	Ctrl + U
Edit active cell	F2	Strikethrough	Ctrl + 5
Cancel cell editing	Escape Key	Add cell borders	Ctrl + Shift + 7
Cut	Ctrl + X	Remove all borders	Ctrl + Shift + – (minus)
Copy	Ctrl + C	**Selecting Cells**	
Paste	Ctrl + V	Select entire worksheet	Ctrl + A
Copy right	Ctrl + R	Select group area	Ctrl + Shift + 8
Copy down	Ctrl + D	Select column	Ctrl + Space
Create cell comment	Shift + F2	Select row	Shift + Spacebar
		Select Manually	Hold Shift + Left, Right, Up, Down Arrow Key

Worksheet Navigation	Shortcut Key	Other Operations	Shortcut Key
Up one screen	Page Up	Find text	Ctrl + F
Down one screen	Page Down	Replace text	Ctrl + H
Move to next worksheet	Ctrl + Page Down	Undo last action	Ctrl + Z
		Redo last action	Ctrl + Y
Move to previous worksheet	Ctrl + Page Up	Create a chart	F11
Go to first cell in worksheet area	Ctrl + Home	Spell check	F7
		Show all formulas	Ctrl + ~
Go to last cell in worksheet area	Ctrl + End	Insert columns/ rows	Ctrl + Shift + + (plus sign)
Go to formula source	Ctrl + {	Insert a new worksheet	Shift + F11
Go to a cell	F5		
		Move between open workbooks	Ctrl + F6
		Autosum	Alt + = (equals sign)

About the Author

Paul Pignataro is an entrepreneur specializing in finance education. Mr. Pignataro has built and successfully run several startups covering several industries, including education and technology industries. Mr. Pignataro also has over 15 years of experience in investment banking and private equity in business mergers, acquisitions, restructurings, asset divestitures, asset acquisitions, and debt and equity transactions covering the oil, gas, power and utility, internet and technology, real estate, defense, travel, banking, and service industries.

He founded New York School of Finance, which has grown into a multimillion-dollar finance education business, providing finance education to banks, firms, and individuals throughout the globe. At NYSF, Mr. Pignataro participated on the training team, and provided training at bulge bracket banks and M&A teams at corporations, and had personally trained funds of high-net-worth individuals worth billions of dollars.

Mr. Pignataro had also developed a semester-long program, the NYSF Advantage Program, based in New York and geared toward business students, which had helped students from top schools, including Harvard and Wharton, and even lower-tier business schools land jobs at the top firms on Wall Street.

Prior to his entrepreneurial endeavors, Mr. Pignataro worked at TH Lee Putnam Ventures, a $1 billion private equity firm affiliated with buyout giant Thomas H. Lee Partners. Prior to TH Lee, Mr. Pignataro was at Morgan Stanley, where he worked on various transactions in the technology, energy, transportation, and business services industries. Some of the transactions included the $33.3 billion merger of BP Amoco and ARCO, the $7.6 billion sale of American Water Works to RWE (a German water company), the sale of two subsidiaries of Citizens Communications, a $3 billion communications company, and the sale of a $100 million propane distribution subsidiary of a $3 billion electric utility.

He graduated from New York University with a bachelor's degree in mathematics and a bachelor's degree in computer science.

About the Website

The companion website contains the model template and solution that accompanies the book. The purpose of the additional model template is for you to gain firsthand practice and to further illustrate the application of skills learned in the book. I encourage you to download the template and work through the model as you page through the book.

The website also contains chapter questions and answers to help aid in your knowledge of the material presented in the book. The questions not only complement each chapter but have frequently been utilized in conducting investment banking interviews. In addition to strengthening your fundamental knowledge of investment banking, the review of questions and suggested answers will help one prepare for such investment banking interviews. Note the practice model and solution on the website, which is a great test of the knowledge learned in the book.

Please note that some of the accompanying models presented in the website were constructed by my colleagues and associates and may contain varying viewpoints. It is helpful to see other types of models from other points of view to illustrate the possible variety. Once core concepts are honed, financial projections are yours to create, and the possibilities are endless. Enjoy!

To access the website, go www.wiley.com/go/pignataro/financial modelingandvaluation2e (password: investment).